THE WHITE
AND THE GOLD

THE WHITE
AND THE GOLD

The French Regime in Canada

THOMAS B. COSTAIN

Garden City, New York

DOUBLEDAY & COMPANY, INC.

To All My Friends in Canada

CONTENTS

MAPS

Introduction

THERE have been many histories of Canada, and some of them have been truly fine, but it seemed to a group of writers, all of whom were Canadians or of Canadian stock, who met a few years ago, that the time had come for something different. We all felt the need for a version which would neglect none of the essential factors but would consider more the lives of the people, the little people as well as the spectacular characters who made history, and tell the story with due consciousness of the green, romantic, immense, moving, and mysterious background which Canada provides. In addition there was a strong feeling—and this clearly was the governing impulse—that Canada's rise to nationhood should be traced to the present day, when the land which was once New France and then the Dominion of Canada promises to develop into one of the great powers of the globe.

This, it will be allowed at once, was what might be termed a rather tall order. However, there was considerable discussion about it, both then and later, and the outcome was a plan to do a formidably long version, all the way from John Cabot to St. Laurent. It was to be the joint work of a number of Canadian writers, one for each volume, and perhaps as many as six volumes.

It fell to my lot to begin, and this volume tells the story of the earliest days, the period of the French regime, concluding near the end of the seventeenth century. It has been with me a labor of love. Almost from the first I found myself caught in the spell of those courageous, colorful, cruel days. But whenever I found myself guilty of overstressing the romantic side of the picture and forgetful of the more prosaic life beneath, I tried to balance the scales more properly; to stop at the small house of the habitant, to look in the brave and rather pathetic chapel in the wilderness, to stare inside the bare and smoky barracks of the French regulars. It is, at any rate, a conscientious effort at a balanced picture of a period which was brave, bizarre, fanatical, lyrical, lusty, and, in fact, rather completely unbalanced.

No bibliography is appended because I found, when the time came to prepare one, that the point of no return had been reached. A list of roughly a thousand items—books, papers, extracts, manuscripts—which had been read or, at least, dipped into, would be of small value because of its very size. I shall content myself, therefore, with the perhaps obvious statement that in writing of this period two great sources constitute a large part of the preparation, that uniquely conceived and organized mass of remarkable material, the *Jesuit Relations*, and the crystal-clear reconstruction in Francis Parkman's splendid volumes.

The second volume, which will deal with the period of the English and French wars, is now being prepared by Joseph Lister Rutledge, for many years editor of the *Canadian Magazine* and a fine scholar with the capacity to keep a great event equally great in the telling.

THOMAS B. COSTAIN
January 1, 1954

THE WHITE
AND THE GOLD

CHAPTER I

John Cabot Speaks to a King—and
Discovers a Continent

1

I T MAY seem strange to begin a history of Canada in an English
city, a bustling maritime center of narrow streets in a pocket of
the hills where the Avon joins the Severn. But that is where the
story rightly starts: in the city of Bristol, which had become second
only to London in size and was doing a thriving trade with Ireland
and Gascony and that cold distant island called Iceland which the
Norsemen had discovered. It starts in Bristol because a Genoese
sailor, after living some time in London, had settled there with his
wife and three sons, one John Cabot, or "Caboote" as the official
records spelled it, a sea captain and master pilot of some small
reputation. He arrived in Bristol about 1490, when the place was
fairly bristling with prosperity and the streets had been paved with
stone and the High Cross had been painted and gilded most elaborately, and out on Redcliffe Street the Rudde House stood with its
great square tower, the home of those fabulous commoners, the
Canynges, as evidence of the wealth which could be gained in trade.

It was not strange that little attention was paid at first to this dark-
complexioned, soft-spoken foreigner. Bristol, aggressive and alive to
everything, had been fitting out ships to explore the western seas in
search of the "Vinland" of the Norse sagas and the legendary Island
of the Seven Cities which had been found and settled more than
seven centuries before by an archbishop of Oporto fleeing the conquering Moors with six other bishops. The waterfront buzzed with
the strange new talk which had been on the tongues of sailors for
years, the suddenly aroused speculations as to what lay beyond the
gray horizon of the turbulent Atlantic. The men of Bristol doffed
their flat sea caps to no one. What had they to learn from a mariner

who knew only the indolent ease of southern seas, most particularly of the Mediterranean, where the leveche blew insistently across from Africa with a dank hot scent?

But then it became known that another of these bland-tongued fellows, one Christopher Columbus, had set sail westward from Spain with three small ships and had found land hundreds of leagues across the gray waters, and that because of this Ferdinand and Isabella of Spain were claiming all the trade of Cathay. Bristol recalled that this man John Cabot had been voicing the same theories which had induced Their Most Christian Majesties to gamble a fleet on such a thin prospect. Cabot also had said that the world was round and that the shortest route to Cathay and Cipango led straight west. They got out their charts and compasses now and with new respect listened to him expound his belief that where Columbus had landed was the midriff of Asia and that the way around the world would be found far to the north. This was heady talk. It meant that there were still lands and seas to which Spain could not yet lay claim, that the flag of England could lead the way to equal wealth and glory. It was decided to seek royal sanction for a venture well to the north of the route which the inspired Columbus had taken.

Henry VII was King of England at this time and he was not exactly popular in Bristol. In the year 1490 he had paid the city a ceremonial visit and had received a truly royal welcome; but on leaving he had shocked them by laying a fine of five per cent on all men worth in excess of twenty pounds. Their wives, he said, had broken some dusty and long-forgotten sumptuary law by dressing themselves finely in his honor. He had called this fine a "benevolence," but the outspoken Bristol men had found other words for it. The seventh Henry, in point of fact, had little gift for winning the hearts of his subjects. The first of the Tudor kings was able and farseeing, but he was cold, withdrawn, hating no man but loving none, incapable of much enthusiasm save for the gold he was accumulating through the efficient raking of the legal fork of Morton, his chief minister.

Henry was eager, it developed, to share in the spoils of the west and so letters patent were issued to John "Caboote" and his three sons, Lewis, Sebastian, and Sancius, to set sail with five ships, to be paid for with their own money, and "to seek out, discover and find whatsoever islands, continents, regions and provinces of the heathens and infidels in whatever part of the world they be, which before this time have been unknown to all Christians." It was stipulated that they were to raise the flag of England over any new lands they found and to acquire "dominion, title and jurisdiction over these towns, castles, islands and mainlands so discovered." The only restriction laid upon them seems to have been that they must not venture into the south, where they would be poaching on the Spanish domain.

The parsimonious King had carefully protected himself from any possible loss, but he stipulated nevertheless that he was to receive one fifth of any profits which might accrue. It was provided in return that the Cabootes were to have as their reward a monopoly of trading privileges and that Bristol was to benefit by being the sole port of entry for any ships which engaged in the western trade. This laid the financial responsibility squarely in the laps of the men of Bristol, and it was not until the following year that they were able to organize their resources for the effort. Early in May 1497 a single ship called the *Matthew*, a ratty little caravel, set out for the west with John Cabot in command and a crew of eighteen men; surely the meanest of equipment with which to make such a hazardous and important venture. It was with stout hearts and high hopes, nevertheless, that the little crew gazed ahead over the swelling waters of the Atlantic, their parrels well tallowed and their topmasts struck to the cap in the expectation—nay, the certainty—of rough weather ahead.

In the fifteenth century the mariner had few instruments to guide him on his course. When the weather was clear he could sail with his eye fixed on the North Star; if it was overcast he had to use the compass. The North Atlantic is more likely to provide fogs and gray skies than clear sunshine, and so it was the compass on which John Cabot had to depend. This meant that he did not sail due west, for the compass has its little failings and never points exactly north. In the waters through which Cabot was sailing the variation is west of north, which meant that the tiny *Matthew*, wallowing in the trough of the sea, its lateen sail always damp with the spray, followed a course which inclined slightly southward. This was fortunate. It spared the crew any contact with the icebergs which would have been encountered in great numbers had they sailed due west; and it brought them finally, on June 24, 1497, to land which has been identified since as Cape Breton Island.

The anchor was dropped and the little band went ashore gratefully, their hearts filled with bounding hopes. The new land was warm and green and fertile. Trees grew close to the water's edge.

The sea, which abounded with fish, rolled in to a strip of sandy shingle. They saw no trace of natives, but the fact that some of the trees had been felled was evidence that the country was inhabited. All doubts on that score ended when snares for the catching of game were found. Perhaps eyes distended with excitement were watching the newcomers from the safe cover of the trees; but not a sound warned of their surveillance.

John Cabot, raising a high wooden cross with the flag of England and the banner of St. Mark's of Venice (that city having granted him citizenship some years before), had no reservations at all. He was certain he had accomplished his mission. He knew that his feet were planted firmly on the soil of Cathay, that fabulous land of spices and silks and gold. Somewhere hereabouts he would find the great open passage through which ships would sail north of Cathay and so in time girdle the earth.

2

It is unfortunate that so many of the great men of early Canadian history are little else but names. John Cabot, who thus had become the discoverer of North America, is wrapped almost completely in the mists of the past. A few dates, a phrase or two from letters of the period, an odd detail shining out of the darkness like a welcome ray of sunshine; these make up the sum total of what is known about him. There is no record of his appearance, whether he was tall or short, stocky or thin. His nationality suggests that he was dark of complexion, but even this remains pure speculation. It is not known when and where he died, although it is assumed that he spent his last days in Bristol.

This much is known: that he and his faithful eighteen, all of whom seem to have returned alive, were given a tumultous welcome in Bristol and that all England joined later in the chorus of acclaim. Cabot became at once a national hero. He was called the Great Admiral and wherever he went, according to a letter written by a Venetian merchant residing in London, "the English ran after him like mad people." He seems to have had a broad streak of vanity in him because he began to dress himself handsomely in silks and, presumably, to affect the grand manner. He distributed conditional largesse with a lavish hand, granting an island (to be chosen and occupied later) to this one, a strip of land to another. He gave it out rather grandiloquently that the priests who had volunteered to accompany the second expedition were all to be made bishops in the new land. From these details it may be assumed that he strutted and posed and made the most of his brief moment of glory.

That much may be said without detracting from the credit due him: he had been cast in the mold of greatness. Before Columbus set out, John Cabot had been expressing the same beliefs and theories as his never-to-be-forgotten countryman and had been striving hard for support in putting them to the test. He had ventured out on the most perilous of voyages in a cockleshell of a ship and with the most meager of crews. He possessed, it is clear, the fullest share of knowledge and courage and resolution. He had mastered the crises of the crossing and had accomplished his purpose before turning homeward. He was entitled to strut a little, to carry his head high, to play the role of destiny's favorite.

It is probable that he had audience with the King before the letters patent for the first voyage were issued, although there is no record of such. That the Great Admiral was granted a hearing after returning in triumph can be taken for granted; and it is likely that more hearings followed. It is known that both the King and the explorer were in London during the early part of August and that the old city fairly seethed with excitement. On August 10 the King recognized Cabot's merit by making him a present from the royal purse of ten pounds!

Henry had been King for twelve years only but he had already begun the systematic sequestration of funds in secret places which yielded on his death the sum of £1,800,000, a truly fabulous estate for those days. Already he was entering into the conspiracy of extortion which his various crafty ministers (most particularly Empson and Dudley, who had succeeded Morton, he of the Infallible Fork) were carrying out. He frequently consulted Empson's Book of Accounts and wrote suggestions on the "margent" for new and tricky methods. It is a measure of the man that out of his amazing hoard he could spare no more than ten pounds for this brave and skillful mariner who had brought to him the prospect of an empire as great as that of Spain.

Henry VII was, however, a man of many contradictions. With his parsimony went a love of ostentation and display. He liked to robe himself with all the grandeur of an eastern potentate, in silk and satin and rich velours, his broad padded coats embroidered with thread of gold and weighed down with precious stones, with massive gold chains around his neck and pearls as big as popcorn on his garters. He maintained a rather brilliant court and he kept a good table, which meant there was an earthy side to him; so good a table, in fact, that Ruy Gonzales de Puebla, the Spanish Ambassador, who was meagerly maintained by that other royal miser, Ferdinand of Spain, dined continuously at the royal board. He encouraged the New Learning and gave passive support at least to Colet and Grocyn at Oxford. He was a steady patron of a commoner named Caxton who was printing books from type for the first time in England. The first king to mint pounds and shillings, which had previously been nothing more than coins of account, he saw to it that his own unmistakable likeness in truly royal raiment was stamped upon them.

Henry was steering the ship of state through waters roiled by hate and conspiracy and imposture, and his success is proof of his capacity for judging men shrewdly. Looking down his quite long Welsh nose with his crafty gray Norman eyes, he must have sized up the Genoese captain, "he that founde the new isle," as a likely instrument for the further extension of his power and wealth. The ten pounds were followed sometime later by the grant of an annuity of twenty pounds sterling. But Henry was not committing himself to this great extravagance. The annuity was to be paid out of the customs of the port of Bristol, and he was not prepared, one may be sure, to countenance any diminution of the sums which reached him annually from that source. The responsibility was laid on the shipowners and merchants of Bristol, and most particularly on the shoulders of one Richard ap Meryk, who held the post of collector, the same relatively obscure official for whom the absurd claim was made later that the new continent of America had been named in his honor.

The King no doubt had many talks with John Cabot, for his enthusiasm showed a steady rise in intensity. New letters patent were issued by which Cabot could take any six ships from any of the ports of England, paying for them (out of his own pockets or the money chests of his Bristol backers) no more than the amount the owners could expect if their vessels had been confiscated for royal use, which would be a pretty thin price. The right was given also to the Great Admiral to take from the prisons of England all the malefactors he could use in the new venture. The King was to get his commission on any and all profits. Henry went this far in lending his support: he would advance loans from the royal purse to those who fitted out ships for the expedition. It is on record that he loaned on this basis twenty pounds to one Lanslot Thirkill of London and thirty pounds to Thomas, brother of Lanslot.

The winter was spent in preparations which rose to a fever point. Not only did the shipping interests of the country show a willingness to invest, but the desire to participate manifested itself in other ways. Men from all levels of society expressed the desire to be taken along. The merchants of London were eager to share in the trading end of the great adventure and sent to Cabot stores of goods to be used in barter with the inhabitants of the newly discovered land— cloth, caps, laces, points (the leather thongs with which men trussed up their leggings and trousers, the forerunners of the suspender, a most doubtful item of exchange with bare-skinned Indians), and many other items and trifles which were thought likely to attract the heathen eye.

The second expedition, which carried three hundred men and so must have consisted of many ships, sailed from Bristol early in May of the following year, 1498. The bold little ships had their holds well stocked with provisions, and with them went not only the hopes of those who had invested their money in the venture and the ardent expectations of all who had received promises of great estates and island domains from the lavish leader, but the support of every Englishman from the acquisitive King to the humblest denizens of hovel and spital-house.

3

The second expedition proved a failure because it started with a faulty objective. Cabot expected to find open water to the north of the new continent which would provide a route around the world. The ships arrived first at Newfoundland, which the leader called the Isle of Baccalaos because the natives used that name for the fish abounding in the waters thereabouts. Later it was learned that the Basque people used the same word for codfish, and this raised the suggestion that Basque ships had preceded Cabot in reaching this part of the world. From Newfoundland the fleet turned north in pursuit of that mirage, the Northwest Passage. They found themselves soon in seas filled with icebergs. This was disconcerting, but nothing could shake their conviction that they must sail ever northward.

Sebastian Cabot, the second son of the commander, was with his father, and it is from a later document, based entirely on his recollections, that the story of the expedition is drawn. Although the season was now well advanced, the majestic icebergs rode the seas in such numbers that there was constant danger of collision. The shores were bare and inhospitable, becoming less and less like the rich lands of Cathay which they sought. At one point, which was believed later to have been Port of Castles, the commander was convinced that he had discovered the mythical Island of the Seven Cities, and there was much excitement as a result. He had mistaken the high basaltic cliffs for the turrets of castles. He persisted in his error sufficiently to report the occurrence later, but it is clear that at the time no effort was made to get closer to where, presumably, the descendants of the seven bishops still lived.

The weather became so cold and uncertain that the northward probe had to be abandoned. Sick at heart and still convinced that the route around the world lay in the north, they finally gave up the quest and turned back.

A determined effort was made then to find some source of wealth in the lands lying south of Newfoundland. The fleet took a southwesterly slant which carried them to Cape Breton and Nova Scotia. Sebastian Cabot, who later achieved a high reputation as a cartographer and maritime authority generally, seems to have possessed the highly unscientific habit of exaggeration. His report of the last part of the journey leaves the impression that the ships from Bristol sailed as far south as the Carolinas, but this obviously was impossible, for they were back in England before the end of the summer. They had found nothing new, they had not seen a single inhabitant, their reports depicted the new continent as bare and grim and, above everything else, silent. They brought back nothing to compensate for the expense of the expedition save cargoes of fish.

On Cabot's return England seemed momentarily to lose interest in North America. This strange land had nothing to offer, no silks, no gold, no precious stones. It had no castles save the glistening towers of ice which floated in the sea. The investors had wasted their money and their ships in an unprofitable venture. Lanslot Thirkill and Thomas of that ilk still had loans from the King to pay off, at a good interest, no doubt. The benefactors of Cabot's freehanded generosity could whistle for their grants of land. The priests who were to have been made bishops returned to much humbler shares in the activities of Mother Church.

Nothing more is known of John Cabot. It is probable that he died within a relatively short time, for there is no record of the payment of the pension beyond the first two installments. His descent into oblivion was rapid and complete. His son Sebastian lived to a ripe old age and held important posts under the rulers of Spain. His boastfulness as to the part he had played in the explorations of his father made him the central figure in bitter controversies centuries after his death; into which it would be unprofitable to enter here.

England had lost a great opportunity. Nothing was done to colonize the lands which Cabot had found, although the fisheries of Newfoundland were developed by enterprising captains from Bristol, St. Malo, and the Basque and Portuguese ports. While Spain was achieving world leadership through the wealth which followed her vigorous conquest of the continent Columbus had discovered, the Tudor monarchs made only ineffectual efforts to follow up the discoveries of Cabot.

Small things have often swayed the course of history. If an arrow shot into the sky had not lodged in Harold's eye, the Normans might conceivably have been defeated at Hastings. Two centuries after Cabot's death a merry little tune, whistled and sung to seditious words and called *Lillibulero,* would play quite a part in ousting a bad king from the throne of England. Perhaps to the list this may be added: that the grant of ten pounds by a parsimonious king to the man who had found a continent may have put a damper on individual enterprise in following up his exploit and so resulted in the temporary loss of this great land which later would be called Canada.

CHAPTER II

Before and after Cabot

1

ALTHOUGH John Cabot had supplemented the discoveries of Columbus by proving the existence of a continent in the North, he was not the first European to set foot on what is now called North America. The Norsemen had discovered Iceland and Greenland long before men of their own race took possession of Normandy, and certainly many centuries before men began to discuss seriously the possibility that the earth was round like the stars in the sky. The rugged men from the North established permanent settlements on both islands. In the year 986 a Viking captain named Bjarne Herjutfson was sailing for Greenland and became lost in foggy weather. He was driven far off his course and came to a land which he knew was not Greenland because it was covered with tall green trees and was very pleasant and warm. Bjarne was so anxious to reach his objective that he made no effort to learn about these strange new shores. After he arrived he told the story of what he had seen and in time it was carried back to Norway. The feeling took hold of the Viking people that some effort should be made to investigate.

In the year 1000, accordingly, a bold young sea captain named Leif, a son of Eric the Red, who had already made his home in Greenland, decided to take the task on his shoulders. He reached Greenland and bought from the less enterprising Bjarne the ship in which the latter had made his voyage, believing, no doubt, that it would bring him luck. With a crew of thirty-five he ventured into the warmer seas which lay to the south and west.

Leif made three landings. The first was on a coast which was cold and flat and snowbound. This he named Helluland and it was, without a doubt, somewhere on the coast of Labrador. After a further venture of several days' duration into the southward they came to a land of much fairer promise. Here there were tall trees and the air was mild and there were beaches of fine sand. Leif called this country Markland. It might have been Cape Breton or Nova Scotia, although it is hard to believe that the ship could have missed Newfoundland on the way. Finally they came to a delightful coast which seemed to the weary crew like the Valhalla where they all aspired to go after death. It was a land, to quote from the Norse saga, where even the dew on the grass had a sweet taste and the salmon were the largest ever to delight the eyes of men. There were vines along the beaches carrying great crops of grapes, and so they called this gentle country Vinland. They wintered there in great comfort and content and returned to Greenland in the spring.

The Norse settlers in the far North were very much excited by the reports Leif and his men brought back with them. In the course of the next few years other parties set out to cover the same course and some of them succeeded in locating Vinland. Leif's brother Thorwald was one of the first and he spent two winters in that land of warmth and plenty. It was Thorwald who located the first natives. They were men with copper-colored skins, of great physical strength and savage disposition. These red men were armed with bows and arrows and they had boats made of the skins of animals in which they got around with amazing dispatch. Thorwald was killed in a brush with them and he was buried, in accordance with his wish, under the green sod close to the shore and within hearing of the slow-breaking combers.

A determined effort to settle Vinland permanently was made a few years later, in 1007 to be exact. A young Norseman named Thorfinn organized a fleet of ships and set out with a considerable company. There were one hundred and sixty men in the party as well as a number of women. They took a herd of cattle with them and they built houses and cleared land for cultivation, after which they turned the cattle out to pasture on the thin outcropping of vegetation along the beaches. Thorfinn's wife had accompanied him, and a son was born to them who was given the name of Snorre and who enjoyed, therefore, the honor of being the first white child born on the continent of North America.

The natives were becoming openly hostile to the efforts of these white-skinned intruders to settle down permanently in their hunting and fishing grounds, and the period during which Thorfinn and his companions remained in Vinland was one long and bloody struggle with the resentful redskins. So many of the Vikings were killed that finally they gave up the effort to remain and returned reluctantly to a grim and iron existence on Greenland's icy mountains.

Just where Vinland was has never been settled to the complete satisfaction of scholars, although it has been conveniently assumed that it was one of the islands lying south of Rhode Island and Cape Cod. Much of the evidence points that way, although grapes could have been found farther north. The remnants of a stone mill, which has been labeled the Newport Tower, have been found on the southern coast of New England and there are clear indications that it was the work of Scandinavians.

There is one point of evidence which inclines some scholars to a belief that the northern part of Newfoundland was as far south as the wandering Norsemen reached. In the *Flateyjarbók,* which is the chief authority for the stories of Norse exploration, it is stated that on the shortest day at Vinland the sun remained above the horizon from seven-thirty in the morning until four-thirty in the afternoon. However, the word used to designate the closing hour of daylight is "eykarstad," and there has been much dispute as to whether this particular word means four-thirty or three-thirty. If the latter is the accurate definition, the shortest day was no more than eight hours long, and that would place Vinland close to Latitude 50. In other words, it must have been somewhere on southern Labrador or the northernmost portion of Newfoundland.

The latest contribution to the controversy has been the finding of mooring holes in rocks on Cape Cod. Now the mooring hole is a device used by the Vikings, and the Vikings only, a hole in the granite boulders of the fiords into which an iron rod would be slipped to keep a vessel fast to shore. This find has been acclaimed by many scholars as proof that Vinland was Cape Cod. It seems a reasonable assumption.

The fact is thoroughly well established, therefore, that the Norsemen found North America and paid many visits to it. Quite recent discoveries hint at more determined efforts on their part to investigate the new continent. There is the Kensington Stone in Minnesota which is covered with runes from the fourteenth century—quite recently relics have been discovered which are unquestionably of Norse origin—heavy battle-axes, swords, spears, a fire-steel of the late Dark Ages. Did the hardy Norsemen, at some date much later than the Vinland adventures, strike far inland and reach the valley of the Red River? It is a fascinating subject for speculation, but until more evidence comes to light it can be nothing more than that.

2

The efforts of the English to follow up the discoveries of Cabot included an expedition sent out in 1501 by the merchants of Bristol. It was headed by three Englishmen, named Ward, Ashhurst, and Thomas, and three Portuguese. Nothing is known about what they accomplished, but it is recorded that Henry VII gave them five pounds on their return. In 1522 there was a different king in England, Henry VIII, and in his forthright way he made it clear to the merchants of London that he expected them to do something about North America. The bluff young king was already spending with a lavish hand the magnificent fortune his father had saved so slowly and carefully, but he had no thought of applying any of it to the proposed expedition. He told the heads of the London guilds that he would be content with nothing less than a fleet of five ships, well manned and provisioned. The merchants were not seafaring men; they were vintners and mercers and goldsmiths, and averse to anything but the management of their countinghouses. They had no stomach for adventure, and it was only in response to the King's hectoring that they finally equipped two of the smallest ships they could find, named the *Samson* and the *Mary of Guildford*. The unlucky *Samson*, caught in a mid-Atlantic storm, went down with all on board, but the *Mary* weathered the blow and conducted a reconnaisance of the American coast which ended off the island of Puerto Rico. Here she encountered a welcome from the Spanish in the form of a salvo of cannon fire. The *Mary* very sensibly turned about and sailed for home.

There was something ephemeral about all the efforts at exploration which followed immediately after the success of Cabot. Many ships crossed the Atlantic without adding anything tangible to the world's knowledge. The thought of colonization does not seem to have entered the calculations of anyone. They were still looking for the magic passage which would give an entrance to Cathay and the easy rewards of gold and precious stones and rich fabrics. One of the most resourceful of the explorers was a nobleman of the Azores named Gaspar Corte-Real, who sailed from Lisbon and was the first to penetrate into Hudson Strait. He packed the holds of his two ships with natives and took them back to Portugal, where they were sold as slaves.

France had no part in this until Francis I came to the throne in 1515. He was twenty-one years old, ambitious and gifted and spoiled by the atmosphere of adoration in which he had been raised by his mother and his older sister. He had a long straight nose and long straight legs and he was a sybarite by disposition. There were two other youthful monarchs sitting on great thrones at this point in history. The burly Henry VIII had been King of England for six years, and it was acknowledged by all his courtiers that he was the best rider, the best wrestler, the best singer and composer, the best player at cards, the best jouster, in fact the best at everything in the whole kingdom of England. Because of the mortality in the family of Ferdinand and Isabella of Spain the succession had come to Charles, son of their second daughter, Joanna, who had married Philip, the heir of the Hapsburgs, and had died in madness. Thus Charles, the fifth of his line, succeeded to all the Hapsburg dominions as well as Spain. He had Austria and Sicily and the Netherlands and all of America, and at the age of twenty for good measure he was elected Holy Roman Emperor. Charles was a reserved young man, with a clear head and a sagacious eye and a jaw which jutted out in an exaggeration of the Hapsburg profile. He might lack the graces of Francis and the swaggerie of Henry, but in point of capacity and unswerving purpose he was without a peer.

Nothing would suit Francis the Sybarite, the finest dresser in all Christendom, but that he must outshine his two rivals. Obviously he could not allow them a monopoly in this matter of opening up the New World in the west. He, the darling of the gods, must project himself into this contest in globe-girdling. Shrewdly enough he fixed his eye on one Giovanni de Verrazzano, who had just returned from a very successful venture in buccaneering in the waters which later became known as the Spanish Main, with plenty of gold and silver in his hold and a price on his head. This bold and able captain was sent out from Dieppe in 1524 with four ships and instructions to establish the claims of France to some slice of the great new continent. Verrazzano found that only one of the vessels, the *Dauphine*, was seaworthy. Leaving the others behind, he reached the coast of the Carolinas in the *Dauphine* and from there made his way north to Belle Isle between Newfoundland and Labrador. He noted the possibilities of a harbor where a broad river (later called the Hudson) came down to the sea. He lingered here a short time and then went on, having been visited with no prophetic vision of enormous white towers reaching up into the sky and streets like echoing canyons. He took back to France plenty of evidence that the northern half of America was rich and temperate and ripe for exploitation; and if the new King had been a ruler of determination and singleness of purpose the result would have been an earlier move to acquire this great new country. But by this time Francis had become involved in a struggle with Charles V and was commanding an army in Italy. Within a year the ambitious dilettante was defeated and captured at the battle of Pavia and carried off to Spain as a prisoner. The American project languished for years as a result. In the meantime Verrazzano came to an untimely end, being captured, according to one report, by the Spaniards and hanged in chains as a pirate.

While this went on, of course, fishing boats continued to ply back and forth each year between the western ports of Europe and the waters of Newfoundland. Bristol was supplying a good part of England with the fish brought back in the holds of her sturdy ships, and the port of St. Malo was doing the same for France. As many as a score of ships went out to the Grand Banks every season. They were content with this small share of the wealth of the new-found continent. No one guessed how close they were to a tremendous secret; that just behind the Island of Baccalaos (this name being still commonly used) there was a gulf shaped like a great funnel of the gods into which a majestic river poured. This beautiful river rolled down seaward from a string of the largest lakes in the world through a transverse valley of more than half a million square miles. Its estuary was so vast that its salt waters exceeded all other river systems put together. The fishermen would have been little concerned if they had known that in the two thousand miles of this new continent a new nation would be nurtured, but their eyes would have gleamed with excited speculation if they had been told of the tremendous stores of gold in the Cambrian shield which bordered the northern rim of the basin.

The stout fishermen set their nets and hauled in their heavy catches. They talked of picking up gold someday on the streets of a mythical Cathay, but the words Quebec and Canada were never on their lips.

CHAPTER III

Jacques Cartier Discovers Canada

1

IT WAS a chill and overcast day, April 20, 1534. Gusts of wind swept across the old harbor of St. Malo, so rich in seafaring tradition. They caused a rustling in the sails of two small caravels, taut at their anchor chains. They were even more audacious, these April winds, for they fluttered the tails of the absurdly wide fur-trimmed cloak of Charles de Mouey, Sieur de la Milleraye, and displayed his wine-colored breeches slashed with yellow, and the jeweled bragetto at his belt. This was a great liberty, for Charles de Mouey was a vice-admiral of France and he stood, it was whispered, close to the King.

The explanation of the ceremony which was being carried out at the harborside was this: Francis had regained his liberty by swearing to certain terms which he repudiated soon after reaching his own soil and now he was free to proceed with other plans. Wondering perhaps if his honor, which he cherished like a maiden lady sighing over faded rose leaves, had survived the breakage of his liberation vows, he had decided to bolster it up by making another effort to establish a colonial empire in the West. The two caravels had been fitted out and provisioned, and crews of thirty men had been selected for each. The commander was to be a relatively obscure man who stood beside Charles de Mouey on this occasion, one Jacques Cartier, to whom the sum of six thousand livres had been granted for expenses.

Jacques Cartier stood high in the regard of seafaring men, so high in fact that Messire Honoré des Granches, chevalier and constable of St. Malo, had allowed his own daughter, Marie Catherine, to marry him. He was now forty-three years of age, a stocky man with a sharply etched profile and calm eyes under a high, wide brow;

slightly hawk-billed as to mouth, it must be confessed, and with a beard which bristled pugnaciously. It was the face of a man who finds philosophic calm in contemplation of the sea but can be roused easily to violent action.

Jacques Cartier presented a distinct contrast to the fashionably attired admiral. He was dressed in a thick brown cloak, belted in tightly at the waist. The tunic he wore under the cloak was open at the neck, where a white linen shirt showed. This was not the garb of a gentleman; it was intended for hard wear and was as unpretentious as the street sign of an obscure glove merchant. His hat had nothing to distinguish it from the flat cloth caps of the crew save three modest tufts in the brim. A sober man, this, fair in his dealings, capable and without fear, and with a hint of power in his steady eyes. There was a thoughtful air about him as he listened to the silky tones of the admiral, whose chief nautical achievement had been, undoubtedly, to sail close to the wind of royal favor at court.

"It is my intention," the great man was saying, "to require this of each and every member of the crews, that you stand before me in turn and swear an oath to serve faithfully and truly the King and your commander."

Everyone knew what was behind this announcement. St. Malo did not favor any further efforts to open up the new continent. It was very pleasant and profitable for them as things stood, with the chance to fish in the most prolific of waters, free of governmental control and supervision. They did not want colonies on the shores of America, and regulations to fetter their movements, and great men like this furred and feathered admiral to keep them in line. Their attitude of sullen opposition was so well known that this oath had been deemed necessary to insure their obedience at sea.

Reluctantly, perhaps, the men came forward one by one and knelt before the admiral. His padded sleeves rustling with each movement he made, Charles de Mouey administered the oath to them. His manner said plainly, "An assistant could do this quite well enough, but I, an admiral of France, desire you to know that I spare myself no effort in the service of our sovereign lord the King, and that the same is expected of you."

It has been said that the caravels were small. They were, in point of fact, quite tiny, not exceeding sixty tons each. They showed some considerable differences and improvements, however, from the equally diminutive vessels in which John Cabot had set out to sea.

They stood higher in the water and the superstructures were elaborately carved. Under the quarter-deck of each caravel protruded four black-muzzled guns. These humble cannon would be of little use in a deadly hull-to-hull sea fight, but they gave Jacques Cartier a fine sense of conviction, that they could be depended on to emit enough heavy smoke and set enough echoes flying to scare all hostile intent out of the copper-skinned natives he expected to encounter.

And so the two little ships took off. The commander, his stocky legs planted firmly on the upper deck, his dark eyes fixed ahead, was convinced that this time there would be results, that he was leading the first practical effort to solve the enigma of the silent continent so far off in the west.

2

It is easy to believe that Jacques Cartier had guessed the great secret of what lay behind the island of Newfoundland. At any rate, he set about the solving of it with a directness which hinted at a sense of the truth. Fortunately he was a man of methodical habit and each night he sat down in his tiny cabin and with stiff fingers and a spluttering pen recorded each step of the voyage. Fortunately, also, he was articulate and so he left for posterity a quite graphic account of what was to prove the discovery of Canada.

It took the two caravels no more than twenty days to come within sight of Newfoundland. It happened that their first glimpse of that mountainous and formidable island was a pleasant one—Cape Bonavista standing up high over the sea with a hint of welcome. Bonavista Bay proved to be blocked with ice, however, and so Cartier found it necessary to shelter in a harbor a few leagues south. In gratitude for the safe ease he found here, the commander named it St. Catherine's Harbor after the loving woman who had condescended to become his wife. His deep affection for her caused him to apply her name to many of the places he encountered in the course of his explorations.

As soon as the ships had been given an overhauling they started out again, sailing north for the narrow stretch of violent water between the northern tip of Newfoundland and the shores of Labrador. The fishermen, who swarmed around the eastern shore of the tall sentry island, had labeled this strait Belle Isle. Ordinarily it was a rough piece of water with the recession of the tides and the strong flow of the waters of the St. Lawrence seeking an outlet to the sea and, to make matters worse, a most unusual storm was raging when Cartier's ships reached the eastern entrance. A violent wind from the west was taking hold of the hurrying current and whipping it into a maelstrom. No sailing vessel could make head-way under these conditions. The caravels were hauled in to anchor-age at what is now Kirpon Harbor and waited there for the storm to subside.

It is easy to believe that the tumultuous flow of waters through the strait had a significance for the commander of the expedition, who was, first of all, a master pilot. It must have appeared to Cartier that he was witnessing the liberation of tremendous waters. Was this, then, the eastern end of the Northwest Passage? One can imagine this man of calm eyes and aggressive jaw pacing his tiny quarter-deck and watching the down-flow with speculative eyes. "This is what I came to find," he would be thinking. "Once we can get through, we will strike straight into the heart of Cathay."

It was not until June 9 that the violence of the winds abated and it was possible to turn the noses of the caravels into the narrow passage. They found it plain sailing now and very soon were through the strait with open water ahead of them. They passed an island which the faithful husband named after his wife (Alexander the Great had set an example by naming six cities after himself) and came to Blanc Sablon. These dangerous shoals were described by Cartier as a bight with no shelter from the south and abounding with islands which seemed to afford sanctuary to enormous quanti-ties of birds, tinkers and puffins and sea gulls. They passed the Port of Castles, but it was clear to them that what Cabot had thought were the turrets of great strongholds were no more than natural cliffs corroded to the shape of battlements; and so the story of find-ing the Island of the Seven Cities was dispelled. One day's sailing brought them to Brest Harbor, where they dropped anchor. Cartier decided to use the ship's boats for a further exploration of the north shore.

He came back disillusioned, realizing that this was not the long-sought-for Northwest Passage. It is more than probable that he was beginning to suspect the truth, that it was the mouth of a power-

ful river. The land of the north shore, moreover, was stony and
barren and thoroughly forbidding. In his notes that night he wrote:

I did not see a cartload of good earth. To be short I believe that this was
the land that God allotted to Cain.

A deeply religious man could think of nothing more damning to
say than that. The land was inhabited in spite of its worthlessness.
Cartier had come in contact with natives for the first time. They had
followed him at a discreet distance in small and light craft which
seemed to be made of the bark of trees. Cartier described them as
"of indifferent good stature," wearing their hair tied on the top "like
a wreath of hay."

At this stage Cartier showed himself the possessor in full measure
of vision and daring. He set sail at once down the west of Newfoundland with the determination to locate the southern shore of
this mighty river. Newfoundland was cloaked in a continuous fog
which would lift occasionally and give awe-inspiring glimpses of
high mountain peaks, stark and aloof and mysterious. It was self-
evident to a pilot with a shrewd understanding of the movements
of water that there must be a second outlet in the south. He was
so sure of it that he did not waste any time in seeking it but turned
his ships and with daring and imagination struck due west, thus
coming in contact with the strong current of the gulf.

His reward came quickly. Sixty miles brought him to an island
of such restfulness and beauty that he put into his notes, "One acre
of this land is worth more than all the New Land," meaning the
shores which up to this time had constituted the whole of the new
continent. Then he continued westward and passed the Magdalen
group and the north shore of what would later be called Prince
Edward Island, coming at last to what he was convinced must be
the mainland.

It was wonderful country. The heat of July had covered the open
glades with white and red roses. There were berries and currants
in abundance and a wild wheat with ears shaped like barley. The
trees were of many familiar kinds, white elm, ash, willow, cedar,
and yew. To the north and west were high hills, but these were
vastly different from the stern mountains of Newfoundland and the
barrenness of the north shore. There was friendliness in their green-
covered slopes and a welcome in their approach to the water's edge.

Because of the heat, which was more intense than they were ac-

GREENLAND

LABRADOR

Belle Isle

Gulf of St Lawrence

Saguenay R.

St Lawrence R.

TERRE NEUVE

NEW FRANCE

Quebec

Three Rivers

Montreal

St Croix R.

St Louis

L. CHAMPLAIN

RICHELIEU R.

Baye Française

Port Royal

LA CADIE

Sable Island

Atlantic Ocean

NEW FRANCE
after map by
Jean Boisseau
1643

palacios

customed to in their own rugged Brittany, Cartier called the bay
where they finally came to rest "Chaleur," and the Bay of Chaleur
it has been ever since.

It became apparent as soon as they made their first move to go
ashore that eyes had been watching them. Canoes appeared suddenly on the water. They kept appearing until there were as many
as fifty of them, filled with fearsome-looking savages who screeched
and yelped with what seemed to be warlike intent. It needed no
more than a glance to realize that they were different from the dark
and somewhat stolid inhabitants of the north shore, who may have
been of Eskimo stock. These were woodsmen, lithe and spare and
strong. The Frenchmen did not like the look of things at all; and
instead of making a landing as they had intended, they turned their
boats about and began to row for the ships which were lying at
anchor some distance away.

As soon as this happened the paddles of the Indians were dipped
into the water with furious energy and the canoes came on in pursuit at a speed which astonished the white visitors. The boat in
which Cartier was seated was surrounded in a matter of minutes.
The natives were now seen to have faces painted hideously with red
and white ocher so that they seemed to be wearing masks.

The commander had prepared for some such contingency and he
signaled back to the ships. Watchers in the shrouds had been keeping their eyes open and had already sensed the danger. The tomkins
had been stripped from two of the little cannon and the waddings
of oakum, which were called fids, had been removed from the black
muzzles. As soon as Cartier's arm was raised the guns were
fired.

To ears familiar with gunnery this was no more than a puff of
smoke, but to the natives it was as though the voices of all the bad
gods had spoken from afar. They took to their paddles in such haste
that in a matter of seconds they were plowing paths of retreat in all
directions. The white men sighed gustily with relief and leaned to
their oars in a desire to attain the safety of the ships.

The Indians were of stouter heart than their panicky retreat would
seem to suggest. Finding that no harm had come to them from the
horrendous uproar of the guns, they brought their canoes about and
began a second approach, this time in a wide and cautious circle.
Cartier decided to take no further chances and, before the canoes
had come close again, he had his men raise their muskets and fire

a volley in the air. This was too much for the redskins. The voice of the distant cannon had been deep and resounding, but the rattle of musketry was sharp and staccato and it shattered the air about their ears with a threat of immediate violence. They made a second retreat, and after that, as Cartier noted in his journal, "would no more follow us."

The next day the savages recovered from their panic and came back with an obvious desire to trade, although they were careful to come well equipped with the stone hatchets they called *cochy* and their knives, which they called *bacan*. There were hundreds of them, including many women and children. They had brought cooked meats with them which they broke into small pieces and placed on squares of wood; and then withdrew to see if their offerings would be accepted. Cartier's men tasted the meat and found it a welcome change from the fish and salted fare on which they had been living. When the natives saw that their gift had been well received, they danced exuberantly and threw salt water on their heads and shouted, *"Napou tou daman asurtat!"* with the best good will. The women were less fearful than the men and certainly more curious, for they came up close to these godlike visitors who had, seemingly, dropped from the clouds. They ran their hands over the wondrous costumes, uttering loud cries of astonishment and delight.

The result was that the two groups, the fair-skinned newcomers, garbed in which seemed to be all the hues of the rainbow, and the almost naked redskins, soon got together for a trading spree. It followed the usual course of all such exchanges. The natives parted with valuable furs and received trinkets in exchange—bracelets made of tin and the simplest of iron tools and "a red hat for their captain"—but were certain that they were having all the best of it and went away happy.

The ships turned north again on July 12 and came to another deep bay which Cartier hoped at first would prove to be the passage through which this great volume of water came rolling down to the sea. Finding that he was wrong, but becoming convinced that he had found the mainland, he had his men construct a tall cross of wood. It proved to be an impressive monument, thirty feet high, with a shield nailed to the crossbeam on which the fleur-de-lis had been carved. At the top, in large Gothic characters, the words had been inscribed:

Vive le roy de France

The cross was erected on the shore with great ceremony in the presence of a large gathering of natives who had emerged from the woods or had paddled across the water in their fleet canoes. As soon as it had been securely fixed, the white men dropped to their knees and raised their arms toward the heavens in a gesture of humility and praise.

This was a memorable occasion. To all with an eye for the picturesque and a desire to see the story of the past dressed out in full panoply, it has seemed the real starting point of Canadian history. The exact spot where the cross was raised has never been ascertained. The tall beam with its antique carving soon began to sag from the buffeting of the winds and finally dropped and in time merged with the soil; but the memory of that impressive moment when it was first elevated against the background of green verdure and blue sky will remain forever in Canadian minds.

The watching natives had some of the imaginative quality which would be displayed so often later. They stood in silent ranks, their dark eyes fixed on the symbol of a strange faith. Instinctively they knew that these thickset men in multicolored clothes were claiming the land for themselves. Storms had been raging and so it is possible that the sun was not out; but the apprehensive savages did not need to see the shadow of the cross stretching out over this fair domain to know that their possession was being threatened. They looked at their chief, a very old man who had wrapped his skinny shoulders in a ceremonial blanket. He had turned his gaze up to the skies as though seeking guidance from the gods who dwelt there. As he made no move, his followers began to shout that shrill demand which would be heard so many times later and in so many ways, sometimes expressed in the blood lust of the war cry, the "*Cassee kouee!*" of the dreaded Iroquois; and always having the same meaning, "Go away! Go away!"

When the ceremony had been completed, the mariners returned to their ships. The Indians followed later in their canoes, and the old chief, standing up in one of them, delivered a long oration. The nature of his talk could be determined from the gravity of his manner and the expressive gestures he used. He was telling the fair-skinned visitors that this land belonged to his people and that they had no intention of sharing it.

Cartier invited the old man and his followers to come aboard the ships. They were feasted and given presents and made much of generally. Two of the chief's sons were given red cloaks and hats, which they donned with childlike eagerness. In the meantime the French leader had succeeded by the use of gestures in convincing the solemn old orator that the cross was intended only as a guide-post. Then with more gestures he invited the two sons to stay and sail back to the land from which the magic ships had come. They assented without any hesitation.

The status of divinity which the deluded natives were always so willing to grant the newcomers was due to many things but above everything else to the wonder of the white man's sails. This was a phenomenon which never failed to entrance them; the breaking out of those great squares of color and then the graceful speed with which the monster vessels swayed and dipped with the winds and so faded off into the horizon.

Not more than half convinced of the honesty of the white men, the savages were still entranced by the wonder of the sails as they watched the departure of these strange gods. Cartier, it may be taken for granted, observed everything carefully from his post on the quarter-deck: the activities on deck and the strutting figures of the clownish sons of the old chief, the doubt in the slow dip of the native paddles. He was glad to be away.

The land receded slowly and the tall cross faded back into the black and green of the trees. Filled with the purpose which had brought him here, Cartier could not have doubted that on this momentous day, on this shore to which he had given the name of Gaspé, he had founded an empire for France.

3

Cartier struck north again and came to a very large island which would be known later as Anticosti. The ships passed to the north of this island and reached the west point with great difficulty. The current here was strong and fierce and an August storm was raging. The final stage of the northern passage was attempted in one of the boats while the ships rode uneasily at anchor. The attempt failed. Thirteen men, pulling furiously against the current, were unable to advance more than a very few feet in an effort which lasted for hours. Accordingly Cartier had himself put ashore and went on foot to the westernmost tip of the island. Here he stood for a considerable time, looking full ahead into that great surging mass of water. The distance from Gaspé to Anticosti had proven that the passage had narrowed appreciably. It must have been clear to him by this time that he was in the mouth of a mighty and majestic river.

Returning to his ship, he summoned all the men of the two crews to a council. In his mind there must have been a consciousness that new concepts of democracy would be developed in this land; at any rate, his notes say that he called in "the sailing-masters, pilots and sailors." They came and stood closely packed about him or on the open deck below, the sailors no doubt in the rear, saying nothing and holding their flat caps in their hands with due respect. The commander outlined the decision which they faced, making it clear first that in his belief they were on the threshold of discovery, that the furiously flowing water against which they had been battling came straight from the heart of this new continent. Conditions made it impossible, however, for them to progress any farther that year. Should they set up winter quarters and be prepared to resume their explorations in the spring, or should they begin at once their return to St. Malo?

The crews seemed to have been unanimously in favor of the second course. They knew nothing of what wintering in this rugged country would entail, and it was clear they had little stomach for the experiment. It would be better, they contended, to sail back without delay in order to escape the equinoctial gales. Cartier may have been of the same mind. He does not, at any rate, record any dissent on his part, and the decision, accordingly, was in favor of an immediate return.

They set sail for the east. With the raging winds of the August storm at their backs, they came swiftly to the shoal waters of Blanc Sablon, where they hove to in order to refit for the long homeward voyage. The trip through Belle Isle was accomplished without accident. And so, in due course, they arrived back in St. Malo with the great news of what they had found.

CHAPTER IV

The Kingdom of Saguenay
—Stadacona and Hochelaga

1

A YEAR was to elapse before Jacques Cartier made his second voyage to the new land, and in that period two minor characters in the drama were to assume considerable importance. They were called Taignoagny and Damagaya, and they were the sons of the old chief, the two zanies who had been so carried away by the colored garments and the red hats given them on that memorable day at the Bay of Gaspé that they had eagerly embraced the opportunity to accompany the white men back to France. They had picked up enough knowledge of the French language to be able to act later as interpreters, and with this command of the white man's tongue they had been talking of their own country, telling the eager questioners of its vast extent and wealth. The portion of their story which created the greatest interest was the legend of the Kingdom of Saguenay.

This, as the dusky pair must have told it, was of a fabulously rich country where the yellow metal could be found in great quantities. It was located far up a mighty river which flowed straight down from the north and joined an even greater one where a city of many hundreds of wigwams called Hochelaga stood on an island. Despite the confusion in the use of the word Saguenay, this description clearly placed this rich country on the Ottawa River, as Cartier was to learn later. The people of this mysterious kingdom, according to Taignoagny and Damagaya, dressed themselves in cloth like that of white men, and they wore ropes of gold around their necks and had plenty of precious stones. This was the kind of thing that everyone wanted to believe about the new continent, and it may be taken for granted that the two hostages were pumped dry.

It is a matter of record that interest in the new continent took an upward leap, and this could not have been due entirely to Cartier's report of what he had seen and found. He did not have anything very sensational to add to what was already known, save the knowledge he had acquired of the great gulf back of Newfoundland and his conviction that this was the passage into the heart of Cathay. A month after his return a commission was issued on behalf of the King by Philippe Chabot, admiral of France, which provided royal backing for a new expedition on a much larger scale to be undertaken as soon as the necessary ships could be fitted out and manned and provisioned for fifteen months. This was to be done at the King's expense, and Cartier was given a free hand in making the necessary preparations.

It may be taken for granted that Francis, who was not freehanded to the point of extravagance and who moreover was burdened with the debts of his interminable war-making, would not have promised the funds for such an ambitious venture if he had not been sure that great wealth would come out of it. He wanted to set up against Spain a rival empire in the western world, it is true, but at the same time his cupidity must have been fired by that magic word, gold. It was the bait of this mythical kingdom of Saguenay which loosened the purse strings of the never too generous Francis.

2

The following year three ships set out from St. Malo. They were the *Grande Hermine,* a leviathan of 120 tons, the *Petite Hermine* of 60 tons, and a pinnace of 40 tons which was called the *Ermillion.* The enrollment for the three crews totaled 112 men. That the imagination of France had been fired to white heat was evidenced by the inclusion of a number of gentlemen of high degree, including Claud de Pontbriant, a son of the Lord of Montreal and a cupbearer to the dauphin, Charles de la Pommeraye, Jean Poulet, and Jean Guyon, all of whom wanted a share in this great adventure. It was on May 19 that the three stout ships put out to sea and set their sails for the west, where, everyone was sure, fame and fortune awaited them.

The *Grande Hermine* outstripped the other vessels and reached Newfoundland alone on July 7. Cartier sailed around the northern tip of the island and dropped anchor at Blanc Sablon, which had been selected as the spot for which all the ships would make in case they lost contact during the Atlantic crossing. There was a long wait, but finally, on July 26, the *Petite Hermine* and the *Ermillion* came limping in together. Three days were allowed for refitting, and then the little fleet sailed out into the gulf and set their course for the west.

It was Cartier's second voyage which brought Canada to world attention, and everything which happened in that memorable year has been recorded at considerable length. As space does not permit full recapitulation, only a few of the highlights of this important stage in the history of the country can be set down here.

Two days west of Anticosti, Cartier's ships came in sight of the twin peaks through which the Saguenay River empties with the swiftness and deadliness of its terrifying depth into the St. Lawrence. The peaks stand up high from the water's edge, marking the end of the gorge through which this unusual river runs. The human eye cannot view these black cliffs without realizing that no orderly proc-ess of erosion could have been responsible for such results, that only a titanic upheavel could have made such a crack in the crust of the earth. Heated imaginations picture a furious rending of the surface, a rocking greater than any earthquake, a roaring like the trump of doom filling all of space. Such thoughts must have filled the minds of Cartier's men as they gazed at the two sentry peaks.

There seems to have been some confusion in the minds of the white men with reference to the legend of the Kingdom of Saguenay. The two hostages must have told them that this was the Saguenay River. Cartier accepted, without a doubt, the assertion of the two Indians that this was the river which yielded the precious yellow metal and where the inhabitants wore clothes of wool and adorned themselves with gold and rubies. He displayed the good judgment, however, of deciding that his duty was to continue westward into the great country which, according to Taignoagny and his brother, bore the euphonious name of Canada (meaning a village) instead of turning his ships into the tossing waters between the spine-chilling black cliffs in pursuit of the chimera of gold. The Kingdom of Saguenay would have to wait. Canada beckoned them on.

It has already been made clear that the first impression of the new continent was always of its vastness and silence. It seemed to rest in repose, waiting for the arrival of man to waken it to fertility. The forests along the shores, tall and dense, seemed both intermin-able and inscrutable. The only sounds heard were the occasional splash of a leaping fish and perhaps a distant cawing from the treetops.

Life, when it finally manifested itself, would be full of surprises. The mouth of a bay would open and there would be a village, a community of wigwams packed with red-skinned people, an exuberant people with painted faces. It would become apparent later that all these natives did not belong in the little village but had gathered there to greet the visitors. Eyes, clearly, had been on the white gods from the start, and the word of their coming had been carried through the forests and up and down the rivers with a speed which defied understanding.

Or it might be that a single canoe would be seen on the water, motionless and silent. Then there would be another and, almost in the winking of an eye, there would be many more. Finally there would be a fleet of them, filled with naked savages who would suddenly explode into excitement and sound. They would stand up in the canoes, waving their paddles and emitting bloodcurdling shrieks. This did not always signify hostility. The Indians, it developed, were always dramatic in anything they did: fierce in war, unrelenting in punishment, mad in their dances. They were graceful and expressive in their gestures, they fairly boiled with eloquence, they were actors in every square inch of their powerful and sometimes rancid bodies; and above everything else they were dramatic in their mastery of surprise.

The silence along the great rivers is understandable in the light of the relatively small numbers of the native population. Most of the tribesmen on the north shore of the St. Lawrence were nomadic, and people who do not sink down roots do not increase and multiply. The Montagnais and the Algonquins, the Indians with whom the French first made contact, were not numerically powerful. Even the Iroquois, who fastened their spell over the forests and the rivers to such an extent that it seemed as if a Mohawk warrior lurked behind every tree trunk, were not a large nation. It was estimated a century later, when the people of the Long House were at the peak of their power, that they could not muster more than two thousand warriors. This would place the total number of the Iroquois people somewhere between ten and twenty thousand. Canada was a silent land because it contained great stretches of country where the naked foot or the moccasin of the redskin had never trod.

Cartier pursued his way along the north shore of the basin, finding that he was indeed in an estuary which was shelving in rapidly. The tip of the great funnel was discovered to be a river not more than a mile in width at its mouth.

Cartier's ships came finally to the most beautiful island on which the eyes of the crews had ever rested. The commander called it the Isle of Bacchus because of the abundance of wild grapes growing on the beaches, but this would be changed later to the island of Orleans. Here a surprise awaited them. Some natives were seen in the woods, and it was apparent that they were going to run away in a great panic. Then they perceived Taignoagny and Damagaya and immediately they began instead to greet the returned hostages with every indication of joy and excitement. It was explained by the pair that this was the tribe to which they belonged and that they had been in Gaspé Bay on a fishing expedition when Cartier landed there and set up his cross.

The safe return of Taignoagny and Damagaya spread confidence in the good faith of the white men. The chief of the tribe, whose name was Donnacona, came forward and extended a warm welcome to the gods from beyond the seas. He and his people lived in a small village on the river near at hand, close also to a huge dome of rock which loomed up on the horizon. Cartier does not record his impressions when his eyes first lighted on these historic heights which would later be called Quebec, but it is easy to believe that some inner sense whispered to him that his eyes were resting on the cradle of a great new country.

A curious change came over Taignoagny and Damagaya as soon as they found themselves united to the members of their tribe. While in France they had been awed by what they saw. The stone cities, the frowning walls, the huge ships, and the booming of cannon had kept them in a perpetual state of wonder, with probably a tincture of fear. Now they became taciturn and sullen, and even hostile to the white men. While the rest of the tribe showed delight in welcoming the newcomers, bringing in their long canoes gifts of corn and pumpkin and fresh meat, and while Donnacona delivered long and flamboyant orations, the two interpreters stood off at one side and glowered suspiciously. Gradually this attitude affected the others. A general silence replaced the rejoicing and there was tensity in the air.

Finally the two hostages were persuaded to give an explanation. Taignoagny, who was more disaffected than his brother, explained that the Frenchmen showed no faith in Indian good will because they never set foot on shore unless armed to the teeth, while Donnacona and his followers had no weapons at all. Later the spokesman for the pair gave another reason, that the French intended to go on to the large settlement at Hochelaga. This, he declared, would not be wise.

The village, which lay near the St. Charles River, was called Stadacona, a small huddle of wigwams in a clearing along the shore. Here the white men remained for some days although conscious of the coolness in the attitude of the natives. Taignoagny continued to assail their ears with protests against their determination to proceed up the river. He even produced three medicine men to indulge in prophecies of the fate which awaited the Frenchmen if they went to Hochelaga. These dusky magicians, to quote Cartier, "were dressed like devils, being wrapped in dog-skins, white and black, their faces besmeared as black as any coals, with horns on their heads more than a yard long." They frothed at the mouth and filled the woods with their incantations, finally giving forth with a prophecy: the cruel god Cudragny had declared to them that the white men would surely die if they went to Hochelaga.

Cartier did not permit himself to be disturbed. "Your god Cudragny," he declared, "must be a fool and a noodle."

Taignoagny asked anxiously if Cartier had sought the opinion of Jesus, and the French commander answered that he had been promised safety and fair weather by the God to Whom all white men prayed.

3

Taking none of the unfriendly natives with him as guides, Cartier and fifty of his men went on in the pinnace. After nine days of easy sailing they reached what is now the island of Montreal. Here they were greeted by a thousand natives with demonstrations of wonder and delight. If Cartier's description is to be accepted, Hochelaga itself was the most formidable settlement in the whole of North America. It stood in the midst of broad cleared fields, at the base of a mountain which he proceeded to christen Mount Royal. The city was round and "compassed about with timber, with three courses of rampires, one within another, framed like sharp spikes." The city had one entrance only, which was kept shut and well guarded with stakes

and bars. Over the entrance, and in many places along the palisades
as well, there was a platform for use in defending against attacks.
The platform was full of stones to be dropped on the heads of
besiegers.

Inside the walls were about fifty houses, built all of wood. Some of
them were fifty paces long and twelve or fifteen broad. They were
covered over with bark "very finely and cunningly joined together."
Each of these houses had a center court for the making of fires and
they were cut up into many rooms, lodgings, and chambers.

The people of Hochelaga gathered in a central court to welcome
the white men officially. Their chief, a veteran so afflicted with palsy
that his legs had lost all power of movement, was carried in on the
shoulders of ten braves and deposited on a stag's skin. The old man
begged the white chief to cure him, and Cartier responded by rub-
bing the afflicted limbs.

The most interesting information gleaned at Hochelaga, by means
of gestures, had to do with the nature of the country. The existence
of the Kingdom of Saguenay was confirmed and was confidently
asserted to lie along the powerful Ottawa, which emptied into the
St. Lawrence at one end of the island on which Hochelaga stood.
Pointing to the silver chain of Cartier's whistle and the handle of a
dagger of copper-gilt dangling at the belt of a sailor, one of the
natives made it clear that these metals were to be found in the
country through which the Ottawa ran. A word of warning accompanied this information. The land where the silver and gold
would be found belonged to *Agojudas,* who were cruel and wicked
people. It was explained also that the country of Canada extended
much farther to the west, that it was enclosed by immense lakes and
guarded by waterfalls of great height.

In the minds of recent historians some doubts have been lodged as
to the accuracy of Cartier's description of Hochelaga. They point out
that he returned there on his third voyage but made no mention of
the place. Furthermore, Samuel de Champlain, who would visit the
island nearly a century later, found nothing there at all, nor has
anyone since discovered traces of the existence of such a large
community.

As a result, there is a tendency to wonder if the report of the sea
captain of St. Malo was exaggerated for a purpose. Could it be that
this section of his report was designed to encourage hopes in King
Francis of great wealth to be found in the New World? Was the

emphasis laid on the legend of the Kingdom of Saguenay a part of the same conspiracy?

A settlement of some importance existed there without a doubt. Cartier's description might very well have been applied to the Iroquois villages which Champlain saw later in the country of the Finger Lakes in northern New York. It could not, therefore, be sheer fabrication. It may have been that a hand other than Cartier's was responsible for certain interpolations which colored the version far beyond the limits of the truth. The mariner of St. Malo was a man of honest purpose, lacking the guile to invent such stories. The fact that in this part of the report there are faulty nautical references which a skilled and meticulous navigator would not use may be adduced as proof that some changes were made after the document was out of his hands. It may be pointed out further that Cartier was dead before the documents were published.

One thing is certain: if Hochelaga existed as set forth in the Cartier report, it soon thereafter vanished. This is understandable in the light of what Champlain found later. There was no trace of either Stadacona or Hochelaga when he followed in the footsteps of Cartier. The Indian tribes which the latter had seen had disappeared from the face of the earth, being replaced by entirely new stock.

Whether or not the Indians living under the shelter of Mount Royal ever built themselves such elaborate defenses and lived under bark roofs ingeniously contrived, there can be no doubt that they were a superior race. They were tall and vigorous, with strongly aquiline features and skins the hue of copper. Cartier speaks with wonder of their strength and powers of endurance. They had considerable skill at agriculture, and the cleared space about the settlement was filled with ripening corn and other cereals. It was indeed a noble prospect spread out before the eyes of the one and fifty brave Frenchmen. This was the time of harvest and the trees were loaded with fruit. A pleasant haze of heat still lay over the land, but the russets and reds and yellows of autumn were already showing themselves. The deep, invigorating waters of the river raced by the shore with the promise of plentiful fish.

Here was a land of plenty, and a better and truer picture to take back to the King of France, grasping though he might be, than stories of a fabulous kingdom where gold could be picked up on the streets and the natives strutted with rubies in their neckbands. If Francis, the great sophisticate, desired an empire across the seas, here it was: a land where men could live and raise fat crops and, in the course of time, increase and multiply, not a run-down and debased civilization which could be squeezed of its wealth and then abandoned.

4

The men who had been left at Stadacona while Cartier made his trip to Mount Royal had utilized the time in building a stockade on the banks of the Lairet, a small tributary of the St. Charles. It was solidly fortified, with cannon from the ships mounted to command all approaches. The commander's first care was to strengthen it still further. He had a moat dug around it and constructed a drawbridge as the only means of entrance. Fifty of the men were selected to garrison this fort while the rest remained on the ships. Watches were set at all hours of the day and night and bugles were sounded to warn the lurking red men that the visitors were vigilant. Here the party settled in for the winter. Perhaps Cartier looked sometimes at the great rocky heights looming up over Stadacona and wished that he had been able to build his fort on that impregnable peak.

From the middle of November the ships were solidly held in the frozen waters of the St. Lawrence. The cold was more intense than the Frenchmen had ever conceived possible and they suffered from it a great deal. Snow fell frequently in considerable volume along the northern shores of France, but Cartier's men had never seen anything to equal the blanket of white in which the world was now wrapped. The flakes came down endlessly, falling from the gray skies in a damp and ghostly silence until no other color was left in the world, and the drifts climbed like besieging foes as high as the narrow slits in the walls where the sentries stood. It turned the trees into white wigwams when it did not bank them over, an implacable as well as a silent antagonist. There was no use in clearing it away, for it blew back incessantly, and what had been an open path at twilight was a great white drift by dawn. Sometimes the snow was incredibly lovely: when the sun was out and the cold set the blood in human veins to pounding furiously and the surface of white was like a vast tray in a goldsmith's shop, sparkling with diamonds.

The chief menace for the closed-in Frenchmen, however, was the lack of fresh food. A disease of which they knew little began to manifest itself early, scurvy, the inveterate foe of seamen. Their gums rotted and their teeth fell out; their limbs became swollen and scarred with clotted blood. Eight men died before the end of the year, and the disease became progressively worse as the rigors of January and February held nature in an iron clutch. The mortality became such that Cartier had to bury the victims at night under the drifts of snow. This was necessary so that the ever-watchful Indians, egged on by Taignoagny, "that craftie knave," would not know how fast the ranks were being depleted. Those who were well enough were set to work at hammering and sawing so that the savages would be convinced a healthy activity existed both on shore and in the hulls of the ships.

It was not until fifty men had perished miserably that a cure was discovered. The disease was also taking its toll in the crowded and stinking wigwams of Stadacona, and Damagaya had been stricken with it finally. One day Cartier, who remained hale and healthy himself, met his one-time interpreter walking on the snowbanked surface of the river, clad in the thinnest of skin coat and leggings. Damagaya explained that he had been restored to full health by the use of the bark and leaves of the white spruce, which made an infallible cure when ground up and boiled.

This medicine was tried with some reservations, but in no time at all—a mere matter of weeks, in fact—all traces of scurvy had left the fort on the Lairet, and the crews on the ships had become normal and filled with new activity and spirits.

During the latter stages of the winter Donnacona and Taignoagny were missing from the Indian encampment. Later they returned, and it was found then that they had been with the more warlike tribes of the south. They had brought back with them a band of auxiliaries, fierce-looking strangers who hid themselves in Stadacona and whose presence was discovered by chance. A sense of mounting fear took possession of the Frenchmen, for it was now clear that at the first opportunity the red men, aided by these grim allies, would launch an attack.

Cartier decided to get away as soon as the river became navigable. He laid his plans so carefully that the natives, crafty and alert, had no suspicion of his purpose. On May 3, when the broken ice was churning and roaring down the great river, he erected another tall cross on the riverbank near the fort with a scroll carrying the words, *Franciscus Primus Dei Gratia Francorum Rex Regnat.* Then he invited a party of the Indians, including Donnacona and the two interpreters, to come aboard the ships for feasting and exchange of presents. The Indians, who were anxious to discover for themselves the state of the French defenses, came willingly in response. Ten climbed the bulwarks and were promptly made prisoners.

The next day, May 6, 1536, the flagship and the little pinnace hauled up their anchors and started off on the return voyage. It was necessary to leave the *Petite Hermine* in a state of emptiness at anchor, the size of the party having been cut down too sharply by the ravages of the disease to make it possible for them to navigate all three. Donnacona and his fellows were allowed to stand on deck and shout reassuringly to the tribesmen who followed sullenly and sorrowfully in their inadequate canoes.

Cartier was taking back the certain knowledge that here was a great continent ripe for settlement, fair land which could be made into the empire so avidly desired by the ambitious King and a rewarding home for the poor of the overflowing cities and towns of France.

CHAPTER V

The Feud between Cartier and Roberval

1

FRANCIS I is said to have listened with deep attention to Cartier's verbal report of the second voyage, studying the sea captain with quick, darting glances of his tawny eyes. Later the monarch talked with Donnacona, who had acquired in the meantime some knowledge of the French language. This was a chance for the unhappy chief to indulge in the lengthy periods and the elaborate metaphors of native oratory; and Donnacona, without a doubt, spoke so warmly of Canada that the royal listener found himself stirred to a deep interest. They presented quite a contrast: the debonair King with his appliquéd and jeweled sleeves puffed out like twin cobras, his slashed doublet of rich hues trimmed with the rare genet which only royalty was permitted to use, his chains of gold and his magnificent rings; and the unkempt red man in his frayed leggings and scanty skin shirt, causing a twitch of distaste at the end of the fastidious royal nose.

From one cause and another Francis became convinced that the continent over the western rim of the world was worth his royal attention. The Spanish Ambassador, whose master wanted to keep the rest of the nations out of America, had the ears of spies at all diplomatic keyholes, and word came to him promptly that Francis was getting ready to act. The French King, he was told, was talking much about the remarkable discoveries which would be made soon in the country of the "River of Cod."

Soon thereafter Francis succeeded in making a truce with Charles of Spain and felt free to consider again the question of America. He had to move cautiously because he knew that Charles would regard any efforts to claim a part of the New World as a hostile act. Time passed, therefore, before the decision was made. Francis decided finally to send a larger expedition to Canada than any his rival had sent out.

Unfortunately he made a serious error in policy. It was the old story again, the need of a figurehead. Inasmuch as it was now planned to send out settlers and artisans and proceed seriously with the colonization of these distant shores, the King felt that a man of noble lineage must be placed at the top. Cartier's work had been above criticism. In commanding the first two expeditions he had shown courage, foresight, moderation, sound judgment; but these were not enough. He was, after all, no more than a sea captain and a master pilot and not fitted to represent the King. Francis looked about him, therefore, for someone who would suit him better, and his choice was one Jean François de le Roque, Sieur de Roberval, a soldier who had distinguished himself in the campaigns of La Marck.

Roberval was not a seaman and he was lacking in the experience needed for leadership in a venture such as this. It soon became apparent that an unfortunate choice had been made.

2

It was inevitable that the Sieur de Roberval and Jacques Cartier would get at cross-purposes. Roberval was haughty and brusque, a man of harsh judgments and almost ferocious instincts. He was soon to prove himself, moreover, a poor administrator and an arrant procrastinator. Cartier, setting himself efficiently but grimly to work on the equipping of the expedition, realized from the first that he could not expect any proper co-operation from his superior.

Immediately on his return from the second expedition, while still anticipating that he would be left in full charge, Cartier had estimated that he would need six ships of 100 tons burden and two barques of half that size. He had reported that provisions should be provided for at least two years and that he should be accompanied by 120 sailors and 150 others, including soldiers and mechanics such as carpenters, masons, lime makers, tilemakers, blacksmiths, miners, and goldsmiths. He had requisitioned in addition six priests, three bakers, and two apothecaries. It was now found necessary, however, to cut down in all directions. Artisans were showing an emphatic unwillingness to take part in the venture; and so, instead of the corps of skilled men Cartier had demanded, he was forced to be content with whatever Roberval was able to recruit by royal mandate.

Early in May 1541, Cartier was ready to sail as soon as the reinforcements promised him arrived. They came at last, and a sorry lot they were, made up almost exclusively of convicts from the prisons, men who had been under sentence of death and had agreed to go in order to save their lives. They arrived in gangs, chained together and under armed guard, a fine assortment of social misfits and dishonest rabble from the stews of the great cities. There were fear and hate and cunning in the eyes of these human culls who were to be the first settlers of the new land. Cartier's heart must have sunk as he watched them come clanking aboard and muttering among themselves. It is recorded that among the lot was a girl of eighteen who was innocent of any crime but had asked to share the chains of one of the criminals. Perhaps she was in love with him; perhaps she had a nobler purpose, the desire to save his soul. The point cannot be elucidated, nor is there anything in the records to indicate what became of the unfortunate girl.

The Sieur de Roberval, it developed, was not yet ready to start. He had supplies of cannon and gunpowder and other goods piled up in all the ports of the Norman coast but was showing himself dilatory in getting them aboard. It was being rumored around that the worthy gentleman had no intention of starting for Canada that year. There was a story, moreover, that he had taken into his employ one Pierre de Bidoux, a notorious pirate, which indicated that the new viceroy of Canada planned to do a little buccaneering before carrying out the King's orders. The ministers of the English King were complaining bitterly of his activities.

Cartier decided finally not to wait for his superior and on May 23 he unfurled his standard and set sail from St. Malo. He reached Stadacona on August 23 after a hard and stormy crossing.

Cartier faced a difficulty at the start. All of the hostages, with the exception of one young girl, had died in France. They had lacked the capacity, seemingly, to face new conditions of living and their lungs had given out. To the eager natives who swarmed out on the waters to greet the ships he explained that their chief was dead but that all the others were in good health and prosperity and had prefered to remain in France. To make his story more realistic, he said that the men had married French wives and were living in great ease and comfort in stone houses. Fortunately for the French, the Indian who had been selected to act as chief in Donnacona's absence was well pleased with the news. It meant that he could remain permanently in his post. He professed to believe everything Cartier said, and his glum followers had no chance to express their feelings.

Despite the friendliness of the new chief, it was clear from the start that the experiment in colonization would be carried out in the face of bitter opposition from the natives. Carter realized that a secure base of operations must be established at once and set his men to work at a point where the Cap Rouge River empties into the St. Lawrence. They built two forts and named the settlement Charlesbourg Royal. The upper of the two forts had a high tower, two courts, a hall, a kitchen, pantries and cellars, and an oven. There were springs close at hand which promised a plentiful supply of water and a well was dug inside the roughhewn walls. Feeling that the high walls of the outer stockade provided security, the leader now put his men to work at tilling the soil outside. They had no difficulty in clearing the land for a garden of an acre and a half. In a time which seemed magically short there were vegetables ready for use.

While these first necessary steps were being taken some discoveries were made which sent ripples of excitement through the rank and file. They found iron deposits and flakes of gold in the sand along the riverbanks. They even found stones which had a sparkle to them and which they optimistically assumed to be diamonds. The spelicans from Paris who had always been willing to slit a throat for a few whites, the codsheads from the provincial jails whose willingness to come with Cartier had won them a reprieve from the gallows were roused now to a greedy interest. There was so much excitement, in fact, that Cartier found it necessary to pack the specimens in barrels of sand and to keep a guard mounted over them.

Before winter set in the commander took a small company of his men, including some of the gentlemen who had accompanied the expedition, and set off on a second visit to Hochelaga. The Viscount de Beaupré was left in charge at Charlesbourg Royal. In his narrative Cartier makes no mention of visiting the large community he had described in such detail earlier, but he tells of the multitude of natives who converged suddenly on the shores of Montreal Island to greet him. It was apparent at once, however, that they were not friendly. His first visit had aroused wonder and curiosity; his second made it clear that he and his men intended to settle down, that they had designs on the land.

Cartier was convinced that the Indians would have attacked at once if he and his men had not been so well armed. He decided it would be advisable to return without delay to the security of the forts, but although he put this decision into effect immediately he was preceded by a party of the Indians under the new chief at Hochelaga. They also were going to Stadacona, and the Frenchmen were thoroughly well aware that their purpose was to plan with the Indian bands at Stadacona for the destruction of the white men.

As they progressed down the river Cartier had one thought continuously in his mind, the hope that Roberval had arrived at Cap Rouge. In this he was to be disappointed. There were no new sails on the river when they drew within sight of the forts; the dilatory nobleman had not held to his promise. It was clear now that a winter of anxious waiting lay ahead of them.

The mariner from St. Malo seems to have lost some of his faith in the purpose of the expedition at this point. His pen was laid aside and the narrative which he had continued faithfully came to an abrupt end with a final entry, in which a note of desperation can be detected, to the effect that the Indians were keeping sullenly aloof. That he did not continue his narrative over the winter, however, is no particular loss. There was probably little new to record. They were anxious days, of course, with scurvy claiming its victims and the malefactors whiling away the hours with gaming and dicing. Perhaps the men who had started for the New World in chains were speculating as to whether death on the gallows might not have been preferable after all to the bitter cold, the privations, the constant state of fear in which they existed.

3

The Sieur de Roberval in the meantime was getting ready for a delayed but quite spectacular start. He had gathered together a company exceeding two hundred in number. Some of them were gentlemen eager for adventure and fame, some were artisans, some of course were reprieved malefactors. There were a number of women and a few children. With three ships of relatively large tonnage Roberval set sail on April 16, 1542, from the port of La Rochelle. The pirate Bidoux does not appear to have been of the company.

It took them a long time to cross the Atlantic, and it was June 8

before the fleet pulled into the harbor of St. John's in Newfoundland. None of the party had been in the New World before and
great was their amazement to find no fewer than seventeen fishing
vessels thereabouts, some French, some English, some Portuguese.
They were still more amazed a few days later when Jacques Cartier
came sailing into the harbor with his three ships intact but his company very much depleted.

The absence of notes from Cartier's pen becomes now a signal
loss. Nothing is known of what happened when the two leaders
came face to face save a brief reference in a chronicle set down by
one of Roberval's men. According to this narrator, the brusque and
haughty viceroy charged Cartier with deserting his post. The man
from St. Malo, equally angry, accused Roberval of negligence in
leaving him, Cartier, to winter alone with insufficient men and supplies, surrounded by hostile natives. Undoubtedly there was a long
and bitter debate between them, the viceroy attempting to carry
things off with a high hand, the sea captain standing up to him and
refusing to accept any blame. This much is known, that at the end
Roberval ordered Cartier to return with him to Stadacona and that
the captain refused to do so. His men were so reduced in number
and in such poor physical condition as a result of the hardships they
had endured that he did not intend to subject them to more suffering. From the course he took, it seems clear that Cartier now doubted
the possibility of establishing a permanent colony.

The outcome of the dispute was that Cartier stole away during
the night. There was no trace of his sails the next morning when
the sun came up over the horizon. He was on his way back to France.
Refusing to be daunted by this desertion, Roberval took his three
large ships on to Stadacona.

A story must be told at this point which gives some insight into
the character of the man who had been appointed viceroy of Canada. His niece was among the women in the party, a handsome and
high-spirited girl named Marguerite. A young gentleman had enlisted with the expedition who was either in love with her to begin
with and went along to be near her or who fell into an infatuated
state during the voyage. The affair reached a stage where there was
much talk about them, and Roberval decided on a drastic form of
punishment for his niece. Off the eastern coast of Newfoundland lay
the Isle of Demons, which, according to report, was inhabited solely

by evil spirits and which all ships avoided. Roberval gave the girl four muskets and a supply of gunpowder and marooned her on this evil island with no one for company save an old nurse who went by the name of Bastienne. Her lover, who apparently was not being punished for his share in the amour, cast himself overboard and swam ashore to join her. The frightened crew saw the devoted couple meet on the shore while all about them could be heard the howling of the expectant demons.

The three victims of this harsh retribution watched the sails vanish over the horizon and then set to work with sinking hearts to build a crude cabin. It is not clear whether the demons possessed any actual physical form or were mere phantoms of the spirit. It is said, however, that they hovered over the unhappy trio, flapping their foul wings and filling the air with their incantations. The hut was finished finally and there in due course a child was born to the lovers. The faithful Bastienne died soon after. The child died also, then the lover, and the unfortunate Marguerite was left alone. It becomes clear at this point that the niece of the granite viceroy had high qualities of courage and resolution. She continued on alone. One day she went out hunting and shot three polar bears, which alone is sufficient evidence of the spirit she possessed. Through everything she refused to be disturbed by the demons, although they gibbered at her through the hole in the roof which served as a chimney.

The denouement of the grim story came two years later, when a fishing vessel, seeing a column of smoke rising from the beach, had the courage to sail in closer. Seeing a woman, clad in the most grotesque garb, signaling frantically to them, they decided to risk the hostility of the evil spirits and went in to rescue her. Marguerite, gaunt and ill but still filled with firm resolution, was taken off the island and sent back to France. She told there the story of her experience, and it seems to have been believed generally. There is one detail which lends some slight degree of authority to this incredible tale. Roberval's pilot, one Jean Alphonse, calls the scene Les Isles de la Demoiselle, a reference, no doubt, to the brave Marguerite.

In the meantime the viceroy and his party reached Charlesbourg Royal and took possession of what was left of Cartier's two forts. Roberval's first thought apparently was to establish suitable quarters for the ladies and gentlemen of his party. He decided to elaborate the upper fort, and the result was a fair imitation of a feudal castle. It had an additional tower, two great halls (one for the gentry, no doubt, and one for the men of low degree), a huge kitchen, a series of storerooms and bedrooms and workshops. The effect of all this magnificence on the watching savages seems to have been a salutary one, for the redskins did nothing to interfere with the white men. It would have been much more sensible, however, if the commander had taken steps to provide something to fill the storerooms. Ground should have been prepared for summer planting in order to supplement the supplies of food. He sent back two of the ships in the fall with a report of Cartier's desertion and of his own intention to winter at Cap Rouge.

The winter proved almost as hard to withstand as the experiences of the probably mythical Marguerite. The stores of food proved inadequate. Scurvy made its appearance early, and the newcomers were at a loss as to what to do to check it. Before the arrival of spring one third of the whole company had died of it.

The Sieur de Roberval quickly demonstrated that he possessed in full degree a stern sense of discipline but no gifts as an administrator. He sat over his people with a grimness of judgment which lends some small credibility to the story of the marooning of his niece. A man named Gailler, one of the malefactors, was detected in theft and promptly hanged. One Jean de Nantes was placed in irons for an infringement of the laws of decency. Women as well as men were sentenced to the whipping post for minor offenses. One member of the party, who later wrote an account of what had happened, asserts that six men were shot in one day and that the situation became bad enough to win the sympathy of the savages at Stadacona.

The balance of the story is largely a matter of conjecture. Spring came and the ice broke on the St. Lawrence and began to grind its way out to sea. Green showed under the fast-melting snow. A land of magic beauty was awakening; but there was no capacity left for joy at the prospect in the hearts of the men and women who had survived that dreadful winter. The Sieur de Roberval reached the same conclusion that Cartier had come to the preceding spring: that the odds were too heavy to overcome and that their mission was doomed to failure. He decided to take what was left of his company back to France.

One version has it that King Francis sent Cartier to assist in bringing them home and that the man from St. Malo performed this duty. The only definite evidence bearing on the winding up of this ill-fated adventure was the holding of a court of inquiry before which both Cartier and Roberval appeared to settle their accounts. The King seems to have been in a forgiving mood and willing to wash his hands of all such expensive ambitions. His strength exhausted by the excesses in which he had indulged all his life, he had only a few more years to live, and this may have been responsible for the apathy with which he passed over the obvious faults and mistakes of the two commanders.

4

Perhaps also the aging sophisticate had become convinced that he had nothing to gain in the New World. The metals and precious stones which Cartier had carried back in his carefully packed and sealed casks had proved to be of little value. The gold was genuine enough, but the captain's report made it clear that the metal existed in such minute quantities that there could be little profit in it. The diamonds were found to be rock crystal. This was a great disappointment and also the cause of much wry joking. For a long period thereafter anything which proved to be valueless was popularly referred to as "a Canadian diamond." The legend of the Kingdom of Saguenay had been dispelled. The dream of finding fabulous wealth in America had been found lacking in substance; the bubble of easy wealth had been pricked.

The Sieur de Roberval was killed in a street affray in Paris near the Church of the Holy Innocents. Cartier spent the rest of his life in a small stone manor house at Limoilou near St. Malo, enjoying the company of his beloved Catherine and the respect of all citizens of the ancient seaport. It was recorded on September 1, 1557, "this said Wednesday about five in the morning died Jacques Cartier."

Fishermen continued to sail every spring to the banks off Newfoundland. In the anterooms of kings and sometimes in the secrecy of royal council meetings there was still talk of conquering and colonizing America. The interest, however, seems to have been largely academic. Spain continued to prosper from the gold which came out of Mexico and Peru, but the northern half of the continent held out no such inducements. Men shuddered at the story of the

lovely and unfortunate Marguerite living alone on the Isle of Demons and of men swinging on improvised gallows outside Roberval's
feudal castle. The appetite for this kind of adventure ran thin for
three quarters of a century thereafter in the veins of Frenchmen
and Englishmen alike.

CHAPTER VI

Samuel de Champlain, the Founder
of New France

1

SAINTONGE lies on the Bay of Biscay and stretches down along the northern shore of the broad Gironde. Farther south, where the Gironde becomes the Garonne and Gascony begins, lies the fair city of Bordeaux, and below that again the magic triangle where the vineyards produce the great Bordeaux wines. Saintonge does not share to any extent in the profitable wine trade with England, but it has had historic connections of long standing with the English people, being part of the inheritance which Eleanor of Aquitaine took with her when she married Henry II in the twelfth century. It was always in view of the marshy shores of Saintonge that the northern fleets passed in their progress down the Gironde to the city which the first Edwards and the Black Prince loved so much, not to mention the unfortunate Richard II, who was called Richard of Bordeaux.

Saintonge's part in this narrative is confined to what might have been a very inconspicuous occurrence. At the small seaport of Brouage in that department was born one Samuel de Champlain in the year 1567. His father was a sea captain and so his biographers have been much concerned about the use of the "de," which is a prerogative of the nobility in personal names. The decision reached has been that the family belonged to the lesser nobility; a matter of small consequence, actually, because Samuel de Champlain had in himself qualities of heart and mind which far transcend any question of the social standing of his father.

Very little is known of his youth except that he was trained for the sea by his father and that he fought through the religious wars which were shaking and impoverishing France. One of the weakest and worst of French kings, Henry III, a son of the Catherine de' Medici who caused the tocsin to ring on the eve of St. Bartholomew's, was on the throne. He was being driven to repressive measures against the Huguenots, the Protestants of France, by his fanatical kinsmen, the Guises. In Navarre, which lay between Frence and Spain, was a young ruler who would become in time France's great monarch, Henry IV. This youth, who was possessed of great ability and great natural charm as well, was the acknowledged leader and hope of the Huguenots. The three Henrys, for the head of the Catholic League which the Guises organized also bore that name, waged a three-sided and bloody series of wars for over twenty years. When both of the other Henrys had been removed from the struggle by the daggers of assassins and the Protestant Henry had reached the conclusion that Paris was worth a Mass and had recanted, the fighting came to an end. Henry of Navarre became King of France.

It is stated that young Samuel de Champlain was an ardent Catholic but at the same time a loyal follower of Henry of Navarre, leaving the impression that he fought under the Protestant banner. This is decidedly confusing. It has been established that he served under three generals, D'Aumont, St. Luc, and Brissac. All three were Catholic generals who went into service with Henry after he became legally the King of France, and so it may be that Champlain did not enter service until after the Huguenot leader had purchased Paris with a Mass. It seems more likely, however, that he would be drawn into enlistment at an earlier age. He was twenty years old when St. Luc fought against Henry at Coutras, and it seems more than probable that the young soldier-sailor was in the ranks there. Coutras was the first great victory for the Protestant cause, and St. Luc had the misfortune to be captured there. Huguenot Henry, who was jovial and easy of temperament and had a great admiration for the fair sex (an understatement of understatements), gave the seventy-eight banners captured in the victory to one of his mistresses, the Comtesse de Grammont, to be used as hangings for her bed. It is probable also that Champlain was with Brissac when he was made governor of Paris; a most important development, for Brissac proceeded to sell possession of Paris to the Navarrese for a million and a half crowns, thereby paving the way for Henry's ultimate success.

In 1598 the Treaty of Vervins brought the fighting to an end and the still youthful Samuel de Champlain had to look about him for some form of employment. He decided to go to sea and found a chance to sail to Cádiz with a fleet taking back the Spanish mercenaries who had been fighting in France on the Catholic side and had been made prisoners. This resulted in his being given command of a Spanish vessel in an expedition to the West Indies, a journey which he described in his first book, called *Bref Discours*. It was an excellent book, although illustrated by the author's own rather ludicrous drawings, and brought him to the attention of the French court, where the new broom of the Navarrese monarch was being busily employed. Perhaps it would have been more profitable for Champlain if the sagacious Henry had decided to use him in an engineering project in Saintonge. Settlers from the Netherlands were being imported to reclaim the salt marshes around Brouage. Champlain would have had a chance here to learn valuable lessons in colonization and also to impress himself on the attention of the King. Wealth and preferment are won in this way; but, as circumstances fell out, the youth from the salt marshes came into close touch instead with certain men who were dreaming again of a successful conquest of the New World. This project fired the enthusiasm and touched the idealistic side of Champlain, and the rest of his life was to be devoted to it.

He failed thereby to attain wealth and ease, but he became the Founder of New France and so achieved lasting fame instead.

2

From a study of the events contributing to the founding of New France there emerges the figure of a man of whom relatively little has been told in Canadian annals. Pierre du Guast, Sieur de Monts, played a larger share than Champlain at the start, and at one critical stage he displayed such firmness and courage that victory was achieved in the face of what seemed sure defeat. To the Sieur de Monts belongs a higher position in the gallery of the great in New World history than he is usually allotted.

He was a member also of the lesser nobility and belonged to what might be termed the moneyman wing, the shrewd and resourceful men who were not averse to dabbling in trade and were ready to gamble their personal fortunes for furs and the fisheries of the west;

the silent partners, in other words, of the sea captains who sailed from St. Malo and La Rochelle. There is a portrait of him in the Massachusetts Archives which shows him to have been a strikingly handsome man with a high wide forehead, arched eyebrows, the delicately chiseled nose of a court dandy, and a glossy goatee. He wears a jaunty hat with a long white plume, a flat collar of elegant lace, an elaborately embroidered cloak, and boots with turned-over tops in what might be called the manner of the Three Musketeers. It may be no more than a likeness of the typical courtier of the period. If it is a portrait, the Sieur de Monts must have resembled his royal master in being a favorite with the ladies.

That he figures in Canadian history at all is due to the fact that Henry IV had been the leader of the Protestant cause. Monts was a Huguenot and ordinarily he would not have been allowed to play any part in the colonization of America, which had taken on from the first an evangelical coloring. Henry, although he had paid for Paris with a Mass, was still at this point a Huguenot at heart. He had already, on April 13, 1598, promulgated the Edict of Nantes, which gave Protestants a protected position, and it was hinted that he sometimes whispered to Huguenot divines in passing, "Pray God in my behalf." He still strove to have some Protestants in positions of trust about him, and among those who enjoyed his favor was the elegant and determined Sieur de Monts.

Henry was too poor and too concerned with restoring conditions in France to normal after the long civil wars to deplete the royal treasury in colonial ventures. He was willing, as the Tudor kings in England had been, to give his blessing to whatever his subjects undertook in that connection—when it was at their own expense. The most spectacular effort was under the direction, and at the personal risk, of a brave French nobleman, the Marquis de la Roche. He landed forty convicts on Sable Island off the coast of Nova Scotia while he proceeded with his ship to make some exploratory casts in the seas thereabouts. A storm drove his ship far out into the Atlantic and left it in such condition that he had to return to France. At home the creditors of La Roche had him seized and thrown into prison, and it was not until five years had rolled around that any attempt was made to rescue the unfortunate malefactors on Sable Island. Eleven of them were found alive, gaunt and weather-beaten Crusoes in shaggy skins with beards to their waists. The survivors were pardoned and given permission to engage in the fur trade in

Canada, where some of them, according to the records, did quite
well. La Roche, a man of gallantry and high purpose, died soon
after in distress and want.

In 1600 a merchant of St. Malo named Pontgravé went into partnership with a sea captain, Pierre Chauvin, as a result of which the
latter took a small vessel to the St. Lawrence Basin and progressed
as far as Tadoussac at the mouth of the Saguenay River. Here the
fur traders, who came more or less regularly to the trading field
which Cartier had opened up, had built a number of small wooden
huts for human occupation and storehouses for supplies. Chauvin
landed sixteen men here to take possession for the winter while he
proceeded to do some profitable trading. He returned to France in
the fall. The next year it was found that the party left at Tadoussac
had found it impossible to sustain the hardships of winter life. Some
of them had died and the rest had gone native and were distributed
among the Indian bands thereabouts.

It was to Aymar de Chastes, governor of Dieppe, that Champlain
turned when the determination formed in his mind to follow destiny
to the New World. It was a fortunate thing for him that he had
earned the regard of this resolute old soldier, a veteran of the religious wars and a close friend of Henry IV, although a moderate,
if staunch, Catholic. On the death of Chauvin after two more abortive efforts, the governor of Dieppe went to the King and begged
of him letters patent to make one more attempt at carrying the flag
of France and the cross of Mother Church to Canada. The King
loved every gray hair which rimed the head of the old soldier and
was happy to grant the necessary permission. No money was forthcoming, however, and De Chastes was not a rich man by any
standard; and so it was necessary to form a new company, admit-
ting all the leading merchants of the seaports, including Pontgravé
of St. Malo.

In 1603 the new company sent out two small ships to begin operations. One was commanded by Pontgravé himself and the other by
a captain Prevert, also of St. Malo. Champlain went along in the
capacity of official observer and historian. While the two ships remained at Tadoussac, he ascended the great river by canoe with a
small company, getting as far as the Lachine Rapids. The country
had changed much since the days of Cartier. Gone were the tribes
which had extended such tempered receptions to the first French-

men. Gone was the palisaded city that Cartier had found at Hoche-laga. The tall natives who had occupied Mount Royal and its vicinity had been replaced by a few wandering bands of Algonquins. But everywhere he heard tales of the great rivers and the gigantic lakes and of the wonder of the country drained by these waters, and he returned to France in the fall more convinced than ever that his life-work was here. At home he wrote a book called *Des Sauvages* which attracted wide attention and focused interest on him as a man who would play an important part in future developments.

When the two tiny vessels, sufficiently loaded with valuable pelts to satisfy the investors, had reached France the old soldier of Dieppe was dead. A new man, Pierre du Guast, who held a court post as gentleman in ordinary of the King's chamber, was besieging Henry to be allowed to carry on the work.

The Sieur de Monts had a new idea which appealed very much to the King and equally to the hardheaded men of the shipping trade. Along the St. Lawrence the country was inhospitable with its cold winters and its unfriendly Indians. Farther east there was the country of La Cadie (a name which stemmed from the Indian word *aquoddie*, meaning the pollock fish), the seaboard section of the continent which took in, to use the names which later came into universal acceptance, Nova Scotia, Cape Breton, New Brunswick, and parts of Maine and Gaspé. For some reason which no one under-stood, La Cadie was blessed with a more gentle climate. The sum-mers were balmy, the soil fertile, the Indians less antagonistic. Why not settle first in La Cadie and sink French roots down into its re-warding soil?

This was a shrewd notion, and the King was easily persuaded to grant a charter to Monts in 1603 by which the latter and his associ-ates were to have a monopoly of the fur trade and in return were to send out settlers at the rate of fifty a year, with all the necessary supplies, and to "represent our person in the countries, territories, coasts and confines of La Cadie from the 40th to the 46th degree."

The holder of the new charter went to work in a thoroughly businesslike way, which showed that he had a level head under his handsome beaver hat and gay plume. He capitalized his company at 90,000 livres and divided the right to participate among the merchants of Rouen, St. Malo, La Rochelle, and St. Jean de Luz. Monts himself took up most of the St. Malo allotment and so held about one tenth of the stock. It may have been that he overreached himself in assuming such a large share, not being a man of great wealth.

The King discovered almost immediately, however, that the religious views of Monts were a serious obstacle. Sully, his chief minister and adviser, was against the charter from every standpoint and had said publicly, "Far-off possessions are not suited to the temperament or to the genius of Frenchmen," which shows how mistaken great men can sometimes be. Administrative France was not willing to deal with a Huguenot, and Normandy refused to register the charter. An even greater difficulty was the opposition of independent traders, who raised a great clamor of protest at being shut out. This was not a matter concerning a few rascally shipowners who operated as mavericks on the edge of things. As early as 1578 it had been reported that there were a hundred and fifty French ships in the waters around and about Newfoundland and in the gulf, and that the number flying other flags totaled two hundred. Most of these independent traders were engaged in the fisheries, but an ever-increasing number followed the Cartier trail and sought the greater profits of the fur trade. They had established bases at Anticosti and Tadoussac, and the natives had fallen into the habit of taking their furs to these two points. It can easily be understood that the tough veterans who made a living by such means were not prepared to be barred summarily from the profitable rivers of Canada; not when they could raise the religious issue and shout "Calvinist" at the man heading the new company.

It was found that concessions would have to be made. Although Huguenot settlers would be allowed to go out if they desired, and might take their ministers with them, the latter were forbidden to have any hand in the instruction of the natives. The number of annual settlers, moreover, was raised from fifty to one hundred. Monts and his associates accepted the new conditions.

Monts knew something of Canada, having made one voyage to Tadoussac. He fitted out two ships, the exact tonnage of which has not been recorded but which obviously were of good size. They were, at any rate, much better suited to the work in hand than any of the ships which had crossed the Atlantic previously. The science of shipbuilding had been progressing with the years. The towering superstructures were being eliminated, thereby giving an increased seaworthiness and decidedly improved maneuverability. Even the convenient galleries around the stern had been abandoned. The new vessels were three-masters with the lateen mizzen thrown in; the importance of sails, in fact, was growing to such an extent that the first test of a sailor—a "yonker" as he was called in England—was his ability to handle himself in the shrouds. There were now two decks, but the conditions below were undoubtedly as bad as ever, so much of the space being given over to the guns and the elaborate cabins of the officers and the gentry. The crews subsisted in the general region of the orlop deck, where the bilge water stagnated in the ballast and the stench was indescribable.

The two ships which set sail from Le Havre in March of the year 1604 carried a distinguished company. The Sieur de Monts himself was aboard, optimistic and aggressive and, no doubt, very decorative, with his commanding height and leonine head. Pontgravé, because of his previous experience, was in charge of navigation. Jean de Biencourt, Sieur de Poutrincourt, a nobleman of Picardy and a substantial investor, had decided to participate personally in the first venture. There were two priests and two Calvinist ministers, and there were the hundred settlers required under the charter, some of whom, alas, had been recruited in the usual way from the prisons and from among the vagabonds on the highways.

Most important of all, as things turned out, was a man in the middle thirties who was quiet and sober in manner but carried about him nevertheless an air of distinction. This member of the company had a broad forehead, a long nose, and the liberal mustache and small goatee which would be fixed later in the memories of men by the great Cardinal Richelieu. This was the official recorder and geographer of the expedition, Samuel de Champlain.

3

It is not strange that everyone, even the scientists and geographers who served kings in their snug little offices and the captains and master pilots who took out ships to buffet the waves and the ocean currents, was mystified by the difference in climate between the part of Canada called Quebec and the provinces which would be called Acadia. The existence of the Gulf Stream was still a secret. On his first voyage to America, Columbus had noted the curious and swift body of warm, light blue water with seaweed in great quantities along its edges, through which he had tossed and struggled before reaching the islands of the West Indies. Ponce de León in his explorations around Florida had been caught in the fast-moving waters between the southern tip of the great peninsula and the island of Cuba. It was clear to all early navigators that the ocean thereabouts behaved in strange ways, but none of them guessed at the truth, that the warm water from the Gulf of Mexico poured out into the Atlantic and then flowed swiftly up the eastern coast of North America before making a broad circular swing and riding down past the British Isles and the Bay of Biscay and washing the shores of the Madeiras and the Azores and the Canaries, ameliorating the atmosphere in a most pronounced way wherever it went.

This strange antic current of the North Atlantic would mystify navigators for another century and a half. One explanation of the discovery of the truth is that in the year 1771 a shrewd American named Benjamin Franklin was in London and decided to investigate the reason for the unconscionable time the Falmouth packets took in making the New York run. He found that the Falmouth captains had not learned how to cope with a current in which they invariably found themselves involved and held up for many days. Whether or not this suggested to the canny Franklin (he is given credit for so many things, so why not concede him this as well?) that the current was the same one which played such tricks around Florida and Cuba, the fact remains that this was the beginning of a long period of investigation in which scientists played a part. A favorite device was to drop bottles in the clear water of the Gulf Stream and to watch for them on the other side of the ocean. They turned up in Norway, along the Irish coast, on the tip of Cornwall, and on the shores of Biscay; proving thereby that the Stream made a circuit of the Atlantic and favored the British Isles most particularly in tempering what normally would be a cold climate. Bottle charts were kept and times were checked, and vessels were sent out to take soundings and to study the behavior of the monster current; and so in course of time the truth about the Gulf Stream came to be understood.

But back in the first years of the seventeenth century all that men like Samuel de Champlain and the Sieur de Monts knew about it was that for some strange reason Acadia had a much milder climate than the rest of Canada and that they were going to take advantage of it. They were taking their two well-equipped ships and their hundred sea-weary settlers to this favored land where the settlers would

ACADIA
and
ADJACENT
COUNTRY

NEWFOUNDLAND

Gulf of
St. Lawrence

St. Lawrence River

Tadoussac

Quebec

RICHELIEU R.

Lake Champlain

ST. CROIX R.

ACADIA

Chignecto Bay

Baie Françoise (Bay of Fundy)

THE FIRST COLONY

Port Royal

Cable Island

ATLANTIC OCEAN

palacios

stay in comfort while the crews went on up to the mighty river to get such profits as they could out of the trade in furs.

4

The importance of the colonies established by the Sieur de Monts was that, after one warlike interruption, they became permanent. The less rigorous conditions had something to do with the success thus achieved, but the credit must be given chiefly to the resolute men who directed the effort. They encountered all the familiar difficulties—and sometimes it seemed that fate was determined to defeat them—but they held on and in the end they won, and around Port Royal the little French farms began to produce and thrive, and the settlers themselves, who became known as Acadians, found happiness there and some degree of peace.

The first crossing proved difficult and tumultuous. The convicts on board were sulky and intractable. The priests and Calvinists were so bitterly antagonistic that on one occasion they came to blows. It was a long voyage, but finally the ships reached the entrance to the Bay of Fundy, which Monts proceeded to name the Baye Françoise. They explored its waters and coasts and were awed by the tidal performances in this tight arm of the sea; the fury with which the in-rolling sea raged about some of the islands and the blood-chilling bore which came in sixty feet high before breaking on the quicksands of Chignecto Bay, while at the same time proving its variability by never achieving more than a height of eight feet in Bay Verte on the northern shore. They sailed into Annapolis Basin and were delighted with its harbor facilities and the beauty of the shores but decided, nevertheless, to establish themselves on an island in the mouth of the St. Croix River on the other side of the bay. Military reasons dictated this decision, for on the island selected the guns of the little colony would maintain some command over the entrance to Fundy.

It proved, however, an unfortunate choice. During the first winter the conditions were so harsh and the winds blew so relentlessly across the water from the northwest that the unhappy people lived in the most bitter discomfort. It seemed impossible to keep warm, and the food supplies proved inadequate. Although they had gone to great efforts in planning their settlement, building a broad and high-roofed house for Monts and his servants and lieutenants on one side of a square and another house on the opposite side where Champlain and the Sieur d'Orville took up their quarters, while the balance of the space was devoted to barracks and workshops and magazines, they had overlooked the need for cellars under the buildings. As a result the food froze in the ill-heated houses and then rotted and became unusable. Scurvy made its appearance early under these conditions, and of the seventy-nine people who made up the St. Croix colony thirty-five died of this loathsome disease.

When spring came at last and fair breezes from the mainland replaced the steely blasts of winter, a sadly emaciated band dragged themselves aboard the ships, taking what was left of their supplies and even the frameworks of the houses. A search was begun for a more suitable location.

The choice fell on the splendid harbor which had been visited first, the Annapolis Basin. The Sieur de Poutrincourt had been so impressed with it at the first glance that he had asked for a grant of it, intending to make it his home and to bring out his family. Monts had agreed to this and had made a legal transfer to his partner. Poutrincourt had then returned to France to bring out more settlers and supplies for his fair domain. As he had not yet put in an appearance, the fear had been growing that he had suffered some mischance and might never be seen again. The survivors, accordingly, proceeded to build homes for themselves on the north shore of the bay.

Two winters were passed here, and in the journals which he kept Champlain makes it clear that conditions were much easier. They seem to have had plenty of food, and even dined together like veritable gourmets by reason of the *Ordre de Bon Temps* (Order of Good Cheer), which he himself originated; a novel idea by which each man in turn was chief steward for the day and wore a collar around his neck. Each incumbent was expected to make great efforts to fill the table with delicate and tasty fare. As a result of this pleasant and thoroughly Gallic form of rivalry, the long refectory table in the Great Hall at Port Royal, the name which Poutrincourt had chosen, always had fresh fish and a variety of game and even rich desserts; and the members sat about the board in ease and content and quaffed their wine with as much pleasure as if seated at the best inn in Paris.

Monts then returned to France and, joining forces with Poutrincourt, who was still there and hampered by financial troubles, he went vigorously to work on even more elaborate plans for the welfare of the colony. The two resolute pioneers purchased a vessel named the *Jonas* and elected to sail from La Rochelle, sending to that port a number of artisans and paying them a portion of their wages in advance. While waiting for the *Jonas* to start, the mechanics lodged together in a waterside tavern and proceeded to spend their advances in drink and carousing, to the scandal of the sternly religious populace. Finally they put to sea with Poutrincourt in charge, Monts finding it advisable to remain at court and mend his fences against the constant assaults of the angry free traders.

Among the new faces aboard the *Jonas* were two men whose names will be remembered always in connection with this gallant venture. One was Marc Lescarbot, a lawyer and poet, who had become convinced of the corruption of the world and longed for the solace and peace of a new kind of existence which he believed could be found in America. He wrote an account of the early days in Acadia which is the source from which much of the history of the period is drawn. The other was one Louis Hébert, who will appear later at Quebec and whose story, which will be told in its proper place, is one of the most stimulating in the annals of New France.

It must not be assumed that all was plain sailing now at Port Royal despite the ambitious setting of the colony: a broad court surrounded on all sides by buildings and with an arched entrance bearing the standard of France and the carved escutcheons of the founders, all of this closed in by a high palisade and bastions in which the cannon from the ships had been mounted. Supply ships invariably were late in the spring, and inevitably there were long faces as the anxious settlers gazed down the rough waters of the bay. The ships would arrive in time, but every period of uncertainty seemed to be building up to a final blow.

In the spring of 1607 the most disastrous of news reached them from the Sieur de Monts. The free traders and the hatters of Paris, who swore vehemently that they could not go on paying the high prices demanded for beaver skins, had prevailed. The charter had been revoked. The news of this disaster was in the form of a letter to Poutrincourt, who had returned earlier and was in command. The latter was directed to abandon the enterprise and bring everyone back to France as soon as the necessary arrangements could be made. On August 11 of that year, accordingly, an unhappy lot of people packed their belongings into the ships and arrived back in France late in September.

This was not the end in Acadia, however. They would come back, these same indomitable people, and under the same leadership. They would establish themselves around Port Royal, and their industry would cause the land to become fruitful.

CHAPTER VII

Champlain at Quebec

1

CHAMPLAIN met the Sieur de Monts in Paris. They were
bitterly disappointed men, for that great silent continent in
the west pulled insistently at their heartstrings. What could
they do about it now? The charter had been revoked and the favor
of the able King, busy with his plans for bringing prosperity back
to France, could be depended upon no longer. Must all thought of
winning the New World for France be abandoned?

Like that remarkable French merchant and promoter of the fifteenth century, Jacques Coeur of green and vivid memory, Monts
also was a promoter; but back of any idea of personal gain was an
idealistic conception. He knew, however, that he faced a crisis in his
affairs. His resources had been seriously strained, and another failure
in America would reduce him to poverty. This he understood fully
when he sat down with Champlain to talk about the future.

The latter had other reasons for hesitation if there had been in his
nature any tendency toward vacillation. His venture up the St.
Lawrence had made it clear to him that conditions had changed since
the days of Jacques Cartier. The fierce tribesmen who had taken the
place of the Indians encountered then would resist to the death any
permanent settlement of white men. He had not come into contact
with the Iroquois, but he had felt on every hand the dread which
they inspired. The Five Nations of the Iroquois, living in palisaded
villages among the lakes of northern New York, were cruel and
strong and, in an angry and arrogant way, ambitious. They were a
conquering race and could not brook any opposition. The *Ongue
Honwe,* they called themselves, "the men surpassing all others," and
their right to such self-praise is backed by a scientific examination of
the skulls of representatives of all Indian tribes; a test from which the

Iroquois emerge as the possessors of larger and more highly developed brain chambers then all the rest, including the native races of the South and West. Champlain knew that to establish a colony on the St. Lawrence would bring him into conflict inevitably with these ruthless red men. It must have been apparent to him that his own life might end in violence if he returned to America. But he wanted to go in spite of such dangers. Destiny was beckoning, and he sought a way to obey that imperious finger.

The meeting in Paris between the two men was one of those moments when history is made. It is easy to picture them together, their eyes fired by the same resolution, even their beards bristling with a determination not to be balked. The outcome of their long talks was a momentous decision. They would not give in. Come what may, they must try again. The Sieur de Monts was willing to risk what was left of his personal fortune in a final effort. Champlain would commit himself to a life of peril and privation.

Monts went then to see the King. It is certain that he got the ear of Henry himself, because the men around the monarch were as cold to America as Sully and they would have seen to it that any proposals filtered through them would come to no favorable conclusion. The King made it clear at once that he could do little, fully sib though he was to the idea. The clamor against monopoly had twisted public opinion. The Church still held aloof from any ventures in which the Huguenots played such a prominent part. The best that Henry could offer Monts was this: a renewal of the charter for one year to enable the latter to establish a permanent trading post in Canada, after which it would have to be a case of every man for himself. One concession could be made, that Monts would not be under the necessity of taking settlers out and providing for them.

If Pierre du Guast, Sieur de Monts, had been of less resolute character he would have pocketed his losses and stopped right there. Small chance for success was offered on such a basis as this. Instead of drawing back he went to the men who had invested in the first company and invited them to share the risk with him. At this high moment in his life it is easy to see the resemblance he bears to that great prince of trade, Jacques Coeur, who was so many centuries ahead of his time that he owned chains of department stores all over France in a day when mercantile vision did not go beyond small shops behind street counters. With the same vigor, the same mastery over the minds of other men which characterized the moneyman of

Charles VI, he sought support for this doubtful one-year gamble. He went first to a pair of affluent merchants in Rouen named Collier and Legendre and succeeded in winning them over. Others began to fall into line, unable to resist his enthusiasm. It was a miracle of promotion and, because he succeeded in talking the tough-minded shipowners of Rouen and St. Malo and even some of the dour Huguenots of La Rochelle into backing him, the Sieur de Monts provided for Samuel de Champlain the chance he could not have found elsewhere.

Enough money was raised to buy and equip three small ships. One was to return to Acadia. The others were bound for the St. Lawrence, and Champlain was placed in command of one of them.

2

A number of factors entered into the success which Champlain achieved finally, and one undoubtedly was his recognition of the importance of the site of Quebec. When his eyes first rested on that great dome of rock standing up like a brooding sentry above the river where it narrows to less than a mile, he knew that here someday a great city would stand. The practical Cartier had been lacking in the imaginative qualities of Champlain. He also had looked at the rock and had then proceeded to build his encampment at Cap Rouge, which had, it must be confessed, some immediate advantages; and now nothing remained of his forts but a fragment of the stone base of an oven. The selection of Quebec as the core and heart of the new effort gave a sense of permanence and dignity to the little colony. For the first time the settlers could look about them and declare, "We are here to stay."

Champlain arrived at this imposing entrance to the river in June of the year following the granting of the extension, 1608. Between the base of the steep rock and the banks of the river was a small space of level ground covered with walnut trees. Here Champlain stood and looked up with awe at the summit which is now called Cape Diamond. Instinctively he knew, one may be sure, that his feet were on important soil. Here he would build his great city and he would call it Quebec from the Indian word *kebec*, which meant a narrowing of waters. This choice of a name suggests that the Founder of New France had been more impressed with this site because of its location on the river than its nobility and its impregnability from a military standpoint. The summit he decided to call Mont du Gas after his splendid friend and backer, the Sieur de Monts. With a peremptory gesture he indicated where the trees must be felled to make way for the fort he planned to raise.

The work proceeded at a pace possible only when enthusiasm is behind every swinging ax and ready wills give impetus to spade and mattock. All joined in, and it took less than a month to finish the task. Champlain has left a record of these first buildings in the form of a drawing somewhat less crude than his illustrations for *Bref Discours* but notably lacking in perspective. This, then, is what we know about the first habitations at Quebec: there were three frame houses, two stories in height and with a three-cornered courtyard in which stood a watchtower. Around this close cluster of buildings was a strong wooden wall with a gallery at the level of the first story and a liberal number of loopholes. A moat lapped the wall on three sides and the river took care of the other. Cannon protruded their ugly snouts at various angles to command the approaches from the water. The leader judged this to be impregnable as far as Indian aggression was concerned.

His next step was to encourage the planting of gardens in the hope of supplementing the food supply. He labored diligently himself with a spade in the space cleared at the west of the fort and sometimes, no doubt, he desisted from his labors and gazed up at Mont du Gas, seeing there, not a jagged outline of bare gray stone, but a tall citadel with the lilies of France flying above it.

In spite of all precautions, the cold months proved disastrous. Cartier's remedy for scurvy had been forgotten, and when that terrible visitor crossed the threshold and hovered over the tables provided with dried and salted food, there was no way of checking it. Pontgravé had gone back to France with a cargo of pelts, leaving Champlain with twenty-eight men. By spring the tiny garrison had been reduced to fourteen. The survivors were a sorry lot, but fresh food brought its remedy and by June, when Pontgravé returned, they were capable once again of looking forward to the future with hope and even a degree of enthusiasm.

Pontgravé's report of events in France was not very encouraging. The year's extension of the monopoly was up and they might expect at once an inrush of independent traders. The men who had provided the funds, and must continue to dip into their pockets if the effort was to be continued, had agreed to go on for another year, on the urging of the ebullient Monts. Beyond that they could do nothing but hope.

Champlain proceeded to make the most of the small margin of time on which he could count. His duty, as he conceived it, was to explore the land westward and learn more about its potentialities, at the same time making friends and allies of the Indians to assure a steady flow to Quebec and Tadoussac of the furs which would keep the wavering investors in line. Leaving Pontgravé in charge at Quebec, he started out on the first of a series of remarkable journeys into the interior.

3

The rivers and lakes of North America were as silent as the coast line. Sometimes a shadow would flit along the edges of the water, made by a birch-bark canoe so skillfully propelled that no ripple marked its passing. At night there might be many such, progressing silently through the hours of darkness. Keen eyes might peer out from the forest depths, but never in daylight would the figure of a bronze warrior be detected at the water's edge.

In June of the year 1609 this for once was changed. A shallop progressed up the Richelieu River, a tributary of the St. Lawrence, which rises in Iriquois country. It was manned by twelve men, each with a short-barreled arquebus slung over his shoulder. At the prow stood the leader who would not abandon his dream, Samuel de Champlain, watching the shore line with the closest interest. In the wake of the shallop came birch-bark canoes in great numbers, all of them filled with the warrior allies of the French, Montagnais, Algonquins, and Hurons. Although the party was striking south to make war on the Iroquois, it traveled openly, which was indeed unique.

This unusual spectacle came close to an ending when they reached a large waterfall beyond which the shallop could not go. Champlain had been most emphatically assured by his dusky allies that the river was open to navigation as far as a great lake much farther along (which he later named after himself), and he realized then how little reliance he could place in anything they told him. In spite of this he decided to go on. He directed that the shallop be headed back to where the Richelieu joined the St. Lawrence. Keeping no more than two volunteers from his company, he told his native companions that he was still prepared to go along with them. The ranks of the

Indians had been thinning rapidly as a result of quarrels among themselves and of a fear which began to possess them as they came closer to Iroquois territory. More left when they realized that only three of the Frenchmen would accompany them. The stauncher decided to keep on, and places were made for the white men in the canoes. With an outward display of confidence they proceeded on their way.

The lake, which they entered through the channel of Grande Isle, proved to be the largest body of inland water on which the three Frenchmen had ever gazed. They studied its island-studded expanse with wondering eyes, refusing to believe when the Indians asserted that much larger lakes lay westward. Proceeding now with the utmost care, they came to Lake George. On the evening of July 29 they sighted off a point of land where later Fort Ticonderoga would stand a cluster of canoes on the surface of the water. The three white men in their soiled doublets and worn leather boots realized that this meant the clash they had come to invite. To their Indian allies the fact that the alien canoes far off in the distance were heavy in the water meant that they were made of elm bark. Only one tribe used the elm canoe. Iroquois!

It was too late to withdraw now. The warriors from the North realized that their boldness had brought them to a dangerous pass. Their savage enemies were out in great force.

What followed bears no resemblance whatever to the established practices of Indian warfare, which were predicated on surprise in attack. The two parties approached each other openly and a challenge to battle was exchanged in jeering voices across the tranquil water. The Iroquois were too well trained in woods tactics, however, to risk a conflict on the water. Having clamored their contemptuous defiance, they took to the shore, and in a very short time there could be seen through the trees the flickering lights of their fires. All through the night the men of the Five Nations danced about the fires and sang war songs, their voices high and shrill and exultant. They were, it was clear, completely confident.

Champlain's companions maintained an equal show of assurance, but they did not venture to go ashore. Instead they lashed their canoes together and spent the night on the water. They returned jeer for jeer and insult for insult, but to Champlain it may have seemed that this was a form of whistling in the dark. It was hard to remain confident in the face of the uproar from the Iroquois camp.

In the morning the three Frenchmen donned their breastplates, which were so highly polished that they caught the rays of the rising sun and sent fingers of reflected light out across the waters of the lake. Champlain himself donned a casque with a white plume as the mark of leadership. The men loaded their carbines and filled the ammunition straps slung across their shoulders. Each of them was equipped as well with sword and dagger. Their fingers were steady and their eyes did not waver as they peered into the depths of the forest where the Iroquois were preparing.

It was arranged that the white men would go ashore in different canoes and keep apart in the battle in order to give more effect to the discharge of their guns. To make their presence a surprise for the overconfident Iroquois, they hid themselves under robes in the bottom of the canoes. On landing they remained in the rear where they could not be seen.

The warriors of the Long House, who had nothing but contempt for their northern foes, came out to do battle with taunting laughter. Champlain estimated their number at two hundred and he was surprised, and perhaps a little dismayed, at their physical magnificence. Tall, lithe, splendidly thewed, they were superior in every respect to the braves from the North. Their voices rang high through the woods, proclaiming their victory in advance. Three chiefs, their heads topped with snowy plumes, strode boldly in the lead, their eyes fierce, their stone hatchets held aloft. The allies, whose response to the exultant howling of the Iroquois had become somewhat forced and reedy, now proceeded in great haste to carry out the plan which Champlain himself had prepared. Their ranks parted and he stepped forward slowly into the breach thus made in the line. Seeing a white man for the first time, the *Ongue Honwe* fell into a startled silence. Their eyes lost for a moment the glitter of tribal hate and became filled with a sense of awe. This, clearly, was a white god who had come down from the sky to fight on the side of the despised Hurons. The stone hatchets, no longer brandished in the air, hung at their sides.

Although Champlain advanced with no sign of haste, he knew that the Iroquois pause was a momentary one, that they would recover their spirit immediately. It was clear to him also that the Huron braves lacked the fighting pitch to sustain a charge from their hereditary enemies, who outnumbered them several times over. The balance between life and death hung tautly in the air. In no more than a second of time it would be settled. Everything depended on him, the steadiness of his hand, the sureness of his aim.

His arquebus had been loaded with four bullets. Taking aim at the three chiefs, who stood together like a group carved by some Greek master, he discharged the contents of the carbine. His eye had not failed him. The spray of bullets stretched all three chiefs on the ground, two of them killed instantly.

The explosion jarred the senses of the Iroquois, but at the same time it had the effect of releasing them from the spell. Although an unfriendly god had brought down thunder and lightning against them, they must fight for their lives and their tribal honor. They reached for their bows and sent a downpour of arrows into the Huron ranks.

At this critical moment one of Champlain's men showed himself on the flank and fired point-blank at the aroused Iroquois. This was more than they could stand. Another god, another roar like thunder in the clouds! They turned and fled with a consternation which never before had been felt in an Iroquois heart. The *Ongue Honwe* had been surpassed at last.

The allies now came to life. With hatchet and scalping knife they sprang in pursuit of the stunned and disorganized foe. Many of the beaten tribesmen were killed and a dozen or more were captured. The fleeing Iroquois took to the shelter of the trees and so everything they had brought with them, even their canoes (which the allies destroyed scornfully), became the spoils of the victors.

That night the excited and madly exultant warriors picked out one of the prisoners for torture. He was a young brave and owed his selection for this grim honor to the hope of the victors that he lacked resolution for the ordeal. They lashed him to a stake set up in a glade of the forest and told him to sing his death song. The unfortunate youth gave out a dismal and quavering chant. The dancing, jeering savages did not allow him to finish but dashed forward and set the wood around the stake to blazing. While the flames licked at the cringing copper flesh they indulged in other cruelties, tearing out his fingernails, pressing red-hot stones to his writhing limbs, ripping deep strips of flesh from his hide after breaking his bones and exposing the tendons.

Champlain stood this as long as he could and then demanded that the torture be stopped. His allies refused to listen at first. It was not until they saw that his friendship might be withdrawn from them that they reluctantly agreed to let him administer the *coup de grâce*. Standing some distance back, the white leader sent a bullet unerringly into the heart of the tortured youth.

A noted historian has pointed out, in dealing with this incident, that there was inconsistency in the revulsion which all white men felt on witnessing the ordeal of prisoners at the stake. In less than a year after this the King of France would die under the dagger of an assassin and his murderer would be put to death publicly with as much brutality as any Indian ever suffered at the hands of his captors.

The point is well taken. Cruelty was not a trait in which the aborigines of America had a monopoly. Ravaillac, the assassin of Henry IV, was subjected to tortures before he was taken out to the Place de la Grève to die, in the hope of getting from him some information as to his accomplices and sponsors. They strapped his leg in an instrument called the brodequin, an iron boot which fitted closely from knee to ankle. Then they proceeded to drive stout wooden pegs between the flesh and the iron. Each blow tore the leg of the condemned man and caused him excruciating pain. By the time three pegs had been inserted the leg of the assassin was a broken, bleeding mass. Ravaillac bore the pain without telling them anything. For the best of reasons; he had nothing to tell. He was the victim of mental delusions and had no accomplices.

In a weakened condition he was carried out to the execution square, where every inch of space was occupied by avid watchers and the housetops were black with people who had paid large sums for the privilege of standing there. Red-hot pincers were applied to the most tender parts of his body and then boiling oil was poured over the wounds. After he had been thoroughly tormented in this way, he was stretched on the ground and his arms and legs were chained to four horses. The straining animals were then driven in the four directions of the compass. His bones snapped and his limbs stretched grotesquely, but the horses lacked the strength, seemingly, to dismember the body. After more than half an hour of this, the crowds swarmed in and, with demoniac din, put an end to his life.

The judges who determined the manner in which Ravaillac was to die and the howling, slavering spectators were not much different from maddened warriors dancing around a prisoner strapped to a fiery stake.

Champlain had joined the northern Indians in this foray into

Iroquois territory, and had enabled them to score an easy victory, as a matter of carefully considered policy. He realized that his efforts at colonization could succeed only if the fur trade proved sufficiently profitable to retain the support of the business associates of the Sieur de Monts in France. It was the Montagnais who brought the fruits of their trapping to Tadoussac, and it was the Algonquins who made up the long flotillas which came down the Ottawa River to trade at Hochelaga. His support must be given to these natural and convenient allies in their never-ending feud with the Iroquois, and the support must be more than passive. He must fight beside them.

In pursuance of this bold policy Champlain took part a year later in a second attack on the Iroquois. They found the enemy, one hundred strong, in a barricade of logs a league or more up the Richelieu. This time the northern allies far outnumbered the warriors of the Long House. The terror inspired by the firearms of the white men paralyzed any attempt at defense, and the screeching allies broke through the barrier, killing all the Iroquois save fifteen, who were carried off to be burned at the stake.

No other policy seems to have been open to Champlain. Propinquity made the northern tribes his natural allies and he needed their immediate friendship. But espousing the cause of the Montagnais, the Algonquins, and the Hurons against the Five Nations was to have bloody repercussions later. The Iroquois could not face the deadly guns of the white men at the beginning. These were years of easy victory for the less vital tribes of the northern woods. But the Long House never forgot nor forgave. They nursed a hatred for the French which the years did not diminish nor the spilling of white blood stale. For more than a century the smoldering wrath of the Iroquois braves would vent itself in furious raids on the settlements of New France. They ranged themselves with the British in the wars between the two white races and struck blow after blow at Montreal and Quebec. Even after the Hurons had been exterminated and the Montagnais had ceased to count, the feud went on. The blazing fires of Lachine were the result of the course which Champlain initiated in the difficult first years of colonization.

CHAPTER VIII

Champlain, Organizer, Diplomat, Explorer, and Indian Fighter

1

THE assassination of Henry IV was a serious blow to the Sieur de Monts and his associates. What hope would there be for a Huguenot to retain any shred of influence at a court over which Italian-born Marie de' Medici, the King's widow, would preside as regent? The new ruler, Louis XIII, was too young to have any voice and there was no reason to assume that, had the power been his, the boy King would have looked with a lenient eye on the enterprise of the merchant adventurers.

Champlain sailed back to France in 1611 to take counsel with Monts and found the latter acting as governor of the city of Pons, a mere dot on the map of Saintonge. This was the clearest indication of impending disaster, that the resourceful Monts had found it necessary to leave court and bury himself in the humdrum details of a provincial post. The truth was that his personal fortune had been dissipated and that he stood on the threshold of bankruptcy when Champlain sought him out. This last glimpse of him which history affords shows him in a favorable light. He did not complain of his misfortunes. He wore his plumed hat as jauntily as ever and his handsome eyes still glowed with resolution. He transferred to Champlain full power to make such arrangements as he might for the struggling colony and urged him not to desist or lose heart. The latter, emboldened by his old comrade's tenacity in the face of adversity, went to Fontainebleau to plead for continued support.

At this point the haughty and sometimes vindictive regent was seated firmly in the saddle of state, with her Italian favorites, the Concinis, pulling strings and amassing a great fortune for themselves. A certain very young bishop from the see of Luçon, "the poorest and nastiest in France," to quote his own phrase, one Armand Jean du Plessis de Richelieu, was most certainly not at court at this juncture, as his election to the States-General would not come about for three years. In any event, this almost adolescent cleric, who one day would rule France with steel-clad hand and put his whole weight behind the colonizing of America, was very discreet and very, very poor (he had to buy a secondhand bed when he took over the bishopric), and the questing eye of Champlain would have passed him over without so much as a pause.

Champlain was working on a plan which no doubt had been hatched in the course of his talks with Monts. The colony must be placed under the wing of someone close to the throne in order to command further help and patronage. The man from Quebec looked about him and his eye became fixed on a cousin of the late King, the Comte de Soissons, a dissolute and supercilious nobleman who was continuously in need of funds. Champlain showed himself in this matter a most resourceful negotiator. He first canvassed the members of the royal council and won support and authorization there for his plan. Then he approached the comte and made a bargain with him by which the noble spendthrift would receive a thousand crowns a year for the use of his illustrious name and his influence at court.

The Comte de Soissons, who was to be named viceroy, did not live long enough to profit from this arrangement. The organization of the new company had not been completed, in fact, when he was struck down with a fever and followed his cousin, the much-mourned Henry, to the grave. Champlain cast about for a successor and fastened his choice on the Prince de Condé, a nephew of the deceased comte and the possessor of one of the proudest names in France. The record of the noble house of Condé was like an agitated sea, majestic heights and wallowing depths following each other in quick succession. It was the lot of the heads of the family to be either sublimely great or completely mediocre and venal. The representative of the line who listened agreeably to Champlain's arguments was to be the father of the greatest Condé, the victor of Rocroi, but he himself was a vain and greedy man who entertained ambitious plans but lacked the capacity to carry any of them out; but who possessed enough influence to put through a matter as relatively small as this. In the spring of 1614, after long negotiations, the merchants of the great ports were brought into one organization under the distinguished, if sterile, patronage of Condé. The latter was to be viceroy with Champlain acting as his lieutenant in Canada. Condé was to receive his thousand crowns a year and the associated members were to send out six families as settlers each season. The monopoly was to extend for eleven years from the signing of the charter.

Champlain, who had been running back and forth between the two continents while the negotiations simmered, returned to Canada now in a jubilant mood. The success of the venture seemed assured at last. The little settlement clinging so tenaciously to the foot of the great rock at Quebec would prosper. Other posts would be started at strategic points. Champlain himself would be able to pursue his explorations and his work with the Indians. And finally the objective which had always been prominent in the minds of those two resolute pioneers, Champlain and Monts (the latter was being given a very humble holding in the new company), would at last be realized. The cassock and breviary of the missionary would be seen along the great rivers and lakes and in the palisaded villages of the savage tribes.

2

In the corner of Ontario which extends northward from Lake Simcoe and takes in all the beautifully wooded and lake-bespangled land around the great arm of Georgian Bay, and which laps over on the east into the present-day playground of summer enchantment known as Muskoka and in the other direction into the northern area of fertile Western Ontario, was the home of the Hurons. It was small indeed to hold a nation of such relative greatness. The Hurons, who numbered about twenty thousand, had provided themselves with more than thirty villages in this irregular triangle of peaceful country. That they were crowded for hunting grounds goes without saying, but the location provided them with one great advantage: they were widely separated from their enemies of long standing, the ambitious and predatory Iroquois. Between the Huron country and the Finger Lakes was Western Ontario, which belonged to the Tobacco Nation, and the western arm of New York, where the Cat People lived. This was neutral land, and although it did not serve as a defense against Iroquois raids it helped considerably.

Between visits to France to smooth the roiled financial waters, Champlain continued his explorations, the work which added more luster to his name than all the confabulations at Fountainebleau and all his diplomatic triumphs over the Condés, the Legendres, and Colliers. It is impossible to tell in detail of the many journeys he made in the long canoes so proudly paddled by his Indian friends and guides, the fleur-de-lis always fluttering at the prow, or to tell of the many far parts of this fair land on which he set foot. The most important of his explorations was a long thrust northward in the summer of 1615 which was prolonged into the next year. He undertook it to fulfill a promise made earlier to the heads of the Huron nation. He ascended the Ottawa River, transferred to the Mattawa, and found himself finally at Lake Nipissing. Turning southward, he came into Huron country and found himself gazing on a body of water of sufficient size and grandeur to make him doubt the accuracy of his senses.

His conviction was that he had reached the great lake of which he had heard so much and which later would be called Huron. Because of this he named the water stretching far out beyond the horizon the Mer Douce, the Fresh-Water Sea. It was, in reality, Georgian Bay.

Progressing southward through the Huron country, which abounded in streams and lakes and waterfalls, he visited a number of the largest villages, coming at last to the most important of them, called Cahiagué, which had two hundred lodges and triple palisades thirty feet high. He found that pandemonium had taken possession of the place. The war kettle had been brought out and was simmering like the caldron of wizardry in the center court. Huron braves from all quarters had been coming in for days, their skulls shaven clean, none wearing more than a breechclout. The crowded lodges at Cahiagué, which will be described in detail later, were now packed as full as caterpillar tents. The warriors were feasting and dancing and singing war songs. The squaws were screaming, the children were joining in, and the innumerable dogs, unlike the barkless canines of Hochelaga, were adding to the din.

The Hurons were taking the warpath on a greater scale than ever before. An allied tribe, the Carantouans, who lived in what is now eastern Pennsylvania, had promised to join them with five hundred men. The plan was to move secretly and swiftly against the main village of the Onondagas, the senior of the Five Nations, and wipe them out once and for all. Now that Champlain, giver of victory, had come with many men, all of them carrying the deadly weapon which killed at a distance, they knew that victory was assured. It was no wonder that the shrill voices rose to a triumphant pitch.

After one of the Frenchmen, a young man named Etienne Brulé (he had come to Canada as Champlain's servant), had been dispatched to the Carantouan country to make sure that the five hundred allies arrived in time, the great war party started. They traveled down the lakes in what is now the Kawartha section and entered Lake Ontario by way of the Trent River. They struck across that great body of water, and as the paddles rose and fell, sending the frail canoes easily along the choppy waves, the white men were told of the great falling waters at the end of the lake and of the huge seas which lay still farther to the west.

The attack was a failure. The Carantouan allies did not put in an appearance, but the defeat was due more to the overconfidence and scatterbrained conduct of the Hurons. First they gave their presence away by attacking a party of Iroquois, women as well as men, who were harvesting their fall crops in fields planted high with rustling corn. As a result of this madness, caused by an irresistible hate which surged up at first sight of the enemy, the attack was delivered against aroused and thoroughly prepared defenders. The village was surrounded by four rows of wooden palisades sloping inward and supporting a gallery which swarmed with jeering Iroquois. Looking the situation over, Champlain realized that the attack would have to be launched with great care. He drew his dusky allies back into the shelter of the trees and set them to work first at making what was called in France a "cavalier," a tower high enough to permit his musketeers to fire down over the heads of the defenders, as well as a number of "mantelets," movable wooden shields behind which the attacking party could advance against the walls.

All would have gone well if the same madness had not taken possession of the Hurons when the attack was delivered. Five hundred strong, and thoroughly convinced that the rifle fire of the French would throw the Onondaga braves into a panic, the Hurons abandoned the shields and dashed madly instead to attack in the open. The arrows of the defenders fell among them like lethal hail and their losses were heavy. The French marksmen in the cavalier took steady toll of the defenders on the gallery, but gunfire no longer held any element of surprise. The men of the Onondaga tribe knew they must expect losses by reason of the magic of the white men. They flinched as their ranks were decimated, but they stood to their posts.

The wild efforts of the Hurons to set fire to the outer palisade failed and they slunk back to the cover of the trees, having lost all stomach for the devastating archery of the Iroquois. After three hours the attacking party decided they were beaten, and Champlain, who had been wounded in the leg by an arrow, could not rouse them to further efforts. All that the disheartened Hurons wanted now was to get back to the safety of their own country so far away. In the retreat which followed, the French leader was carried in a basket on the back of a powerful brave. He suffered intense pain, his unhappiness increased by speculation as to what effect the disaster would have on his unstable allies.

Sullen in defeat, the Hurons made it clear that they had lost faith in their white friends. Why had the long iron tubes failed to bring the Iroquois to their knees? The mutter of discontent which filled the canoes after they had reached Lake Ontario held no trace of self-blame. They had crossed the lake in ease and supreme confidence, but they made the return in better haste and with many a frightened backward glance.

It had been arranged that canoes would be provided to take the French to Montreal Island immediately after the expected victory. Now none would volunteer for the task, pointing out the danger of being picked off by the bands of Iroquois who would soon swarm in the woods. Champlain, who understood the Huron moods, realized that there was more than this back of the attitude of the chiefs. They expected the enemy to attack in turn and they needed the help of the white men and their muskets.

Champlain saw that, whether they liked it or not, he and his men faced the necessity of spending the winter in the Huron country.

3

The failure of Etienne Brulé to bring the Carantouan contingent was not due to any fault of his own. He had made a quick descent of Lake Orillia and down the Humber River (thus becoming the first white man to visit the side of the city of Toronto), at which point he and his Huron aides crossed Lake Ontario. They skirted the Iroquois country cautiously and reached in safety the upper waters of the Susquehanna River. The chief Carantouan village was located close to the site of the modern town of Waverly, and here they found the Carantouan chiefs. The latter were friendly but inclined to be

dilatory. Days were wasted in useless powwows and council meetings. They finally got the warriors out and on their way to join the
Hurons, but it was then too late. They arrived two days after the retreat of the Huron war party.

Of all the Frenchmen who listened to the call of the wild, Etienne
Brulé was perhaps the most rash but also the most daring and enterprising. The records do not supply a description of him, but it is not
difficult to achieve a mental picture of this wild and unfortunate
man. It is known that he was extraordinarily strong. In his last appearances among white men he was dressed like an Indian, his
powerful torso bared to the waist and tanned as brown as walnut.
His hair, it may be guessed, was shocky and coarse. His eyes, when
he became angry, which was often, had a reddish glint in them. He
had gone native, living as the Indians did, taking brown-skinned
wives wherever he went and putting them away as his fancy dictated. Father Gabriel Sagard, who was his friend, acknowledged
sadly that Brulé was "much addicted to women."

After the failure of the expedition against the Iroquois, Brulé
began on the travels which would have made him famous if his
achievements had not been blotted out by a final act of treachery.
He went down the Susquehanna and reached the northern tip of
Chesapeake Bay. On his way back he was captured by the Iroquois
but made his escape by a lucky accident. He had been the first to
ascend the Ottawa, crossing to the Mattawa and following its course
to Lake Nipissing and the French River, thus establishing the route
to the Huron country. He had also been the first to set eyes on
Georgian Bay. Making his way through the Inner Passage, he had
reached Lake Huron.

His failure to return to Quebec convinced Champlain that his one-
time servant had been killed. No one could have been more completely alive and active. Brulé's first move after returning to the
Huron country was to lead a party past Michilimackinac and so out
to the waters of Lake Superior, the Grand Lac. Some historians believe that to his list of "firsts" should be added the discovery of
Lake Michigan. If he failed to reach it, Michigan was the only one
of the Great Lakes that he overlooked. He saw all the others first.

He took no notes, he drew no maps, he wrote no stories of his
travels; but the verbal reports he gave of what he had seen left no
doubts as to the truth of his statements. In all probability there was
no serious purpose back of his wanderings. He liked to be on the

move, to have a paddle in his hands, his eyes fixed on the farthest horizon. Had he shared the scientific interest of the men who came after him and followed the trails he blazed, his name would have headed the list of early American explorers.

This phase of the life of Etienne Brulé is the bright side of the picture. There will be more to tell about him later, and it will be, unfortunately, a quite different story.

4

The six months which followed for Champlain, amounting to a form of detention, were lived through at first with the keenest distaste, but gradually the leader saw that the situation held compensations. He came to know the Indians with a thoroughness which would not have been possible under any other circumstances. His busy mind was never allowed to rest. While the disgruntled braves lolled on their lice-infested platforms and smoked the time away in uneasy speculation as to when and in what form the ire of the Iroquois would manifest itself, Champlain watched and talked and asked questions. What he learned was put down on paper, a wealth of information which makes possible an understanding of many phases of Canadian history.

It is probable that the long cold months were lived through at Cahiagué, where the blow, if it came at all, was most likely to fall. It has already been said that the village consisted of two hundred lodges, and the description that Champlain supplies makes it clear that they were community houses, some being as long as two hundred feet. They were made of roughhewn boards bent inward to form an arch. Inside they were regions of bedlam, with long platforms a few feet above the ground on each side and with a narrow open space between. These platforms were divided into spaces for the various families; and here they lived and ate and slept and performed all the natural functions with a lack of privacy equaling that of the animals in the Ark. Down the center of these malodorous caverns there was a series of family fires belching forth sparks and smoke which stubbornly refused to leave by the open space between the ends of the planks above and thus established a murkiness of atmosphere through which the brown skulls and fierce features of the inmates loomed dimly like denizens of the nether regions. In the dark and drafty upper reaches unshelled corn hung down on long lines looped from section to section, with the family clothing, the skins, cured and uncured, the dried fish, the weapons, and the rather pitiful prized possessions of these primitive people.

Champlain's first consideration, of course, was to improve the defenses, making sure that guards were always mounted on the galleries and that supplies were kept of stones and water to be used in case of attack. He realized by this time that he had espoused the weaker side in this agelong feud. Nothing the Hurons could do would ever put them on an equality with the Iroquois in the making of war. The men of the Long House were the great warriors of America, dauntless, hard, and with all the cunning of wild animals. Some authorities have advanced the opinion that the Iroquois brave, for courage and craft and power of endurance, has never had an equal, placing him even above the mounted bowmen of Genghis Khan, who were truly terrific fighters, and the inspired Ironsides of Cromwell.

The Iroquois reprisals did not materialize and the winter was spent in the most deadly monotony. The food, always flat because the Indian did not understand the use of salt or any form of seasoning, became so bad as the winter progressed that the civilized stomachs of the unwilling guests were revolted by the dreadful messes prepared by the toothless and quarrelsome squaws. There was always a shortage of the dog flesh which was a staple article, and very rarely did the hunters bring in venison or bear meat. Usually a meal consisted of heavy concoctions of dried corn, sometimes called sagamité and sometimes migan, the latter a combination of corn meal with smoked fish, which gave it a peculiarly offensive odor. Perhaps the Frenchmen witnessed something which later caused the missionaries the most extreme revulsion. The young boys of the tribe devoured the cooked hearts of captives who had died bravely at the stake, under the impression that they would acquire thereby some of the same brand of fortitude themselves.

Champlain had known before that in striking a balance between the virtues and faults of the red men their morals had to be placed on the debit side. The Huron men were lazy, they were natural thieves, they were treacherous and unpredictable. They were inefficient even in the few duties they took on themselves. The women, after a few years of unbridled license and passion, were hopeless drudges, busy all day at plodding tasks and becoming in time more cruel than the men. Jacques Cartier had reported a custom at Hochelaga of turning all girls at puberty into a community brothel, where they remained until they chose a husband. The Huron custom was based on trial marriage. A girl, after receiving a gift of wampum, would live with a man for a long enough period to decide whether they suited each other well enough to make a permanent partnership of it. The more attractive of the dusky belles made as many as a dozen experiments before settling down, and gathered as a result a very handsome store of wampum and other gewgaws for the adornment of their plump brown bodies. This fickleness did not weigh against them. It was a recognized approach to matrimony and, if they never again allowed their fancy to stray after settling down, they were as well regarded as the young squaws who had been less adventurous.

The most interesting possession in all Indian tribes was wampum, belts or strips of skin covered with designs in small shells of many colors. Wampum was like money in the sense that it served as a commodity of exchange, but it was much more important than that. It was used as well as a means of recording historical events. In treaty making, wampum was employed as a pledge and proof of the decisions arrived at, each side carrying away strips which illustrated what had been decided. Champlain may have seen with his own eyes the first stage in the making of wampum. A dead body, usually that of an antagonist who had been killed in battle or had perished miserably under torture, was slashed with long deep cuts on the belly and buttocks and other fleshy parts. The body was then lowered into deep water and left there for a considerable length of time. When brought to the surface, it would be found that small shellfish had buried themselves in the cuts. From the inner surface of these barnacles the handsomely tinted pieces of shell were cut which served in the designing of the wampum.

Even at this early stage of relationship between white man and red the taciturnity of the latter was fully recognized. On most occasions the Indian had no more to say than the customary "Ho!" of greeting, but in the winter evenings it was a different matter. As they crowded around the fires and blinked with their smoke-filled eyes (most of them developed diseases of the eye early in life), their tongues unloosened and they cackled and laughed and boasted and lapsed into the broadest of humor. The elders orated and were given always an attentive hearing; the women sat about and listened, their fingers busy at some task. Champlain took full advantage of his opportunity, asking questions and making notes later of the answers.

It is not surprising that the shell of the Huron taciturnity cracked wide open, because this was the season of talk. It was, in fact, the only safe time for the braves to indulge themselves in loquacity. The gods were imprisoned in winter in blocks of ice and so lost all contact with living men, whereas in summer they roamed the woods and sat at the shoulders of men and heard everything that was said, so that it behooved everyone to speak warily because the gods took offense easily and were prone to wreak vengeance on anyone spreading tales about them.

The Hurons were prepared even to speak of their religious beliefs. Out of the information given him Champlain asserts that they had no conception of one god. In this he was misled. They had a conviction of the immortality of the soul, these benighted inhabitants of the deep and inhospitable forest, as well as a belief in one great god above all others (called by the Iroquois, who also believed, "He who lives in the sky"). The Hurons had a theory of their own, that the spirits of dead warriors took a long journey along the Milky Way, racing at top speed, so fast that no enemy could overtake them, the winds blowing fiercely at their backs to help them on, until they came to the Happy Hunting Ground. The Hurons were certain that their favorite dogs had souls but they would not concede as much to their women. The Algonquins, a gross and licentious race, were sure that after death the souls of warriors lived in a heaven where they feasted and danced through all eternity.

It is certain that the Hurons kept from the constantly questing Champlain a secret about themselves which was ascertained much later. They had an understanding of picture-writing. Racial legends and beliefs were set down in symbols on flat pieces of wood, and these were preserved and handed down from one generation to another. Among the stories thus preserved was a version of the beginning of things. A literal translation of the start of their saga of the making of the world ran as follows:

At first there were the great waters above all the land,
And above the waters were thick clouds, and there was God the Creator.

The arrow wound in Champlain's leg had healed (fortunately only the Cat People used poisoned arrows in war) and so he was able to venture out into the open, where the air was sharp and damp and penetrating. It was a constant amazement to him that his hosts went about in semi-nakedness, oblivious of the cold which froze the ears and noses of his Frenchmen. The women were not as hardy as this and preferred to bundle themselves up warmly in robes made of the skins of wild animals, the unmarried ones being particularly partial to this kind of luxury. It was not uncommon to meet young squaws looking very handsome in coats of fox or ermine or otter which would not have looked out of place on the backs of European princesses. They were openly flirtatious, and some of them did not seem to have a thought in their sleek brown heads of demanding wampum.

When spring came it was apparent to the Huron chiefs that the white men could not be kept as their guests forever if the friendship between them, which the northern nations prized above everything, was to be maintained. The Iroquois had not struck and it might be that they had decided not to attempt so bold a reprisal. At any rate, the canoes and the necessary crews were produced for the return trip, and early in April they set out. As they progressed at high speed down the rushing waters of the Ottawa, the mind of Champlain was busily at work. The defeat sustained provided him with plenty of reason for serious reflection, and it is possible that the specter of future wars was constantly before him. A more pleasant thought may have occupied his mind at intervals. This long thrust he had made into the unknown wilds must have appeared to him as the first of countless other ventures. Perhaps the certainty entered his thoughts that Frenchmen had a special liking, and a great natural capacity, for the adventurous kind of life. It is pleasant to assume that he had visions of what would follow: of Frenchmen, bold and gay, venturing out in long canoes of their own to open up the North and West, singing to the dip of the paddles, living and dying on the trails of the forest and the great waters, and creating legends which would never die.

5

It must not be assumed that while Champlain conducted his bold explorations all was plain sailing in France. It is true that the company began to make money, paying profits of 40 per cent one year. The new viceroy received his thousand crowns annually and a share of the profits without lifting one of his delicately white hands to earn such a reward. In fact, this rather stupid scion of an illustrious line proceeded to destroy whatever value he had for the syndicate by getting at odds with the administration.

Condé had married Alice de Montmorenci, one of the great beauties of France, and in the last years of the life of the amorous Henry IV he had found it expedient to live in exile with his lovely mate. Only on Henry's death did he venture back to pick up the threads of a normal life, and it might be thought that even an ordinary degree of caution would have prevented him from getting embroiled in the political feuds of the day. Unfortunately he had no political sagacity and became involved almost immediately in intrigues against the ministers of the young King. Soon after his appointment as viceroy of Canada he became deeply committed in these conspiracies. In 1616, at a time when his wife had decided to seek a divorce from him, he was placed under arrest and packed off to the Bastille. The fair Alice then decided it was her duty to stand by her spouse and she went to the great prison which held turbulent Paris in awe to share his rigorous confinement—with several body servants and footmen, a cook, a barber, and a confessor! Here they remained for three years, and the boy who became the great Condé was born as a result of this reconciliation.

Despite the prosperity of the company, Condé decided as soon as he regained his liberty to rid himself of this connection. He sold his post as viceroy to Montmorenci, the admiral of France, for eleven thousand crowns. This, as it turned out, was a good thing, the admiral proving himself a man of parts and decision.

At no time did Champlain have any peace. The investors in the company, having no concern for anything but the profits they could make, refused to assume the expense of sending out settlers as provided by the charter. Champlain complained so bitterly about this that he was subjected to continuous attacks from a cabal in the ranks of the company who wanted to oust him from his post at Quebec. There was one troublesome gadfly in particular, a merchant named Boyer who had made himself a pest through all the years of control by the Sieur de Monts. Boyer now established himself as the active leader of the opposition. He even went to the length of having Champlain barred from a ship sailing for Canada when he wanted to return in the spring of 1619.

The founder of Canada was not the kind of man to accept rebuffs of this nature in silence and allow his great project to be ruined by the greed of grasping individuals. He laid all the facts before Montmorenci. The admiral reached the conclusion that the time had come to cut away from the greedy shipowners, the niggling money lenders, and the noisy faultfinders. Obtaining the necessary support in the King's council, he transferred the monopoly to two brothers in Rouen, Guillaume and Emery de Câen.

This drastic move stirred up in the maritime world of France a most bitter controversy. To attack what had been done, the ousted merchants seized on the fact that the Câen brothers were Huguenots. All the great ports rang with the dispute. It became so bitter that finally a compromise had to be reached. There was a reorganization, and the former partners were given five twelfths of the stock in the new syndicate, an arrangement grudgingly accepted because it left them in a minority position. Champlain, standing between the two parties because his innate sense of fairness would not allow him to see either side robbed by the other, had to exercise all his diplomatic skill to keep things on an even keel. That he succeeded is proof that he possessed in rare degree the qualifications of a peacemaker.

CHAPTER IX

A View of Quebec in the First Days—
Louis Hébert—Champlain's Romance

1

QUEBEC in 1620. It must be confessed at once that the cradle of New France was little different from what it had been at the start. Perhaps the dreams and hopes and determinations of the loyal souls who clung to the base of the rock had already created an atmosphere of solidity, but physically it was far removed from a realization of Champlain's vision. Seven years later the resolute founder gave the population as sixty-seven, including children, and so it may be assumed that at this stage there were no more than fifty people in the settlement.

The huddle of hastily constructed buildings still stood among the walnut trees, but they were beginning to leak and show signs of collapse. Other houses had grown up around them, all of which were just as unsubstantial and dreary. Along the waterfront were wharfage facilities and some rude storage sheds.

Between the summit towering overhead and the little settlement hugging the riverbanks there was nothing but a steep, winding path; in summer nothing to break the browns and greens, in winter no cheerful glimmer of light against the solid blanket of snow. The summit was bare also. Some efforts had been made to clear the ground, and the stumps of what had once been noble trees now cluttered that lofty expanse, waiting for the settlers who would haul them out and set oxen to plowing the ground.

Off to the east the high line of the hills sank rather sharply until it leveled off in a thick tangle of woods where the St. Charles joined the St. Lawrence. Here, where Cartier had built his forts, the Récollet fathers had established themselves in a log building surrounded by a square palisade. The Récollets were an offshoot of the Franciscans, the order which St. Francis of Assisi had conceived to aid the lowly and tend the sick and cheer the downtrodden. The original purpose of the founder had been obscured over the centuries, and the Franciscans had become powerful and even wealthy. The result of this had been the breaking away from the parent body of dissenting groups for the purpose of getting back to the original conception. The most rigid of these were the French Récollets, known sometimes as the Franciscans of the Strict Observance, a mendicant body wearing the pointed capuche and dependent on charity for their daily bread. It happened that a Récollet convent had been established near Brouage, and on one of his visits to his home Champlain went there and made clear how much the colony needed spiritual assistance. The Récollets agreed to send out a group of their members, but with the understanding that the expenses of the venture would be provided, they themselves having not so much as a single coin. Champlain at this point stood at the peak of his organizational powers. He visited Paris, where the States-General was in session, going from bishop to bishop and stating his needs. The leaders of the French Church, despite a feeling of contempt among them for the lowly friars, subscribed the sum of fifteen hundred livres to be used in the purchase of vestments and supplies. Four of the friars had volunteered eagerly for the mission, Joseph le Caron, Jean d'Olbeau, Denis Jamay, and Pacifique du Plessis.

The people of Quebec, starved for the activities of their former life and particularly for the solace and the ritual of their faith, received the Récollets with every manifestation of delight. The first Mass ever heard in Canada was celebrated by D'Olbeau before a rude altar raised in great haste, with the settlers kneeling in humility and thankfulness and the Indians watching from far off.

With their own toil-callused hands the friars then raised the palisades and hewed out the logs and cut the stone for their severe habitation on the St. Charles. This much accomplished, they were eager to be about their mission. Not waiting to acquire any command of Indian languages, Jean d'Olbeau betook himself to Tadoussac. He existed there through a severe winter, living in a birch-bark lodge with the Montagnais, who were particularly primitive in their ways. Later he accompanied a roving band of the Montagnais up into the North, where they went for fur. His delicate frame was ill suited to the hardships of the trail and he became partially blind in the smoky atmosphere of the native lodges, but he came back in the spring and went on with his work.

Joseph le Caron was consumed with an equal eagerness to begin and attached himself to the Hurons. Champlain found him there when he paid his visit to the Huron country which has already been described. The others remained in Quebec for the time being and ministered to the spiritual needs of the settlers.

Although vegetables and grain and some fruit were now being grown and the waters thereabouts yielded fish in considerable quantities, the people of Quebec often found themselves close to the edge of actual want. In other ways their life was far from diverting or useful. They diced and gamed and quarreled, and stern discipline had to be maintained over the unattached men. The women probably suffered the most. The men could hunt and fish, but their wives sat in idleness within their own four walls. Even when the ships arrived in the spring there was nothing much in the cargoes to interest them, certainly none of the latest fashions from Paris and none of the newest fabrics. Even the issues of the *Mercure Gallant,* which had begun publication in 1611, were more than three months old when received.

The shut-in settlers were now denied the interest which the independent traders had supplied. In the earlier years, when no monopoly had existed, the adventurers from the seaports had flocked out in crowded ships, avid for a share in the riches of the new continent. They lived in the dilapidated cabins on Anticosti or in the ships anchored off Tadoussac. They even risked the passage of the St. Lawrence and swarmed about the Place Royale, as Champlain had named the trading post he had established at Hochelaga and which was becoming the most active of trading centers. It was here that the great fur flotillas of the Hurons and Algonquins brought their pelts for barter, sweeping down the swift Ottawa.

The independents had always been an obnoxious lot. They were greedy and dishonest and drunken and a continual nuisance to the authorities at Quebec, where they paused on their river trips. They ogled the women and they caroused in the supply sheds at the waterfront. Noisy and rambunctious, they were unrestrained in all their habits; a filthy, heavy-bearded crew with the instincts of pirates. They were, in fact, the most deadly birds of prey, utterly without scruples, ready to risk their own scalps for beaver skins and quite prepared to do murder for gain. Later they would be responsible for the first steps in debauching the red men. It was from the free traders that the Indians had their first taste of alcohol, and from these transients, also, the red warriors obtained guns and learned to use them.

Champlain's head was filled with plans. He would have a stone citadel on the crest, a series of streets and squares, broad and clean and airy, churches with lofty spires, a hospital. He even dreamed of houses climbing up the steep path, a waterfront of enduring stone; of orderly days and secure nights, and church bells tolling the hours. But he would not live to see the realization of more than a fraction of his fond hopes.

This, then, was Quebec in 1620, a meager settlement indeed to represent the desire of the French people for a share in the colonization of the New World. But small and poor though it might be, it was there to stay. The few inhabitants were inured to the difficulties of the life and schooled in pioneering ways. Not even the interruption supplied by the English in 1628, which will be told in due course, could do more than temporarily dampen the faith and determination of these hardy people.

2

The time has come to speak of the man who is rightfully called the first Canadian settler and whose brief sojourn in Acadia has already been noted, Louis Hébert.

"I hope the cutting is good. Now for the sewing," said Catherine de' Medici, Queen Mother of France, after her favorite of the three sons who succeeded each other on the throne, the weak and vindictive Henry III, had seen to it that his chief political opponent, the Duc de Guise, was assassinated. The Queen Mother seems to have had grave doubts about the sewing. She had long been in bad health, and there were many who declared that after the massacre of St. Bartholomew's, which she instigated and managed, she never knew real peace of mind. Whether or not the ghosts of the slaughtered Huguenots came back to haunt her dreams, it is certain that she strove hard to keep at a distance the one enemy she feared, death. She kept about her always a large staff of physicians and listened hungrily to the advice they gave her. All to no avail: she did not live to see the results of the sewing (they were most disastrous) but died thirteen days after the body of Henry of Guise lay stretched on the floor of the royal anteroom.

One of the physicians who thus failed to do anything for the guilt-ridden Queen bore the name of Hébert. He had a son called Louis, and it is likely that the boy had opportunities to see court life with his own eyes. It was not an edifying spectacle at this point in French history, but it had one advantage: the royal chambers buzzed continuously with talk of the great country across the Atlantic. The boy grew up with a deep desire to keep far away from royal courts and to have a personal share in the settling of Canada.

He followed his father's example and became an apothecary, perhaps as a means to an end. At any rate, he was the first to answer the summons and sail with the Sieur de Poutrincourt when that gallant gentleman voiced the need for an apothecary in his company for Acadia. The disastrous ending of that venture did not lessen Hébert's enthusiasm. He reopened his shop in Paris, but his mind was fixed on a land where mighty rivers flowed through the silence of great forests and he took little interest in the mixing of laxatives and the rolling of pills. When Champlain came to him in 1616 and offered what seemed like splendid terms to go to Quebec as resident physician and surgeon for the company, he accepted gladly. He was to be maintained for three years and receive a salary of two hundred crowns a year. Hébert promptly sold his shop and his house in Paris and the next year took his wife and family of three to Honfleur for embarkation.

Here a shock awaited him. The Boyer element was in the saddle at the moment, and the only sentiment which prevailed was the desire for more and still more profits. The bewildered Hébert was told that Champlain had exceeded his authority and that the agreement would not be honored. He would receive only one hundred crowns a year for the three years, and after the term of the arrangement expired he must serve the company exclusively for nothing. He must never dabble in the fur trade, and if he became a raiser of produce he must sell everything to the company at prices they would fix.

The brusque gentleman who informed him of this late change of heart on their part had an agreement drawn up for Hébert to sign. He realized that he had no choice in the matter. He had disposed of his shop, he had cut loose from his snug moorings, and now he could not turn back. He signed the scandalously unfair paper and took his worried family aboard the ship for the New World.

The ship landed at Tadoussac on a warm summer day, with the sun bright overhead and an invigorating breeze blowing across the majestic river. The first settler went ashore with hopes so high that no thought of the chicanery of the directors came up to disturb him. It did not matter that the chapel in which a Récollet father said Mass was a flimsy structure made out of the branches of trees and that a cloud of mosquitoes descended upon them. It did not matter later that the Indians who watched them land at the dilapidated supply sheds in Quebec were dirty and practically naked and openly sullen. This was the New World, and to stout Louis Hébert the great wall of rock above the tumble-down houses in the grove was a symbol of the new world which would rise about it. He was so anxious to begin that he could not tolerate a day's delay. Up the steep pathway he led his family to inspect the ten acres which had been allotted to him on the crest. There they spent the first night under a tree. The exact spot where the tree stood is still pointed out to curious visitors.

Louis Hébert soon demonstrated that he was of the true pioneering breed. No repining for him over the lost ease of his comfortable shop on a fashionable street in Paris, no sulking over the bad faith of the company. He set to work at once and cleared a considerable stretch of the land. The temporary house he set up for his small family and the one domestic who had followed them out was soon replaced by a permanent one, a substantial structure of stone. All that is known of this first real house to be reared on Canadian soil was that it was of one story, the length thirty-eight feet, the width nineteen feet.

Here the Héberts seem to have been happy. Certainly they were industrious. The vegetables they grew on their fertile acres soon supplied all of the less fortunate families on the riverbanks; and for this, under the terms of the unfair agreement, they received no pay. At the same time the head of the family acted as physician and dispenser to the whole colony.

With Champlain he was always on the best of terms, not blaming the founder for the repudiation of the first agreement. It is said that Champlain, who was now fifty years of age and was beginning to fill his doublets with a degree of amplitude, plodded up the steep path frequently to visit the Héberts, his dog Matelot at his heels. There was another reason for the frequency of his visits: he liked to look down over the river and the country which stretched to the south and to think of the day when all this land would be as thickly settled as Normandy or Touraine.

As physician to the colony Louis Hébert had his reward in the love and often expressed gratitude of the people he served. Fortunately he was to receive more tangible evidences. In 1621, when a proper legal system was inaugurated in Quebec, he was appointed King's procurator in the first court of justice. In 1623 he was given full title to the land on the summit and was admitted to the ranks of the minor gentry. The following year he received an additional grant of land on the banks of the St. Charles, with which went the title of Sieur d'Epinay. He had become reasonably prosperous. His children had grown up and married and had built around the comfortable parental home. Paris had become no more than a dim memory; the new life had been infinitely more satisfying than an existence on the edge of the royal court.

The first Hébert daughter, Anne, married Etienne Jonquit but died soon after in 1620. The second daughter, Marie Guillaumette, married Guillaume Couillard in 1621, a carpenter who had arrived in Quebec a year before the Héberts. They raised a family of sturdy children, and from this fine stock a line descended which has never been broken and has played a prominent part in French-Canadian history.

It was a severe loss to the colony when Louis Hébert suffered a fall and died on January 25, 1627.

3

There had been no time for romance in Champlain's life. During the years when a man usually seeks a wife he was campaigning actively in the religious wars under the brave St. Luc and the scheming Brissac. Then came his Spanish journeys and the writing of *Bref Discours,* and finally he had involved himself in long absences in Canada. Nevertheless, he had been married in Paris in 1610 under circumstances which might have led to a highly romantic married life. Returning to France after his first victory over the Iroquois, when he was forty-three years of age and at the very peak of his career and his physical powers, he had contracted a matrimonial alliance with a daughter of the secretary of the King's chamber, one Nicholas Boullé, a wealthy Huguenot. Hélène Boullé was only twelve years old when they took the vows together in the Church of St. Germain l'Auxerrois. Because of her age the marriage contract stipulated that she must remain with her parents for at least two years before joining her husband in Canada, and it is easy to believe that Champlain looked forward with ardent expectancy to the time when his young bride would arrive in Quebec.

Nicholas Boullé gave a dowry of six thousand livres to his daughter, which was quite a handsome one for that period. The Sieur de Monts was one of the witnesses, and it is certain that the union had the full approval of the King. It was understood that the bride would become a Catholic before the time came to join her husband.

Then the knife of the assassin Ravaillac struck down the great King Henry and, as has already been recorded, trying days began for the Canadian colony. Champlain may have been too exclusively concerned with the heavy pressure of his duties to bring his young wife out at the time stipulated. It is more likely, however, that he considered the future of the little settlement too uncertain for her to be involved in its struggles and privations. Whatever the reason, she remained in France for ten years after the wedding. His relationship with her was limited to the brief visits he could pay her during those harassed periods when he progressed back and forth between the court at Fontainebleau and the seaports.

Madame de Champlain was, therefore, twenty-two years old when she finally came to Canada. She had become a mature woman, thoughtful and intelligent, a devout Catholic, and an ardent believer in the cause to which Champlain was committed. She had long desired to see the fabulous land of which she had heard so much and to take her place beside her now famous husband. The once slender and dark-eyed girl had become an attractive woman, still small, still gay in manner. Having been a Parisienne all her life, she knew how to dress herself expensively and well.

Champlain, by way of contrast, was now fifty-three years old. The time had passed when he could venture boldly on journeys into hostile Indian territory. His hair was sprinkled with gray and lacking in the bristling quality it had possessed when he first assumed the responsibility for the colonizing of a continent. The long years of struggle, were beginning to show.

The arrival of the young wife was auspicious enough. She was accompanied by four women who are generally supposed to have been her own servants. It is improbable that the realistic Champlain would think of setting up such an elaborate household in the midst of the primitive colony, and so it is more likely that some of the women had come out to find husbands among the unattached men. They were all much of an age, and a sense of expectancy and excite-

ment had helped them over the hardships and illnesses of the long
crossing. The ship in which they had sailed held a large company,
including a brother-in-law of Madame de Champlain, a Monsieur
Guers, who was coming as commissioner for Montmorenci, and
three Récollet fathers.

The wife of the founder came ashore at Quebec in a flurry of
excitement. She had brought many trunks with her, filled with the
beautiful clothes which a ransacking of Paris shops had yielded.
Much of her trousseau—this was a bridal voyage, although she was
a married woman of ten years—was white, for the latest fashions in
Paris ran to that most becoming of all colors for the young and fair.
There had been, in fact, quite a revolution from the ugly extremes
of the sixteenth century, when ladies appeared in the extravagance
of Catherine-wheel farthingales and skirts so absurdly wide and so
firmly wired that it was difficult for the lovely creatures to squeeze
themselves through doorways. The farthingale was seldom seen any
more, and it may be taken for granted that it would not be found
in the rich assortment of clothes and accessories and trinkets which
filled the young wife's trunks. Even the wide neck ruffs, stiffly
starched and pleated, had given place to the rebato, a much smaller
type of collar. Daintiness was now the order of the day, and it was
the prevailing note in the wrist cuffs of point lace, the graceful
slashed sleeves, the barred petticoats, and the trim polonian shoes.

Madame Champlain frequently wore a gold chain around her
neck with a small mirror. The Indians, who became much attached
to her, counted it a great privilege to look at the mirror and see
themselves reflected there. They believed this meant that she always
kept them in her heart.

The wives of the little settlement gazed with famished wonder
and delight at the gaily bedecked mate of their dignified leader and
the excited bevy of young women who followed at her heels, equally
gay with their many-colored falles and buskes and puffs. As there
was always a fresh breeze on the river, they would be wearing the
rakish hats which had taken France by storm a year before, made
of beaver and almost masculine in size. Under the brim of her hat
of this variety, handsomely plumed and feathered and banded,
Madame de Champlain glanced about her with curiosity in her dark
eyes. Perhaps there was a shade of dismay in them as they rested
on the tipsy walls of L'Abitation, Champlain's official home, and took
note of the dilapidated wharves and the mud of the streets.

It should be explained that there were only eighteen artisans in the colony, and these had been employed in helping the Récollet fathers with the raising of their walls and the construction of stalls and pens for the cattle, sheep, pigs, and chickens. Champlain had his plans drawn for the stone citadel on the crest, but the need of the friars had been more pressing and he had delayed the start on the fortress. Under these circumstances there had been no possibility of repairing any of the dwelling houses.

This was unfortunate. The hasty foundations of L'Abitation had been sinking, and as a result the floors were so uneven that it was like living in a ship's cabin in rough weather. The doors and windows fitted so badly that the place was full of drafts and could not be properly heated in wintertime. The roof leaked, allowing water to run down the walls, so that there was about the house a close and unpleasant odor of mildew.

Perceiving his wife's instant reaction to her new home, Champlain withdrew some of the artisans from their labors with the Récollets and set them instead to repairing L'Abitation. It is unlikely that they were able to do anything about the topsy-turvy walls and the uneven floors, but they succeeded in making the house dry and warm.

The first winter was a period of difficult readjustment for the delicately reared young woman from Paris. There was very little for her to do. Housework was negligible. The beautiful snow, greeted at first with delight, began very soon to dampen her spirits, for there is no loneliness like that of a cold open space where no life stirs and the clouds are gray and low and menacing. In this strange white world she was like a prisoner. The summit, where the stone walls of the friendly Héberts showed against the skyline and at night a light twinkled across the drifted snow of the narrow path, was difficult to achieve, but there was no other place to go, and many times she trudged slowly up the winding trail.

Champlain did the best he could, no doubt, to ease the strain of life under such circumstances. It is not on record that he started anything like the *Ordre de Bon Temps* to add spice to the dull existence of his pent-up wife, but he had at any rate seen to it that the larders were sufficiently stocked to keep the dreaded scurvy away from the door. It was a relieved man who wrote in his notes of May 6 that work had been started at last on the foundations of the citadel and that "the cherry trees have begun to open their buds and the hypaticas are springing from the soil." Some days later he noted down other pleasant items of news. The raspberries were budding and the elder bushes were showing their leaves. "The violets," he exulted, "are in flower and the chervil are ready to cut."

At last winter was over and the miracle of spring had begun.

4

It should be stated that in reality very little is known about the married life of Champlain and the unhappy woman who was his wife. He avoided the subject in the journals he maintained so faithfully, setting down the fact of her arrival and the date when she left, nothing more. The sparse references of the elderly husband are supplemented, fortunately, by stray bits of information from other sources; and the random glimpses thus afforded of the pair are as useful as the single bone of a prehistoric monster from which scholars are able to reconstruct the whole frame of the long-extinct animal.

It is certain that the marriage was not a success. If there had been less disparity in their ages, if it had been the good fortune of the young wife to have taken her place by his side earlier, the situation might have been different. Madame de Champlain had character and courage, and it is pleasant to indulge in thoughts of what might have been; of his young wife accompanying the founder of Quebec on some of his ventures into the western wilds, sitting in the prow of a canoe, her eyes as filled with excitement as his with the beauty and wonder of the new continent.

The years that she remained in America were punctuated with excitement of a kind. There was an anxious period when the Indians camping near Quebec killed two Frenchmen and, fearing reprisals, decided to take the initiative and wipe out the whole colony. The purpose of the savages came early to the ear of the commander, and he took steps to improve the defenses. There were many watchful days and nights before the fear subsided and friendly relations were established again.

She was in Quebec also when two Iroquois braves arrived to discuss a treaty of peace between the Five Nations and the French—a ferociously painted pair, most haughty and contemptuous. The settlers, who had been fed for years on tales of their fighting power and their cruelty, watched with anxious eyes. It developed, after a great deal of desultory talk, that the visitors had undertaken the mission on their own initiative and could not claim to represent their tribes. The suspicion grew then that they had come to spy out the land. It was a good thing that work on the citadel in the meantime had progressed to the stage where its turreted walls frowned above the crest and the boom of cannon at dawn and sundown gave warning that a vigilant watch was being maintained. The emissaries were allowed to see that the fort was large as well as strong—thirty-six yards in length with wings of twenty yards, towers at the four corners, and a ravelin in front to command the approaches, the whole circled with a moat.

After much feasting and dancing and more futile palaver, the two braves took to their canoes and vanished up the river. They had in all probability accomplished their purpose. Nothing more was heard of a peace treaty, but no war parties came to attack the settlement.

At the end of four years it became known that Madame de Champlain would accompany her husband back to France. The glum colonists watched while her trunks, packed tight with all her finery (for which she had found so little use), were carried aboard the ship. They watched with open regret when the slim figure climbed the swaying rope ladder. She stood at the rail and waved to them in farewell, knowing that it was a final one.

She never came back. Having become deeply religious, she desired to enter a convent. Champlain refused his consent to this, and it was not until after his death that she carried out her purpose of becoming an Ursuline nun, taking the name of Sister Hélène d'Augustin. She founded a convent at Meaux and died there in 1654.

CHAPTER X

The Coming of the Jesuits—The Formation of the Company of a Hundred Associates

1

I N HIS last years Henry IV of France came under the influence of
the Jesuits. His confessor was a member of that order, Father
Coton, a man of remarkable character. It was due to Coton's
earnest prompting that the King decided to attach Father Pierre
Biard, a professor of theology at Lyons and a zealous Jesuit, to the
first Acadian colony. The leaders of the venture, Monts and Poutrincourt, shared the suspicion general in France that the order was a
Spanish institution and closely allied to the Inquisition. By some
skillful contriving the ship which was supposed to take Father Biard
to America managed to leave him behind in the port of Bordeaux,
and there he remained for a year in mounting indignation and wrath.
He succeeded finally in getting himself aboard another ship and
reaching Acadia. He was just in time to figure in the bitter days of
the Argall raid, which will be described later.

After the death of Henry a coterie of court ladies carried on the
movement to place spiritual control of Canada in the hands of the
Jesuits. The Society differed from the Franciscans in an important
respect: it appealed to the middle and upper classes, while the
gentle friars labored almost entirely among the poor and lowly; and
so it is not hard to understand that the ladies in question had a great
deal of influence. The Queen Regent was of the number, as was also
one of Henry's mistresses and, of more importance still as things
turned out, a very lovely and virtuous lady with whom the amorous
King had been deeply but unsuccessfully in love, Antoinette de Pons,
Marquise de Guercheville. The marquise, still lovely and more virtuous than ever, was a widow and the possessor of great wealth with

which she was prepared to support the followers of Loyola in the New World.

In 1625 the Duc de Ventadour assumed the post of viceroy of Canada in succession to his uncle, the Duc de Montmorenci, and in the new incumbent the determined ladies found a most willing ally. This deeply religious young man was titular head for a short time only, but he left his mark on the colony.

A story about the Duc de Ventadour must be told at this point. His religious convictions took such hold on him early in life that he shunned the court. During the years when he acted as viceroy he was one of a group of earnest young men who met weekly at the Capuchin convent in the Faubourg St. Honoré to discuss ways of alleviating the lot of the poor. Out of these meetings was to come the establishment in 1630 of a society known as the *Compagnie du Très Saint-Sacrement de l'Autel,* which was shortened in time to *Compagnie de Saint-Sacrement.* Its purpose was to initiate and give impetus to worthy causes, such as the improvement of prisons and hospitals and lazar-cotes, as well as to supply relief in individual cases. The members were for the most part men of the highest rank who could always reach the right ears, even as high as the King's, and command all sources of wealth. Ventadour was the moving spirit of the organization, but he had with him such men as the Marquis d'Andelot, the Archbishop of Arles, the French Ambassador to Rome, Henri de Pichery, who was the royal maître d'hôtel, and Father Suffren, who acted as confessor to both the King and the Queen Regent.

The success of the society, which was quite amazing, was due largely to an early decision of the founders. Instead of beginning with a great fanfare and an open appeal for support, they kept their affairs secret, believing they could best employ their influence by avoiding all publicity. None save the members knew where or when the society met. None of the members mentioned it or acknowledged affiliation. Members never signed the letters they sent out. Secrecy can become a more potent weapon than publicity. All France began to whisper about the society, to speculate as to who belonged and about the real aims back of it. In time they even began to fear it.

Certainly the society grew to have tremendous power, and in the early stages it did a very great deal of good. It has been said that the beloved "Monsieur Vincent," who was canonized as St. Vincent de Paul, was one of the members. There is no proof of this, but the society was of great assistance to him in the noble work he did with his Congregation of the Missions.

The success of the *Compagnie de Saint-Sacrement* was so great, and public interest in it was fanned so briskly by its self-imposed cloak of secrecy, that inevitably it drifted from its true course. After the original members died, it became an instrument of punishment rather than charity and devoted itself largely to the detection and suppression of heresy. Becoming known in time as *La Cabale des Devôts*, it was suppressed in the next reign by Cardinal Mazarin.

Such, then, was the Duc de Ventadour, who now took into his hands the reins of the viceroyalty. He was already convinced that religious teaching in New France should be exclusively in the hands of the Jesuits. It has been said, in fact, that it was on the advice of Father Philibert Noyrot, his confessor and a Jesuit, that he had assumed the post. Shortly thereafter Father Noyrot joined the Jesuit group in Canada, where the work was still being shared with the Récollets and where, moreover, the Huguenot influence was strong because of their predominance in the company membership. When Father Lalemant, the Jesuit Superior in Canada, sent Noyrot back he wrote to Ventadour, ". . . in order to finish what he has started. He is the most capable one for this affair." It had been apparent for some time that the Récollets were not strong enough to carry on the work in Canada unaided, and Ventadour saw to it that the burden was transferred to the willing shoulders of the black-cassocked Jesuits.

Three truly remarkable men formed the Jesuit advance guard, Charles Lalemant, Jean de Brébeuf, and Enemond Masse. Filled with courage and burning with a zeal which nothing could daunt, they were to play great parts in the early history of New France. They arrived without ostentation and found that no provision had been made for their reception, Champlain being in France and the Huguenot Emery de Càèn acting in his place. It was necessary for them to take up their quarters temporarily with the Récollets on the St. Charles River. Although the kindly friars knew that they would be relegated to a secondary part, they welcomed the newcomers cordially.

The vigorous intent of the order became apparent soon thereafter when two more priests arrived with ample supplies provided by the unfailing purse of the widowed marquise and accompanied by a corps of workmen. They then proceeded to build themselves a simple

but stout house behind a palisade of tall timbers in the neighborhood of the Récollets. Impatient to be about the work which had
brought them to the New World, and thirsting perhaps for the
martyrdom which beckoned, the staunch fathers set forth into the
wilds as soon as their base had been established. Lalemant and
Brébeuf went to live with the Hurons, where they labored and
suffered for many years. Soon Brébeuf was writing to the General of
the Society in Rome: "They [the Indians] are frightened by the
torment of hell. Enticed by the joys of paradise, they open their
eyes to the light of truth . . . We have baptized more than 90."

This expressed much of the philosophy which governed the activities of the Jesuits. They were avid for results and at all times showed
a keen interest in the statistics of conversion. One of the lesser-known
priests, Father Raymbaut, who struck far north and lived among the
Nipissings, was at the point of death and said to one of the natives
about him: "Magouch, thou seest well that I am about to die; and
at such a time I would not tell thee a lie. I assure thee that there is
down below a fire that will burn the wicked forever." Magouch
replied, "Beyond a doubt, I must obey God." He became thereafter
one of the most convinced and eloquent of converts.

Because of the nature of the work they were doing, the Jesuits
in the wilderness felt themselves close to God. The solitude in which
they existed added to their mysticism. Even Father Brébeuf, who
was a giant physically and a man of simple and gentle spirit, began
to have visions. Once he saw a great cross in the sky. This was in
1640, when the Iroquois had declared open war on the French and
were stalking the forests. The cross was in the south, above the land
where the men of the Long House dwelt. It seemed to be moving
toward him.

He called his comrades and told them what he could see. "How
large is it?" asked one after gazing in the direction indicated and
seeing nothing.

Father Brébeuf did not reply at once. He continued to stare up
into the sky and finally he sighed deeply.

"It is large enough," he said in a low voice, "to crucify all of
us."

The missions in the Huron country had much success. It was at
Brébeuf's direction that they decided to center their activities at
Ihonatiria, and here they built a chapel which was a constant source
of wonder to the dark-skinned people. It was thirty feet long, sixteen

wide, and twenty-four high, and the vestments were costly and beautiful. In the otherwise bare house of the priests were many objects which caused astonishment among the credulous men of the woods. There was, for instance, the clock which they began to call the Captain. The priests were willing to capitalize on the effect produced by the striking of the clock. If it happened to be ten they would cry out immediately after the tenth stroke, "Stop!" and when the Captain obeyed, the red men would slap their thighs with horny palms and shake their heads in delighted wonder. "What does it eat?" they asked, convinced that the mechanism was alive. Some years before a young Huron who was called Savignon had been taken to France as a hostage when Etienne Brulé remained in Indian hands. Savignon came back full of awe and reported that he had seen the golden cabin of the French King rolling along the ground, pulled by eight moose without horns, and that he had also seen a machine which spoke and told the time of day. Here was a proof of his veracity and one of the reasons why the Hurons examined the clock with particular interest.

The Captain proved very useful to the hard-worked priests. They told the Hurons that each stroke conveyed a command and that when it reached four in the afternoon the order was "Go home!" At four o'clock, therefore, all the Indians would rise obediently and leave the lodge.

Every piece of equipment the mission contained was equally potent, a magnifying glass in particular. The dusky visitors never tired of looking through it and crying out when the figures of ants and bugs grew to an unbelievable size before their eyes. They watched the magnet with due awe, believing that a *manatu* of great power dwelt within it and compelled objects to draw near.

There was one occasion when, like the Connecticut Yankee at the court of King Arthur, the Jesuits made capital of an eclipse. There was this difference in the two incidents, that far up in the Huron country it was the light of the moon and not the sun which was conveniently dimmed. This happened during the night of December 31, 1638. The priests consulted their books and told the members of their flock to watch for what was coming. The fading out of the light of the moon at the moment predicted raised a panic among the natives; and ever after they believed the Black Gowns capable of commanding the coming and the going of light. This anecdote was contained in a letter written by Father François Joseph le Mercier from the Huron village of Ossossané.

The history of these early years is based to a great extent on the long letters which the priests faithfully indited and sent to their superiors in France and Rome. It is from these priestly epistles, written with weary fingers after the Captain at four o'clock had ordered the natives to depart, when the cares of the day, beginning always at four in the morning, were over, that most of the story of the long and ferocious Indian wars are drawn. They told the blood-chilling incidents of a great Huron victory. The northern warriors did not follow the Iroquois custom of giving notice of the number of prisoners captured with a loud halloa for each as the canoes came within sounding distance of the home villages. This would have been difficult on the occasion in question, for the number of Iroquois who had been brought back as prisoners was so great that the woods would have echoed and re-echoed to the signals of triumph. The Hurons, however, had a custom of their own. They carried upright sticks in their canoes to signify the number, and for good measure they placed on the ends of the sticks the scalps they had taken. The exultant squaws and the stay-at-home old men and children were driven to a frenzy of excitement by the fact that one hundred poles had been raised in the canoes of the victorious party!

A sequel to this must be told. The torturing of the prisoners began at once, and as each man died his remains were roasted and devoured. The priests strove desperately to stop the slaughter but found their charges so carried away over their victory that they paid no attention. The Jesuits protested so long that finally the Indians became angry and tossed the hand of one of the victims through the door of the mission lodge. The Jesuits had been allowed to baptize each prisoner before he was led out to the stake, and so the hand was sorrowfully buried in consecrated ground.

The most regular correspondent was Father Paul le Jeune, who became the Superior at Quebec. Father le Jeune had the capacity to convey in what he wrote the fervor which animated the men in the field. His letters, filled with stories of their trials and triumphs, began to attract attention in France. This gentle priest had a sense of humor as well as a burning zeal and he told many stories which added to the interest in his reports. He did not hesitate, for instance, to tell of one difficulty the Jesuits encountered in learning Indian languages. A habit of some interpreters caused them much trouble, a tendency to teach obscene words in place of the right ones, which resulted in the unwitting priests sending their listeners into spasms of mirth. He told also of the Indian tendency to interrupt all discourses. In the middle of an address one of the elder statesmen would be likely to interject some such remark as: "Listen, young men, do you understand clearly what the father is telling us? You are not doing right; mend your ways!" When they approved of what was being said, the whole company would wag their heads and declaim, "*Ho, ho!*" or "*Mi hi,*" which meant "That is good," or even "*Me ke tiang,*" "We will do that."

The priests had no conception at first of the interest these epistles were creating in France, not knowing of a daring experiment which had been decided upon by the Superior of the Society in France. The latter made up his mind that the letters of Father le Jeune should be published so that they would be made available to everyone, and accordingly he effected an arrangement with Sébastien Cramoisy, the most prominent of the printers of Paris. The Cramoisy colophon was known as *La Marque aux Cicognes,* two storks, one feeding the other in flight. The printers proceeded to produce the letters with the utmost care in vellum-bound volumes, small octavo in size, and put them on the market at twenty *sols.* The sales proved nothing short of phenomenal. The distribution was so great, in fact, that it was decided to put out a volume a year and to call the series the *Relations.* Publication was kept up for over forty years, the scope of the series being extended to take in all letters from priests and many incidental papers relating to affairs in Canada. Cramoisy continued as publisher and printer most of that time. After his death his grandson carried on the work under the firm name of Sébastien Fabre-Cramoisy.

Not since the publication of the *Imitatio Christi* two hundred years before had such a wave of spiritual fervor been evidenced.

The writer of the letters, Paul le Jeune, received his first intimation of what was happening when a vessel from France arrived at Quebec and delivered to him huge packets of letters. He began to open them in wonder and discovered that they were from people who had read the *Relations* and whose concern in the work of the missions had been so stimulated thereby that they desired to help. They carried the signatures of men and women of the highest rank, of great diplomats and soldiers, of men prominent in the administrative departments, of priests and nuns, of lowly people who could not be of financial help but had felt impelled to write through feelings of gratitude. It was made evident that in every religious college in

France, in monastery and nunnery, ardent souls were thirsting for a chance to join in the work.

To his great astonishment, Father le Jeune discovered that he had become famous. Everyone was reading his letters, everyone was talking about him and about the work he depicted so graphically. That he was gratified goes without saying, but at the same time he was clearheaded enough to realize that a checkrein was going to be needed. He wrote to the Father Provincial in France, "They [the Ursuline mothers] write me with such ardor . . . that if the door were open a city of nuns would be formed and there would be found ten sisters to one pupil." He was equally well aware of the poor quality of the settlers who were being sent out to the colony. On this point he wrote, "Every year the ship brings us many people; this number like coin is of mingled gold and base alloy; it is composed of choice and well-selected souls, and of others indeed base and degraded."

The success of the *Relations* stimulated the missionaries to further efforts. More priests were sent out to join the hard-worked fathers in the field. Sometimes workmen were sent with them. An outstanding example of the collaboration which developed was the importation into the Huron country of nearly a score of artisans to build the chapel at Ihonatiria. The carpenters and joiners went in canoes over the water trails for many hundred leagues, carrying their tools and some of the materials with them.

It was thus made abundantly clear that, of all men, the Jesuits were the best fitted for missionary work among the Indians. Individually they were brave, resolute, unflinching, and ready for any sacrifice. As a body they were backed by great wealth and influence.

Quebec had continued to grow in the meantime, but very slowly. The population was now slightly in excess of one hundred, but the settlement had not learned to be self-supporting. Champlain, adroit and resourceful though he was, could not make useful citizens out of the dregs who were sent to him by his profit-mad partners. These misfits and unfortunates hunted and fished sporadically; they loafed, they drank, they diced, and continued as hostile to honest toil as they had been when plucked from the stews and prisons of Paris.

The truth of the situation finally reached the one man in France who was capable of finding the solution. Armand Jean du Plessis de Richelieu, the young Bishop of Luçon, had left his mean episcopal

palace and had attached himself to the service of the lumpish, lazy,
and vindictive Queen Regent. Although the fall of her favorites, the
Concinis, to whom Richelieu had paid lip service, set him back for
several years, he was soon in the saddle again and in full charge of
foreign affairs. A man of such relentless will and transcendent ability
could not be checked once he was in a position to display his gifts.
Richelieu, who had now received the red hat from Rome and was
called thereafter the cardinal, moved with consummate skill through
the conspiracies of the corrupt court and in time gained a complete
ascendancy over the weakling son of Henry IV who had succeeded
to the throne as Louis XIII.

The once sickly and sullen son of the great King had grown up into
a very strange and far from healthy young man, as different from
his illustrious sire as any human being could be. He took little interest in affairs of state, except for sudden gusts of unpredictable energy
which made it necessary for the cardinal to exercise all his skill in
order to retain his hold on the reins. Ordinarily the capricious young
King concerned himself with boyish fancies. He was very much interested in cookery and became quite expert in the making of garlic
spreads for bread and salades with sauce rousse. In a court noted
for the beauty and immorality of its women, the young King showed
no tendency to emulate the gallantry of his father. He took little or
no interest in New France.

Richelieu soon became convinced that the control of the French
colony must be assumed by the government and he acted then with
characteristic vigor.

2

A frail man in the red robe of a cardinal sat behind his desk on
a gusty day which the calendar registered as April 29, 1627. Before
him lay a document from which the title seemed to spring out and
command the eye.

Acte pour l'Etablissement de la Compagnie des Cent Associés.

The Company of One Hundred Associates! This organization with
the euphonious name which has impressed itself firmly on the pages
of Canadian history was the answer which Richelieu was supplying
for the problem of Canada.

The man behind the desk was thin and austere. His face fell away
from a fine wide brow to a chin so delicate and pointed under its

small beard that it suggested a sensitive nature (which was completely misleading); and the result would have been to give his ample nose too much prominence if it had been possible to notice anything about this extraordinary man but the uncanny power of his unblinking pale eyes. The Richelieu eyes, it was currently believed, could look through anything: the most astute politician who might face him, the walls which surrounded him, the knotty problems he had to solve. His hands had an almost feminine daintiness, but in their capacity to seize and hold and rend they more nearly resembled the talons of a bird of prey. There was uncanniness also in this man's gift for knowing everything that went on about him, for knowing instinctively the right course to pursue, for the perfection of his choice of words in convincing those about him, for his unerring judgment of men. He was utterly unscrupulous and, of course, without kindness or pity. No other great minister of state ever quite equaled him; not Wolsey or Fouquet or Colbert, not Bismarck or Disraeli.

The slender forefinger which rested on the front page of the charter had assisted in cutting with vigorous surety through all obstacles in the way of the measure. The cardinal had abolished the office of admiral of France and had set up a new post in its stead, the Grand Master and Superintendent of Navigation and Commerce, assuming the duties himself. The prevailing charter held by the Càens and their associates had been revoked.

This bold measure may have originated in the brain of another man, that strange figure who stood so often at the shoulder of the cardinal and whispered in his ear—François Leclerc du Tremblay, the Capuchin who was called by the populace Father Joseph of Paris and sometimes *L'Eminence Grise,* Gray Eminence. Father Joseph became the "familiar spirit" of Richelieu, his sword blade in diplomacy, his director of intelligence and spying. He followed the great minister everywhere; but whereas Richelieu traveled in state with a long train of prancing horses, the silent, glowering Capuchin followed on foot, striding tirelessly on bare feet over the rough and muddy roads. A man of the most intense faith, he was nevertheless the most consistent exponent of the theory that the end justifies the means. He was created Apostolic Commissary of Missions by Pope Urban VIII, and his influence can be detected in the course which Richelieu was now following.

With no further evidence than this to draw upon, it is clear that the unseen fingers of Father Joseph had been at work on the skeins, shaping the destiny of a distant land sometimes called Canada.

It is probable that in the long room where the cardinal worked so steadily hour after hour, day after day—with its candles guttering in long silver sconces and its blood-red curtains looped in silver brackets—were some of the men who had already agreed to become members of the new organization. In respect to social position they were decidedly a mixed lot. All men of ministerial rank were included, some of the nobility, some merchants, some men in holy orders. The name of Cardinal Richelieu headed the list. Somewhere— far down on the page, no doubt—was a man too far away to be consulted, Samuel de Champlain. Each member was obligated to pay three thousand livres.

A reading of the act makes it clear that this was no halfway measure, no hastily contrived piece of legislation to correct defects in the present situation. It conferred on the company the whole of the North American continent from Florida to the farthest northern point, and from the Atlantic seaboard to the western sources of the St. Lawrence River. The fur trade was to belong to them exclusively for all time, and they were to control the trade of the colony, with the exception of the coast fisheries, for a term of fifteen years. No duty would be charged on the goods they would import to France. In return the Associates engaged to send three hundred people to Canada each year and to bring the total to four thousand by the expiration of the fifteen years; supporting the settlers, moreover, for three years and providing each community with three priests.

No point seemingly had been overlooked in this thorough document. It was provided that the members of the nobility might become Associates without any prejudice to the dignities which formerly had excluded them from participation in trade. On the other hand, twelve patents of nobility were to be distributed among the men of lesser degree, the merchants and the shipping heads. All settlers sent to Canada were to be French and Catholic. The government was to stand back of the company and to provide immediately two warships fully equipped for service.

As an understanding of the situation in France is necessary to any familiarity with what was to happen in Canada, it may be of interest to tell more of the cardinal and the background he was developing for himself. He had become already an enormously wealthy man as well as a powerful one. The house where he lived and carried on the affairs of state was known as the Hôtel de Richelieu, but it would not serve him much longer. Some part of his keen and active brain was already occupied with the planning of a magnificent new establishment on the same busy site: across from the Louvre where the Rue des Bons Enfants turned into the Rue St. Honoré, directly across from the inconspicuous stone building where that equally remarkable man (but in a far different way), Monsieur Vincent, conducted his little college. To obtain the room he needed, the cardinal would tear down two other buildings, the Hôtel de Mercoeur and the Hôtel de Rambouillet, and on the enlarged site he would erect the imposing building now known as the Palais-Royal but which in his lifetime was called the Palais-Cardinal. This four-storied proof of the importance of its founder would contain *La Galerie des Hommes Illustres*, with twenty-four portraits of the great figures of French history, including Jeanne d'Arc, the brave Dunois, Bertrand du Guesclin, Olivier de Clisson, the cardinal himself, and two kings, Henry IV and Louis XIII, the balance of the kings being deemed worthy of no more than representation in a row of small busts.

Inasmuch as the King had a company of musketeers (including in their ranks a certain Monsieur d'Artagnan) as his personal body-guards, it had seemed fitting to the cardinal that he also should be adequately protected; and so young guardsmen in the scarlet and meline livery of Richelieu stood always at the front entrance, on the staircase, and in the anterooms, an air of vigilance and suspicion about them, long swords clanking against their muscular calves. In these crowded anterooms the old nobility rubbed shoulders with vulgar place-hunters and exchanged confidences with mere merchants and lowly priests; confidences which invariably were expressed in whispers because it was well known that spies were everywhere. The cardinal had come a long way since his unhappy days in the palace at Luçon where all the chimneys smoked and the cold rooms were dirty and filled with malarial odors rising from the sea fens.

Richelieu was creating for himself and for his master, the King, and the kings who would succeed him, the absolute power in which he believed. The nobility had ceased to carry weight. Concentrated authority for a long time thereafter would be vested in the King, to be exercised by the ministerial departments organized around the throne. Canada was to be governed by rules laid down in the cabinets

of the new autocracy. Documents signed with the flourish of busy
and supercilious pens would determine the lives of the men and
women who braved the rigors of pioneering across the seas. Every
step would be charted, every detail of existence dictated. Free will
was to be denied to governor and trader, to explorer and habitant.

3

Champlain's reaction to the formation of the new company was,
naturally, one of complete accord and delight in the magnitude of
the new conception of things. With the news of the sweeping changes
Richelieu had initiated came word that a fleet of twenty transports
was being gathered and that four ships of war, under the command
of Admiral de Roquemont, would convoy this large flotilla to
Quebec. The transports were to be filled with the right kind of settler
—family men with wives and children and trained to a trade or to
work on the soil—and loaded with supplies of all kinds. Cannon to
the number of one hundred and fifty were to be sent out for the protection of new settlements. Here indeed was a realization of the
dreams which had always filled his mind.

It is doubtful that he had any conception of the disadvantages in
this turn of events, that he perceived dangers in the ambitious planning of the cardinal. What Richelieu had done was to fix a pattern
from which France would never thereafter deviate in the handling
of New France. Regimentation would go hand in hand with colonization. The habitant would never be allowed to work out his own
destiny, to do with his life as he pleased. Instead he would be an
automaton, jerked this way and that by strings in the hands of
bureaucrats, every detail of his ways determined by writ and provision, unable to think for himself, even subject in marrying and giving in marriage to king-made restrictions and controls.

Richelieu was unequaled as a statesman and organizer, but he
lacked in knowledge of the human heart. He did not realize that the
impetus to great deeds springs from the spirits of men who control
their own destinies, that the feet of strong men who go out to reclaim
the wilderness and win the far frontiers of the earth must be un-
fettered. He had misled himself into thinking that the miracle of
success in the New World could be achieved by the remote control
of men of thin blood sitting behind comfortable desks.

CHAPTER XI

The Start of the Long Wars with the English

1

WHILE the pioneers of Quebec were still fighting for an existence around the great rock, dependent on the support of profit-mad merchants, the English had been establishing themselves in the South. In 1607 the London Company, operating under a charter granted by that great dispenser of charters, James I of England, landed a party of settlers at a place ,in what is now Virginia and which they loyally named Jamestown. After a rigorous first year the colony came under the direction of one John Smith, sailor, soldier, and adventurer extraordinary with a penchant for writing books. Smith is best remembered through the association of his name with that of Pocahontas, the daughter of an Indian chief. A captive of the tribe, Smith was rescued from death by the intercession of the lovely Pocahontas. He was a brisk and efficient administrator, and the little colony prospered under his hand. Even at this early stage there was a realistic note to the colonial operations of the English, a determination to consolidate their holdings and to concern themselves more with driving the Indians out than in catering to their immortal souls.

The second great venture in colonization came thirteen years later, by which time the Virginians were firmly established. The same John Smith had voyaged along the rock-bound coast of Massachusetts in 1614 and had made maps of it which were much more accurate than those Champlain had drawn some years before. It was by chance, however, that a landing of settlers was made in the Land of the Cod. A party of religious Separatists, now called Pilgrims, had been driven from England by the intolerance which developed during the reign of James and had taken refuge in Holland. Being granted permission to settle in Virginia by the London Company, they set sail from

Holland in the year 1620 in a ship called the *Mayflower,* an earnest and utterly inexperienced body of men and women numbering no more than a hundred. Bad weather drove them off their course and they landed at what is now Provincetown on the long arm of Cape Cod. Despairing of reaching their objective, they decided to remain in this northern part to which, it seemed possible, the hand of Providence had directed them. They settled themselves across the bay at Plymouth. Upheld by a faith which survived every trial, here they clung to their precarious base in spite of the most bitter hardships and the continuous menace of the hostile Indians.

The next point settled was Salem, and then a third sinking of the roots of colonization occurred on the peninsular arm which formed the land protection on the north of what is now Boston Bay. The town of Boston, so named in 1630, grew with more rapidity than any of the other settlements and gradually became the center of the ever-widening effort to take over and break to the plow the lands which are now New England. Thus, at the time of Champlain's death, Quebec had a flourishing rival. Boston, small and stern and determined, faced Quebec, which shared all these qualities; and it was inevitable that in the course of time the two would clash.

The United Netherlands claimed the country along the Hudson in 1609 as a result of the explorations of Henry Hudson in the *Half Moon.* In 1615 the first efforts at colonization were made by the Dutch with the settlement of a trading post on Castle Island near Albany, but it was not until 1624 that they went seriously about the task. In 1626 Peter Minuit bought Manhattan Island from the Indians, and Fort Amsterdam was erected there. The arrival of the Dutch made the rivalry for possession of North America a triangular one. As they had been farseeing enough to make a treaty with the Iroquois in 1617, there was a period when it seemed possible that the sturdy Dutchmen would pre-empt all of the New World which is now included in the states of New York, New Jersey, and Connecticut.

King James of England had a way (which he shared with the French) of granting vast claims to such of his subjects as desired to venture into the west. On the authority of one such charter an English sea captain named Samuel Argall (the same commander who abducted Pocahontas in Virginia and allowed a member of his crew, John Rolfe, to marry her) cruised up the coast from Massachusetts with the intention of expelling the French from their Acadian possessions. He had no difficulty in capturing them, as the French were taken by surprise. The buildings at Port Royal were burned and some fourteen members of the colony, including the Jesuit priest, Father Biard, were carried off as prisoners, to be released later. The rest scattered and lived as well as they could off the land.

The Argall raid was the first open conflict between the English and the French. The war would go on, never completely quiescent even when the mother countries were at peace, for a century and a half. Much blood would be shed and many gallant deeds would be performed (and many black and terrible deeds as well) on both sides before the struggle came to an end when Wolfe captured Quebec.

2

The Argall raid had been a minor clash. It remained for two pedantic Scots to bring about the first fighting on a large scale. One was James I, the other Sir William Alexander; and of the pair, it was said that "James was a king who tried to be a poet and Alexander was a poet who tried to be a king." It may be stated at the outset that both failed.

James I was the son of Mary Queen of Scots and succeeded to the throne of England on the death of Elizabeth in 1603. He had already won for himself a reputation that culminated in the description, "the wisest fool in Christendom." Riding eagerly away from the poverty of his native Scotland, he took with him into England a whole train of Scots whose heads were filled with knowledge and ambition but whose pockets were woefully empty. One of these was William Alexander of Menstrie, whose patrimony was not large and who had been acting as tutor to Prince Henry, the oldest of the royal children. He was the most prolific of poets (his *Doomes-Day* ran to eleven thousand lines, most of them very dull indeed), and this brought him into close contact with the pawky monarch who thought he could do great things with words also. It was Alexander who sat at the royal elbow when James began to compose his metrical version of the Psalms. The attempt was not a very happy one and it was not until after the death of James that the royal version was published. The King's son, who succeeded him as Charles I, granted permission to Alexander "to consider and reveu the meeter and poesie thereof," but it is not known to what extent he availed himself of the opportunity.

Alexander, being a man of vision, was unwilling to spend his life in the writing of verses and tutoring of princes. His eyes had become fixed on the west, and it was partly as a result of his urging that King James elected to make his liberal gestures of annexation. In 1621 the King made a grant to Alexander of all Nova Scotia, which was assumed at the time to include Newfoundland, Cape Breton, Acadia, Maine, New Brunswick, and a large slice of Quebec. In a later confirmation Alexander was empowered to "erect cities, appoint fairs, hold courts, grant lands and coin money."

It remained for the poet-tutor, thus royally endowed, to find the wherewithal to take possession of his vast domain and to build the cities where the fairs would be held and the courts convened. King James had a favorite device for raising funds, to make baronets out of men who could pay a fat price for the honor. On his journey to London to claim the crown, he had created them with as lavish a hand as a queen of the May tossing posies. Now he decided to adopt the same plan in the occupation of North America. A new order was created, the Knights Baronet of Nova Scotia. Any man of property who could make a voyage to that country, or pay down instead the sum of one hundred and fifty pounds sterling, would get his title and a grant of land six miles by three. He would have the right to wear about his neck "an orange tawney ribbon from which shall hang pendant in an escutcheon argent a saltire azure with the arms of Scotland."

Nothing much came of this save the settling of small groups here and there around the Bay of Fundy and the creation of much ill feeling between the newcomers and the French at Port Royal. After the death of James the Company of Merchant Adventurers was founded in London by Sir William and a number of London financiers and merchants. One of the members was Gervase Kirke, who had married a Frenchwoman and had always taken a great interest in matters concerning North America. The company had an ambitious purpose, the seizure by force of arms of all Canada. War had started between England and France because of Richelieu's determination to break the back of Huguenot solidarity. The new dictator of France struck at the heart of Calvinism by besieging La Rochelle. In the reign of James there had been a handsome court favorite named George Villiers who gained such an ascendancy over the bumbling old monarch that he was created Duke of Buckingham. "Steenie," as James had affectionately called him, had continued to wield a great influence over the new King. He even succeeded in persuading Charles to take the part of the Huguenots. War accordingly had been declared on France and Charles had sent a fleet under Buckingham to relieve La Rochelle. Buckingham was a man of glittering personality and an almost diabolical degree of charm, but he possessed neither military capacity nor experience. The expedition was a signal and dismal failure.

When the war began the Company of Merchant Adventurers raised the sum of sixty thousand pounds to equip an expedition against the French in Canada. Three ships set out early in 1628 under the command of Captain David Kirke, a son of Gervase. Word had reached England that the armada promised Champlain by the Company of One Hundred Associates was ready to start. Kirke made his first objective the interception and capture of the fleet.

Kirke and his two brothers, Lewis and Thomas, started for Canadian waters, carrying letters of marque from King Charles. They found Admiral Roquemont and his armada in Gaspé Bay, where he had been compelled to take refuge by heavy storms sweeping over the gulf. It was clear to the English captains at once that the French admiral had been taken by surprise. All his ships were deep in the water with the weight of the cargoes they carried. The new guns were lashed in the holds of the bigger ships and the few that were ready for use were of small caliber. Even the decks of the four warships were black with the passengers they were bringing out—men, women and children, soldiers and mechanics and Jesuit priests. To see English sails on the horizon was the last thing the admiral had expected.

De Roquemont looked about him with a desperate anxiety. The Company of One Hundred Associates had lived up to their promises. The bay was dotted with sails, for in addition to the four convoy ships he had twenty transports in his charge. Everything that the colony at Quebec needed had been loaded into the holds with a lavishness in contrast to the penurious methods of the now defunct trading companies. Could he let this wealth of supplies, which meant life to the struggling colony, fall into the hands of these buccaneering ships which had suddenly emerged out of the blue horizon?

De Roquemont was a good sailor and a brave man. He decided not to give up without a struggle, and the order to prepare for defense was hastily flown from his masthead. The struggle, however, was a brief one. The three English ships came in under a spread of canvas but otherwise stripped for action, the shrouds filled with musketeers, the muzzles of heavy cannon protruding from the portholes. David Kirke brought his ship alongside that of the admiral and raked the hull of the French flagship with a broadside. Throwing out their grappling irons, a boarding party of the English came over, their cutlasses in their teeth. With the most valorous of intentions, the French found themselves unable to put up any effective resistance. To spare the lives of his helpless passengers, De Roquemont had to strike his colors. The other French vessels, seeing the uselessness of further resistance, surrendered also.

Kirke burned some of the transports and took the rest, heavily loaded with the spoils of victory, into Newfoundland harbors. From here he sailed back to England, taking the most prominent of his prisoners with him.

England hailed the victors with delight. France seethed with indignation and dismay. Stuffed effigies of the three Kirke brothers were burned on the Place de la Grève.

3

A despairing Champlain paced the ramparts of the citadel on the heights after receiving this bitter news. He had learned of the capture and destruction of Roquemont's ships from Indian scouts. The French colony, he was convinced, was now doomed. There was nothing to prevent the English from seizing Quebec and expelling all the French settlers. Old and bent and unhappy, he kept an eye on the eastern reaches of the river, expecting to see at any moment the sails of the English ships coming triumphantly to his undoing.

Champlain was fully aware of the weakness of his position. Never an engineer, he had proven himself a poor builder. The houses he had raised among the walnut trees had been flimsy and had fallen into dilapidation and disrepair in the course of a few years. His great pride, the stone citadel, was now going the same way. The walls showed signs of decay and insecurity; the masonry had developed dangerous fissures; two of the corner towers had collapsed, filling the moat with rubble over which an attacking force could scramble to victory with the ease of Joshua and his men charging into Jericho. The mouths of his few cannon protruding above the battlements looked little more dangerous than broomsticks poking out from the white walls of a boy's snow castle.

Expecting attack, Champlain had moved the people of Quebec into the fort. The food supplies were inadequate for a siege and so he had found it necessary to reduce the daily ration to a small supply of peas and "turkey corn," as the Indian maize was called. The people grumbled and in their hearts perhaps hoped that the English would come soon to free them from such privations.

But the English did not come. Winter settled in. With the freezing of the streams and the falling of the snow, the sufferings of the little garrison became pitiful indeed. The cellars of the now fatherless but always thrifty Héberts yielded considerable in the way of grain and vegetables, but the total supply could not fill so many hungry mouths. When spring came at last there was no joy over the violets in flower and the chervil which was ready for cutting. The daily ration by this time had been cut to seven ounces of pounded peas per person. The settlers were gaunt; the children were thin and spiritless in their patched and ragged clothes.

Throughout the winter the unhappy colony had been cut off from the outside world. The Kirkes held control of the waters about Newfoundland and the gulf. Champlain did not know, therefore, that the defeat had precipitated a serious situation in France. The Company of One Hundred Associates hovered on the brink of bankruptcy.

Returns made to the government in 1671, after the final dissolution of the concern, showed that it had been bankrupt almost from the first. The cost of the great fleet had almost exhausted the amount raised. All subsequent reorganizations did no more than fend off the ultimate failure. After the first days of incredulous rage when the effigies of the three Kirkes smoked on Execution Square, there had been talk of equipping more ships for the relief of Canada, but the preparations had proceeded with great slowness. Champlain, in the dark about all this, still expected relief in the spring.

The settlers do not seem to have shared his optimism. The men of the colony, no longer content to exist on starvation rations and anxious as well to ease matters for their families, began to scatter into the woods. Some joined bands of roving Indians, some took to boats and vanished down the river in the direction of the fishing banks. Their wives and children remained in the fort, begging piteously for the food which the unhappy commander could not supply. When the English finally came, Champlain had no more than sixteen men with him in addition to the priests on the St. Charles.

Two ships came into sight from behind the Isle of Orleans, flying the English flag. David Kirke had returned from England with four ships, the *Abigail* of three hundred tons and the others of two hundred tons each, the *William,* the *George,* and the *Gervase.* The first two named had been left at Tadoussac, and it was the *George* and the *Gervase* which had been sent to attack the citadel. As it happened, this was not going to prove a difficult task. At the moment there was no man in the fort save the stooped and sad-eyed commander, all of his sixteen men being in the woods in a desperate search for food. Champlain, standing despondently on the battlements, watched an English officer climb up the narrow path under a white flag. The moment he had foreseen with so much dread had arrived.

The sails of the ships had been seen from the woods on the high declivity, however, and now the men of the garrison were hurrying back. As they straggled in they were ordered to go at once to their posts. When the English officer reached the summit, he found the fort well manned. Soldiers with muskets on their shoulders paced the crumbling ramparts, and the sound of sharp military orders reached his ears. It must have been apparent to him, however, that all this was no more than a brave pretense; that in reality destitution perched on the sagging walls and the sharpness of the voices held an edge of despair.

Realizing that to offer defense would be futile, Champlain nevertheless held out for terms. He insisted that the commander of the attacking force must first show his commission from the English King, that no effort be made to come ashore until all terms had been agreed to, and that one of the two ships be used to convey his people back to their own country, including all the priests and two Indians; and above everything he demanded that fair and courteous treatment be accorded to all.

The commander of the English agreed to these terms. And so on August, 9, 1629, Champlain formally surrendered Quebec to the invaders. It is worth noting that the company of English officers and men who came ashore and raised their flag over the citadel found no food in the place save one tub filled with potatoes and roots.

What thoughts filled the mind of Samuel de Champlain, watching the fluttering of the fleur-de-lis as it was hauled down from the flagpole on the battlements? Was he remembering the struggles of the long years, the disappointments, the triumphs? Did he think of the meeting at Fontainebleau when he and the Sieur de Monts had pledged their lives to the cause, come what might? Did he pause to recall his many explorations which had accumulated knowledge of the vast extent of this wooded empire, this wonderful domain which France was now yielding to her hereditary foe? Perhaps he was too old and tired, too beaten down by the seeming finality of the blow, to experience the poignancy of such regrets. Perhaps he said to himself no more than "This, then, is the end of it all" as he turned and hobbled down the uneven stone steps to the cobbled courtyard of the citadel, where his word had been law for so many years.

4

It was known to Champlain that Kirke's ships had been guided up the St. Lawrence by Frenchmen, and he encountered two of these renegades when he reached Tadoussac as a prisoner on his way to England.

The English commander had left a garrison at Quebec under Lewis Kirke and was taking all his important prisoners of war with him. Champlain, the most unhappy and weary of men, was allowed to go ashore when they reached the mouth of the Saguenay, and it was here that the two men were pointed out to him as having belonged to the party of four who acted as guides to the enemy. The governor's indignation caused him to approach the guilty pair, who hung back with a shamed air and seemed anxious to get away. To his astonishment and sorrow, he recognized one of the brown and unkempt fellows as Etienne Brulé!

Champlain's ire mounted to such a height that he proceeded to berate the pair at great length. A full version of what he said is contained in the *Relations*. It unquestionably has been rephrased, for it is a well-rounded and somewhat stilted harangue and not in the heated terms in which Champlain probably expressed himself. The picture of the scene that is given, however, can be accepted as an accurate one. It is recorded that Brulé, holding his head down and shuffling in the extremity of his embarrassment, made no defense save to say that he knew the French garrison had no hope of resisting successfully and so it had not seemed to him wrong to act with the English.

The former servant of the governor, whose exploits in the field of exploration had been so creditable and, in fact, astounding, but who now would be remembered chiefly for this act of treachery, slunk away and was never seen again by men of his own race. Word of his doings reached their ears, however, and it is possible to tell briefly of his last days.

When he guided the English ships up the estuary to the foot of the rock, his period of achievements and, yes, glory came to an end. From that stage on he failed to add anything to his record. Apparently the urge to set out on new quests had left him. No longer was he filled with a desire to plant his moccasined feet on new trails or to dip his paddle in strange waters. He went back to the Huron country and spent the balance of his days there, a slothful and degraded existence. Perhaps he became bitter of temper and quarreled with the tribesmen in whose midst he lived. He had settled down in the village of Toanché on Penetanguishene Bay, a spot of great natural beauty. One day the Indians turned on him and by force of numbers (he was a man of considerable personal strength and could not have been worsted in single combat) succeeded in beating him to death. Having killed him, they decided they might as well benefit in the usual way. They cut up his body and boiled it in the kettles, and then they gathered in a wide circle and proceeded to consume all that was left of this ungovernable young Frenchman (he was only forty-one when he came to his end) who, in spite of everything, deserves to be remembered for the greatness of his exploits.

Sometime afterward Father Brébeuf recorded in one of his letters that he had visited Penetanguishene Bay where the tragedy occurred and that an intuitive flash of his own death had come to him. "I saw the spot where poor Etienne Brulé was barbarously and brutally murdered," he wrote, "which made me think that perhaps someday they might treat me in the same manner, and to desire at least that it might be while we were earnestly seeking the glory of the Lord."

5

On April 24, a month after the second fleet left England to complete the conquest of Canada, peace had been declared between England and France. When word came back from Canada of the success of the Kirkes, the French Government made an immediate demand that Quebec be restored and that restitution be made for all the losses the French had sustained. King Charles agreed to this.

The Kirkes found on their arrival that their King had appointed
a commision made up of a panel of legal baronets to take possession
of everything they had brought back, with the intention of turning
it over to the French Government. A warrant had been issued to seal
the warehouses of the Company of Merchant Adventurers, the purpose being to seize and deliver to the French all the beaver skins
and other pelts which were stored there.

The victors protested vigorously. They pointed out that they had
sailed under a royal commission and that the purpose of the expedition had been discussed and approved. Their claims, in spite of this,
were coldly received and as coldly brushed aside. No attention was
paid to the fact that the men who backed the expedition had spent
sixty thousand pounds in equipping the ships and that they now
stood to lose every penny of it. Even the statement of Kirke that
only thirteen hundred of the seven thousand skins he had brought
back with him had been taken from the French, the rest being the
result of his own trading with the Indians, was disregarded. When
he went to the length of taking forcible possession of the warehouses
and refusing to yield them to the Crown, the sheriffs of London received orders from the King, or from the ministers acting in his
name, to use force in regaining possession. This was done.

The raiding of a thieves' den in Alsatia, the section of London
where the crooks gathered and the authority of the Upright Man
(the name applied to criminal bosses) was recognized above the law,
could not have been conducted with less lack of consideration.

It developed later that King Charles had decided to employ the
restitution of Quebec as a weapon to compel the French Government to pay him the balance of the dowry of his Queen, who had
been Princess Henrietta Maria of France, which amounted to eight
hundred thousand crowns. He was in desperate need of money, having already embroiled himself with Parliament and so being without the financial supplies usually voted to the heads of state. The
deal with the French Government was carried through. King Charles
received the balance of the dowry and Quebec was handed back to
the French.

The merchants of London lost every shilling they had invested in
the effort to add Canada to the overseas possessions of the English
Crown. Alexander, it is true, was elevated to the dignity of Earl
of Stirling, but some years later he died in London in an insolvent
condition. David Kirke was knighted for what he had done, but it

is not on record that any of the family received as much for their
services as the ten pounds which another king had given John Cabot
as his reward for discovering North America.

Twice Canada had been within the grasp of the English. Twice
the great prize had slipped away from them.

6

Canada was officially handed back to France by the Treaty of
St.-Germain-en-Laye, signed in March 1632. The Company of One
Hundred Associates was teetering on the verge of dissolution at
this point, but Cardinal Richelieu needed it for the carrying out of
his plans in Canada. The official bellows were used to blow new life
into it, and Champlain was sent back to Quebec to resume his lieu-
tenancy.

The willing veteran, who had now reached the age of sixty-six,
was received with delight by the few settlers left, among them the
widow of Louis Hébert with her children and grandchildren. The
guns boomed from the dilapidated citadel, and the happy inhabitants shed tears of gratitude. The Indians showed their delight at
the return of the grand old man by holding a meeting. Long orations
were delivered, in the course of which it was stated that "when the
French were absent the earth was no longer the earth, the river was
no longer the river, the sky was no longer the sky."

In spite of his advanced years Champlain went briskly to work
to repair the damages of war. He saw to it that new houses
were built for the settlers who would be arriving. He repaired and
strengthened the citadel, raising new towers and mounting larger
cannon on the battlements. He erected a new chapel and called it
Notre Dame de la Recouvrance as a token of gratitude for the
restoration of Canada to the French people.

The atmosphere at Quebec had changed. The chaffering of free
traders was no longer heard, nor the rough language of convict-
settlers, the loud songs of men who lived in idleness. The Jesuits
were in full control. The Récollet fathers had been released from
captivity in England as soon as the treaty was signed and had been
sent back to France. There they had found that they were not to
resume their work in Canada. The Black-Gowns, as the Indians
called the Jesuits, sat in council with Champlain and shared in his
plans.

Champlain seems to have enjoyed some of his earlier vigor. He began to plan campaigns against the English, the Dutch on Manhattan Island, who were becoming active rivals in the fur trade, and the Iroquois, who were demonstrating the bitterness of their hatred. The last letter he addressed to Richielieu was a request for one hundred and twenty soldiers to defend the colony and police the Great Lakes. He raised a fort at Three Rivers and he willingly issued commissions to anyone desiring to explore the country to the west.

It was in the midst of such activities that death came to him. While his mind remained brisk and vital, his heavy frame had been showing the effect of his advanced years. In the fall of 1635 he was stricken with paralysis. He lingered for several months, unable to stir from his couch. It is to be hoped that as he lay in his narrow stone room in the citadel awaiting the slow approach of death there came to him for consolation a prophetic glimpse of the greatness which would grow out of the work to which he had devoted himself so loyally and so long.

He died on Christmas Day. Where he was buried has remained a mystery and has led to much research and earnest pursuit through the records of the day. The conclusion to which most historians have given their assent is that he was laid away in the Mountain Hill Cemetery which adjoins the chapel of Notre Dame de la Recouvrance. The chapel was burned in 1640 and Champlain's successor, the Sieur de Montmagny, erected a new one in its place. It is generally believed that this edifice was raised over the grave in which the brave and able leader had been buried.

The unhappy colonists would have restrained their tears, which flowed so freely and generously, if they had known that the death of the founder was a happy release from humiliation. As he lay on his last couch the Company of One Hundred Associates was meeting in Paris to choose his successor.

Why it was thought necessary to replace the man who had devoted his life to New France and whose faith alone had kept the fleur-de-lis flying over the high eminence of Quebec has never been explained.

CHAPTER XII

Three Resolute Women and the Parts They
Played—Madame de la Peltrie—Marie
de l'Incarnation—Jeanne Mance

1

THERE was born at the castle of Vaubougon in Alençon in France in the year 1603 a daughter to the Sieur de Chauvigny and his wife. The child was named Marie Madeleine and became in course of time an attractive and intelligent young woman. Although not strong, she had a will which enabled her to rise to every emergency. Sometimes she was cheerful and gay, sometimes thoughtful and somber as her thoughts turned from the purely mundane details of existence. It is always difficult to gain an accurate mental picture of people who live in the shadows of bygone centuries, and reliance has to be placed on chance phrases in letters and in small and seemingly unimportant bits of evidence which survive. In connection with Marie Madeleine de Chauvigny, who has come down in history as Madame de la Peltrie, there are enough such clues, and one in particular which is worth recalling. When she had succeeded in founding the Ursuline convent at Quebec she was so obsessed with the need of strengthening the institution as well as the small colony which existed outside its walls that she once said she would go out and plant corn herself. An old Huron Christian who overheard the remark said, "Tell lady that corn planted by hands so delicate take long time to ripen."

Marie Madeleine de Chauvigny had the desire early to devote herself to the Church. Her family, particularly her father, were very much against the idea. So much pressure was brought to bear that she gave in and married a man much older than herself, Charles de la Peltrie. She seems to have been happy enough in the conjugal relationship. Her husband died when she was twenty-two years of age and left her all his property. Secure now in her status of widow, she resisted the pressure brought upon her to marry again. The time had come when she intended to give herself to the role for which she had always longed. She had decided to join the Ursulines and devote her life and her property to the establishment of a convent for children in Quebec.

Her decision created a family storm, the outcome of which was that her sister and brother-in-law brought suit to have her declared incompetent and her property removed from her control. It is at this stage of her life that the firmness of will possessed by this outwardly gentle and delicate young woman becomes clear. To circumvent her insistent relatives she entered into an engagement to marry a gentleman of her acquaintance, one Monsieur de Bernières, who was royal treasurer at Càèn. The worthy treasurer had no desire to wed her or anyone else, but he entered into the engagement on the promise that it was a subterfuge. When this failed to lull the family suspicions, the determined young widow actually talked the reluctant Monsieur de Bernières into becoming her husband, with the understanding that it would be nothing more than a marriage of convenience. Her father had died in the meantime, but the antagonistic sister and her acquisitive husband suspected her design and even questioned the validity of her marriage. They went to court again, and at first it looked as though the family harpies would win. There was a long and despairing interval before a countersuit was declared in her favor. From that moment the zealous young woman, whose personality seems to have blossomed as difficulties grew up about her, proceeded with her plans.

It was at Tours, where she had gone to visit the Ursulines, that she met a woman of equal zeal and determination who was to join the enterprise and become in course of time its chief prop and stay.

2

Marie Guyart was born in the year 1599 at Tours, which claims to produce the most beautiful girls in France and can advance much evidence in support of its pretensions. This daughter of the old city could not be called beautiful, however, though she was tall and somewhat stately and distinguished by fineness of feature. She was dark and in expression rather intense, in which respect her appearance matched her character, for she was the possessor of great will power and a capacity for ceaseless application. She was married when quite young to a worthy citizen named Claude Martin and within a very few years was left a widow with one son and a bankrupt business on her hands. Faced with the necessity of providing a living for herself and her son Claude, she entered the household of a brother-in-law named Buisson in a role which can best be described as manageress. She did so well that her indolent employer decided she might as well assume charge of his mercantile business. Taking over without any hesitation, she began to manage all the details, all the problems of employment and cartage and bookkeeping, displaying a sure head and a level sense of judgment; receiving, however, in return for the increased prosperity she brought to the crowded warehouses and dingy offices no substantial reward at all.

It was not this unfairness which turned her thoughts to serving another master in a far different field. She had always wanted to give herself to the Church. Even when overburdened with responsibility and work, she had been severe in her penances, wearing a hair shirt and flagellating her back with a knotted cord. For a few years she was held back by the need to provide for her young son. The latter, it seems, was at first much opposed to her idea of entering a religious order.

When Claude became old enough to go to a Jesuit college, Marie Guyart became a novice in the Ursulines at Tours. This was in 1631, and two years later she took her first vows, assuming the name of Mère Marie de l'Incarnation. It was at this time that Madame de la Peltrie came to Tours. The old archbishop, who had been watching the new member of the Ursulines and knew that her desire was to go to Canada, suggested to Madame de la Peltrie that here was an instrument who might prove of great use. The two women seem to have understood and liked one another at first sight, and out of the meeting grew a partnership which would leave its mark on many of the pages over which historians ponder. The energy and perseverence as well as the truly saintly quality of self-abnegation which Marie de l'Incarnation would display in remarkable degree were to prove the most potent factors in the success of the institution.

It should be recorded that Claude ultimately joined the Benedictines and became Assistant Superior General in France. Before attaining that post he was offered a secretaryship under Cardinal

Richelieu but declined that great honor in the belief that he could be of more service in his work with the order.

3

The two zealous founders left France on May 4, 1639, sailing from Dieppe in a ship called the *St. Joseph*. They were accompanied by two nuns in the costume of the Ursulines, gray under a black tunic. One of the nuns was a delicate and pretty girl who also had met Madame de la Peltrie at Tours, Marie de la Troche of St. Bernard. She was a great blessing to them all on the long and arduous journey, her cheerful spirits introducing a bright note into the grim days when the little ship was in the grip of Atlantic gales.

On the *St. Joseph* also were three members of the order of Hospitalières who were sailing to carry out the plan conceived by Richelieu's niece, the Duchess d'Aiguillon, for the establishment of an Hôtel-Dieu (the French name for hospital) in Quebec. Three Jesuit priests were on board, one of them Father Vincent, who had been chosen to succeed Paul le Jeune as Superior of the Society in Canada.

The party was enthusiastically received, although it soon became evident that little thought had been given to the question of their accommodation. Unaware of the difficulties they would have to face, the devoted young women, happy to have reached the scene of their mission, went down on their knees and kissed the soil of New France. They were then taken to a settlement a few miles above Quebec where Christian Indians had been established, with a church of their own, a mission house, and a small hospital, all of which had been made possible by funds from Noel Brulart de Sillery, a wealthy court official in the household of the Queen Mother. In this small community, which had been named quite properly Sillery, the newcomers remained for several days until other arrangements could be made for them. Then the Hospitalieres were lodged in a house on the summit of the rock and the Ursulines were moved to a small frame building on a wharf at the mouth of the St. Charles River.

It was a very small house. There were two cramped rooms and a shed which was nothing more than a lean-to. Madame de la Peltrie took one look at it and then said with a laugh which may have had a hint of ruefulness in it that it undoubtedly should be named the Louvre. The defects of their new home were so apparent that the

name was adopted and "the Louvre" it became to all members of
the party.

The walls of the Louvre were not weatherproof and the interior
was damp and drafty. The roof leaked so badly that it was impossible to keep candles lighted when rain was falling. The lean-to,
which had been converted into a chapel, was so cold that in winter
they could not go there to pray. But the greatest fault this charming
habitation had to offer was a lack of room. There was accommodation for no more than eight pupils, but the number of dark-skinned
and sober-eyed charges who came soon exceeded that number several times over. Privacy became a word with no meaning whatever.

Madame de la Peltrie took to the care of the children with a
wholehearted devotion. She loved them all and in her spare moments her fingers were always at work with a needle. In a very
short time she had them dressed in crimson camlot, a uniform which
delighted them beyond measure. In the meantime the devoted
women were learning the Indian language. Marie de St. Bernard,
who had taken the name Mère St. Joseph and was often called the
Laughing Nun, was quick at this, with Madame la Fondatrice (the
Foundress) a close second. Mère Marie de l'Incarnation had more
difficulty. Writing to her son, she said that "the words rolled like
stones in my head."

The parents of the pupils had a habit of dropping in for visits.
They had little knowledge of French and so did nothing but stand
around and wait for refreshments to be served. The nuns always
kept a pot of sagamité on the fire, a dish which has already been
mentioned as a favorite with the Hurons. For the more important
occasions, when they entertained many visitors, the nuns went to
considerable trouble and expense to provide food to the liking of
the voracious parents. One recipe, which seems to have been a special favorite, has been preserved. They would take a bushel of black
plums (which were raised in large quantities in the fruit groves),
twenty-four pounds of bread, a large quantity of Indian corn and
ground-peas, a dozen tallow candles melted down (for reasons
which good housewives may possibly understand), and two or three
pounds of fat salt pork. This conglomeration, which certainly must
have had a distinctive flavor, was very much liked by the dusky
guests. When provided frequently, however, it cut into the meager
income of the convent.

The endowment which Madame de la Peltrie had provided had

seemed large enough, although it came to no more than nine hundred livres a year. It was apparent at once that it would be impossible to save anything out of the income for the new building of stone which they were planning to erect on the summit. New funds must be raised, and the task devolved on the indefatigable Marie de l'Incarnation. After working all day long, this remarkable woman would settle herself down at night with a single candle (when the weather was dry) and her fingers would race over the sheets of paper for long hours. She wrote mostly to women of position and wealth in France, telling them of the difficulties of the poor little institution and begging financial assistance.

Gradually the dream came to fruition. The letters of Marie de l'Incarnation, who had become the vital spark of the institution, brought the needed assistance. A stone convent was planned, and for this purpose the governor granted them six arpents of land on the summit. Workmen were brought over from France on a three-year contract and were paid a wage which came to thirty cents a day. The cornerstone was laid as early as 1641, and within three years of their arrival in Quebec the framework had been completed. The three-storied building of dark-colored stone which the leaders had raised for the continuation of their efforts seemed to everyone a structure of real magnificence. It was ninety-two feet long and twenty-eight broad and it contained a chapel which was seventeen by twenty-eight.

The raising of the walls had exhausted the funds, and nothing could be done about the interior save the putting up of some plain pine partitions. There were four large fireplaces which consumed 175 cords of wood the first winter but did not keep the place warm. Despite these difficulties they were delighted to be in their new home. They were particularly glad to escape from the discomfort of the muddy road which led to their river-front house. With their happy tendency to make light of all difficulties, they had named this road the *Grande Allée*.

Because of the lack of heat the first winters spent in the great stone convent were a test of endurance, a point which the busy fingers of Marie de l'Incarnation stressed in the ever-increasing number of epistles she sent to likely contributors in that land of loving memory so far away. The furnishings were primitive in the extreme, and the uncomplaining women had to use narrow beds which closed up like chests when not used. This type of bed, which can still be found in use, had a double advantage. It occupied only half the space of a regular bedstead and could be used as a seat during the day. It is easy to understand that in these first years the gaiety of the little Marie de St. Bernard was sorely needed to keep up the spirits of her companions.

4

The third member of the trio, Jeanne Mance, was born in 1606 at Nogent-le-Roi in Champagne. Her family belonged to the lesser nobility and her father held the post of King's procurator. She was, it seems, a continual source of puzzlement and speculation to her family and friends. Because of abundant good looks she could have been the belle of the community: a delicate but lovely girl, vividly dark, with a handsome mass of curly dark hair, expressive brown eyes, and fine features. In spite of all her advantages, she remained aloof from social activities. What those about her did not understand was that she had yielded to the wave of intense spiritual conviction which was sweeping over France, fanned by the deep interest in the Jesuit *Relations*. She had made up her mind that she wanted to go to Canada and devote herself to mission work.

She became of an age for matrimony but showed no inclination to accept any of the numerous suitors who appeared for her hand. Then she paid a long visit to Paris, and envious friends declared that her purpose must be to place herself in a more advantageous position on the matrimonial market. Nothing could have been farther from the truth. Jeanne Mance was taking advantage of the opportunity to let her desire for a life of service become known in the highest circles. Her purpose gave her prominence at once. Women of high rank whose thoughts were tending in the same direction came flocking to see her, including the Princess de Condé. The Queen, the lovely and unhappy Anne of Austria, summoned her to an audience.

It was to be a lesser-known woman, however, that Jeanne was indebted in the end for the chance to fulfill her destiny. Madame de Bouillon, widow of the Superintendent of National Finances, became deeply interested in her. Claude de Bouillon had proved himself so extremely able and useful in his official position that, in addition to his regular salary, Cardinal Richelieu sent him on the first day of each year the sum of 100,000 livres as a bonus. When

he died he left everything to his widow, who thus became a very
wealthy woman. After many long and earnest talks she and Jeanne
Mance decided that the purpose they must accomplish jointly was
the establishment of a hospital in Canada. The generous widow
promised the fullest financial support and made one stipulation
only, that her name was not to be used. She was to be referred to
only as "the unknown benefactress."

While in Paris Jeanne saw Father Lalemant, who had returned
from Canada. He encouraged her in her purpose but, for a curious
reason, was unable to give her any specific suggestions. That very
day he was leaving for Dauphiné to negotiate a most important step
in the organization of the Company of Montreal, about which much
will be told later. Inasmuch as he could not be certain of the success
of his mission, he said nothing to the beautiful young woman from
the provinces of the opportunity which might thus be opened to her.

With the assurance of generous support, Jeanne set out for La
Rochelle, from which port a ship was sailing for Canada, she had
heard, on a very special mission. After paying a visit to her home
to bid her relatives and friends good-by, she rode all the way to the
seaport on horseback. In her purse was the first installment of the
funds promised by "the unknown benefactress," the sum of twelve
hundred livres to be used for her personal expenses.

At La Rochelle, which impressed her as a sordid city because of
its crowded and shabby streets packed tightly about the waterfront,
she reached an important stage in her great adventure. The telling
of what happened to her there must wait, however, for its proper
place.

CHAPTER XIII

The Story of Ville Marie
and How It Came into Existence

1

IT WAS not strange that Hochelaga exerted a deep influence on those who saw it. Here two mighty rivers meet. The St. Lawrence, carrying on its broad bosom the excess waters of the Great Lakes, flows in a northeasterly direction on its majestic way to the sea. The Ottawa, rising in the northern wilds and gathering volume from the tributaries which empty into it, comes down to mingle with the St. Lawrence.

It is not a peaceful union. The Ottawa, as though angry that it must surrender its identity, flings itself into the waters of the parent stream with tumult and violence. So much impatience and anger cannot be confined within a single entrance like the stately pouring of the Saguenay River into the St. Lawrence. The Ottawa plunges down so bitterly that it cuts the land into many channels, thus forming islands at the point of union. To increase the drama of its last phase, it tears out hills and broadens into lakes and cuts gorges through the high ground, and in places it tumbles so excitedly over rocky bottoms that it forms rapids where the lashing white waters boil and foam and set up a continuous roaring.

The islands thus created are, by way of contrast, peaceful and lovely; and the most peaceful and the loveliest of them all is the island of Montreal. It is the largest of the group, oval in shape and thirty miles long, with a hump in its center like a great natural sentry post, which is called the mountain. It was ordained from the first to be the site of a great city.

Montreal Island was known as Hochelaga when Jacques Cartier visited it and found so much to astonish him in the size of the Indian village at the base of the mountain. The beauty and fertility of this island on the sun-drenched slopes appealed equally to Champlain, although Hochelaga village had disappeared. The free traders who came up in their barques and bateaux, trolling their earthy songs and slavering for a share of the furs, were likewise impressed and awed. Here, they all agreed, was one of the natural crossroads of the earth; and here, if anywhere, the wealth of the new continent would collect so they could lay their avid hands on it. Here, in other words, was the greatest natural trading post the continent had to offer.

The story of the island which had been formed in the death throes of a powerful river had a magical effect in France as well. But it was for a far different reason. Men and women spoke of Hochelaga with reverence. They read the published letters from the priests who had gone out into the wilds, and they pictured the meeting of the two rivers as a place which God had created for a much greater purpose than the stimulation of trade. Here the Deity had appointed that white men and red should meet, to the end that the souls of the natives might be saved.

2

Two stories must be told to explain how Montreal came to be settled. The first is a commonplace one, well authenticated and open to acceptance without question. It deals with human frailty and the play of selfish motives behind the scenes.

The annual meeting of the Company of One Hundred Associates was held on January 15, 1636, in the Paris house of Jean de Lauson, who held the post of intendant. The attendance was not large, for it had been provided, in order to facilitate the transaction of business, that all authority was to be vested in a board of twelve members. In any event, the company still teetered on the brink of bankruptcy and most of the members regarded their association as a liability, particularly as they never knew when they might be called upon for fresh support by that most demanding of men, the gimlet-eyed cardinal. One of the chief items of business at this meeting was the granting of large tracts of land in Canada. The Sieur de la Chaussée was given the island of Montreal. One Simon le Maître was allowed a seigneury which afterward was known as the Lauson. Jacques Castillon was allotted a large share of the island

of Orleans. The most important of the grants, however, was to the
eldest son of Monsieur de Lauson. He was given an enormous tract
of land around the union of the two rivers, sixty leagues of frontage,
no less, on the St. Lawrence, with exclusive navigation and fishing
rights. The tract thus turned over to the young Lauson was a kingdom in itself. To it was given the name of La Citière.

A short time thereafter Monsieur de Lauson resigned his post as
intendant of the society, and the holders of the three grants first
mentioned made them over to him. It had been no more than a
scheme to feather his own nest while he was in a position to do so.
It seems to have been the usual thing. At any rate, it is not recorded
that there was any protest, official or otherwise.

The second of the two stories cannot be authenticated save by the
evidence of the deeply religious men who were concerned in it.
Although it cannot, therefore, be accepted as easily as the first, it
conveys such a depth of conviction that it has been told and retold
and believed down the centuries; and in no other way can the beautiful story of the founding of Montreal be explained.

Here, then, it is. There was in Anjou, which is called sometimes
the home of hardheaded men, a certain Monsieur Jerome de Royer,
Sieur de la Dauversière, who was receiver-general of taxes at La
Flèche but whose head was not hard enough to banish the visions
which filled it and whose heart was so large that he thought only
of doing good. He was a plump little pumpkin of a man with a
turned-up nose and an unimpressive mustache. He seems to have
been sickly. At any rate, he spoke in a slow and halting voice. No
hero he in appearance, but there was a staunchness about him
which showed in his steady eye and in the purposes which possessed him.

He became early a devoted reader of the *Relations*, and as a result
a picture began to form in his mind. He could see the beautiful
islands where the two rivers came together, and in particular the
island of Montreal with the slopes of the mountain bathed in sunlight.
There had not been any description of this part of Canada in anything published, and the Sieur de la Dauversière had not spoken to
anyone who had been there; but he saw everything in such minute
detail that he could make others see it as well. It was as though he
had been carried in spirit to the great crossroad in a dream and had
heard the hoarse booming of the waterfalls and had seen the tossing
manes of the white horses in the rapids.

The vision dwelt so continuously in his mind that he went finally to his confessor, Father Chauveau, who was rector of the Jesuit college at La Flèche. The latter was convinced at once that the vision had been granted him for a purpose and that he should devote the rest of his life to the christianizing of the savages. "Dismiss all doubts," said the priest.

At this time a friend was staying in the Dauversière household, one Baron de Fancamp, who also was piously inclined. The two men talked long and earnestly and finally decided to visit Paris. Here they hoped to found an association for the purpose of establishing a mission on Montreal Island. This led to an all-important meeting between Dauversière and the Abbé Jean Jacques Olier, a young man engaged in country missions who was later to found the Sulpician Seminary.

It was in the galleries of the Château de Meudon that the two men met. It was completely by chance, neither having any idea of the identity of the other. Nevertheless, they stopped at once and stood for several moments in silence, the intent priest and the insignificant man, looking into each other's eyes. It was, they said later, as though a great light had illuminated everything for them. Each could see into the mind of the other.

"I know your design," said Monsieur Olier. "I am going to commend it to God at the holy altar."

Later the two men met again, this time in the park of the same château. The priest handed to the Sieur de la Dauversière a purse containing one hundred pistoles (a popular name for the *louis d'or*, having a value slightly under that of the English pound) and said, "Take this to commence the work of God." They talked for three hours, planning the movement to form a Montreal company. The same white light seemed to play over them as they conversed, keeping their minds in full accord and giving a divine direction to the conclusions they reached.

And now the threads of the two stories drew together. The Montreal Company could not be started as long as the island was owned by the acquisitive Monsieur de Lauson and his son. The ex-intendant had gone to the Dauphiné after resigning his post on the board of the Associates and was acting there in an administrative capacity. Dauversière and Fancamp journeyed, therefore, to Vienne and met Monsieur de Lauson. They received from him a prompt and emphatic answer in the negative. This hardheaded man of affairs saw

no reason for giving up such a valuable grant, particularly to two
strangers. They impressed him, no doubt, as a pair of addlepated
visionaries.

But it was known that Monsieur de Lauson had not fiulfilled any
of the terms on which the grant had been based. He had not sent
out a single settler, nor had he invested the smallest coin in colonization efforts. Perhaps this had some bearing on the decision he made
later, although the credit for his change of heart is given to Father
Charles Lalemant, who had returned to France as procurator of the
Jesuit missions. Father Lalemant went to Vienne (on the day, it will
be recalled, that he talked to Jeanne Mance) and persuaded Lauson
to relinquish his rights to the island.

On August 7, 1640, the cession was made legal and thus the island
of Montreal passed into the hands of Dauversière and Fancamp,
acting for the company which already was taking definite shape.
The agreement was confirmed in December of that year at a general assembly of the Company of One Hundred Associates held in
Paris.

In planning the Montreal Company the same secrecy was observed as in the case of the *Compagnie de Saint-Sacrament*. It was
known that Fencamp and Dauversière were the prime movers, but
the men who provided the funds remained in the background. Not
until years later, when the need for a reorganization was felt and
Jeanne Mance returned to France to urge that it be done at once,
did the backers of the company permit the use of their names.

The need was now faced for a man to act as governor of the proposed colony. It was realized that the right man would be hard to
find, that in addition to being a good soldier and administrator he
must be animated by a religious zeal in keeping with the spiritual
aims of the founders. Dauversière went to Father Lalemant for
advice and found the latter ready with a candidate. "I know a
gentleman of Champagne," said the Jesuit procurator, "who may
suit your purpose." He then mentioned the name of Paul de Chome-
day, Sieur de Maisonneuve, a soldier who had fought with distinction in the Dutch wars; a man, moreover, of high character and
clean heart.

It happened that the Sieur de Maisonneuve was in Paris at the
time and living at one of the larger and more reputable inns. In
order to judge of his merits at first hand, Dauversière took lodgings
there also and made a point of eating his meals in the common

room. One day the company around the long table was joined by the man who had already been pointed out to him as Paul de Chomedey. Dauversière watched the newcomer as he took his place at the other end of the board. It was clear that he was a gentleman, for his blue doublet was of excellent material and an immaculate frilled shirt showed at his neck; a soldier also, wearing his sword and carrying himself with muscular ease.

Dauversière began at once to speak to the company of his plans for the new mission. He talked in glowing terms, overcoming the slowness of his utterance, trying to make them see the things he perceived so clearly; and as he went along he allowed his eyes to rest often on the face of the quiet man at the other end. It was a grave face and one of unusual quality; a strong nose and jaw, the slightly receding forehead so often found in soldiers, eyes well spaced and thoughtful. Maisonneuve was on the right side of forty and seemingly in the best of health. He was eating little and listening intently.

Dauversière, not even pretending an interest in the food on his plate or the glass of wine at his hand, turned the discussion to the difficulty of finding the right leader. Out of the corner of an eye he considered the effect this was having on the silent Maisonneuve, and it was with dismay that he saw the latter rise from his place and leave the room.

"I have failed," he thought. "I have found the right man but I have not been able to interest him."

But when Dauversière also rose from the table he found the grave-faced soldier waiting in the corridor with an invitation that they go to his apartment. Maisonneuve opened the conversation by saying that he would gladly participate in the expedition to Montreal and the work of the mission there. He told Dauversière of his experience as a soldier and even went into the matter of his finances. He had, it developed, a yearly income of two thousand livres, which made him independent and in a position to serve without compensation. As the only son of an old and wealthy family he would in time come into a substantial inheritance. He would be prepared, he said, to devote to the cause everything he possessed.

The right man had been found. Dauversière had no doubts now on that score, nor had any of his associates when they met Paul de Chomedey. He was shortly thereafter appointed governor with authority to collect equipment and stores and to aid in selecting volunteers.

3

In the early summer of the year following Champlain's death a new governor had come to Quebec, Charles Hualt de Montmagny, a knight of the Maltese Order. He was accompanied by his chief lieutenant, Bréhaut l'Isle, who belonged to the same order, and they looked most imposing in their black robes with white crosses of eight points on their breasts. The company which came ashore on the heels of the commandant was large and distinguished. There was a secretary named Piraube, one Juchereau des Chatelets, the factor of the company, and two gentlemen staff officers, Repentigny and St. Jean. There were several gentlemen, including the Sieur de la Potherie, who had been granted seigneuries and were arriving to take possession of their land. Of more importance in the eyes of the always apprehensive people of Quebec, Montmagny brought with him some soldiers and settlers, forty-five in all.

The new governor was an urbane and pleasant gentleman of high courage and Christian ideals and an instinct for organization. He was welcomed with enthusiasm, particularly as he displayed his religious zeal from the first moment of his landing. Father le Jeune was a witness to the arrival of the party and wrote his impression of the scene in rhapsodic terms. "It was a sight to thank God for," he said in describing the newcomers, "to behold these delicate young ladies and these tender infants issuing from their wooden prisons like day from the shades of night." The good father must have been carried away by his publishing success, in thus referring fancifully to the six lovely and unmarried daughters of two of the new seigneurs, Monsieur de Repentigny and Monsieur de la Potherie.

Quebec at this stage was entering what might be termed its first boom. This sudden renaissance showed itself in building activities rather than in a great increase of population. True, the number of inhabitants had doubled, but the total did not yet exceed two hundred. There seemed to be a conviction that if churches and schools and hospitals were provided the necessary worshipers and scholars and patients would be found to make use of them. The flimsy houses of the early days were giving place to stone. Private residences were being built. The Sieur Giffard, the first holder of a fief to do homage, lived in Quebec and directed his seigneury at Beauport from there. Already buildings were lining the route to the summit and the winding path had become an important thoroughfare. At night a cheerful series of lights marked its course up the rock.

There were other residents who had brought out rich possessions and lived with the degree of elegance which might have been expected of Frenchmen of distinction and background. The name of only one finds its way into the scant records of the day, Pierre des Puiseaux, who had made a great fortune in the West Indies. He had reached the advanced age of seventy-five, and it is not easy to understand his reason for electing to spend his last days in this hazardous outpost. He had provided for himself two houses. In the oak forest back of Sillery he had a habitation called Ste. Foye, but he himself resided in a quite luxurious house, the finest in Quebec, which was called St. Michel. Situated beyond the flat plateau known as the Plains of Abraham, St. Michel was a handsome stone structure with high chimneys and rooms of considerable size; and here an atmosphere of gracious living was maintained under candles set in glass chandeliers, with fine silver services for the table and the whitest of napery. It is interesting to note that part of the walls of this house, so remarkable for the time in which it was built, are still incorporated in one of the great houses of modern Quebec.

The new governor set to work at once to enlarge and strengthen the fort and to lay out streets around it. A new chapel was built back of the fort and named after Champlain, in close proximity to a home of frame construction for the Jesuits. This proved a mistake, for both chapel and house were burned to the ground shortly thereafter and had to be replaced by structures of stone. The Jesuits had received a gift of six thousand crowns from the Marquis de Gamache for the founding of a school for Indian children and had already erected a frame seminary in the neighborhood of the citadel to which small red-skinned recruits were coming.

A noteworthy addition to the permanent buildings of the town was the Hôtel-Dieu which the Hospitaliéres erected on the summit overlooking the valley of the St. Charles.

In spite of this rather remarkable development there was a reverse side to the shield. The atmosphere of Quebec was troubled and tense. The shadow of Iroquois hostility hung over the colony like a black cloud. The warriors of the Five Nations had held a solemn powwow at Lake St. Pierre and had declared war on the French in belated revenge for the defeats they had suffered at the hands of Champlain. They swarmed along the rivers and in the forests and it was no longer safe for a white man to venture out. Fear was felt for the safety of the little settlement at Sillery and the few seign- euries which had been established along the St. Lawrence.

Somewhat later the aggressive Iroquois would develop a plan for the extermination of the white men. With considerable military acumen they established a line of fighting posts along the river from the neighborhood of Three Rivers, where the small French post existed in a position of extreme jeopardy, to a point near the water- fall of the Chaudière on the Ottawa, thus cutting the white men off from their Huron and Algonquin allies. To carry out this bold plan, the Iroquois leaders divided their forces into ten bands. Two of these fighting divisions were located at the Chaudière to prevent any sorties across the blockade on the part of the Hurons. Four divi- sions were stationed around Montreal Island, the strategic impor- tance of which was fully realized. A seventh was maintained at Lake St. Pierre, an eighth on the St. Lawrence near Sorel, a ninth near Three Rivers. The tenth, the largest and most formidable, was re- served for the purpose of striking at the main settlements when an opportunity arrived.

This plan of campaign was typical of the wily Iroquois, who did not believe in committing their best fighting men to engagements in which, even if they emerged the victors, their losses would be heavy. They depended on stealth and surprise attack, and the objective of their campaign was to pick off French parties and gradually reduce their strength in readiness for the day of the major stroke.

In the carrying out of this crafty plan they had one asset which thoroughly alarmed the French garrisons. The red warriors had guns. Some of the fire pieces had been acquired by trading with illicit dealers, but most of them had been supplied by the Dutch, who had established a trading post at Beverwyck on the site of what later became Albany. Actuated by a desire to cement their alliance with the Iroquois, and prepared to assist in the elemination of the French as rivals, the Dutchmen had not hesitated to sow the wind by plac- ing this deadly weapon in Iroquois hands.

This was known in Quebec. The French could not tell how skillful the dreaded warriors of the Long House had become in the use of "the club which kills at a distance." Fortunately they were not very adept at first. Gradually, however, they would become expert, and so the long wars would carry this added menace.

It was not only "the delicate young ladies and the tender infants" who slept uneasily in the French strongholds because of the war with the Iroquois. The governor and his staff spent weary hours and sleepless nights over the problem of defense.

4

When Jeanne Mance arrived at La Rochelle she discovered that not one ship but three were sailing for Canada. She went first to Father La Place, a Jesuit, and there she was introduced to Fancamp. The baron had come to the seaport to superintend the preparations for departure, and so she learned for the first time of the plan to found a mission on Montreal Island. Later she met the Sieur de la Dauversière at church and from him received further details. The originator of the movement was in a state of high satisfaction over the progress which was being made. Enough money had been collected to fit the expedition out on a complete scale and seventy-five thousand livres had already been spent. With his halting speech he succeeded in conveying a full measure of his enthusiasm to the receptive neophyte, and she declared her desire to go with the party.

One difficulty presented itself. She would be the only woman, and this caused her some qualms of uneasiness. Almost immediately, however, it was learned that two of the artisans who had volunteered to go were now loath to leave their wives. It was decided to lift the prohibition which had been placed earlier, and the men were told to bring their wives with them. Thus Jeanne Mance, to her entire satisfaction, found herself committed to the adventure.

The expedition left in due course. The ship to which Jeanne had been assigned was the first to arrive at Quebec, having lost contact with the others. Much to the surprise of the party on board, they were received with tempered enthusiasm. As head of the colony the Sieur de Montmagny felt that the plan of the Montreal Company was an infringement of his prerogatives. This attitude on the part of the governor had communicated itself to the residents, and the only one who seems to have shown warmth in greeting the newcomers was Madame de la Peltrie. That ardent espouser of causes found her imagination fired by the new movement. She took an instant liking, moreover, to Jeanne Mance. These two delicate but high-spirited women had much in common, and it was not strange that they became friends. Madame de la Peltrie seems to have taken things into her own hands by arranging for Jeanne to be lodged at St. Michel, the luxurious residence of Pierre des Puiseaux. Later she moved there herself.

The willingness of the foundress of the Ursuline convent to absent herself from the work in this way caused much discussion in Quebec. Although the cornerstone of the new building had been laid, the walls were going up most deliberately and the nuns and their charges were still lodged at "the Louvre." The ever-faithful Marie de l'Incarnation remained in control during the temporary absence of the titular head, so that in reality no serious interruption to the work came about.

The ship on which Maisonneuve had sailed was the last to put in an appearance. It limped into sight on August 20, a much-battered vessel with tattered sails and leaky hull. The governor of the new mission saw at once that he had stepped into a situation of mounting tensity.

5

The Sieur de Montmagny was a gentleman of courage and high ideals, but he was also a stickler for his rights. He was affronted and also a little nonplused by the situation in which he found himself. He had not been consulted about the Montreal venture at any point and certainly he had not expected to find Maisonneuve entrusted with powers which amounted almost to complete autonomy. The newcomer held a warrant from the King to control the destinies of the Montreal colony, to train and command troops, to make his own appointments. It was clear enough that he would look to France for his instructions rather than to Quebec. Monsieur de Montmagny found this little to his liking, and it is not strange that during the months which followed there was much bickering over such matters as the firing of salutes and the exercise of authority.

There was thunder in the air when the two men met for the first time in the rebuilt citadel on the summit. Montmagny stated his objections to the new venture openly and emphatically, but he seems to have skirted the issue of divided authority by basing his objections on what he termed the folly of settling at Montreal under the conditions which existed.

"You know that war with the Iroquois has commenced," he said, his eyes cold and withdrawn. "You cannot, then, in any reason think of settling in a place so far removed from Quebec. You must change your resolution. If you wish it, you will be given the island of Orleans instead."

Maisonneuve answered in quiet but firm tones. "What you say, Excellency, would be good if I had been sent to Canada to choose a suitable site. But the company which sends me is determined that we shall go to Montreal. My honor is at stake. You must not take it ill if I proceed with the plans as made."

No amount of expostulation had any effect. Although he knew that the crossroad lay 180 miles to the westward and that the Iroquois infested the country thereabouts, Maisonneuve could not be convinced that the plan should be changed. The only concession he would make was to delay their departure until the spring. This was a wise postponement, for the season was already far advanced. There was no possibility of getting settled on the distant island before winter set in.

The Quebec governor called a general meeting of the residents of Quebec as well as the members of the Montreal party to discuss the situation. Maisonneuve listened to the vehement protests but remained adamant. He had his orders and he intended to carry them out. "Were all the trees on the island of Montreal," he declared, "to be changed into so many Iroquois, it is a point of duty and honor for me to go there and establish a colony."

A soldier himself, the Sieur de Montmagny must have understood the position taken by Maisonneuve. Perhaps secretly he had come to approve it. The opposition to the plan, at any rate, was abandoned.

The winter was spent in preparations for the move in the spring. Pierre des Puiseaux placed his property at St. Foye at the disposal of the Montreal leader, and from here Maisonneuve directed the building of the river boats which would be used in the ascent of of the St. Lawrence. They constructed a pinnace of the three-master type, two shallops which were half-decked and with a single sail, a barge which was probably on the order of the river bateaux with their high-bowed and narrow-bottomed style of construction which made them particularly useful in running rapids and in the navigation of shallow water, and a still smaller vessel which is designated as a *gabare* and was undoubtedly on the order of the modern scow. All of these different varieties of craft were equipped with weathering, a device similar to the nets which ships of war used on going into action to keep their decks concealed.

The work progressed all through the winter. The sound of the busy axes could be heard in the woods back of St. Foye, where oak trees were being cut down and trimmed and dressed. No unnecessary chances were being taken. Sentries with loaded guns on their shoulders kept an eye on the water, and scouts roamed the woods to pick up any hint of approaching war parties.

In the meantime Maisonneuve had joined the congenial company at St. Michel. The veteran owner had been completely won over and was heart and soul with the leaders of the Montreal project. He was so enthusiastic, in fact, that he once said to Madame de la Peltrie, who continued to reside with him: "Madame, it is no longer I who lodge you. I am nothing here. It is Monsieur de Maisonneuve to whom you are obliged. He is master." There was talk of conveying all his property to the cause, but later he changed his mind and asked for a restoration. This, of course, was arranged.

They were all very content, it seems, with the life at St. Michel; the comforts, the inspiring talk in the evenings before roaring fires, and the glimpses over the drifted snows on what would be called at a later day the Plains of Abraham. There was, above all, a meeting of minds. When spring came they were all eager to start. The boats were ready; the plans were laid. Madame de la Peltrie had talked down all opposition and was going with them. Even Pierre des Puiseaux, bent and gray with the years, was to accompany the advance guard.

The defection of Madame la Fondatrice had helped to widen the breach between the residents of Quebec and the party for Montreal. The issue had become already a burning one, and it would continue to smolder between the two cities all through the years of the French regime; and, in fact, can be detected in a sense of rivalry which still persists. The energetic and vivacious Madame de la Peltrie was roundly criticized. Even Mère Marie de l'Incarnation said in one of her letters to France: "She afterward took back her furniture and many things which were used for the church and which she had given us. To say she did wrong, I cannot before God." Then her great goodness asserted itself and she added, "I cannot doubt that her intentions are good and holy."

The attitude of Madame de la Peltrie was due in some degree to the friendship she had conceived for Jeanne Mance, in a still greater degree to her desire to be in the thick of things. The work at Quebec had settled down to a steady routine, while the call to Montreal was like a bugle blast. Later she would plaintively but determinedly beg permission to go into the Huron mission field, a request which the head of the Jesuits denied with even greater determination.

6

Montmagny stood beside Maisonneuve in one of the shallops at the head of the procession of boats. Standing on the half deck, they were the first to see the island of Montreal stretching ahead of them in the dusk of early evening. They had started from Quebec on May 8, and it was now May 17. This was a great moment for the brave men and women who had crossed the Atlantic to turn an idea into an actuality and who were persisting in it despite the dangers which pressed so closely about them. They had come all the way up the St. Lawrence without seeing so much as the shaved head of a Mohawk brave or hearing the excited gabble, much like the clucking of angry turkey cocks, in which the dreaded warriors were prone to indulge. Was this a happy augury? Would the founding of Montreal be carried out with less hazard than had been predicted?

The next morning they landed near a spit of land now known as Pointe à Callières. It was a truly gorgeous day. The records, usually silent on such welcome details, indicate that Nature excelled herself in extending a welcome to the newcomers. The early morning sun touched the flat top of the mountain and lighted up the thick forests. It was a warm sun for so early in the season, and a grateful one to the company, who felt a cheerful lift of spirits after the gusts and raw winds of spring which they had suffered in their cramped quarters on the boats. They were happy that the long journey had thus come to an ending in a setting of peace and beauty.

It was not a large company which came ashore: the two governors and their staff officers, alert and anxious with so much responsibility on their shoulders; a number of Jesuit priests, including Father Vimont and Father Poncet, the latter having been assigned to duty at the new settlement; Madame de la Peltrie and her faithful maid, Charlotte Barré, Jeanne Mance, an exalted group; Pierre des Puiseaux and a few other visitors from Quebec; all of the twenty-one settlers who made up the rank and file, conspicuous among them the sturdy figure of Nicholas Godé, the joiner, with his household of six.

As the feet of Maisonneuve touched the soil of the island he fell to his knees, and his example was followed by all of the company. A prayer was said and then their voices were raised in a hymn of thanksgiving.

They had landed on a flat piece of land, damp from the inundations of the spring floods. It was a low-lying stretch formed by the waters of the St. Lawrence and a small stream which they named later the St. Pierre. This tiny tributary dried up long ago, and the exact spot of the landing is vaguely identified under the tall buildings of the modern city. The name of "the Common," which they applied to the meadow where their feet first touched, soon passed out of use, although an echo of it remains in the Common Street of today. But of this we may be sure, the memory of that first scene never faded in the minds of the participants. The officers had donned their finest garb and the priests had assumed their vestments for the first Mass. On the altar, which the women of the party had raised, were the sacred vessels. The soldiers, some few of whom were to remain, stood on guard at the edge of things, their muskets ready for use.

After Mass had been said Father Vimont raised his voice. "That which you see," he said, "is only a grain of mustard seed. But it is cast by hands so pious and so animated by faith and religion that it must be that God has great designs for it. He makes use of such instruments for His work. I doubt not that this little grain may produce a great tree, that it will make wonderful progress someday, that it will multiply itself and stretch out on every side."

The rest of the day, which remained fair, was spent in preparing the first crude living quarters. Tents of birch bark were pitched, and the work was started of cutting down trees for the palisade behind which the small settlement would nestle. It is recorded that, having neither candles nor oil for the lamps, the women caught fireflies and placed them in glass phials to provide some illumination.

Work began in real earnest the next morning. A ditch had to be dug behind which the wooden palisade would be raised, and the Sieur de Montmagny was the first to take spade in hand. This much accomplished, and the island having been formally handed over to Maisonneuve as the representative of the Company of Montreal, the governor boarded one of the ships. He must have been glad to be returning, for the purpose of the new company had meant misunderstandings from the first and much back bristling and hard feelings. There must have been in his mind, however, a sense of reluctance, of pity for the resolute group. It was such a small company which remained. They stood, it seemed, on the rim of the world. The sun still shone warmly and a slight spring breeze stirred in the heavy cover of trees, but danger and the black face of catastrophe hovered above them.

Neither time nor space allows of telling in detail the story of the first days in Montreal. A few facts must suffice: how reinforcements arrived on September 15, consisting of fifteen men under Monsieur de Repentigny and including Gilbert Barbier, a carpenter, who was to prove one of the most useful members; how the boats continued to ply up and down the river, bringing on the supplies which had been left at Quebec; how a habitation capable of holding sixty people and a chapel were erected inside the now formidable palisade; how the season waned and winter came; and how on January 6, the Feast of the Epiphany, Maisonneuve had a path cleared through the snow to the top of the mountain and placed there a great wooden cross which would stand for many years, a symbol of the faith which had brought these fine people across the ocean and set them down in their crowded sanctuary on the bottom lands.

During these first months nothing was heard of the Iroquois, although it was taken for granted that they lurked somewhere in the huddle of islands at the junction of the rivers and that their angry eyes often surveyed the life going on behind the high rampart of logs. Maisonneuve and his followers expected an attack every day, and they counted each hour of delay a respite granted them by a beneficent God.

But the Iroquois did not strike and the tall cross continued to look down reassuringly from the top of the mountain.

CHAPTER XIV

The Start of the Wars with the Iroquois—
An Ineffectual Peace—The Tragic
Story of Isaac Jogues

1

VILLE MARIE de Montréal, as the devout band called their rude little settlement, was the farthest outpost and on that account the danger spot in the war with the Iroquois. The Indians left them alone at first, but this did not lend any sense of security. The garrison could feel the blow poised above them and ready to fall.

There was no longer any security along the St. Lawrence. On August 3, 1643, a party of Huron converts, more than a score, were making their way up the river. With them was Father Jogues and two young Frenchmen; Isaac Jogues, scholar and saintly figure, delicate of body and gentle of spirit, one of the best beloved of the Jesuits. Hugging the shore for safety, they neared Lake St. Pierre and here they found themselves in a nest of small islands, a reedy and overhung part of the river. Here came to reality the picture Maisonneuve had conceived of Montreal. Each tree trunk rising out of the water became a Mohawk brave, each bulrush a hostile toma-hawk. Forty naked figures sprang at the startled occupants of the canoes. In a brief conflict many of the Hurons were killed. The savages carried off as prisoners the three Frenchmen and a score of their terrified allies.

The captives were taken to the village of the victorious Mohawks. Goupil, one of the young companions of Jogues, was killed, and the other, Couture, was drafted ultimately into the tribe. The Hurons were burned at the stake, two or three at a time. Father Jogues was tortured continuously and with fiendish zest, becoming no more than a mutilated shell. With the assistance of Dutch traders, nevertheless, he managed to escape and was smuggled down the Hudson to the fur post at Albany. Later he was put on a boat and sent home to France. Time had not succeeded in patching him up; the nails had been torn from his fingers, his hands were shapeless stumps, his arms had been sawed to the bone with ropes. It was no more than a wraith of humanity that the French people received in reverent acclaim. The Queen expressed a desire to see him and, on his entrance, she went down on her knees and kissed his unsightly hands. Convinced that duty called him back, Father Joques returned to Canada the following year and willingly undertook the most dangerous of all assignments.

The Mohawks, always the most belligerent and relentless of the Five Nations, had finally been brought to an agreement of peace with the French. It was felt that a representative should be sent among them and, as Father Jogues was thoroughly familiar with the language and the customs of the tribe, he was selected to go. In addition to acting as an ambassador, he was to establish a mission for which, prophetically enough, a name had been selected, the Mission of the Martyrs. It seemed at first that his errand had been carried out with complete success. The Mohawks were disposed to be friendly at last. They listened to the harangues of the frail little priest and they accepted the belts of wampum he had brought and the other gifts, one of them a box which he left with them on starting back as a pledge that he would return.

Leaving the box proved to be a mistake. The Mohawks were divided into three families, the Bear, the Wolf, and the Tortoise. They were already at loggerheads among themselves over continuing the peace. The Bears were savagely determined to start the war afresh, and the pacific inclinations of the other families had no weight with them. After the departure of the mission, the medicine men of the Bears began to say that the box contained spells and that they were responsible for the famine from which the tribe was suffering. It was not hard to convince the savage rank and file with such a story.

In the meantime the question was being debated at Quebec as to whether the Mission of the Martyrs should be continued immediately. At first it was concluded that Father Jogues should remain in Montreal for the winter at least. A short time after, the decision was reversed and the good father received orders to repair to the

Mohawk country. He obeyed without question but with a presentiment that death awaited him at the hands of the antagonistic Bears. This feeling was expressed in a letter he wrote to a friend in France. *Ibo et non redibo,* he declared. "I go but I shall not return."

On the way Jogues and his one white companion, a zealous young *donné* named Lalande, were warned by friendly members of the tribe that it would not be safe to proceed. The Hurons who accompanied them deserted at once, but the valiant little priest and his courageous aide decided they must carry out their instructions.

The warning delivered had not been an idle one. A war party of the Bears waylaid them before they reached the heart of the Mohawk country and carried them to their own village in triumph. Here they were beaten, and one of the belligerent braves cut strips of flesh from the back of the priest.

"Let us see," he cried, "if this white flesh is the flesh of an *oki* [a bad magician]."

"I am a man like yourselves," answered Father Jogues. "Why do you treat me like a dog?"

That evening the badly wounded missionary was summoned to a feast at the lodge of the new chief of the Bears. He arose at once, knowing that a refusal would be a mortal offense. At the entrance to the lodge Father Jogues bowed his head in going in, and an Indian standing just inside sank a tomahawk into his brain and then hacked his head free of his body. In the morning Lalande was dispatched in the same way.

The bodies were disposed of, but the heads were triumphantly elevated on the palisades of the village; a practice, as all familiar with the history of more civilized countries will recall, generally followed after executions.

Thus died Father Isaac Jogues, the first of the martyrs, the most gentle and perhaps the most to be pitied of all the brave band who were to give up their lives.

Before this tragic episode Governor Montmagny had planned to establish a fort where the Richelieu River empties into the St. Lawrence, this being the route the Iroquois war parties most often took. He arrived at the spot with a party of nearly one hundred men, including forty well-trained soldiers who had been sent out by Cardinal Richelieu the previous year. It was just eleven days after the unfortunate priests and his companions had been carried off, and the exultant tribesmen had paused long enough to elevate poles along the riverbanks with the heads of the slain. Bark had been stripped from some of the trees and scenes had been daubed crudely on the trunks, including a likeness of the captured priest.

Victory had so emboldened the warriors of the Long House that they attacked the new fort before the palisades were completed. Two hundred strong, screeching their war cries and armed with their newly acquired guns, they charged right up to the walls and fired through the sentry holes at the surprised garrison. It was touch and go for some time, but after a furious struggle the white soldiers finally prevailed and drove the redskins off. The Iroquois, fuming in defeat, retreated to a fort of logs they had built three miles up the river.

The new fort did not accomplish its purpose of keeping the St. Lawrence clear. The Iroquois cut overland and the terror on the river continued to mount. With a gun in his hands the Iroquois warrior was irresistible against the Huron with nothing better than an iron tomahawk. The allies of the French deserted the territory along the river, retreating far back into the woods or huddling ab- jectly in the proximity of the forts. The St. Lawrence was so unsafe that the mail boats were intercepted three times. By a curious chance some of the letters thus seized came into the possession of Father Jogues during his captivity and were taken by him to France.

Later in the summer six men from the Montreal colony were sur- prised while cutting wood at the point on the river where Chambly now stands. Three were killed and the others were carried off. Two of them died at the stake and the last one made his escape, bringing back to the settlement the grim story of the fate of his comrades.

It was with a feeling of relief, therefore, that the little colony heard of special measures which the King was putting into effect for their assistance. He presented to the Montreal Company a ship of 250 tons, named the *Notre Dame de Montréal*, and it was dispatched at once with more settlers and supplies. There was added encourage- ment for them in the knowledge that the King, who in another year was to die at the early age of forty-two, wrote to the Sieur de Montmagny at Quebec with positive instructions "to assist and favor in every way in his power the Seigneur de Maisonneuve in such manner that there shall be no trouble or hindrance." The reinforce- ments arrived at Montreal under the command of Louis d'Ailleboust, the Sieur de Coulanges, and the colony took fresh courage at once. The new-coming officer was a trained military engineer and one of his first tasks was to strengthen the defenses of the camp. He deepened the moat and raised the palisades. Two new bastions were built which commanded the approaches to the walls.

It is essential at this point to pause and consider the motives behind the Montreal venture and the considerations which caused the settlers to persevere in the face of such conditions. The determination to found a mission at the meeting place of the rivers had stemmed from the visions of Dauversière, and it was therefore one of the spirit rather than the mind. Because that insistent and fanatical little man had seen the green mountainsides and the vast forests and had heard the roar of the rapids, those who rallied to his support would not listen to any change of purpose. The divine finger had pointed at Montreal, and so Montreal it must be. Common sense would have dictated acceptance of Montmagny's advice and the selection of a location close to Quebec. It must be said that in the plans of the new company common sense had no place, not so much as the millionth part of a grain. Montreal lay so far out in the wilderness that a concerted attack by Iroquois forces would almost certainly have carried the walls. It was encompassed by such deadly peril now that the friendly Indians did not dare visit it, which prevented the settlers from accomplishing the purpose to which they were dedicated. Nevertheless, they refused to give up. Far away from all chance of immediate succor in the event of an attack, ill equipped and vulnerable, they waited serenely for whatever might befall. It was fanaticism in a high degree. But also it was magnificent; and it was to lead in the end to great things.

Having said this, the story leads at once to a prime example of the lack of reality in the control of the colony. The wife of Louis d'Ailleboust, who is generally referred to by her maiden name of Barbe de Boulogne, had accompanied him; with great reluctance, it must be said, and after refusing three times to do so. On arriving at the island she fell at once under the spell of Jeanne Mance and became completely imbued with the spirit which prevailed. Her husband had brought news for Jeanne which set the two new friends to excited planning. It was from the unknown benefactress, a contribution of forty-two thousand livres for the building of the Hôtel-Dieu.

This was the situation at the time. There was no room inside the palisades for a new building of this size; and, in any event, the site was proving unsuitable because of the spring inundations which flooded the flatlands. It would be necessary to build the hospital outside the walls, where it would be vulnerable to attack. There was urgent need to strengthen still further the defenses of the fort and little enough time in which to do it. There was no immediate need for a hospital because the Indian allies were giving the island a wide berth and there were no patients. Here the fanaticism of the little group shows itself conspicuously. It was decided, in spite of all the reasons to the contrary, to proceed at once with the new building.

The fort, it will be recalled, stood on the west bank of the St. Pierre River. On the other bank the ground stood well above the high-water mark of the spring floods. Back of it and flowing in a westerly direction to join the St. Pierre was a still smaller stream known as St. Martin's Brook. The higher land, therefore, was better suited to defense and perhaps should have been selected for the mission in the first place. Here it was decided to raise the walls of the hospital.

Louis d'Ailleboust saw to it that the new structure was strongly built. It was sixty feet long and twenty-four wide and contained four rooms. One (a very small one) was intended for Jeanne Mance, one for her assistants, and the others were for the patients. There was a chapel attached to the main building. It was quite small, but it was of stone construction and had a weatherproof roof. A suitable home had at last been found for the gifts which had been sent out from France. There was a handsome chalice of silver. A ciborium was suspended at the altar, the type of communion cup which resembles in shape the Egyptian water lily. There were costly candlesticks of silver and gold and lamps like those which swung from the ceilings of the Tabernacle; three sets of vestments, a piece of burgamot tapestry, and two carpets.

In the rooms for the patients were furnishings which had been carefully and lovingly made, including a beautifully carved long table for the keeping of drugs, bandages and supplies, and the crude surgical instruments which were in use at the time. The wards were airy and light and filled with the clean smell of new wood. The walls were weather-tight, the window frames well fitted, the hearths of ample size.

When the slender woman looked about her with her dark and rather tragic eyes, she saw in this small frame building the realization of a dream. Here the bodily ills of the savages would be tended and the seeds of service planted which would raise a great harvest of conversion. Did it matter that adverse conditions were curtailing the number of patients and that certain material needs had seemed to demand attention first? Not to Jeanne Mance; and not, it is only fair to add, to any of that devoted band. The men and women of Montreal looked over their inadequate walls at this institution of mercy standing so boldly alone on the high ground across the stream and did not begrudge the effort which had gone into it.

The hospital, of course, had been provided with as much protection as possible. A high palisade had been raised around its four acres of land in which already two oxen, four cows, and twenty sheep had been turned out to graze. A strong bastion had been erected over the entrance.

Jeanne Mance, happy at last, took possession at once and waited for the patients to come. A few soldiers from the fort were assigned to the hospital.

The second winter arrived. The colonists saw in the change of season a further protection, for surely now the hostile bands would cease to lurk in the woods and betake themselves to the shelter of their own log houses. It was to prove a severe winter. The snow fell incessantly and covered the earth with great drifts. Then the bitter winds from the Ottawa country began to batter the sides of the mountain and to assault with unabated fury the settlement huddling on each side of the St. Pierre. To the sentries who paced the platforms behind the wooden barricades and breathed through beards white with frost, it seemed impossible that the scantily clad enemy were still on the prowl.

This was underestimating the determination and the powers of endurance of the Iroquois. They had not given up the offensive. In spite of the intense cold they still swarmed in the woods, waiting a chance to pick off anyone who ventured out. Sometimes they were so close to the cockleshell defense of the walls that their voices could be heard, the high-pitched gabble which Frenchmen were learning to dread.

At this critical stage in the life of the infant settlement the garrison was indebted to a four-footed friend for much of the immunity enjoyed. A faithful female dog named Pilot had set herself the task of patrolling the woods. She had a nose which unfailingly scented the presence of the Iroquois. After giving birth to a large litter, she taught her sons and daughters to follow her example. At all hours of the day and night the ubiquitous Pilot and her growing family maintained their ceaseless watch. Whenever their keen noses caught the acrid scent of hostile Indians, they would come to a halt like bird dogs on point and send up such a clamor of warning that the garrison would rush at once to the gun posts.

There was no danger of a surprise attack as long as Pilot and her eager pups continued this unremitting patrol, but the advantage thus provided was almost thrown away through the impetuosity of the garrison. Irked by the close confinement and confident they could drive the Indians out of the woods if given the chance, the men kept begging to be allowed to sally out. Much against his better judgment, Maisonneuve finally gave in to them.

On March 13 the sun was hidden behind heavy clouds and the cold was so intense that any step on the hard surface of the snow sounded clearly for some distance. Pilot and her noisy brood were on their rounds. They drifted in and out of the woods, sometimes venturing so far back into the cover that the occasional excited yipping of the young ones came faintly to the listening ears behind the barricades. Suddenly the deep baying of the mother could be heard. This could mean one thing only, that the pack had caught the scent of painted warriors hiding in the woods.

The garrison collected about the governor and pleaded to be allowed the chance to give battle. They were certain they could teach the redskins a lesson.

"Get ready then!" said Maisonneuve. "I shall lead you myself."

A party of thirty men, armed with muskets and hunting knives, issued from the enclosure behind the commander. They were brimful of confidence. Not even the difficulty of wading through the deeply drifted snow (only a few had donned snowshoes) dulled the edge of their desire to come finally to grips with the red men.

No sooner had they entered the woods, however, than it became evident they had walked into a trap. The Iroquois were out in full force. The war whoop of the enemy sounded all about the little party. Arrows whistled through the woods, and the sharp rattle of musketry warned the startled Frenchmen that the enemy had plenty of guns.

Maisonneuve shouted an order: they must take cover behind the trees and fight the Indians with their own methods. This did little good, however, for it was soon demonstrated that the white men were outnumbered. The Indians were spreading out and outflanking the French on both wings. Making a hurried calculation, Maisonneuve decided there must be close to a hundred Iroquois in the party. He shouted another order, this time to retreat.

In the construction of the hospital a track had been made into the woods for the hauling out of logs, and in their scramble for shelter the French found this of great assistance. The Indians now burst from the woods in complete disregard of the guns of the retreating white men, and their spine-chilling cries of *"Cassee kouee!"* filled the air triumphantly. Musket balls and arrows whistled by the panic-stricken whites and kicked up snow like spume on each side. Three French-men were killed and a number wounded. It was certain now that the governor's estimate of the number of the foe had not been far wrong. They seemed to be everywhere, leaping over the drifts, brandishing their weapons in derision, and shouting in wild abandon.

To the frightened watchers in the fort it seemed impossible that the plodding soldiers could reach safety before the screeching Iroquois closed about them. D'Ailleboust ordered the men who had remained behind with him to fire at the Indians over the retreating whites, but at that distance this did not prove effective. Perhaps the whine of the bullets had the effect, nevertheless, of slowing up the pursuit. The Iroquois did not succeed in their efforts to encircle the French. The doors of the Hôtel-Dieu received the racing whites with the smallest possible margin of safety. Maisonneuve was the last man in, having risked capture to cover the retreat of his men. The heavy portals swung to behind him.

The episode had one result: it provided Jeanne Mance with her first patients.

The Indians remained in the woods throughout the whole course of the winter. Sometimes at night the baying of the faithful Pilot would be heard and the members of the watch would hurry to their posts. Here they would remain, straining their eyes for any sign of a rush of fleet copper figures across the white of the snow. The women would dress and sit in the darkness in anxious prayer.

2

It must not be assumed that the hands on the clocks stood still while the Iroquois besieged the French settlements like the goblins to whom they were compared by Father Jerome Lalemant in one of his letters. Somehow business went on and native canoes, in lesser quantity than ever, reached Three Rivers and Quebec with furs for barter. The fall fleet departed for France on October 24; "laden," said the *Relations*, "with 20,000 pounds weight of beaver skins for the habitants, and 10,000 for the general company, at a pistole, or ten or eleven francs, a pound." This statement makes it evident that plenty of private trading was carried on in spite of the efforts of the company to suppress it.

Nor did the Iroquois invariably have things their own way. The Hurons, who sprang from the same racial stock as the indomitable warriors of the Long House, fought bravely enough when danger faced them. The Algonquins were a fierce and cruel race who in the past had bested the Mohawks, the most relentless among the Five Nations. To the Algonquins, moreover, belongs the credit of producing the greatest individual warrior of that day, whose name was Piskiart.

Piskiart lived in the Ottawa country and had become a Christian; almost certainly, it was said, with an eye to receiving the musket which the French sometimes felt safe in confiding into the hands of converts. If the great Piskiart had taken the vows with an ulterior motive in the first place, he made up for it later by becoming thoroughly devout in his declining years; and certainly he made good use of the musket. He was a tall fellow with the agility of a panther and the face of an eagle; a lone wolf, moreover, for he preferred to fight alone. His greatest feat was when he stole down into the enemy country, a war party of one. Reaching a Mohawk village after night had fallen, he located a huge pile of wood at the edge of the nearby forest and made for himself a hiding place under it. Then he stole into the village and killed all the occupants of one lodge, men, women, and children, never using more than a single blow to split open a skull. In his secret and convenient niche under the woodpile he heard the commotion next morning when the catastrophe was discovered: the lamentations, the shouts of rage, the departure of parties to track him down, the return of the discomfited avengers empty-handed.

The second night, believing that the killer would not dare to return, the village sank again into heavy slumbers, and Piskiart repeated his sanguinary feat by slaughtering the occupants of another lodge. The second day was a repetition of the first, but when the insatiable and confident Piskiart emerged from his woodpile the third night, he discovered that a string of sentries had been set about the village. Having to be content with killing one of them, he raised a wild cry of triumph and departed. The Iroquois sent a party after him. This time he made no effort to conceal himself but boldly set

out for his own country. All through the day the chase went on. The
pursuing braves followed the usual plan of taking turns at setting
the pace, so that he was forced to travel at high speed through most
of the day. Among his other accomplishments Piskiart seems to have
been the fleetest of runners. At any rate, he showed his heels to the
lot of them. The pursuing party finally gave up and settled down to
a night's sleep in a state of complete exhaustion, upon which the
bold Algonquin slipped back and brained them all with his well-
reddened tomahawk.

None of the paladins of European legend, the heroes of chivalrous
annals, performed greater deeds than copper-skinned Piskiart. It is
unfortunate that more is not known about him.

It came about, therefore, that the men of the Five Nations, who
were as shrewd as they were brave, decided to give themselves a
space of time for recuperation from a war which had been exhaust-
ing and, up to this point, not too rewarding. They announced their
intention of offering peace to the French, using as a pretext the
magnanimity of Montmagny in saving the lives of two Iroquois
braves who had fallen into the hands of the Algonquins; another
feat of the great Piskiart. In July of the year 1645 a party of Iroquois
leaders arrived at Three Rivers to begin negotiations. The spokesman
was an arrogant chief named Kiotsaton, who came ashore swathed
in wampum ("completely covered with porcelain beads," was Father
Lalemant's phrase), and haughtily announced his intention to discuss
terms. He addressed the Sieur de Montmagny by the name which
the Iroquois people, who had a gift for poetic imagery, had selected
to designate the leader of the French—"Onontio," meaning Great
Mountain.

"Onontio, give ear," he orated with graceful gestures. "I am the
mouth of all my nation. When you listen to me, you listen to all the
Iroquois. There is no evil in my heart. My song is a song of peace."

Kiotsaton was playing a part. In his heart there was nothing but
double-dealing. Nevertheless, he worked out a basis of peace with
the French and their allies, the Hurons, the Algonquins, the Montagnais, and the Men of the White Fish. He produced seventeen
collars of wampum and handed them over one at a time, with a
burst of oratory to describe the clause in the proposed treaty which
each of them symbolized. The collars, which were very handsomely
decorated, were then strung on a line between two poles so that they
could be seen by everyone.

It was all very dramatic and convincing. The French were happy to see a period of rest from the fierce aggression of their terrible foes stretching ahead of them. The Indian allies cried, "Ho! Ho!" in heartfelt assent.

Piskiart had been selected to make a gift of furs to Kiotsaton and his fellow envoys. When the arrogant voice of the Iroquois spokesman had fallen into silence, the mighty warrior of the Algonquins stepped forward. He was wearing leggings of new buckskin and moccasins which were handsomely beaded. There was a tuft of plumes rising above his shaved poll. His eyes swept the peace party with a gleam which told them he had not forgotten the one-man raid he had carried out at their expense. Perhaps also there was in his mind a shrewd estimate of how little reliance could be placed in the high-sounding phrases of the Mohawk orator. He proceeded then to demonstrate that he was a spellbinder in his own right.

"O Kiotsaton!" he said. "Consider these gifts as a tombstone that I place above the graves of those who died in our last meeting. May their bones be no longer disturbed. May revenge be though of no longer."

The Iroquois departed then in a final outburst of oratory. Kiotsaton turned to the French. "Farewell, brothers!" he cried. For the Indian allies he had a somewhat contemptuous admonition. "Obey Onontio and the French. Their hearts and their thoughts are good."

In the following year, having given themselves a chance to rest and restore their strength, the Iroquois went out on the warpath again. Forgotten were the seventeen belts of wampum which had been exchanged as the symbols of peace; most particularly the eighth, which was designed to bind together as one man and for all time the Iroquois, the French, and their Indian allies. They were acting on a plan which had been shrewdly debated over secret council fires. It was their purpose, as a first step in the destruction of all their enemies, to concentrate on the Hurons and exterminate them so completely that not even the ashes of a hunting party would be left to tell where that ancient tribe had lived.

The Destruction of the Huron Nation
—The Jesuit Martyrs

1

THE Jesuit missions had been making remarkable headway in the Huron country. Of all Indian tribes, the Hurons seemed to respond most readily to Christian teachings, and in each of the four tribal families into which they were divided, the Bear, the Rock, the Cord, and the Deer, the number of converts had been rising in a steady tide. The pagans were still in a majority, but counts made in the forties varied from Father Bressani's estimate of eight thousand to a more conservative figure of thirteen hundred baptisms. The mission of La Conception, which was in the teeming village of Ossossané, where Point Varwood protrudes out into Nottawasaga Bay, had been almost one hundred per cent successful in its labors. At the time when the Five Nations decided on their campaign of extermination the hope was high in priestly minds that the whole nation would soon be united in the Faith.

This reduced the effectiveness of the Hurons as war allies. The converts, accepting the teachings of Christ with the wholeheartedness depicted in the *Relations*, had ceased to respond to the urge for war. They became gentle and asked nothing better than to hunt and fish and tend their maize and pumpkin patches and to follow the injunctions of their spiritual fathers. As a further handicap, few of them had firearms. By this time the Iroquois were well supplied with guns and had acquired skill in the use of them. It followed that the men of the northern tribe were no longer capable of withstanding the attacks of the *Hotinonsionni*, as they called the Five Nations. When the latter laid their plans to devastate the Huron country, the result was a foregone conclusion.

The Jesuits had established twelve missions in this beautiful country. It was a small corner of Ontario, somewhat less than forty miles deep and twenty miles wide, a land of rolling hills and many rivers (there were five emptying into Matchedash Bay), with a maze of villages around which the land had been cleared. An attempt had been made to beautify the chapels because the natives responded quickly to anything that pleased the eye. Each mission had a bell or as a substitute a kettle or any other utensil of metal from which sounds could be produced. Sometimes, through lack of towers, the bells had been suspended on the limbs of trees, but they were always effective in attracting large congregations. Crosses had been raised in forest glades and at junction points of the trails so that the eyes of the natives would be continuously filled with reminders of the Faith which held out its arms to them.

The main mission, which served the double purpose of an administrative center and a retreat for the priests, was that of Ste. Marie. It stood near the mouth of the Wye River where it empties into Gloucester Bay, a group of buildings of impressive size.

There has been enough interest in Ste. Marie to attract many archaeological parties to its site during the past century. Chiefly as a result of exceptional and exhaustive efforts carried out by Mr. Wilfrid Jury of the University of Western Ontario and his associates, it has been found that this Jesuit center was a quite amazing accomplishment. Although supplies and tools had to be brought in by canoe over many hundred miles of water, the engineers and their mission helpers not only erected and fortified a cluster of substantial buildings but supplied them with ingenious defense measures, the most astonishing of these being an underground passage in which canoes could be kept without being seen. The construction of this passage has created much speculation.

The water entered under the northern curtain of the walls from the aqueduct and into the center of the compound, behind the screen of the stone walls. As the fort stood well above the level of the river, the water had to be raised by a series of three small locks. The water channel in which it was raised and lowered was securely boxed in with a wooden casing.

The canal lock, which was invented in the latter part of the fifteenth century (Leonardo da Vinci is named as one of the earliest users of the principle), was not supposed to have been introduced

into North America until the close of the eighteenth century. Here,
however, is belated proof of an astonishing fact, that far out in the
wilderness a miniature lock system was constructed and used in the
first half of the seventeenth.

The clump of frame buildings on stone foundations which made
up the chief part of Ste. Marie was surrounded by a series of walls
and bastions of considerable strength. Behind these walls the European compound was divided from the Indian by the water channel
rising through the medium of the locks, as already explained. A gate
in the wall connecting the eastern bastions served as the main entrance. It will be recognized at once that this was a far cry from the
wood palisades which had been the main feature of fortifications up
to this time. Everything, in fact, had been carried out in accordance
with European practice, and it was believed that the mission could
be held against any Indian attack.

Within the walls were two main buildings, the larger being a two-
story structure which undoubtedly was used as living quarters for the
priests. It had a main chimney twenty-eight feet high which provided
the fathers with a hearth of such size that all members of the staff
could sit within comfortable range of the fire on cold evenings. In
front of this main hearth was a pit two feet deep. This had been used
as a storage place for books and documents, the Indians being so
intensely inquisitive that such measures were necessary.

The other main building was the chapel, which was sufficiently
impressive to make it, in the eyes of the natives, the first wonder of
the world. There were also sundry structures of lesser size, kitchens
and service buildings including carpenter and blacksmith shops.

This was only the inner core of the mission. The outer portions,
which provided adequate quarters for the natives, were enclosed by
a double wooden palisade of irregular construction. Four buildings
stood inside the palisades, including an Indian long house where
the dusky visitors slept, a hospital of European construction with
a large stone fireplace, and a chapel with a high peaked roof which
accommodated large congregations. In this enclosure the hospitable
fathers had looked after as many as seven hundred Christian Indians
in a two-week period, feeding them three bountiful meals a day as
well as serving their spiritual needs. It was the desire to be tended
in illness and buried in death which brought most of them to Ste.
Marie. There was a large and well-tended cemetery within the high
palisades.

The COUNTRY of the HURONS

palacios

The mission, over which Father Ragueneau presided as Superior, had a rather considerable European population. The highest number recorded was in 1645, when the total reached fifty-eight, which included twenty-two soldiers. In addition to the priests, who numbered eighteen and were absent generally at their posts throughout the country, there was a full complement of lay members. Robert le Coq was the business manager, although no title of the kind was applied to him. It was one of his duties to make yearly trips to Quebec to arrange for the necessary yearly supplies. Charles Boivin was the master builder and carpenter, Joseph Molère the apothecary, Ambrose Brouet the cook, Louis Gauber the blacksmith, Pierre Masson the tailor, and Christophe Regnaut the bootmaker. These men were either *donnés or engagés*. The former were lay members who received no pay but were supplied with food, shelter, and clothing. It was promised the *donnés* that they would be supported by the Society in their old age. The *engagés* were volunteers who served without pay but were permitted to engage in the fur trade while working for the Society.

Around Ste. Marie were great stretches of tilled land where crops of grain and vegetables were raised and fruit trees of all kinds. In the fields the white workers were assisted by converts, and the agricultural branch was so well handled that in the spring of 1649, when the threat of Iroquois aggression obscured the sky like a dark cloud, a surplus of food was reported sufficient for three years.

2

It was to this active center of missionary effort that alarming rumors came during the winter of 1647–48. The Iroquois had broken the peace. A war party of unprecedented size—the Huron scouts said it numbered twelve hundred braves—had ascended the Ottawa and was wintering in the country around Lake Nipissing. This could mean one thing only, that the main attack was to be directed against the Huron people.

This intelligence inspired so much terror that free communication with the French settlements in the East came to an abrupt stop. The fur fleets, with their noisy show, did not go down the Ottawa as usual. However, the Huron hunters used up their supplies so quickly that they were dependent on the French for their metal weapons and utensils (they believed that the King of France held his rank because he made the largest kettles). It became necessary to reach Quebec, and in the early summer an effort was made to get in touch with the East. So great was the fear inspired by the Iroquois that an escort of two hundred and fifty warriors was provided. The departure of this large body of fighting men, which was a serious mistake on the part of the Hurons, served as a signal to the enemy to begin operations. They came silently down the river, traveling by night, their fierce eyes turned to the west where the nation lived which they had sworn to destroy.

The most vulnerable of the Huron villages was St. Joseph, or Teanostaiae, because it lay on the extreme south border and could not obtain assistance quickly. Normally it was the largest, having two thousand inhabitants, but at this tragic moment many of its able-bodied men were with the party going by way of the Ottawa to Ville Marie. The mission at St. Joseph was a large one, with a highly devout priest, Father Antoine Daniel, in charge.

On July 4 Father Daniel was celebrating early Mass, and an unusually large gathering filled the chapel. It promised to be a warm day, and already a strong sun was flooding through the windows and lighting the interior. Suddenly the resonant voice of the priest was interrupted by a cry from the palisades, "The *Hotinonsionni!* The *Hotinonsionni!*"

Father Daniel raised his hand as a signal that the service could not be continued and then hurried to the door of the chapel. To his dismay he saw that the Iroquois had already made a breach in the palisade and were pouring into the town. Naked warriors, armed with guns and mad with blood lust, were pouring through the breach. The din was unearthly, horrible, indescribable.

The priest realized that this was the end, for the village, for his flock, and for him. He went back to the front and baptized the panic-stricken people who crowded about him, pleading for protection. Then, in his white alb and red stole, and carrying a large cross in front of him, he strode out again to the entrance.

By this time the Iroquois were in almost complete possession and the work of butchery had begun. The screams of the victims mingled with the bestial cries of the attackers. It is said that the Iroquois paused when they first glimpsed through the furious confusion the figure of the fearless priest emerging from the chapel with unhurried steps, raising the cross high above his head. If they did, it was for a moment only. They surged about him, and an overzealous arrow (the accurate aim robbing them of what they desired most, a Black-Gown as a captive) struck him down.

The town was set on fire and for a day and night thereafter a heavy pall of smoke rose above the treetops to tell the rest of the Huron country that the foul hand of aggression had struck. The victors then made off as fleetly and silently as they had come, taking with them seven hundred terrified prisoners. The mind recoils from contemplation of the orgies which followed when they reached their villages among the Finger Lakes.

The summer passed with no more than small and sporadic attacks, but in the fall a second Iroquois party made its way up the Ottawa to winter in the woods of the North. This meant another attack, and the Hurons had no difficulty in deciding where it would fall. The eastern frontier was open to attack and the enemy might be expected to cross the Severn and, putting the North River and the Coldwater behind them, fall upon St. Ignace and St. Louis and the nest of smaller villages scattered about them. An idea of the compactness of the Huron country is supplied by the fact that St. Ignace, which was regarded as dangerously exposed, was in reality no more than eight miles east of the stone ramparts of Ste. Marie.

3

Had a little more time been granted, the village of St. Ignace would have been made impregnable to any attack the Iroquois might launch. It was situated on a high flat ridge, six acres in extent, which protruded from the wooded hills behind it like the blunted head of an arrow. The sides of this elevated ground were so steep that they could not be scaled. To defend the relatively level approach, the elder statesmen of the community had planned strong fortifications across this strip, which was no more than one hundred yards wide. There were to be triple palisades with bastions extending out far enough to cover all approaches, and the main entrance was to be massive. It was intended, in fact, to make St. Ignace an outer fort of great strength for the whole of the Huron country. The extensive archaeological investigations carried on here by Mr. Jury indicate that many buildings of considerable size were under construction when the blow fell which wiped out the village for all time. Two of them were long houses, one hundred feet long and thirty wide. These were the largest, but of the twenty-six houses which made up the community many were of major size. Several of these were not finished, and some which seemed to have been ready for occupation gave no indication of having been lived in. Obviously the village was not feeling the need for such extensive additional accommodation to meet normal growth. It was being readied for a purpose, which quite clearly was the protection of the vulnerable eastern flank of the country; to become a garrison town to meet the first shocks of Iroquois aggression.

Such was the plain. There had been much procrastination during the winter months, however. The men of St. Ignace had hugged their fires according to custom and had done little. This must have dismayed the two priests who were responsible for the welfare of the nest of villages which lay behind St. Ignace. Father Brébeuf, who has been mentioned often, had this part of the country in his charge, with the assistance of Father Gabriel Lalemant, a nephew of Jerome Lalemant.

St. Louis lay halfway between St. Ignace and Ste. Marie, and here the two priests had established themselves. Often during the long winter the brave pair left their small fire at St. Louis and tramped over the rolling hills to the outpost village to urge that the work be continued. They presented a marked contrast, these two faithful shepherds. Father Brébeuf was a massive man, far above the average in height and strongly built. Father Lalemant was small and of uncertain health. The older man always strode ahead, his puny assistant following at his heels. The Hurons had great respect for each of them, but nothing could stir them out of their apathy, not even the prospect of an attack when the snows melted.

Jean de Brébeuf was, without a doubt, the best loved of all the missionary priests. A Norman by birth and of good family, he had joined the Society early. He had now been twenty-two years in the mission field and during that time he had been unfailingly kind and brave, bringing to his work the devotion of a sublime faith. As the years rolled on and the shoulders of the tall priest became a little bent and his dark hair and beard turned to gray, the Hurons grew so attached to him that his absence would seem the greatest of misfortunes. They called him affectionately *Echon*. Once he had been away from them on a long journey, and when his tall figure in its tight black soutane was seen approaching through the woods, they rushed out to greet him.

"Here is Echon come again!" they shouted.

Everyone in the village saluted him, touching his hand and saying over and over, "Echon, my nephew, my brother, my cousin, hast thou then come again?"

It is pleasant to think of them flocking about him, the sober brown children fearing to touch so much as the hem of his garment, their elders nodding their heads and throwing their usual taciturnity to the winds as they assailed him with questions. In all the villages where duty took him, they knew the sound of his solid footstep, they loved the deep notes of his voice.

He was, above everything else, a modest man. On joining the Society he had been so conscious of what he deemed his shortcomings that he asked to be no more than a brother coadjutor instead of a full member. On the trail he always took the heaviest loads at the portages and made the most frequent trips. He rowed or paddled without stopping from the start to the finish of the day.

"I am an ox," he would say, referring to his name, "and fit only to bear burdens."

He would speak at times with great power and even eloquence, but ordinarily he was inclined to slowness of thought and speech. When men of quicker perceptions goaded him with their sharpness, he never lost his dignity or benignity; his answers would be kindly and fair, and to the point.

Because he often said, "God has treated me with so much mildness," it was in his thought that he would die by violence. At times he had been visited by a recurring vision, Death attached to a post with hands bound behind. Because of this, it was clear in his mind that death would come to him through the instrumentality of those insatiable conquerors, the Iroquois.

4

The blow fell on the morning of March 16 of this sanguinary year, 1649. Although they were prepared in Huronia for an attack from the war party wintering in the North, there was no thought that the attack would come as early as this. The ice had not yet broken up on the rivers; there was still heavy snow on the ground; the winds from the north still blew with relentless vigor. The elder statesmen at St. Ignace drowsed over their pipes, and the permanent palisades had not been raised over that hundred-yard strip. There was still some time of peace to be enjoyed: let the inevitable tragedy be faced at its appointed time! So many of the able-bodied men were hunting in the woods that most of the houses were unoccupied except for the very old and the very young.

The Hurons had never been blessed with much imagination and even less initiative. They never understood the deep cunning of the Iroquois mind nor prepared themselves for the new methods of surprise which those fertile military brains devised.

The tall priest and the puny one were at St. Louis, having walked over together the night before from a week end of retreat and contemplation at Ste. Marie. The community was roused before dawn by the frantic cries of three Hurons who came racing through the woods, their faces filled with terror. The Iroquois had struck St. Ignace, scaling the makeshift walls before anyone in the doomed village was awake. These three alone had been able to get away, and the answers they gave to the hysterical questions showered on them contained no grain of comfort. The men of the Long House were as numerous as the empty shells on the shore (there were, it developed, a thousand Mohawk and Seneca warriors in the party) and they were all armed with guns. They would soon be swarming through the woods to add the destruction of St. Louis to the sacking of St. Ignace.

The terrified trio were right on the last point. As the sun came up over the trees with the promise of a day which would be clear and fresh and untainted with evil, save the evil that men would do, the topknot of the first Mohawk was seen in the woods; and in a matter of seconds the space around the palisades of the village was filled with terrifying figures. The Iroquois had smeared the blood of the dead at St. Ignace over their heads and faces and they were screeching with great frenzy for more victims.

There were only eighty Huron warriors in St. Louis, but with a courage which amounted to rashness they had decided to stay and fight it out instead of seeking sanctuary behind the stone walls of Ste. Marie. Stephen Annaotaha, one of the bravest of Huron chiefs, was there and had been firm in the resolution to fight. The sick and the old had been routed out and sent to Ste. Marie.

"My brothers, save yourselves!" the chief had said to the two priests. "Go now, while there is time!"

Father Brébeuf must have known that at last the fate he had apprehended had found him out, but he knew also how great would be the need for him before this day of blood was over. He would not leave. Father Lalemant, whose delicacy of constitution had made life in the wilds an incredible hardship, was equally determined to remain with the doomed flock.

It did not take long for the attacking party to make a breach in the walls. They swarmed into the village, a thousand strong; and the eighty Hurons, fighting doggedly and repelling the first thrusts, were soon killed or captured. Brébeuf and his companion were in the thick of it, tending the wounded and administering the last rites to the dying. Unfortunately for them they were not killed as Father Daniel had been. They were captured and led away when the screeching horde decided to enjoy their victory orgies at St. Ignace.

5

Jean de Brébeuf and Gabriel Lalemant were led out to the platform which had been raised for the torturing of the prisoners, raised up high so that all of the bloodthirsty mob could watch and take delight in the "caressing" of the victims. The two priests had been stripped to the skin, and the younger man, conscious of the boniness of his frame and filled with a sense of shame, quoted to his companion the words of St. Paul, "Truly, this day, Father, we are made a spectacle to the world, and to angels and to men."

Father Brébeuf was to die first; Lalemant, for a time, was to watch. The tall priest kissed the stake before they chained him to it, and in a loud voice he exhorted his companions in misfortune to keep stout hearts. He was first scorched from head to foot with blazing torches and all the nails were torn from his fingers. A Huron renegade, who had been baptized by the good priest, cried out, "Echon, thou sayest that the sufferings of this life lead straight to paradise: thou wilt go soon, for I am going to baptize thee." The renegade then took kettles filled with boiling water and poured them over the gray head which was held so high, crying out with a mad delight, "Go to heaven, for thou art well baptized."

The most frightful of all the tortures practiced was the application of the collar. This was not new. It had been used often enough by the Hurons and Algonquins as well as the Iroquois, and it seems to have been with all of them their favorite refinement of cruelty. This was how it was done: they took a large withe of green wood and attached to it six hatchets which had been heated white-hot over the flames. This they hung over the shoulders of the man at

the stake. If the victim leaned forward to rid his chest of the excruciating pain of this diabolical necklace, the sizzling iron sank
deeper into the back; and so every move, every instinctive shrinking
of the flesh, added to the torment. There was intense excitement, a
depravity of slavering jowls, among the capering, jeering braves
when this infernal instrument was placed around the neck of Father
Brébeuf. The smell of scorching flesh could be detected at once,
but that indomitable man disappointed them by making no move,
by uttering no sound.

Then they proceeded to encase his mutilated body in a bark
weasand belt which had been made inflammable with pitch and
resin, and to this they set fire. His flesh, already torn and scalded,
began to roast in this sheath of fire, but his deep voice never faltered
or broke as he then began to exhort the watchers and to beg forgiveness for them. To stop that brave voice the angry tribesmen cut off
both his lips and part of his tongue. Then they stripped the flesh
from his thighs and arms, roasting it in the fire which was consuming
him and eating it before his eyes, in which a faint spark of consciousness still burned.

Father Brébeuf had been the most conversant of all the priests
with the native tongues, and one of his labors had been the translation of the Lord's Prayer into Huron. Perhaps the strange words
came back into his tortured mind and, while his lips still held a
power of utterance, he began to pronounce them; a final act of devotion as the shades closed about him:

"Onaistan de aronhise istare. Sasin tehon . . ."

Father Brébeuf, the much-loved Echon, was tortured from noon
of that red and wrathful day until four in the afternoon. When his
heart had been torn from his body and eaten—it was scrambled for
because he had died so bravely—they threw his broken body into
the flames; but the embers were dying down about the stake, and
what was left of him, resolute even in death, refused to be consumed.

The frail body of Father Lalemant, who was called by his flock
Atironta, resisted death for eleven hours.

Huron survivors of the deviltries of St. Ignace, one of them with
an arrow in his eye, reached Ste. Marie and told what had happened.
When the Iroquois war party made an unexpectedly sudden departure, as will be recounted later, the sorrowful fathers went to the

smoking ruins of St. Ignace and found there the bodies of the two martyrs. The condition of the remains confirmed everything the eye-witnesses had told of the tortures to which the brave veteran and his frail companion had been subjected.

Included in the party was one of the *donnés*, Christophe Regnaut, who served as bootmaker at Ste. Marie. He made a report on what they found, which read in part as follows: "We buried these precious relics on Sunday, the twenty-first day of March, 1649, with much consolation. . . . When we left the country of the Hurons, we raised both bodies out of the ground and set them to boil in strong lye. All the bones were well scraped, and the care of drying them was given to me. I put them every day into a little oven which we had, made of clay, after having heated it slightly; and, when in a state to be packed, they were separately enveloped in silk stuff. Then they were put into two small chests, and we brought them to Quebec, where they are held in great veneration."

Thus Christophe Regnaut was much privileged. He had made the shoes in which the great tall priest and the brave small one had gone about their duties in the rolling slopes of the forest about St. Ignace and in which, no doubt, they walked that day to their deaths; and in the end he was allowed to tend what the fires had left of that devout pair.

6

Following the capture of St. Louis and the killing of the two priests, Huron warriors from other parts of the country came up to assist in repelling the attacks. The largest band came from the populous village of Ossossané, the headquarters of the family of the Bear. Ossossané was a little less than nine miles south and west of Ste. Marie and most picturesquely located on the shores of Notta-wasaga. It was here that the mission of La Conception had been so successful that it came to be called "the Believers Valley," and it followed that the rescue party was made up very largely of Christians. They passed the southern tip of Lake Isaragui (now called Mud Lake) and struck due east, the sooner to reach the scene of the fighting. They were three hundred strong and at first they took the upper hand. They drove the invaders who had remained at St. Louis back into the smoking ruins of the stockade. Iroquois scouts carried the word to St. Ignace, where, after his long hours of torture,

Father Lalemant had finally found escape in death. The men of the Five Nations, glutted with blood and their victory feast, turned savagely to meet the attack. The Bear warriors found themselves outnumbered three to one and were surrounded in turn. They fought bravely and the struggle lasted for the better part of a day. In the end, of course, numbers prevailed and all but thirty of the Hurons were killed.

This bold effort, without a doubt, saved Ste. Marie. Since the tragic moment when the smoke of St. Ignace had first been visible above the treetops, the Frenchmen had stationed themselves on guard on the stone walls, forty in all. They expected to be attacked at any moment and had small hope of withstanding a siege by such a large band. At one stage they sighted Iroquois scouts in the edge of the forest, and they looked well to the priming of their guns, thinking that the moment had come. At this point, however, the rescue party from Ossossané struck at St. Louis, and the struggle there engaged the full attention of the invaders until the brave Christians had been subdued.

It was then that a strange misapprehension took possession of the Iroquois leaders. They had everything in their own hands. Only a few small Huron parties remained at large in the woods. Somehow the invaders became convinced that large forces were gathering to hem them in, and a sense almost of panic showed itself in their councils. It was decided that they had accomplished as much as they could hope to and that the time had come to retire to their own country. They moved with extraordinary speed to carry out the withdrawal. At one moment their advance scouts swarmed in the woods, and the only question seemed to be where the blow would be struck; the next, seemingly, all was silence in the forest and the smoking ruins of the villages were deserted. It was hard for the weary men who had been standing guard on the walls of Ste. Marie for so long to believe that fate, or an ever-watchful Providence, had stretched forth a hand to save them. Finally they became convinced that the enemy had disappeared. The Iroquois were racing eastward again and would cross the Coldwater and North rivers in a mad haste to reach the neutral country which lay beyond the Severn. With savage temper they were driving their prisoners before them, dispatching any who showed physical weakness or an inability to hold the pace.

The unexpected withdrawal of the Iroquois came too late to save the Huron nation. Certain that the relentless warriors from the Finger Lakes would come back, and keep coming back until no one was left to oppose them, the despondent Hurons began to scatter. The Believers Village was deserted so completely that no sound was heard there save the lapping of the waves on the shore. Not knowing what to do, the homeless Christians, most of them women and children, wandered into the Petun country and begged to be taken in. Others migrated still farther south, after burning their villages and destroying their crops, to find sanctuary with the Neutrals and the Eries. The few who remained betook themselves to Ste. Marie, where the busy mission staff had to serve six thousand meals in the first few days.

No will to remain in their own land animated the few survivors. They moved to an island off the northern tip of Nottawasaga which the French named later St. Joseph's. It was a large island and capable of accommodating the refugees. The thoroughly demoralized Hurons, believing they would be safe there, urged the mission staff at Ste. Marie to follow them.

With the utmost reluctance the Jesuit fathers at Ste. Marie decided they would have to move. Their charges had deserted them and they could serve no good purpose by remaining in the desolation to which this once populous land had been reduced. On May 15 they set fire to all the buildings and removed to the island, using for the purpose one fishing boat and a very large raft for the transportation of their livestock. The move was a major operation, for a large stock of possessions had accumulated at the mission headquarters over the course of the years. They had domestic animals, which could not be left behind, and a surplus of corn and vegetables; enough of a surplus, it was believed, to last for three years.

It became apparent at once that the food surplus would be needed. The poor Hurons, who seem to have lost all energy and initiative, were subsisting on acorns and a very bitter root they called *otsa*, sometimes being reduced to living off garlic, which they baked under ashes. Fish abounded in the waters about the island, but they lacked boats to take advantage of this and were not attempting to build any new ones.

The Jesuit fathers took matters in hand. They provided food for the starving refugees and they began to build a very strong fort, which they named Ste. Marie II, against the possibility of future attacks. They had the one reward for which they might have asked.

The Hurons, in their despair, turned to the teachings of the missionaries. During this tragic period more than fourteen hundred were baptized and admitted to the Church.

Thus it came about that the first objective of the forward-looking Iroquois had been achieved. The Hurons no longer existed as a nation. Scattered in all directions, they would never again draw themselves together. A few remained permanently on the islands of Georgian Bay, and more still moved westward to Mackinac Island at the northern end of Lake Huron. Those who had taken refuge with the Neutral Nations gradually lost their identity. For twenty-two years the missionaries had labored among them, and now not a single living soul was left in all of that once beautiful land. The forests were as silent as before the coming of man. The only evidences left of Huron occupation were the trails through the forest, the blackened ruins of villages, and at St. Ignace, perhaps, the charred stake where Jean de Brébeuf had given up his life.

7

During the summer of that blackest of years stray parties of Hurons continued to find their way to St. Joseph's until the refugee population numbered seven thousand. This made the situation a serious one, for the resources of the island were not sufficient to feed so large a number. Despite the efforts of the Jesuit fathers, there was starvation during the winter which followed, and epidemics carried off a large part of the disorganized and disheartened Hurons. In the spring they began to scatter again, many of them going still farther west to join a kindred tribe, the Wyandots. This led to a decision which was taken later, to transport as many as possible of the Christian natives to Quebec.

In the meantime the Iroquois had returned to the attack. The only missionaries left in the field were among the Algonquins who lived along the northern shores of Georgian Bay and in the Petun country, where three mission posts were maintained, St. Matthieu, St. Jean, and St. Mathias. The Iroquois decided to break the neutrality they had maintained up to this point with the Petun tribe and on December 7 they attacked St. Jean. It was so unexpected that no measures of defense had been taken and the inhabitants were all slaughtered, including one of the mission priests, Father Garnier. Another priest, Father Chabanel, had left St. Jean to escort a party of the homeless Hurons to St. Joseph's, and they had progressed a short distance only when a war party closed in on them. All of the party left the priest and scattered for safety, the last to depart, a renegade Huron, killing him and disposing of his body in a stream.

The list of martyrs was mounting fast—Jogues, Daniel, Brébeuf, Lalemant, Garnier, Chabanel—but more were to join the roll call of glory. Father Garreau was shot later while on his way to join the Algonquins, and others died as a result of the conditions which the Indian wars imposed. The Iroquois, in the meantime, continued to make war on all tribes within reach of their conquering bands, the Neutrals, the Eries, the Cat People. They became so much feared that all tribes along the eastern seaboard paid tribute to them.

Conditions became so impossible on St. Joseph's that it was decided finally, and after much thought and heartburning, to abandon it as a mission center. On June 10, 1650, they began the homeward trek, sixty Frenchmen and several hundred Hurons. After an arduous journey of nearly two months they reached Quebec. The following year the Hurons were moved to the island of Orleans, where, it was believed, they could live in security and peace.

The efforts of the Jesuits had not come to an end. They were as determined as ever to accomplish the christianization of the native stock. But it was apparent that until the power of the Iroquois was broken or the war could be brought to a lasting end their work would be confined to the scattered Indians who subsisted close to the fortified centers or who had removed to the far North.

CHAPTER XVI

Richelieu Dies and Mazarin Takes
His Place—A Troublesome Period Is Reached
in the Affairs of New France—
A Strange Feud in Acadia

1

CARDINAL RICHELIEU was dying, and the news of his impending demise was received in New France with forebodings. He had been the father of the new policy which took the control of affairs out of the hands of grasping merchants and vested it in the state. Although stern and exacting, he had striven to assist the struggling colony, even though the cost seemed far out of proportion to the slow progress being made.

The great cardinal was now fifty-seven and his frame, always frail, was wasted with disease. His right arm was paralyzed, his body was covered with ulcers, his eyes seemed unhumanly large in the sunken framework of his face; but his intelligence burned as fiercely as ever and his will had lost none of its iron quality. He kept as closely in touch with every phase of governmental activity as he had done in his prime, even to the extent of following the campaigns in Flanders and the South. To do so the dying man had made extraordinary arrangements.

This is how the inexorable and unforgiving churchman kept himself in the heat and pressure of things when by all the rules he should have been dying in his great bed, canopied with purple taffeta, in the Palais-Cardinal. He had a movable apartment made for his use, a truly amazing cabinet which was large enough to contain a replica of his regular bed as well as a table and a chair for his confidential secretary and a small anteroom as well. The cardinal, being a lover of color and a sybarite in general, had insisted that the cabinet be upholstered with scarlet velvet. It was carried on wheels over the roads which led to the fronts where French armies were locked in conflict with the Hapsburg forces, or on boats plying up and down the rivers. On water he would be accompanied by a fleet of river boats and barges, all carefully guarded by his own musketeers in their scarlet livery, on shore by a long cavalcade of mounted men and carriages with supplies. Such arrangements must have strained an income even as large as the cardinal's three million crowns a year.

At night it would be necessary to find accommodations for the dying statesman and his huge mobile establishment. The castle or inn selected for the honor would be adorned with hangings of rose and velvet damask and with the costly furniture which was brought for the purpose. Then the apartment would be taken off its wheels or removed from the barge, carried by a special corps of trained servants. It was usually too wide to go through doors, and a hole would be torn in a wall to admit the cardinal on his wide bed.

Affairs of state were conducted in this way as thoroughly, if not quite as expeditiously, as though the great man had remained in his ostentatious Paris headquarters, the Palais-Cardinal. Couriers rode up on smoking horses, carrying dispatches, and others rode away with the answers. Secretaries took down the whispered instructions of the sick man; clerks scribbled and copied letters. Spies waited in the anteroom to make their reports (the cardinal was one of the ablest spy masters of history); the nobility came with haughty and withdrawn faces, but carrying their plumed hats in their hands, to pay their respects to this man they both hated and feared.

Late in the year 1642 it became apparent that the cardinal would have to yield to his inevitable conqueror, although the star of his power was as high overhead as ever. The latest conspiracy, the famous Cinq Mars affair, had been scotched and his enemies had scuttled into their uneasy mouseholes. The main conspirators were going to the block, where so many top-ranking nobles had already been sent. The power of the nobility had been broken. The citadel at Perpignan had fallen on September 9, thus bringing the Spanish campaign to a most satisfactory conclusion. Returning home to die, the cardinal took the route of the Rhone River with all his circus-like trappings and came at last to Paris with so little life left in his emaciated body that even the light in his terrible eyes seemed to be failing. His devoted niece, the Duchess d'Aiguillon, who will be remembered as the sponsor of the Hôtel-Dieu in Quebec, remained faithfully and affectionately by his side, disregarding his orders to spare herself by leaving.

When the last rites were administered, he was asked the usual question:

"Do you forgive your enemies?"

There was a pause, and then the dying churchman answered, "I have no enemies but those of the state."

These few words summed up the guiding policy of the renowned statesman. The state, absolute in its authority, above challenge in its operations, had been his creation. The supreme power he had vested in the Crown would be maintained throughout the long reign which followed, the outwardly splendid period of the Sun King, Louis XIV. Those who opposed him were in the mind of Richelieu enemies of the state, dissenters from his dream of a triumphant France.

When the news reached them that the cardinal had breathed his last on December 4 of that year, it seemed to the settlers of New France that they had lost their best friend. Viewing the question with the easy perspective of three centuries, it is clear that the opposite was the truth. His interest had been aggressively addressed to the growth and prosperity of the colony, but he had established the policy of control by the Crown, and the ministers thereof, so firmly that nothing thereafter could change it. He had been the architect of ultimate failure.

Having said this, it must be granted that New France under his successor, whose attitude was one almost of indifference, came to a very bad pass indeed.

2

It had been understood that the cardinal's successor would be Father Joseph of Paris. That very able man, however, had preceded his master to the grave by a narrow margin of years. The matter of a successor had become at once of paramount importance, because Louis XIII was also marked for an early translation to a realm where kings are not supposed to enjoy any privilege above their personal deserts. The fevered orbs of the determined little minister had fixed themselves, therefore, on another churchman, a Sicilian named Giulio Mazarin, who had been drafted into the French service three years before and had so distinguished himself on several diplomatic errands that his reward had been a red hat from Rome; thus becoming the famous Cardinal Mazarin of romance and history. He was a man of quite enormous ability and the equal, or nearly so, of Richelieu in diplomacy and administrative skill but not possessing the same full measure of genius.

Mazarin was a personable man, forty years of age, with curling chestnut hair and beard, a fresh complexion and fine eyes, and a pair of hands remarkable for their whiteness and delicacy. Women were partial to him, as will become apparent later.

Mazarin was at the bedside when the great cardinal died, and the next day King Louis XIII sent instructions to all the departmental officials to make their reports thereafter to the new chief minister. The King himself had only a few more months to live and so his acknowledgment of the succession was of the greatest importance.

But how would the new incumbent impress the Queen, Anne of Austria? It was understood that on the King's death she would be made Queen Regent for the minority of her young son. As things turned out, there was no need for worry on that score. That lady of gentle spirit and quiet beauty (who was becoming, alas, a little plump now) had already met the new cardinal. Authorities disagree as to where or when the meeting occurred, although it is generally believed that it took place at a court function and that Mazarin was looking resplendent in purple vestments. It was generally believed also that the warm and romantic heart of the Queen, which had been only slightly stirred by the handsome, long-legged Buckingham, began to flutter as soon as she saw the cardinal. At any rate, when the King died on May 14 of the following year, the promptly appointed Regent overlooked her own special supporters, who had expected to bound into office, and confirmed Mazarin in his post.

New France was to suffer for many years thereafter as a result of ministerial lack of interest. Not until the new King had grown up and attained his majority and had surrounded himself with able ministers, Colbert in particular, would the handling of New France be placed on a stronger basis.

It was not surprising that Mazarin failed to take the same interest in the colony as his illustrious predecessor. He was new to the complications and vexations of colonization, the politics within the ranks of the Hundred Associates, the greed, the fears, the continuous pressure of free traders who still rebelled against monopoly. The company had been bankrupt almost from the start. With a grandiose gesture, dictated no doubt by Richelieu, they had invested their total capital in the fleet under De Roquement and had seen it lost when the Kirkes captured all their ships. Several plans had been followed since to provide new funds, but the company had continued in a condition best described as moribund. In 1641 the directors had found it necessary to place an assessment on the members and in this way raised 103,500 livres; a measure which had caused a great deal of grumbling. The situation had become temporarily more satisfactory, however. The beaver population of North America was estimated by various authorities at ten million. The Hurons and Algonquins, released from fear by the spurious peace treaty offered by the Iroquois, began to bring beaver skins to the French trading posts in enormous quantities. In Europe every ruffling gallant and every stout burgher wanted a beaver hat. The value of the trade at this point rose to 300,000 livres a year.

Then the Iroquois struck again, and the first result was that the Hurons as a separate race passed out of existence. The officials appointed for the colony might have been capable of providing a reasonable peacetime administration, but they were completely unfitted for the situaton which now developed.

The men of the Five Nations were actuated by more than hate for the northern tribes. The war they waged was, in a broad sense, a beaver war; colloquially, a "castor" war, that being the name applied to the beaver skin. The heads of the Iroquois realized that, having cast their lot with the Dutch and the English, they must divert the fur trade from the French. With their usual sagacity they saw that the Ottawa River was the key to the situation and so their largest war parties patrolled the Ottawa country, making it impossible for the northern Indians to form their giant flotillas and convey the year's take of furs to the St. Lawrence.

For two years after the great blow which wiped out St. Ignace and St. Louis and led to the dispersal of the Hurons the beaver trade came temporarily to an end. Not one pelt arrived at Montreal. It was then that the French began to meet the situation by going out in small parties to the source of supply. The *coureurs de bois*, picturesque and gallant, came into existence. The Iroquois could prevent the running of the great fleets, but they could not control all the northern rivers where these French traders, filled with a love of adventure as well as a desire for profit, began to appear. It was in recognition of this new development that the Associates relinquished their exclusive hold on the fur trade to the more powerful inhabitants of New France, the seigneurs of the St. Lawrence—Giffard, Repentigny, Godefroy, Des Chatelets. It was estimated that the profits which accrued to these traders who had the advantage of operating at close range amounted annually to 325,000 livres, laying the foundation for the wealth of the seigneurial class.

It was not plain sailing, however, for the new fur princes of New France. The men who braved the dangers of the northern trails, who were to venture as far north as Hudson's Bay and westward beyond the Great Lakes, these men quite properly thought themselves entitled to a large personal share of the profits. They began to find ways of smuggling furs out of the country. It became the practice for even the lesser employees, the men who tended the warehouses and posted the books, to desert to the fishing fleets, taking large supplies of pelts with them.

The affronted Associates came to realize that monopoly was a losing proposition. They closed their books finally, and their doors, in 1663.

This was a hornets' nest which Mazarin found above his door. He was not successful in handling the situation, the chief reason being the caliber of the men who were sent out as governors at this trying period. Montmagny was recalled, and out came Jean de Lauson, the one-time intendant of the Company of One Hundred Associates and the first owner of the island of Montreal. A civilian filling a post which called for soldierly qualities, Lauson was seated in the Quebec citadel at a particularly dangerous stage and proved himself a complete failure, as will be told later.

3

No attention has been paid to Acadia while these events were transpiring along the St. Lawrence, but it must not be assumed that there is any lack of interest in the events occurring in the wooded inlets around the Bay of Fundy. A quite extraordinary situation had developed there.

A son of the Sieur de Poutrincourt had been left behind when the settlers at Port Royal were carried off in the Argall raid. With a handful of followers he roamed in the woods. They lived like Indians, subsisting on game and fish and dressing themselves in animal skins. The young leader, who is referred to in the records as Biencourt, finally succeeded in constructing a small fort among the rocks and fogs of Cape Sable, to which he gave the name of Fort Loméron. Here the band remained for a number of years, waiting impatiently for sails on the horizon.

It came about that this resolute young man died before the pennons of France came into view. He left all his lands and possessions and rights to one of his followers, a highly ambitious Norman named Charles St. Etienne de la Tour; at least La Tour declared that the cession had been made in his favor. There was, however, a strong suspicion in French governmental circles that La Tour was playing a double game by negotiating with the English, who still held to their claim that they owned all this part of the world. It is doubtful if La Tour, who adhered to what he considered his own with a grip of iron, had ever been prepared to hand over his lands to the English, but it was established that he had been made a baronet of Nova Scotia by Charles I of England, a most suspicious circumstance. It was not strange, therefore, that the French Government was very cautious in the matter of recognizing any of his claims.

Under favorable conditions La Tour might have become one of the great colonizers and trail breakers. Certainly he possessed many of the qualities required, the determination, the resourcefulness, the unbridled ambition. Shrugging off the coldness of the administration, he proceeded to widen the scope of his operations by building himself another fort. This time he selected as the site a highly strategic point, the mouth of the St. John River on the other side of the Bay of Fundy.

The government finally decided to take action and in 1632 sent out Charles de Razilly to take formal possession of Acadia after the country had been ceded to France by the Treaty of St.-Germainen-Laye. Razilly died three years later and nominated his chief associate, one Charles de Menou d'Aunay Charnisey, to take over his duties. D'Aunay, as he is called in the records, seems to have been a man of the best character. He was both courageous and devout, courteous in his dealings, a loyal servant of the government. That he developed aggressive and even arrogant traits in the course of his long duel with La Tour cannot be denied, but it must be taken into account that he was dealing with an opponent who would go to any lengths. D'Aunay had, it must also be said, a touch of the grandiose in him, a willingness to dramatize his importance. At any rate, he set himself up at Port Royal like a great suzerain. He brought out a wife, with countless barrels and bales of possessions, and a great many settlers to resume cultivation of the fertile land. Port Royal became a feudal stronghold; a fort with a garrison, a seminary with no fewer than twelve Capuchin friars, a harbor dotted with the sails of ships, a settlement with a constant coming and going of Indians with furs to trade.

La Tour and the men about him considered all this an infringement of their rights. They had upheld the sovereignty of France through the long bleak years (said La Tour), living lives of hardship, with no support from home and little hope to bring them comfort. They refused to acknowledge the authority of D'Aunay, and so began one of the most curious struggles in history.

It would take a whole volume to tell in detail the ups and downs of this struggle, the attacks that each side made on the possessions of the other, the bitter controversy their adherents waged in France, the backing and filling, the hatreds and cruelties. La Tour would not have been able to keep up such an uneven duel if he had not secured the aid of the English settlers at Boston. Plausible and adroit, he convinced the hardheaded Pilgrims that their best interests would be served by helping him to get the upper hand, and they went to the length of sending ships and men to aid him in his efforts. He also brought out a wife, a courageous Amazon named Marie Jacquelin, but as she was the daughter of a barber of Mans, she did not have the rich wardrobe or the fine possessions with which the highborn Madame d'Aunay had brought refinement and distinction to the somewhat baronial halls of Port Royal. She proved so strong a partisan, however, that La Tour left her in charge of the fort at St. John when he made one of his visits to Boston.

D'Aunay took advantage of his rival's absence to besiege the fort. Madame la Tour fought to the last ditch, encouraging the men of the garrison when they began to lose stomach for more resistance. When the place was taken finally, D'Aunay hanged some of the garrison and kept Madame la Tour a prisoner until she died. In his report D'Aunay declared that the resolute lady "died of spite and rage."

Shortly after this tragic occurrence things took a turn. D'Aunay was immersed in the cold waters of Annapolis Basin when his canoe upset and died of the exposure. He had enjoyed the full support of the administration in his long struggle with La Tour, but after

his death there seems to have been a school of thought at Fontainebleau which favored putting the control of the country in the hands
of the latter. La Tour came out with the claim that he had been
appointed governor, although he does not seem to have produced
any written proof of it. It is a fact that the government took no
steps to protect Madame d'Aunay when a merchant of La Rochelle
named Le Borgne claimed that the estate owed him 260,000 livres.
A lawsuit that he brought was decided in his favor, and the widow
was left penniless with her eight children. Perplexed, unhappy, desperate, the poor widow ended by marrying that resourceful widower,
La Tour; a most unexpected turnabout in events indeed.

There was no longer a feud to keep the Acadians at war among
themselves, but they were not to enjoy peace. The struggle with the
English now entered on an active stage and the country would be
taken by the English twice more, only to be ceded back to France
by treaty.

La Tour died in 1666, bringing to an end a most colorful and
fantastic page of history. There have been supporters of both La
Tour and D'Aunay to proclaim belief in the merits and honesty of
each of the embattled leaders. The controversy will probably never
end, although it does not seem to possess anything but academic
interest now. One thing seems certain: that both men loved the
land over which they fought, that they loved it enough to prolong
the struggle when they could have relinquished their part in it and
returned to the ease and comforts of civilized life. Between them
they maintained a hold on the country through long years of hardship and discouragement.

CHAPTER XVII

The Iroquois Gain the Upper Hand—
The Mission to the Onondagas

1

THE Iroquois did not owe their supremacy over the other Indian tribes to their courage and ferocity as much as to the size and shape of their heads. With their great physical strength they combined a high degree of intelligence; and from the roomy cranium which had been given them they derived a capacity for organization which the others lacked. The hit-and-miss Huron, the lackadaisical Neutral, the erratic Erie were creatures of impulse. The men of the Five Nations proceeded always according to plan. They had created a parliamentary procedure for arriving at decisions, and this led to a Spartan-like unity of purpose in carrying out what they had decided.

The chiefs of the Five Nations were chosen by a system which was partly hereditary and partly selective. A dead chief's successor was never chosen from among his sons—there was always some doubt of paternity—but from his relatives on the distaff side. If none of the cousins and nephews seemed strong enough to suit the opinionated and outspoken rank and file, a council would be called to select the warrior best fitted to assume charge. This entitled the new chief, among other privileges, to sit in the supreme upper council of the Five Nations, which was made up of fifty sachems, each of the tribes having a definite allotment. It was in this upper chamber, this meeting place of senators, that all matters of importance were decided, particularly the questions of war and peace.

The fifty sachems gathered by established custom in the council house at the Valley of Onondaga, the Onondagas being the tribe centrally located. Generally the whole Iroquois population would move out of the rolling hills and valleys of their fruitful country and follow their leaders to Onondaga, there to sit in dense groups and hold their own conclaves while the great men talked in the council house. The concerted wisdom of these open-air forums, including those of the women who were always given a hearing, would be conveyed by delegates to the solemn council of the sachems and would be fully considered before any final decisions were reached.

Once made, a decision had the unanimous support of all the Five Nations. There was no such thing as conscription, however, and a man who did not want to fight was not compelled to do so. If war had been decided upon, the braves would leave with their tiny supplies of ground corn and maple sugar (it was their custom to live off the land), their guns and tomahawks, knowing that each stage of the campaign ahead of them had been thought out in advance. Nothing had been overlooked. The Iroquois were incapable of such desultory conduct as the Hurons of St. Ignace had shown, smoking the winter months away and dreaming of the strong defenses they were going to build.

It was an intense pride of race which made them conquerors. In the early years of the eighteenth century they admitted to their confederacy a tribe which had been forced out of South Carolina and had migrated to the North, the Tuscaroras. They called themselves thereafter the Six Nations, but their attitude toward the Tuscaroras was always condescending and resentful.

It was not difficult for a race as well organized as this to prevail over the shiftless and scatterbrain tribes around them. After the Hurons had been eliminated, the Five Nations struck savagely at others nearer to hand. The following year they captured the main village of the Neutrals and drove the vanquished people into the woods, where most of them died of starvation. The Eries, who lived in the fertile country south of the lake of that name, were the next victims. Carrying their canoes as shields, the Iroquois boldly rushed the palisades and then employed the canoes as scaling ladders. Such resourcefulness could not fail of success. They swarmed over the walls and in a single day of blood and fire they wiped the Eries from the face of the earth. The Andastes proved more worthy opponents and it took years to subdue them; but finally the plans hatched by the fifty wise men in the council house at Onondaga proved effective, and the Andastes also ceased to exist as a separate tribe.

The French at this stage were going through a period of weak and fumbling leadership, and it was not strange that their Indian foes, combining sagacity with ferocity, took the initiative into their own hands and never lost it until a climactic stage had been reached. They made peace when the mood seized them; they went back to war when they thought the time ripe, always striking without warning. They called the tune; and the Frenchmen, as well as their witless allies, danced to it.

2

It so happened that there was a brief moment of peace in the early months of 1653. The Mohawks had been beaten in an attack on Montreal. Two hundred warriors made a surprise attack on the hospital which stood on the high ground across the little St. Pierre River. Jeanne Mance was alone in the place, but a brave soldier named Lambert Closse, who had come out a few years before and had become second-in-command to Maisonneuve, went to the rescue with sixteen men. From six in the morning until six at night the little band held the redskins off, and when the attacking party retired it was in a chastened mood. It was largely due to this defeat that a peace of sorts was patched up.

The Onondagas selected this moment to send a party of eighteen chiefs to Quebec with a singular proposal. They wanted the French to show their friendliness and good faith by establishing a colony among them as had been done earlier with the Hurons. The French were puzzled and dismayed by the suggestion. There was behind it, they were sure, some inexplicably malign purpose. To send settlers down into the heart of the Iroquois country might be condemning them to death, but to refuse would undoubtedy be accepted by the belligerent redskins as an affront and lead to an immediate resumption of hostilities. The Iroquois had made it very clear that they never needed a pretext for war-making. Why, then, this demand that the French step like flies into the diabolical parlor of the spiders on the Finger Lakes?

The Jesuits were more disposed to the idea than the civil officials of the colony. Since the dispersion of the Hurons, they had been weighing the possibility of setting up missions among the Iroquois. Danger to them was an enticement rather than a deterrent. "The blood of the martyrs," they cried, "is the seed of the Church." When

Father Ragueneau wrote in the *Relations* defending the idea of establishing a colony by citing the practical reasons which might have influenced the Onondagas, he was no doubt repeating arguments which they had already used to urge an acceptance. He pointed out that the strong fort the French would raise would serve as a rallying point if the village were attacked by other foes. The Onondagas were thinking also undoubtedly of the training they could get in the use and repair of firearms, which they badly needed. The main reason might very well be, however, that the Iroquois man power had been so seriously impaired by the continuous fighting that they needed new blood and were hoping that Indian allies would follow the French into the Valley of Onondaga and agree to adoption into the tribe.

It was decided as a first response to this disturbing invitation to have a survey made. The Jesuits agreed to send Father Simon le Moyne, a wise choice, for this brave priest had already spent some time with the Mohawks and was "tenderly beloved by them." Ondesonk, as he was called by his Iroquois friends, returned with a favorable report, despite the fact that danger had stalked him at every turn. Jean de Lauson, a Mazarin appointee, was governor at this critical stage and was finding the decision beyond him. He hesitated and temporized and finally decided to send more envoys. Two Jesuits went this time, Father Dablon and Father Chaumonot. The latter was an Italian and the possessor of a silver tongue. The headmen of the Onondagas listened to his harangues with both fascination and delight, but they began nevertheless to underline the felicity of their invitations with open threats: Come down into the Valley of the Onondaga or know our anger. Father Dablon returned to Quebec to report while Father Chaumonot remained to please the braves and assuage their impatience with the gentle fancy of his metaphors.

On receiving Dablon's report, the governor could no longer evade the issue. The risk of establishing a colony in the Iroquois capital must be taken, he decided. The Jesuits planned to send four of their number, and Fathers le Mercier, Dablon, Ménard, and Frémin were selected. The fine temper of the men of New France had never before been so warmly displayed as at this point; between thirty and forty of them volunteered to go with the party into the valley of the shadow. They were organized under the command of Major Zachary du Puis, and on May 17, 1657, they set out in two large boats and twelve canoes.

The jealousy of the Mohawks, strangely enough, had been aroused by the decision of the French. If there was to be a settlement of the white men, why should it not be with them? Although a treaty of peace had been entered into and was still officially in force, they immediately sent a war party of three hundred braves down the St. Lawrence. After the departure of the boats for Onondaga, they passed Quebec in the stillness of the night and at dawn made a surprise attack on the Huron settlements on the island of Orleans. They killed a few of the docile Christian Indians and carried off more than eighty of them as prisoners, many of them women.

Jean de Lauson, most pusillanimous of all the long succession of governors, stood on the safe ramparts of the citadel of St. Louis and watched the war canoes of the Mohawks, filled with terror-stricken Hurons, their arms raised in supplication to the white gods whose religion they had embraced, pass the French capital in broad daylight. The jeering warriors raised their paddles in mock salute and even maneuvered their craft up and down in front of the town. As a final insult they made their captives stand up and sing.

Not a move was made to rescue the helpless Hurons, not a shot was fired from the guns of the fort. Lauson considered in gloomy speculation the risks of interference and decided finally he must respect the peace, allowing the poor captives to be borne off to torture and death. But the peace had ceased to be a peace long before.

Houses straggled out from under the walls in all directions. The people who lived in them, frightened by the spectacle of war canoes on the river, had already rushed in for shelter. Before departing, the Mohawks sent parties ashore and with much whooping and maniacal laughter they ransacked the houses, taking whatever seemed to them of value. Lauson still did nothing.

The prestige of the French had been dealt a severe blow. The jeering Mohawks took away with them the conviction that Onontio had come down from his high mountain, that he was no more to be feared than a disused garment stuffed with leaves and elevated over a maize field. The young men had thrown their defiance in his teeth. For a long time thereafter the Five Nations carried off things with a high hand, showing no manner of respect for the authority of France.

In the meantime the party for Onondaga proceeded on their way. They changed to canoes at Montreal and finished the journey behind a large banner of white taffeta containing the word JESUS. If a sense of duty gave them some elevation of spirits, the presence of Mohawks on the edge of the flotilla dampened them again—tall, sulky fellows who needed only wings on their ankles to look like woodland gods. The Mohawks had death behind their scowling brows, but because the Onondagas restrained them they had to be content with an almost daily murder among the Hurons of the party, braining the women and dragging the men out of the canoes to be carried away and burned.

When the canoes had crossed the eastern end of Lake Ontario and had entered the Oswego River, the watchful whites saw that they had come to a land of great promise. Here the harvests had been good. The trees were heavy with fruit, with stoneless cherries and apples shaped like goose eggs, with chestnuts and walnuts. The long lakes, stretched out like the fingers of a human hand, were alive with fish. The Valley of Onondaga, they found, lay in the heart of the Iroquois country—the Oneidas and Mohawks to the east, the Senecas and Cayugas to the west—and it was high, rich land.

Father Chaumonot had selected for the settlement a place on the highest lake, in the midst of salt springs and with a view of all this rich rolling country. The party was escorted there at once, with the French soldiers in their blue coats piping and drumming to keep up their courage and making a brave enough show of it, and copper faces on every hand like a forest of masks, the Indian drums joining in the tumult.

The Jesuit fathers went on at once to Onontagué (Onondaga) to begin their work. They found they had arrived at a moment of considerable drama, the Five Nations having assembled for a tribal council. The sachems smoked their pipes and orated in the secrecy of the council house. Outside, as far as the eye could see, were dusky warriors and their wives, squatting among the withered pumpkin vines and the tall stalks of maize, debating the same issues. The question under consideration might very well have been the fate of the newly arrived party.

The orators who had extended a welcome had done so in extravagant terms of friendship. "Farewell, war!" they had cried. "Farewell, arms! In the future we will be brothers." But the arrival of the priests caused a lowering of heads to conceal the message of hatred in the eyes. Some of the natives could not conceal their emotions.

"I have killed Black-Gowns!" cried one.

"I have helped burn them!" contributed another.

Back at the lake, the newly arrived Frenchmen were feeling some of the emotions that Protestant converts had experienced on being dragged to an auto-da-fé. It was only too apparent that soon the fires would be lighted for the most terrible orgy of murder by torture in which these past masters, the Iroquois, had ever indulged. Fear lent urgency to the axes and speed in the construction of the walls. They hardly dared draw breath until the tall timbers of a palisade closed them in. Now they could, at any rate, sell their lives dearly.

Inside the palisade they built a house capable of accommodating them all, a chapel and such smaller buildings as were needed. They called this the Mission of Ste. Marie of Gannentaa.

The Jesuits met with success at first, and their reports to the *Relations* tell of two hundred baptisms, including five chiefs. Chaumonot went to the Senecas, who were the most numerous of the five tribes, Ménard to the Cayugas. The number of converts rose to four hundred. Had there been an honest desire, after all, for a mission?

Conditions in the beautiful country around the outstretched fingers bore out one contention of the Jesuits. The Iroquois, whose fighting strength at the peak of their power had been very little in excess of two thousand warriors, had been very much depleted by the bloody victory over the Eries and the long struggle with the Andastes. A plan of enforced enrollment was being carried out. In Onondaga were captives from eleven alien tribes, all existing in graded scales of slavery. The women, kept for lust and drudgery, were on the lowest scale and could be killed at any time by an irritable tomahawk.

It was apparent almost from the start that death, imminent and terrible, ringed the colony about. The Frenchmen were kept informed of what was going on by the whispers of the slaves. They knew when a special meeting was called in the valley to debate the questions of the time and method of their end, and that the hand of extermination was held back only because D'Ailleboust, who had taken over the duties of government from the feeble Lauson fingers until a new appointee could arrive from France, had boldly seized twelve Mohawk warriors and was holding them as hostages.

3

Winter arrived and a dying captive gave the fifty-odd Frenchmen, cooped up like livestock marked for slaughter behind their palisade,

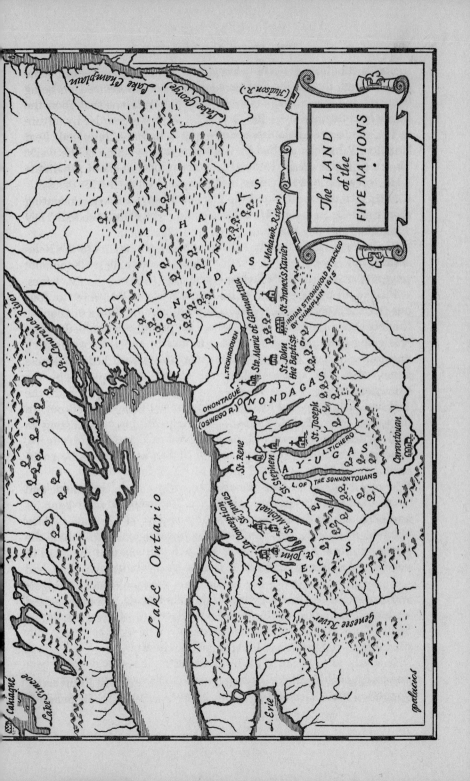

The LAND
of the
FIVE NATIONS
.

MOHAWKS

ONEIDAS

Lake Champlain

Lake George

(Hudson R.)

St Lawrence River

(Mohawk River)

L. TECHIROQUEN

Ste Marie of Ganuentaa

St. Francis Xavier

INDIAN STRONGHOLD ATTACKED
BY CHAMPLAIN 1615

St. John
the Baptist

ONONTAGUÉ

(OSWEGO R.) ONONDAGAS

St. Joseph

L. TICHERO

CAYUGAS

St Rene

St Stephen

L. OF THE SONNONTOUANS

Carantouan

Conception St James

St Michael

St. John

SENECAS

Lake Ontario

Cahiagué

Lake Simcoe

L. Erie

Genesee River

petacios

the truth about the plans of the Iroquois. They were to be allowed to exist through the winter, but they would be killed as soon as the ice went off the rivers and lakes, by which time the hostages would surely be redeemed by guile.

The condemned colonists spent many long hours discussing their situation. What chance had they of extricating themselves before the blow fell? It was unsafe to show as much as a nose outside the timber wall, for a close watch was being kept. Winter had gripped the country in fetters of ice; and the first sanctuary, Montreal, was many scores of leagues away. How long could they withstand an assault when the fatal day arrived?

A plan was made finally. All through the winter, which for once seemed much too short, the French labored secretly to prepare themselves for one of the most unusual escapes in history.

First of all they began to build boats. Every night parties slipped out into the woods and carried back with them the limbs of trees. In the loft above the main house, where no prying eye could see what was going forward, they succeeded in making two large open boats and four elm-bark canoes. March came, and with it the promise of open water. The second half of the stratagem was then put into execution.

It had been proposed by the youngest member of the party, whose name was Pierre Esprit Radisson. Coming with his parents from St. Malo when fifteen years old, he had lived at Three Rivers and had been captured by a prowling band of Mohawks while hunting with two young friends. Adopted into a Mohawk family and most affectionately treated, he had managed to escape and had sailed from Manhattan in a Dutch ship for France. Returning to the colony, he had been among those who had volunteered for the journey into the Onondaga country. This youth will reappear again and again as the history of New France develops and will start many bitter controversies and do many remarkable things. Bear him in mind.

The plan was to invite the Indians to a great feast and stuff them with so much food that they would fall into a coma. These feasts had an almost religious significance for the natives of North America. Such an invitation could not be refused, even though the guests were planning to butcher their hosts immediately after.

It is safe to say that in all Iroquois history there had never been one to equal this. All the male population of Onondaga came at the appointed time. They could not be allowed inside, of course, and so large fires had been set blazing in front of the gate. The guests said "Ho!" the ceremonial greeting, and seated themselves at one of the fires. There they waited.

It was a curious scene: the tossing tops of the trees strongly etched against the black sky by the light of the fires, the silent braves squatting cross-legged on the ground with no trace for once of enmity, the young Frenchmen entertaining the guests by singing and dancing and playing on musical instruments (young Radisson played a guitar and proved himself quite adept), the smell of hot food from the courtyard setting copper-colored jaws to spasmodic movements. Although the Indians contributed no sound whatever, the din was tremendous.

Then the gate swung open wide and the food was carried out. The Indians never seasoned their food with salt or pepper or herbs of any kind, and it might be supposed that the French cooks would attack those starved palates with highly spiced dishes. Fortunately they knew enough not to do this. They were aware that the doughty sons of the forest were creatures of habit, that they liked the way their squaws prepared food for them. Salt made things bitter to the Indian taste. According to a writer in the *Relations*, they "abhorred Dutch cheese, radishes, spices, mustard, and similar condiments." Accordingly, the long succession of dishes which emerged from the kitchens and the fires in the courtyard were cooked in the manner to which the squatting guests were accustomed.

The French cooks could be trusted, however, to prepare a tremendous variety of dishes. All the pigs belonging to the colony had been butchered, and this provided a wonderful base for the meal. Corn and a kind of mincemeat were brought in first, followed by kettles full of broiled bustard and chicken and turtle. Next came eels and salmon and carp and a sagamité of thickened flour filled with vegetables. These were dishes the Indians understood. They allowed themselves to be served great spoonfuls of everything. No dish passed them untouched. As young Radisson put it in his diary, "they eat as many wolves, having eyes bigger than bellies."

It was Radisson who whispered to one of the other Frenchmen as the orgy continued unabated, "They do not cry *skenon* [enough], but soon we will cry *hunnay* [we are going]."

It was customary for the hosts to abstain from eating, and so, while the feasting went on, the French beat on their drums and blazed away on their instruments and so made it impossible for the gorged warriors to detect certain unusual sounds which came from the rear of the enclosure. The drums beat faster when the appetites began to slacken. It is possible that some drug had been put in the food, although none of the records available mentions this. Nature finally took a decisive part. The overstuffed stomachs of the warriors brought sleep to their eyes. One by one they toppled over.

A last loud salvo on the drums brought all sound to an end save for the rhythmic snoring of the guests.

When the fires died down, the sleeping Indians were wakened by the cold. Some of them stirred, sat up, and then roused the others, not with the ceremonial "Ho!" but with an urgent gabble of words. It was not yet dawn, and the stars were still in the sky. The gate of the Mission of Ste. Marie was closed with an undefinable hint of finality, an effect increased by the silence reigning over it.

One of the additional senses which men of the wild possess told the aroused Indians that something was wrong, but they made no effort to get at the truth of things until the end of the day. In the meantime no hint of sound came from the cluster of buildings, not the snuffle of a dog or the cackle of hens. When dusk began to fall the warriors could no longer be restrained. They broke down the front gate and rushed into the enclosure.

They discovered at once that their suspicions had been well founded. The place was deserted. Everything had been cleared out and the rooms were bare. All the livestock was gone save a few lonely hens on their roosts.

Footprints led from the rear of the mission to the shore of the lake; a great many of them, suggesting to the trained eyes of the angry Iroquois that they had been made by men in a great hurry. The French had departed, then, by water. But how? They had no boats. Had some magic vessel, with white wings like a monster bird, dropped from the sky to take them out of danger's way?

The ice on the surface of the lake was unbroken. There was no way of knowing that the white men in departing had broken the ice before them as they made their way out from the shore, using axes and the butts of their muskets, and that it had frozen over behind them.

On April 3 the heavily loaded craft reached Montreal. The hungry and weary people, who had braved the winds of March for a fort-

night without cover, went eagerly ashore for rest and food. On April
23 they arrived at Quebec. The population turned out in excitement
and delight to welcome them back. It was clear they had given up
the adventurers into the Onondaga Valley as lost, although there
were some who contended that Zachary du Puis and his band had
given in to their fears too easily.

4

At Three Rivers that resourceful young man, Pierre Radisson, went
ashore to join his family. Here he met for the first time a man ten
years his senior who was destined to become his partner in some of
the most unusual exploits in history, one Médard Chouart des
Groseilliers. This newcomer had married Radisson's half sister
Marguerite, the widow of the Sieur de Grandmesnil. The title "Des
Groseilliers" had become his in the first place as a joke. Chouart had
acquired a corner of land at Three Rivers overrun with brambles and
gooseberry bushes; hence the name, which, bestowed in jest, became
accepted seriously later.

Médard Chouart was born on July 31, 1618, at Charly-sur-Marne.
Coming to Canada at an early age, he went first to the mission at
Lake Nipissing with Father Dreuillettes. After that he turned up in
Huronia as an *engagé* and lived through the bitter days of the war
of extermination, returning with the last of the party to leave the
island of St. Joseph. Coming to Three Rivers after the departure of
young Pierre with the Onondaga party, he met Marguerite Hayet
Véron, who had been left with three children when her first husband
died. He married her and seemed disposed for the first time in his
life to settle down.

It was a natural thing for a man of his disposition and antecedents
to come to Three Rivers, which owed its name to a mistake made by
Pontgravé. He had been led by the splitting of the St. Maurice where
it joined the St. Lawrence into believing that it was due to the junction there of three rivers. This small settlement had become the
meeting ground of the hardy spirits who had an itching of the foot,
the *coureurs de bois*. Quebec was the port, the administrative center
of New France; Montreal was a brave experiment, an outpost existing in a state of spiritual fervor; Three Rivers was the starting point
of exploration. Woodsmen had fallen into the habit of making it their
winter quarters.

Its importance was due largely to its strategic position. By taking
the route of the St. Maurice, which joins the St. Lawrence at Three
Rivers, and crossing to the Gatineau, one of the more important
tributaries of the Ottawa, it was possible to reach the upper Ottawa
and the rich hunting country of the North without encountering the
risks and dangers of the junction of that river with the St. Lawrence.
It was a short cut and, for a time at least, free of the interference of
the Iroquois. As a result it was much in favor with the fur brigades.
Turning off into the Gatineau with their heavily loaded canoes, the
Indian trading parties escaped the steaming rapids and were free of
what seemed to them the dark and bloody land around Montreal
Island. For many years the fur trade centered at Three Rivers.

Wealth began to accumulate there, and the first men ennobled in
Canada were residents of Three Rivers: Boucher, Godefroy, Hestel,
and Le Neuf.

Marguerite Hayet Véron must have been a comely woman to attract the eye of this born wanderer. He even showed a tendency to
settle down and raise a second family with the young widow. It soon
developed, however, that Marguerite was a determined woman, one
of the managing kind. The soft light in her eye could change in the
fraction of a second to a steely glint. She managed the property her
first husband had left her, she ran a small shop, she trained her three
children and brought into the world five more during the much-
interrupted span of her married life with Chouart. For good measure
she indulged in feuds with neighbors and spent much time in court.
She was quarreling with her new husband over his attitude toward
her first children when young Pierre came home.

The two men took one look at each other and realized that there
was a kinship between them more enduring than the conjugal tie
which bound Groseilliers to his family. A spark passed from eye to
eye. They were birds of a feather, animated with the desire to leave
no horizon unexplored, the soles of their feet always having the itch
for exploration. Neither was of the kind to settle down to the humdrum existence of a little frontier trading post, burdened with household cares and the squalling of young children. The old English
couplet applied to both:

> And ever sang they the song they wrought,
> "Why standee we, why go we not?"

Before long they were off together for the West, Radisson leaving
his parents, who had come to expect little from him but his absence,

Groseilliers abandoning for the time being his buxom Marguerite to the cares of their growing household.

They departed secretly, for a number of reasons. The governor at Quebec had promulgated a law that no French subject could devote himself to the fur trade without a permit, and permits were hard to come by. The number issued each year was limited, the total at first being twenty-five. To obtain these much-coveted and striven-for permits would have meant an open avowal of their intention to leave and a prompt negative from Marguerite of the dark brows and the unbending will.

Luckily for them, Groseilliers had been elected captain of the borough of Three Rivers. One night the pair took to the water and paddled down the St. Maurice. When they came to the lookout post at the entrance to the St. Lawrence, they were challenged by the night guard. Groseilliers answered in his capacity as borough captain and was allowed to proceed.

Radisson and Groseilliers! These became magic names, names to create visions in the minds of other young men; visions of the far North and the mighty inland sea known as Hudson's Bay, of the far West and the country of the Great Lakes. An important moment in history, this; Radisson and Groseilliers off on their first journey to-gether. Let the masterly Marguerite stir uneasily in the couch she must occupy alone. What would it matter that officials frowned over the fact that a pair of young fellows had taken to the woods without permits? Two of the greatest and least appreciated men in Canadian annals were beginning their rocketing career together.

5

The success of the *Relations* had been teaching the Jesuit fathers something about popular tastes, and they had begun to vary the fare, injecting matters of a lighter nature in the course of more serious dis-cussions. Conscious, perhaps, that so much talk of Indian wars might weary the reader with its repetition of horror, Father Ragueneau injected into his reports at this stage a chapter on Indian customs as compared with French. Perhaps for the same reason it may be advis-able to pause also and review briefly what he tells.

The habits, the beliefs, the likes, the dislikes of the aborigines of North America were, of course, diametrically opposed to those of Europeans. The Indian found the smell of grease and oil, which he daubed all over his body, most agreeable to his senses, whereas it was like carrion to the French. On the other hand, "the rose, the pink, the clove, the nutmeg are insipid to him." The same divergence was to be found in all respects.

Civilized music was nothing but a confusion of sound in the savage ear. The warrior, who never seemed to sing except when under torture or at the approach of death, considered his own heavy and dismal songs "as beautiful as the blush of dawn." There is an amusing story in this connection, drawn from another section of the *Relations*. Once a party of haughty Iroquois chiefs arrived at Quebec to discuss terms of peace. They were in a belligerent mood, and it occurred to the French leaders that a little music might soothe their savage breasts. They conducted the peace party to the seminary of the Ursulines, where Madame de la Peltrie's little Indian charges lined up and sang a hymn for the visitors. The Iroquois listened with no hint of pleasure or approval on their scowling brows. In fact, they scoffed openly at the efforts of the children and then lined up themselves to demonstrate what music should be, intoning in concert some mournful dirge. The children responded with another song, a gay madrigal. The chiefs expressed even deeper scorn and gave another sample of their preference in music. And so it went on for some time, the bitter chiefs determined to prove their superiority; and departing finally, convinced that they had done so.

In the matter of food the Indian liked his meat smoked, which, to the French palate, gave it a taste like soot. "Yellow porridge," the Indian term for mustard, was the most obnoxious of all foods to the Indian since the day when one of their number, offered a dish of mustard, scooped up the whole contents and took it down at a single gulp. Tears which he could not check poured from his eyes, but otherwise he concealed his suffering like a victim at the torture stake. From that moment, to proffer yellow porridge was a deadly insult. The Indians had a weakness for eggs but preferred them when they contained a bird nearly ready to hatch. Meat bones were seldom given to the eager dogs because of a superstition that they made animals harder to catch. Only when a dog's master was dining on the flesh of an animal which had allowed itself to be caught easily would the bones be held in sufficient contempt to be tossed down to the hungry beast.

The Indians admired their own small black eyes and long features. Contrary to the general impression, they disliked the white skins of the French. They found curly hair grotesque, while beards seemed to them nothing short of loathsome. A savage would often look into the face of a bearded Frenchman, shudder and say, "Ugh, how ugly you are!" The Indians were surprised at the roughness of European skins; their own were soft and delicate, as a result of the constant application of oil and grease.

Father Ragueneau tells a story to illustrate the peculiarity of the Indian attitude toward dress. A pretty Indian girl, on leaving the seminary at Quebec, was given a dress by the Ursuline mothers. As she had been a favorite with them, they went to great pains to make it attractive. It was a white gown and no doubt had ribbons and a touch of lace and unquestionably a very fine sash. The girl was married immediately after, and to the dismay of the donors the husband was seen soon after decked out in his wife's finery. They tried to tell him that the white gown was not suitable for masculine wear, that it was for his wife's use only. He shook his head emphatically. If anyone was to wear anything as fine as this, he as the head of the family was the one. He strutted and posed about the streets, and when white people laughed at him he accepted their raillery as proof of their approval.

The natives, in fact, wore anything that suited their fancy. The good father had seen a tall Huron warrior wearing a boat pulley about his neck with open ostentation. Another wore a bunch of keys. As the keys had been stolen, this prideful display proved unprofitable in the end. The women tried to dress in ways which accentuated their size. One of their habits was to wear two belts, the first above the stomach, the second around the waist. The fold of the dress was allowed to hang out between, thus serving a double purpose: it made the wearer seem buxom and provided a convenient pocket.

The worthy priest then proceeded to speak of the country. The soil was so productive that in a few years the husbandman not only found himself free of need but in a position to make money out of his crops. The streams abounded with fish and most particularly with eels, the latter an important item, for Frenchmen love a stew of eels above most dishes. During the months of September and October, when the eels reached a fine stage of fatness, an expert plier of the spear could catch from forty to seventy thousand, thus assuring a supply for the whole winter. A good huntsman could go out into the woods during the winter and kill moose by the score. The air, more-over, was so clear and healthy that men attained to a great strength. Few children died in the cradle as they did in France. They grew up straight and tall and strong, and filled with a rare degree of courage.

This review of the wonderful possibilities of the great new land which they still proudly called New France but would be equally proud later to name Canada led the narrator to speak of the one factor which nullified all the advantages, the hostility of the Iroquois. "We chanted the *Te Deum*," he wrote, "with much feeling, it is true, but with conflicting emotions; for we seemed to hear at the same time our captive Frenchmen singing on the scaffolds of the Iroquois."

Later he added: "A rumor is current that all the Europeans oc-cupying the long coast line from Acadia to Virginia, incensed against the Iroquois, the common foe of all nations, wish to form an alliance for their destruction."

He did not say, because no resident of New France had any inkling of the truth, that while Europeans contented themselves with thoughts of concerted action, the wily and determined men of the Long House were going much farther. They were planning a cam-paign which, they were sure, would result in the destruction of all the Frenchmen in America and the burning of their settlements.

CHAPTER XVIII

*An Uneasy Peace—Charles le Moyne
and the Beginning of a Great Family—
Jeanne Mance Takes Matters into Her Own Hands*

1

A LULL before the storm. Through the middle fifties peace had come to the St. Lawrence, a temporary peace while those implacable and unpredictable foes, the Iroquois, mulled over their savage plans and waited to strike again. It was also an uneasy peace, for the French still suffered from weak leadership and their allies had been massacred and dispersed by the hammer blows of the Iroquois confederacy.

But in Montreal, the French spearhead, there was no perceptible lull. The town at the meeting of the two rivers had been growing, but the mere fact of growth had added to its vulnerability. On his last trip to France, Maisonneuve had returned with 114 men, some of them artisans and some soldiers, and this had increased the population to well over the two hundred mark. It is recorded that there were 160 ablebodied men altogether. A third of them were married and inevitably were raising families. This had created a need for more houses. It was no longer possible to build behind the walls which surrounded the fort, and so the town had moved out into the open. Between forty and fifty houses had been built on a road to which was given the name of Rue St. Paul and which ran almost due east and west, first following the bank of the St. Lawrence and then bending to the course of the St. Pierre, passing the Hôtel-Dieu and the well-palisaded frame structure of three stories which served the double purpose of a home for Maisonneuve and an administrative center. At right angles to this road was a narrow and muddy passage which cut between these two main buildings and ran north to what would become the Place d'Armes and then to St. Martin's Brook. To this road was given the name of Rue St. Joseph. In 1657 a small chapel had been erected in the open at the extreme east end of the Rue St. Paul, and this had been given the name of Bonsecours.

The governor's greatest problem had been to devise some measure of defense for the straggling line of small houses, and he had solved it as well as he could by erecting forts and redoubts at intervals. At the extreme eastern point, above the Bonsecours chapel, he had constructed a strong stone fort which was called the citadel. At the other extreme, south and west of the original fort, there was a windmill which was well loopholed and capable of resisting attacks. In addition there was a series of log redoubts behind which the little houses clustered. These had been named by the devout Maisonneuve, and so we find the *Redoubt of the Infant Jesus, St. Gabriel, and Ste. Marie.*

The houses, necessarily, were small and of frame construction, but they followed the architectural ideas which were to be more fully developed later, the habitant type; the roof always peaked to the shape of a witch's hat to prevent the accumulation of snow in winter; the framework an industrious white, relieved by doors of bright colors, red or blue or even purple (but never yellow, for that shade had come to denote a traitor or a deceived husband), according to individual tastes; the oven outside, constructed of wickerwork, plastered inside and out with clay or mortar and raised four feet from the ground. Some of the houses had palisades of their own for defense purposes.

The men who built the houses were far different from the dregs and spews who had been brought out to Canada in the early days. They were showing the first signs of becoming a new race, the French-Canadian. They were straighter and much stronger, their shoulders and arms hard from the unceasing swing of ax and dip of paddle. Even their voices were starting to change, the soft note of the French provinces giving place to a higher and clearer note which carried over long stretches of water and through the forests, and with a musical ring to it, particularly when they sang to the heave of the busy axes such songs as *Rossignolet Sauvage, La Norrice du Roi,* and *Dame Lombarde.* Their eyes were clear and alert, as indeed they had to be with peril all about them; but there was nothing timorous, nothing furtive. They seemed capable of looking far into the distance, of seeing beyond the encircling forest the open plains of the far West and the icebound waters of the North.

The qualities found in these industrious workmen would become accentuated as time went on. They would animate the men who would soon be starting out for all parts of the continent: down the Mississippi to the Gulf, north to Hudson's Bay, west to the great prairies where the buffalo roamed.

As environment had changed them physically, it had led also to distinctive ways of dressing. The men of Montreal wore long-skirted coats tied at the waist with worsted scarves. In Quebec the scarves were red and in Three Rivers white. Their legs were covered in winter with *chaussettes* of wool, their heads well protected in warm woolen coverings called *bonnets rouges*. The custom had already developed of wearing a birch-bark case around the neck containing the wearer's knife for eating, it being a habit to set out only a fork and spoon for guests.

The character of the town was changing. In the hearts of the devout Maisonneuve and the resolute Jeanne Mance the flame of dedication still burned brightly, but there was no denying the destiny of a settlement with such a situation as this. Montreal had been intended from the first by the forces which control such matters to be a great trading center. It could not be bypassed by the canoes from the north and west which brought the winter's catch down to the market. More and more traders were starting in business and doing well for themselves. The region lying between the Rue St. Paul and the muddy *Commune* bordering the course of the St. Lawrence was filling up with mercantile establishments, stores, trading posts, warehouses. A census taken in 1665, just five years beyond the point in time which this narrative has reached, would show a jump in population to 525. Two years later it would be 766. This growth, which seems infinitesimal in the light of modern statistics, was quite fabulous when compared to the slow increase in the first twenty years. The fur trade was to be thanked for what was happening at the junction of the rivers.

Men were becoming wealthy, and the life of the seigneurial class and the better-established merchants was taking on some of the refinements and the opulence of the leisure classes in France. The freight received from France was no longer made up of sheer necessities. There were bales of rich materials for clothes and the niceties of attire which Paris created for the world; for the ladies, *considérations*, which were panniers to be worn over skirts, head-dresses of *étamine, contouches* with bows of red ribbon down the front, lacy robes of *gorge-de-pigeon*, skirt stiffeners called *criardes;* for the men, *tapabord* hats, which had turned-up brims and silk linings, and *claques*, which were three-cornered and very handsome indeed, *bretelles* (a primitive form of suspenders), and knee-length *capots*. The finest furniture was being sent out as well: walnut commodes with marble tops, serpentine tables, *armoires* of sassafras wood, and fine crystal chandeliers. The best of wines were available in the stores and very much in demand.

This increase in trade was not an unmixed blessing. The fur merchants had discovered that one commodity was irresistible to the Indian, that he could be parted easily from his furs for brandy. The liquor traffic was beginning to split the colony wide open. The clerical heads fought it bitterly but, in the long run, unsuccessfully. Already in 1660 Montreal had witnessed Algonquin hunters, stark-naked and roaring drunk, staggering down the Rue St. Paul.

There was no real security for a community as exposed as this. The Iroquois studied the straggling rows of houses from the depths of the forest or the opposite bank of the river; their small black eyes intent, their cunning minds at work. When the time came for the big effort, this wide-open town could be carried by assault. They were sure of this, although they knew it would be a costly matter. In the meanwhile they carried on a policy of attrition, lurking in the woods and attacking any whites who ventured too far from the town.

They became progressively bolder and even hid themselves among the houses. The people of the town learned to their sorrow that a lurking shadow was likely to be a Mohawk and that a sound outside the house had to be investigated warily, for it might mean an Onondagan concealed in the woodpile. Sometimes the daring redskins hid themselves in the gardens of the Hôtel-Dieu, prepared to kill any nun who ventured out.

Fighting might occur at any time in the neighboring woods or in the town itself. The shrill *"Cassee kouee!"* of the Iroquois became as familiar to the harried whites as the cawing of crows in the spring. The nuns at the Hôtel-Dieu sounded the tocsin whenever they heard it, summoning all the men of Montreal to the scene of the trouble. The wily Iroquois did not expect they could capture the town by such casual attacks. They were content to wear the garrison down, to keep nerves taut and fears high.

2

Ville Marie de Montréal had lost two of its first pioneers. Pierre des Puiseaux had grown so old that he had returned to Quebec and had gone from there to France to spend his last years in peace. After eighteen months in Montreal, Madame de la Peltrie had been summoned back to Quebec by the heads of the Ursulines, a step precipitated, no doubt, by the increasing tension between the two towns. She had gone with great reluctance. It was not that she had lost interest in the original venture. She still loved the solemn little charges of the seminary and held the staff in affectionate esteem; but distant frontiers and the adventurous life still beckoned her, and she had not recovered from her disappointment at being barred from the Huron missions.

It is unfortunate that so little is known of this unpredictable lady. A closer acquaintance would reveal complexities of character and, no doubt, contradictions as well. The physical promise of her youth had been more than fulfilled and she had become a woman of considerable beauty. A contemporary describes her as follows: "Her whole person presents a type of attractiveness and gentleness. Her face, a wonderful oval, is remarkable for the harmony of its lines. A slightly aquiline nose, a clear-cut and always smiling mouth, a limpid look veiled by long lashes . . ." She must have possessed a rare degree of charm, and it is easy to conceive of her as out of place in a land where austerity governed life and people existed always in the shadow of death.

She obeyed the summons and built herself a tiny house, barely large enough for two people, next to the stone seminary of the Ursulines. Here she would spend the rest of her life, working long and faithfully. She had never become a member of the order and so could not wear their uniform. Her instinct for the dramatic, however, made it necessary for her to be different from the rather drab housewives. She planned a gray uniform for herself and never thereafter wore anything else. It lacked any individual touches, and as the years rolled by and her resources became more scanty she appeared in a threadbare and much-patched version of it.

3

The time has come to introduce an important and colorful member of the Montreal community, a young Norman named Charles le Moyne, the son of an innkeeper of Dieppe. He had accompanied the first company to the town at the age of seventeen and had made himself felt almost from the start. The first mention of him is found in the *Relations* when he was serving as an interpreter with the Huron missions. He became known soon after as a guide and a fearless Indian fighter. His name figures in all the exciting stories of conflict with the Indians around Montreal. He played such a bold part, in fact, that the Iroquois began to fear him, and to the white settlers he became a legend. In later years a favorite story was told about him which always began this way:

For years the old women of the Long House had been gathering wood to burn Charles le Moyne at the stake. Akouesson, they called him . . .

The story goes on to explain that this valiant Frenchman was captured finally on the Richelieu River. They could hardly wait to take him back to the old women and their fagots. They dipped their paddles in the water with triumph in the ripple of their muscles.

But after a time they were much less sure about the wisdom of what they were doing. Charles le Moyne was talking to them. He was familiar with the Iroquois tongue and he knew how to play on their feelings. He began to tell them of the disasters which would befall the people of the Long House if they killed him. His people would come in canoes which were higher than the highest trees of the forest and with guns so big that they would silence the thunder. He kept repeating this over and over again until finally some of the cocksureness went out of the arms of the Iroquois.

They stopped and held a council among themselves, whispering and glancing at him over their shoulders. The outcome was that they paddled back in haste to where they had captured him, and there they turned him over to some friendly Indians.

When he came of age he was granted a tract of land on the opposite bank of the St. Lawrence, and he named his little seigneury Longueuil. It had a frontage on the river of fifty arpents and was double that distance in depth. It was located in a dangerous spot, for it was through this neck of land that the Iroquois passed on their way from the Richelieu. This did not frighten the bold young Le Moyne. He began to develop his land and built a house there, although after his marriage in 1654 he occupied a small home on the Rue St. Joseph in Montreal. His bride was Catherine Primot, who proved a most faithful and devoted helpmeet. She presented him with eleven sons, ten of whom lived to maturity, and two daughters, and it is chiefly because of the remarkable exploits of these unusual sons that the name of Le Moyne is stamped indelibly on the pages of Canadian history.

On the occasion of his marriage Charles le Moyne received an additional grant of ninety arpents of river frontage. His fortune began to mount rapidly at this point. With his brother-in-law, Jean le Ber, he entered the fur trade, and between them they had shops and warehouses running south of the Rue St. Joseph to *La Commune*.

Two years later the first of the valiant sons arrived and was named Charles. He was destined to succeed his father and become not only the head of the family but the financial genius who would supply the sinews of war for the remarkable schemes of expansion which they carried out. He developed Longueuil into one of the most important of the seigneuries of Canada and built an unusual structure which was fort and château in one, and which will be described fully on later pages as the saga of the Le Moynes develops. After his father's death, Charles was created Baron of Longueuil and acted for a short period as governor of the colony.

In 1659, just as the Iroquois storm threatened to break over Montreal, a second son was born and was given the name of Jacques. In 1661, after the storm had dissolved, a third son would put in an appearance. This lusty infant would be given the name of Pierre. The temptation to cast ahead into the future becomes irresistible at this point, for the sturdy third son of the family was destined to become the great paladin of New France, the forever renowned fighter on land and sea who is known in history as Pierre le Moyne d'Iberville. A still further cast ahead would introduce a boy born in 1680, the eighth of the line, who carried the name of Jean Baptiste le Moyne de Bienville to lasting fame as the founder of New Orleans and the lifelong governor of Louisiana.

All of the sons who survived had careers distinguished by bravery of the highest order; a truly fantastic family, representing the finest qualities of the French-Canadian people and earning for them-

selves the title of the Canadian Maccabees, for reasons which will
soon become apparent.

4

During the first half of the year 1660, when the clouds hovering
over Montreal reached their blackest stage, the colony lacked the
inspiring presence of two women who had come to typify the religious side of the settlement, Jeanne Mance and Marguerite Bourgeoys.
The latter, a resident of Troyes in Champaigne, had come to Montreal to found a school for girls when she was thirty-three years old.
She was practical, zealous, and hard-working and made a perfect foil
for the spirituelle and inspiring Jeanne Mance. Soon after the hospital
had been built, the continuous pounding of the Iroquois had made
it necessary temporarily to use the building for defense purposes.
The patients had been moved into a low building of two rooms near
the fort, an arrangement which continued for four and a half years.
The house contained a low attic and, for lack of anything better,
this had been turned into a schoolroom for Marguerite Bourgeoys
and her students. It was cold and drafty, with a small hearth and
a tiny cupboard. The house had been built of green wood, and
cracks in the walls had opened through which the winter winds
whistled and the snow drifted. The food had to be kept in front
of the small spluttering fire to keep it from freezing. The pupils sat
in huddled misery at the raised planks which served as desks, their
hands numb, their noses blue. They were not acquiring education
easily, these unhappy children.

A somewhat similar situation prevailed belowstairs, where there
were always more patients than beds and no place for the nuns to
sleep. It was in the hope of obtaining additional funds and better
equipment that the two heads had decided to pay a joint visit to
France.

Jeanne Mance seems to have had a genius for communicating her
enthusiasm to others and spurring on to action all with whom she
came in contact. Gentle of manner and soft of speech, she was a
seventeenth-century Florence Nightingale, nevertheless, filled with
a deep pity for the ill and the poor and ready to batter down walls
in her desire to aid them. The hardships of ocean travel were beyond
description, and it was folly for her to undertake a journey at a time
when she was suffering from the worst of health. She refused to

be deterred by such considerations. She, and she only, could get the help so badly needed.

On a previous visit to France she had succeeded in effecting a reorganization of the Montreal Company, something which needed doing very badly. Borrowing the policy of secrecy from the Duc de Ventadour and his order of Saint-Sacrament, the company eschewed the use of names except those of Dauversière and Fancamp. These two men of single purpose and fanatical zeal had been allowed to exercise all authority in connection with the affairs of the company and, as neither of them possessed any administrative capacity whatever, they had reduced things to a sorry tangle. Arriving on the scene, she went promptly to work and convinced the chief contributors that a change would have to be made unless they were content to have their contributions wasted. The silent partners of the company gave her authority to make changes. The names of all the main partners were given out. Jean Jacques Olier was made president and Louis Seguier secretary. The displaced pair were not very happy about this new policy, but they could not check the thoroughly aroused and determined Jeanne Mance. She continued to have her way; and this turned out to be a very good thing for the people of Montreal.

It was agreed also that the company would convey ownership to the hospital of two hundred arpents of land with the understanding that this would be divided up into tracts of thirty arpents each for any individuals who would take possession and cultivate the land. Under this arrangement the owners developed a system of co-operation by which they helped each other in clearing the land and building houses.

With this same decisiveness and clarity of vision Jeanne Mance proceeded on her arrival in France to fight for the lives and the well-being of her fellow residents. She went to Madame de Bouillon first of all. The unknown benefactress, who seems to have been entertaining doubts as to the wisdom of devoting her charitable efforts so exclusively to this one purpose, was won back to enthusiastic support. The glowing eyes, the eloquent tongue could not be withstood. In perfect accord once more, the kindly patroness and the young evangel of kindness and mercy made plans between them for the extension of the work and also for the bettering of the defenses of the town. As a first installment of the funds promised, Mademoiselle Mance carried away with her twenty-two thousand livres. This was a big sum for a woman to have in her possession. Highwaymen haunted the roads and cutpurses lurked in the dark streets of the cities. She decided to keep two thousand livres for the immediate needs she would encounter on returning to Montreal and confided the remainder to the Sieur de la Dauversière for investment.

The final step was the selection of new helpers. Three young nuns were chosen from among the members of a nursing community which Dauversière had established at La Flèche. Marguerite Bourgeoys was equally successful at Troyes, where she found three recruits who were willing to face the rigors of pioneering life, Sisters Châtel, Crolo, and Raisin. There was some difficulty at La Flèche, where the story had spread among the townspeople that Dauversière was sending the young nuns out to Canada against the wishes of their parents. This, of course, was not true, but the rumor gained so much circulation that a mob gathered at the gate of the convent to prevent the departure of the party. Force had to be used to clear the street.

The party gathered finally at La Rochelle, including men who had been recruited to aid in the defense of Montreal and a few young women who were going out to find husbands in the colony. Before sailing time Dauversière put in an appearance to give them his blessing. He was in very evident bad health, which showed itself in the pallor of his cheeks and the unsteadiness of his gait. Under the skirt of the semi-clerical garb which he had begun to affect he displayed something about himself which had never before been observed, a pair of wide clay feet.

After expressing his hopes to the hospital aides that they would enjoy their work, he was asked by one of them, who was acting as treasurer, what steps she should take to receive in due course the interest on the money which had been left with him for investment.

Now it happened that the tax collector of La Flèche had become involved in financial difficulties and had already applied the twenty thousand livres to this personal deficit. He showed some embarrassment in answering.

"My daughter," he said finally, "God will provide for you."

The money was never paid back, and as a result Jeanne Mance and her helpers lived at their hospital for years thereafter in such poverty that they were never able to afford new gowns. The clothes they wore were so patched and repaired that before they were discarded it would be impossible to tell of what material they had consisted when new.

The ship made a slow crossing, but the party reached Montreal in time to participate in full in the most trying days of the Iroquois encirclement.

CHAPTER XIX

Adam Dollard and His Magnificent Stand at the Long Sault

1

THE North American Indian had evolved over the ages a few tools and weapons, a few conceptions of tribal organization, a few vague beliefs; and with these he had been content until the white man came along and upset everything. But he made two remarkable inventions, the snowshoe and the bark canoe.

The canoe remains today one of the few nearly perfect vessels. It can be handled easily, it develops great speed, it skims over shoal water, it races down rapids with grace and daring. It is so light, moreover, that it can be carried with relative ease. It was the canoe which opened up the continent to the white man. It carried him up and down rivers and over lakes and it traveled on his head when he encountered the need to cross land. The *coureur de bois* thought nothing of setting out from Three Rivers or Montreal to winter along Lake Michigan or in the rich country north of Lake Superior. The French-Canadian explorers, who so often wore the black gown of the Jesuit, did not consider Hudson's Bay or the Mississippi beyond the range of their efforts. The canoe was like a pair of seven league boots.

But there were times when even the canoe failed its master, and one of the hardest of obstacles was the Ottawa River. In earlier stages of world's history, long before a two-legged creature named man had been evolved and had constituted himself its historian, the Ottawa had served as the outlet of a vast sea which lapped the base of the Laurentian range. It remained a stream of furious power, which was augmented as one tributary after another drained into it. It joins the St. Lawrence at the southwestern tip of Montreal Island through four passages like the fingers of a hand. The Ottawa has variety to offer at every turn; it is full of fancies and surprises, and it is always rough in its play. It broadens between wide shores and becomes deceptively passive, it gains in depth and impetuosity as the shores narrow, it roars through close defiles.

Entering the Ottawa from the St. Lawrence puts a strain on even the strongest of arms. After negotiating one of the four passages and crossing the Lake of Two Mountains, the first serious obstacle is encountered in the Carillon Rapids. The name does not derive from the sound the river makes at this point, for the deep bass voice of the Ottawa has none of the soft and dulcet tone of bells. After the Carillon come the rapids of Chute à Blondeau. Still farther along on the broad westward sweep of the stream the entrance to a lake is reached, and this proves to be the most formidable of the many bottlenecks along the lower course of the brawling river. The water pours in roiling fury down a long narrow passage which is called the Long Sault.

The Long Sault, always a menace and a source of delay, made it necessary to unload canoes three times in an ascent. It had grown in importance since domination of the Ottawa had become a part of Iroquois strategy. When parties of Frenchmen approached it from either direction it was always with the expectation of finding Iroquois bands hidden along its banks; and the shoe was on the other foot when it was the Iroquois themselves who were on the move.

The Long Sault will never be forgotten because here was enacted the great epic story of early Canadian history.

2

There was in Montreal at this time, in the capacity of an officer of the armed forces, a young man named Adam Dollard (sometimes, but erroneously, called Daulac), Sieur des Ormeaux. He had come out from France three years before, at the age of twenty-two, and it was generally believed that some kind of shadow had settled on his name at home. In fairness to this brave soldier, whose exploit places him on a level with those two great holders of historic gaps, Leonidas at Thermopylae and Horatius on the bridge at Rome, there is nothing in the records to warrant the assertion save a statement by Dollier de Casson in his story of Montreal. Dollard was seeking a chance, declared the Sulpician historian, "to be of use to him on account of something which was said to have happened in France."

It may have been that Dollard himself had talked of the matter or at least that he had dropped a hint. Certainly this was not the kind of rumor or canard which would have been invented in the years immediately following the great stand at the Long Sault, when all New France rang with praise of the little band. More likely the story would have been suppressed, and banished from all minds, if there had been any feeling that it could cast the slighest shadow on this new-made grave. Dollier de Casson arrived in Montreal six years after the event and doubtless heard the story then, told without rancor or any desire to detract from the glorious record of Adam Dollard. Certainly Dollier de Casson would not have invented it. That gentle ex-soldier, with his big generous heart in his huge frame, was incapable of such malice.

Here, then, was Adam Dollard des Ormeaux, looking eagerly for a chance to strike a bold blow for New France and perhaps to win something for the bare shield of a seventeenth-century Tor. He went to Maisonneuve and told him of a plan he had formed. The war clouds had been getting denser and lower all the time. Iroquois warriors had wintered on the upper Ottawa, several hundreds of them, and a still larger concentration was under way along the Richelieu. At least a thousand braves were out on the warpath. Would it not be the best kind of defense to go immediately on the offensive? Dollard proposed to the governor that he be allowed to recruit a small band of men and make a stand on the Ottawa in the hope of preventing a junction of the two forces.

Such, at least, was the story accepted and loudly extolled during most of the years which have elapsed: that Dollard led his men to the Long Sault, knowing they would all die but believing that a bold enough stand might give Montreal more time to prepare and even perhaps raise a doubt in Iroquois minds as to the possibility of succeeding in their main objective. If this was the plan he outlined to the governor, it was indeed a sublime act of sacrifice and one of the great and unforgettable audacities of history. It might reasonably raise doubts, however, as to the good judgment of the commander who allowed them to go. Maisonneuve could not fail to recall the near disaster which followed when he undertook a sally into the woods at Montreal against his better judgment and walked into an ambush. So small a band as Dollard proposed to take might easily be destroyed by a large Iroquois war party, and thus they would throw their lives away uselessly. They could be employed to better advantage behind the defenses of Montreal, where in the event of a concerted attack every pair of eyes capable of sighting a musket would be needed and no heart of good resolution could be spared.

The facts seem to indicate that Dollard's plan was a less ambitious one. A close checking of the dates involved led to the conclusion that he could not have known of the Iroquois designs as early as this; that, in fact, no one in Montreal had yet heard. The first hint of the plan was given at Quebec when a Mohegan warrior, who had become a naturalized Mohawk, was being burned at the stake. He let it be known that eight hundred Iroquois braves were gathering at the mouth of the Richelieu and waiting only for word of the coming of the party from up the Ottawa. Montreal was to be attacked first, then Three Rivers, and finally Quebec. It was in the early part of May that the captive told his story, but it was in April that Dollard proposed his plan to Maisonneuve.

It seems certain that Dollard's suggestion was that he would take his party up the Ottawa and pick off as many as possible of the hunting parties as they returned down the river. This plan was a reasonable one. Maisonneuve listened and gave his assent.

But, conceding that Dollard did not expect to face the heavy odds which he was doomed to encounter, the plan he proposed was both bold and patriotic. It achieved, wittingly or not, the great result which early chronicles declared to have been in his mind from the start, the salvation of Montreal. The glory he won is not dimmed if we conclude that he did not plan in the beginning to commit himself and his comrades to the certainty of death. The heroes of the Long Sault deserve all the praise and the adulation which have been accorded them down the slow-turning calendar of the years.

3

Charles le Moyne came over from Longueuil when he heard what was afoot. He wanted to join the party, but he was strongly of the opinion that it would be better to wait until he and the other settlers thereabouts had finished with the sowing of their crops. What would be the use of beating the Iroquois, he asked, if there would not be flour and vegetables that winter in the food warehouses along *La Commune?* It was early to make any move, he contended also. No Iroquois parties would be encountered on the Ottawa for at least a fortnight. On these points both Lambert Closse and Picoté de Belestre, fighting men of proven courage and sagacity, agreed with the young seigneur of Longueuil.

Dollard refused to wait. Perhaps this was due to a sense of urgency, a fear that the opportunity would be lost if they delayed. Perhaps—and this is the reason most generally accepted—he was concerned because he would have to surrender the command of the party if these men of established seniority joined. He felt that the plan was his and that he should have the responsibility of carrying it through. Whatever the reason, he convinced his followers that they must leave at once.

He had recruited sixteen men, all as eager as he was to risk their lives in the common cause. The gallant seventeen made their wills, confessed, and received the sacrament in the little stone chapel of the Hôtel-Dieu.

The band who knelt before the altar were almost pitifully young. There was one among them who had reached his thirty-first year; the rest were in their twenties, for the most part the early twenties. Their earnest faces carried the flush of youth and an exultation due to the fineness of the cause. They were not men of knightly rank venturing out to a deed of high emprise; they were of humble stock, soldiers who had come with the last contingent, artisans, tillers of the soil. The list of their names, which is still preserved and honored, testifies to the low social level from which most of them sprang.

Because they were not experienced woodsmen, they lost time in negotiating the swift and treacherous currents around Montreal Island; a delay which Charles le Moyne could have saved them. It was a full week before they managed to enter the mouth of the tumultuous tributary. The task continued hard as they battled the swift-flowing waters. They passed the Carillon and then the Chute à Blondeau. It was only after nearly two weeks of backbreaking effort that they came to the narrow passage where in a white fury the roaring waters of the Long Sault rolled by.

This was on May 1, and none of the Iroquois had yet come down the Ottawa. Here they decided to wait.

A short distance back from the angry waters, on the eastern side of the Sault, they found an abandoned stockade. It was no more than a rough enclosure of logs, high enough to give protection to crouching men but not reinforced in any way and already showing signs of disintegration. This was indeed a stroke of luck, for all the heaviest work involved in creating a fort had been done. A little

more effort would have turned the stockade into a tight island of
defense against which an Iroquois wave might beat in vain. If Dollard and his followers had been expecting a large war party to come
down the river against them, they would have taken advantage of
this spell allowed them to raise the walls and strengthen them in
every way. As it was, they did nothing. They even raised their kettles
along the bank of the stream and did not stock the fort with provisions or water. This is the second reason, a conclusive one, for sup-
posing that Dollard and his young companions had not anticipated
the proportions of the risk ahead of them.

At this point a large party of Indian allies joined them. There
were forty Hurons under a wise and brave chief named Anahotaha
and four Algonquins from Three Rivers led by Mitewemeg. They
had arrived in Montreal and had heard of the bold venture of the
seventeen Frenchmen and had conceived a desire to take a hand.
Apparently there was open talk of Dollard's plan in Montreal, and
this would not have been the case if it had been regarded as a matter
of high military strategy; nor, for that matter, would the Indian
allies have been venturing along the St. Lawrence if they had known
of the Iroquois concentration at Richelieu. Maisonneuve had given
the chiefs a letter to Dollard to serve as their credentials.

Dollard seems to have welcomed the newcomers and the unexpected augmentation of strength they gave him. For two more days
they waited.

4

At last the hour struck. The scouts placed at the head of the Sault
brought down word that two canoes, filled with Iroquois, were in
sight. Dollard now gave proof of his capacity as a soldier. He selected a spot where he judged the Iroquois would land, and here
his men concealed themselves in the underbrush. The ambush had
been shrewdly planted, for the two elm-bark canoes, containing five
Iroquois braves, pulled in here. As they came ashore the concealed
Frenchmen fired a volley. Unfortunately one of the Iroquois escaped
unharmed and carried the word back to the main party.

Almost at once, it seemed, the narrow stream became filled with
canoes manned by savages eager to avenge the attack. The startled
Dollard, making a hasty appraisal of the enemy strength, saw that
there were forty or fifty canoes in the water. This meant a force of

not less than two hundred warriors. For the first time, perhaps, he realized the extreme jeopardy in which he and his companions were placed. He ordered a retreat to the shelter of the fort.

The Iroquois swarmed ashore like angry hornets. Without making any attempt at organization they came down on the stockade in an immediate attack. The Frenchmen and their allies poured volley after volley into them, killing and wounding many. The Iroquois chiefs soon realized from the firmness of the resistance that such a hasty onslaught would not succeed. They drew their men back out of range. A council was held, and then several of the furiously discomfited warriors came forward to open a parley.

The heat of the conflict was in the blood of the little band behind the loosely constructed log wall. Without pausing for thought, they fired on the Iroquois emissaries, killing several of them. Those who escaped rejoined the waiting warriors in the woods above.

Anahotaha is reported to have given his head a grave shake at this. He said to Dollard: "Ah, comrade, you have spoiled everything. You ought to have waited the result of the council our enemies are holding."

The state of mind which now possessed the Iroquois braves can easily be conceived. This interruption to their plans was a complete surprise. They had lost many of their number, shot down in that first angry attempt to clear the daring Frenchmen from their path, and there was in the men of the Five Nations a sense of loyalty which made the sight of their dead the most potent incitement to increased effort. If any serious delay resulted here, they would be late for the appointed rendezvous with the large concentration near the mouth of the Richelieu. The hasty council they held, therefore, was not marked by deliberate and rational discussion; it was, rather, an explosion of furious talk. Being wily tacticians, even when roused to the highest fighting pitch, they concluded that another frontal assault would be too costly. Perhaps they were misjudging the size of the force opposed to them; at any rate, their next step was to begin building a fort of their own farther up the river.

This gave Dollard and his men an opportunity to accomplish the task they should have set themselves to as soon as they arrived and found the log barricade. They reinforced the wall by cutting branches from the trees about them and binding them around the stakes and the crosspieces, thus turning the shaky structure into a solid circular wall. All gaps were stuffed with earth and stones, leaving only small loopholes. Realizing the dire peril in which they stood, the young Frenchmen worked in desperate haste; and as they worked they could see bands of the Iroquois ranging up and down the shore of the noisy Sault, smashing the canoes they found there (thus destroying the last chance of the French to make a dash for safety) and demolishing the kettles suspended over the ashes of the last fire.

The second attack was launched from all sides and with the suddenness and weight of a thunderbolt. The men of the Long House rushed boldly out from the cover of the trees, leaping in the air as they ran and screaming in hate and rage. They strove to build a fire against the stockade, using for fuel the bark of the French canoes. Inside the fort there was no trace of panic. Dollard's voice in directing the defense was clear and confident and amazingly cool. The Frenchmen at their small loopholes poured a devastating fire into the close ranks of the enemy. The Iroquois, failing to set the wall ablaze, retreated in a sudden confusion. Their chiefs rallied them and they came back a second time; with the same result. A third attack was broken and repulsed, and then the chagrined warriors returned to their own rude fort for a second council of war.

The result of the Iroquois debate was proof of the bewilderment and dismay they were feeling as a result of the unexpected firmness of the French stand. They came to the conclusion that their strength was not sufficient to clear the path unassisted. Messengers were sent off to the main concentration, asking for reinforcements.

For five days there was a lull, but this did not mean that the Iroquois were idle. They kept a close watch on the stockade, sniping with matchlock and bow from behind the trees, maintaining at all times a threat of attack so that the defenders were never permitted a moment's ease. This was typical of Iroquois methods. Equally typical was the plan they carried out to split the defense forces. Renegade Hurons in the attacking force kept up a constant verbal assault on the followers of Anahotaha. The whole of the Iroquois strength was coming, they shouted gleefully, they were coming in their hundreds and thousands. The water would be black with their canoes, the loud roar of the rapids would be lost in the great battle cry of the Long House.

"Come!" they cried. "Save yourselves while you have the chance. Come over to us!"

The gallant Frenchmen behind the earth-chinked logs had no

illusions. Death faced them, swift and inexorable. They had one
consolation left: that they still had it in their power to make the
Iroquois victory a costly one. In the hope of diverting attack from
the vulnerable little town at the meeting place of the rivers, they
would fight on. But their Indian allies had no such consolation, and
it is not surprising that the followers of Anahotaha began to hearken
to this invitation dinned so insistently into their ears. If there was
a shred of hope left for them, it was in heeding the forked tongues
of the renegades. One by one the Hurons began to climb the barricade.

The Indians who remained jeered as the deserters sprang over
the top and scuttled across the open space, which was now heaped
high with the bodies of the dead. This, as it turned out, was sheer
bravado. None of the Hurons caught in this deathtrap had any
stomach left for fighting. Even as they jeered they were edging up
to the barricade in order to join the exodus. In the end the brave
Anahotaha was the only member of his party who remained. The
four Algonquins, to whom no promise of clemency had been held
out, remained with their chief when the last of the Hurons had vanished. But they were a badly shaken lot.

The position of the small remnant was a desperate one. Rest was
denied them, for the foe maintained the threat of attack through
the hours of darkness. They had no water, and their thirst became
so great that they could not force down their throats the dry rations
which remained. Hungry, thirsty, unnerved by lack of sleep, the
gaunt young men stood at the loopholes and prayed constantly to
the God in Whom they placed their trust.

On the fifth day the warriors from the Richelieu concentration
arrived, more than five hundred in all. The din of their arrival, the
triumphant war whoops which echoed through the woods, the formidable massing on all sides accentuated the hopelessness of the
odds: seven or eight hundred trained fighting men, filled with hate
and rage, against seventeen weary Frenchmen and six native allies.
The defenders were starved, maddened with thirst, their nerves
raw. The end, it was only too clear, could not long be delayed.

But in an area as restricted as the ground over which the small
redoubt could be attacked, the law of diminishing returns came into
operation. Eight hundred Iroquois could do little more, when it
came to a frontal attack, than two hundred, save to assure replace-

ments and an unrelenting persistence. The first attack, delivered to the eldritch clamor of hundreds of threats, was no more successful than the earlier ones. The desperate defenders treated the charging tribesmen to such a welcome of lead that the Iroquois charge curled back like a spent wave, broke, and receded. This check was so unexpected that an Iroquois council was held immediately after, and the suggestion of abandoning the contest was seriously debated.

Second thoughts prevailed, however. The Unbeatable Men, the *Ongue Honwe,* as they still proudly called themselves, could not concede their inability to break down the resistance of a mere handful. The stockade must be carried, no matter at what cost in lives. For three days they busied themselves with preparations, keeping up an incessant all-day and all-night aggression. The white of complete exhaustion began to show under the two weeks' accumulation of beard on the faces of the defenders. Staggering from lack of nourishment, they were barely able to keep their positions at the loopholes.

The Iroquois chiefs then produced the packages of sticks. This was always a solemn moment in the Spartan ritual of war which the men of the Five Nations observed. The sticks were strewn on the ground near the simmering food kettles. No exhortation was delivered, no form of compulsion employed. Each man willing to attack in the van was expected to come forward and pick up one of the sticks.

There was no delay, no holding back. The tall, proud volunteers stepped up and each selected his stick. These bold spirits were then given shields which had been fashioned out of the trunks of trees during the three days of preparation. Behind these they crouched, waiting for the signal to advance, another Birnam Wood ready to move on Dunsinane.

The charge was delivered from all quarters. Nothing could exceed the dread and horror of the scene on which the eyes of the little white handful rested. First came the Men of the Sticks, bold, vengeful, crouching like tigers behind their rough shields, lighted torches in their hands to be applied to the logs of the barricade; behind this vanguard the less bold spirits, fierce nevertheless in their war paint, wildly vocal. If the defenders cast despairing glances upward, they were robbed of a last glimpse of the sun, for the smoke of the torches and the burning fuel, which was being dragged forward, had already mounted above the tops of the trees. It was impossible to exchange a word, for the air was filled with the wild screeching of the embattled braves. Only one consolation was left, and each of the gallant young men took advantage of it, without a doubt, to say a brief prayer. Perhaps each made a special intercession, "O God, in Thy mercy, let me die in the fighting!"

The charge did not succeed at once, so stoutly were the loopholes manned. It was the recoil of an experiment which gave the Iroquois their chance. Dollard had crammed a musketoon with powder and bullets, intending to toss it over the barricade so that it would explode in the close ranks of the attacking redskins. His aim was not good; the handmade grenade struck the top of the logs and fell back into the enclosure. The explosion which followed killed several of the defenders and nearly blinded the rest. In the confusion thus created, the Iroquois gained possession of some of the loopholes and began to fire through them at the surviving members of the little band.

It was soon over then. The Men of the Sticks climbed the barricade, tomahawks out and ready, scalping knives bare in their belts, screeching in triumph. Dollard was one of the first killed. In the hand-to-hand fighting which ensued the Frenchmen were soon cut down. All but four died in the struggle, and of the survivors, three were so close to death that the savages dispatched them where they lay. The fate of the fourth has never been determined definitely. He may have succumbed to his wounds before he could be carried away to die on a torture platform; and even after a lapse of three centuries it is impossible to suppress a shudder at the thought of the terrible retribution which may have been exacted of one unfortunate man.

The Men of the Sticks tossed their improvised shields on the fire which licked at the barricade of logs. They had gambled with death and now they could strut in the insolence of pride in their home villages, each with his stick suspended around his neck. The Iroquois losses had not been heavy on this last day, but it is much to be doubted if the leaders of this great concentration took satisfaction out of the result. They had won, but at a bitter cost in men, in prestige, in the complete dislocation of their plans for driving the French into the sea.

5

A few days after the finish of the struggle a trading company came down the Ottawa in canoes loaded with fur from a profitable winter of hunting and trading. In the van were the two eager young men who had slipped out in the dead of night through the harbor guards at Three Rivers, Radisson and Groseilliers.

For the most part, they had spent the winter in the country north and west of Lake Superior but had penetrated far enough south to see where a certain forked river had its source. Radison's notes indicate that this river was considered of very great importance among the Indians of that district, and so some historians have seized on his reference as meaning that it was this ingenious young trader who discovered the Mississippi. Whether or not the eyes of the eager pair had rested on the Father of Waters, there is no denying that they had spent a fruitful time. They were bringing back news that the country north of Lake Superior was thickly populated with an especially fine species of beaver and that the Indians of all the western lands were eager to trade with the French. They were full of information about the northern waters and had evolved a new theory with reference to the approach to Hudson's Bay. They were convinced that instead of running the gamut of Iroquois interference along the Ottawa, the bay could be more readily reached by sailing north of Labrador and cutting in through an entrance from the Atlantic. A more specific result was the heavily loaded condition of the canoes. It developed later that the value of the furs they were taking to the market reached the handsome total of 140,000 livres.

When the home-coming traders reached the Long Sault a terrible sight greeted their eyes. Before leaving on their morose and far from triumphant return to Iroquois land, the victors had trussed up the bodies of the French dead to posts along the line of the shore. It is not known whether the hunting party removed the bodies from the posts and buried them, although it seems certain they would do so. This much they did, however—they counted the bodies. There were sixteen. Not seventeen; one was missing.

The last day of the attack could not have been later than May 11. Ten days later one of the Huron deserters, a Christian who had been baptized and given the name of Louis, arrived at Montreal, having

managed to make his escape. He told the story of the uneven struggle, providing the details which could come only from an eyewitness.
The circumstantial narrative which has been set down is based
largely on what Louis told of the epic adventure and on corrobora-
tive bits of evidence which developed later from other Huron prisoners who escaped, one of whom was actually tied to the death stake
and had suffered the first tortures when a violent storm drove his
tormentors into shelter and gave him the opportunity to free himself from his bonds.

The first inventory of the wills and possessions of the brave young
men was made in May 27. On June 3 their deaths were entered on
the parish records. They were now officially dead, even the one
who had not been fortunate enough to have his lifeless body nailed
to a post along the boiling waters of the Long Sault.

The Iroquois forces returned to their own country without striking
another blow, and the conclusion has been accepted that they had
lost faith in the feasibility of breaking down the bristling redoubts
of Montreal. Their confidence had been shaken by the difficulty
they had met in carrying a flimsy barricade with no more than a
handful of boys behind it. The French crops were planted in peace,
and in the fall there was a bountiful harvest to carry the settlers
through the long winter.

It does not matter whether or not Adam Dollard enlisted his band
with a sure knowledge of the fate in store for them and an advance
knowledge of Iroquois plans. The important thing is that they did
save the colonies. They held the gap long enough, even as Leonidas
did at Thermopylae.

CHAPTER XX

The Transfer of Montreal Island to the Sulpicians—
The Appointment of Bishop Laval Leads to Clerical War
and Begins a Great Chapter in Canadian History

1

BEFORE the gallantry of Adam Dollard and his companions brought about a temporary lull in the hostility with the Iroquois, there had been developments of a highly interesting nature in the colony of New France. As a result of the reorganization of the Company at Montreal, in which the spirituelle but strongminded Jeanne Mance had played a big part, it had been recognized that the original founders were no longer capable of providing satisfactorily for the needs of the growing town and that a more direct form of control was desirable. The newly created Seminary of St. Sulpice was invited in 1657 to assume the task. They accepted, and so there began an association which was highly successful and which has left indelible traces on the city of Montreal.

It was an unusual step to put the affairs of a frontier town in the hands of a religious organization, but those responsible for the move had shown a high degree of imagination as well as sound judgment. The Sulpicians were secular priests and without exception gentlemen of property. Anyone who eschews the advantages of living comfortably on inherited wealth and joins an order where he dons the white rabat of the parish priest and devotes all his time to the service of the people who lack the privileges he could be enjoying is certain, in the first place, to be of a high heart. He must have courage and resolution and, above all, a sense of imagination. *Les Messieurs de St. Sulpice,* as they were called, were not driven by fanaticism nor filled with gloom and doubts. They walked in the sunshine. They considered the service of mankind a joyous mission.

As their funds were ample, they were in a rare position to do much good.

But the transfer of Montreal Island to the Sulpicians, which was not completed until four years later, was not to be brought about without difficulty. The first contingent, consisting of four members, reached New France late in the summer of 1657, having been delayed by the death of the founder of the seminary, Monsieur Olier. They found themselves involved at once in a sharp flare-up of the strained feelings between Quebec and Montreal. There had been a growing realization of the need for a permanent head of the Church in Canada. As the vows of the Jesuits precluded any of them from accepting a bishopric, it occurred to the messieurs of the seminary that one of their number might reasonably be selected. They moved quickly to secure for one of the original four, the Abbé de Queylus, the approval of the Assembly of the French Clergy. This seems to have been accomplished before the Jesuits bestirred themselves in the matter. The latter had not been concerned prior to this, but they began now to see the disadvantages of a bishopric vested in another order; particularly in view of their great services to the colony and the extent of their sacrifices. They started quietly to use their enormous interest at court. They used it to such good advantage that Mazarin temporized and delayed his sanction of the appointment of the Abbé de Queylus.

Queylus was a man of high character and undoubted capacity. He had considerable personal wealth and had become noted for his generosity. On the surface he was an excellent choice for the new post of Canadian bishop. In the situation which developed, however, he proceeded to demonstrate that he lacked at least some of the qualities which would be needed in the exercise of such wide powers. He was both aggressive and ambitious and quite lacking in discretion. These weaknesses showed when he paid a visit to Quebec soon after his arrival and preached two inflammatory sermons. The lack of wisdom he thus displayed was due to his receipt while in Quebec of letters from the Archbishop of Rouen appointing him vicar-general for all of Canada. The archbishop had been taking the position that Canada was under his jurisdiction because most of the ships bound for the colony sailed from ports in his diocese, and his appointment of Queylus was his first move to have this recognized. The latter now considered himself safely seated in the saddle, and he resented the opposition which was apparent immediately in the attitude of the Jesuit fathers. He lashed out at them so vigorously from the pulpit that they retaliated in kind, declaring that the abbé was warring on them more savagely than the Iroquois.

In the meantime there had been a stirring under the surface in France. Largely due to the influence of Anne of Austria, Pope Alexander VII conferred the new post on François Xavier de Laval-Montmorency, Abbé de Montigny. He was a relatively young man, having reached the age of thirty-six years, and although his family was both wealthy and great ("as noble as a Montmorency" was a common saying in France), he had devoted himself to good works and had lived an extremely ascetic life. The Queen Mother was delighted with the appointment. She set aside for him from her own funds a pension of one thousand livres annually and she wrote personally to Governor d'Argenson in Quebec, "I wish to join this letter to that of the King, my son, to let you know that, according to his inclination and to mine, you must have the Bishop of Petraea acknowledged as vicar-apostolic all over the country of Canada under the power of the King."

In making this appointment the Pope had shrewdly kept in mind a conflict which was sharply dividing the Church in France into two camps: the Gallican party, which believed that all temporal power belonged to the King, and the papal party, which considered the Pope supreme in everything. The Jesuit order was strongly committed to the latter view. In appointing Laval vicar-apostolic instead of bishop, the Pope placed him directly under papal supervision. The bishopric of Petraea was given him as well. This ignored the Concordat of Bologna, which had placed the appointment of bishops in the Pope's hands but with the understanding that the nominations must come from the King of France. It was true that in this case the nomination had come from the King, but specifically for the post of Bishop of Canada. The royal assent to the lesser title granted was both reluctant and uneasy. The papal party had won a victory. Laval came to Canada, therefore, with the somewhat halfhearted backing of the King but the wholehearted approval of the Jesuit fathers.

The young appointee, who was destined to be one of the most controversial figures in early Canadian history and eventually one of the best loved, arrived at Quebec in June 1659. It was six in the afternoon when the ship warped into its moorings, and a rosy stream of sunlight from the west fell on the battlements of the citadel and the metal roofs of the episcopal buildings along the crest. The little city had already gained an atmosphere of its own. It looked old, as though memories and traditions clung to its crooked streets. The vicar-apostolic, realizing the need to make an impression, had arrayed himself in his pontifical vestments, and Father Jerome Lalemant, who stood beside him, wrote later in one of his letters, "He looked as an angel of heaven."

It is possible, however, that the young Vicomte d'Argenson, who had come down to the moorings to extend an official greeting, felt some misgivings when he observed the stern and exacting dark eyes of the new head of the Church, the strong and somewhat massive nose protruding from the pale face with more than a hint of the masterful nature of its owner, the forehead which combined intelligence with nobility, the thin lips which told of an unbending will. It was inevitable that this inflexible cleric would clash on points of authority with the soldierly aristocrat who represented the King. Marie de l'Incarnation, who was as active and zealous as ever in the direction of the Ursulines, seems to have cut to the core of things in one of her long letters to her son; the letters which did so much to lend posterity a clear insight into the currents of thought which stirred in the colony. It was clear, she wrote, that he (Laval) was the choice of God if not of man. She was quite right in her estimate of the role he was to play. No one lacking the qualities of Laval, the stern will, the determination to have his own way, which he believed to be the way of God, could have succeeded in the new post.

The immediate arrangements made by the newcomer were an indication of the character of the man. He showed no inclination to set himself up in state. After staying for a short time with the Jesuit fathers, he rented from the Ursulines the small house which Madame de la Peltrie had built for herself beside the seminary. That lady of many contradictions refused to listen to his protests and moved out at once so that he could have the tiny two-story stone house which was no more than thirty by twenty feet. It might have been expected, in view of her gentle upbringing and refinement, that she would have invested it during her years of occupancy with some degree of charm, perhaps even a hint of elegance. Those who had seen her crossing the ice in her bare feet on the freezingly cold night when the seminary burned down in 1650 to help in the rescue of her pupils would not have been surprised when it was found that such was not the case. The bishop fell heir to two plain wooden bedsteads with straw mattresses, two worn quilts, a few yards of fustian serving as bed curtains, a plain wooden table with two books, *The Epistles and Gospels* and a *Selection of Meditations,* a straw-bottomed chair, a stool, and a crucifix painted on wood.

In this modest dwelling, therefore, the new head of the Church established himself, sharing the inadequate space with three priests and two male servants, a valet-cook and a gardener. He built a high paling around the small garden in which it was set, but otherwise he does not seem to have made any changes.

Another immediate demonstration was given of the character of Laval. In Montreal the Abbé de Loc-Dieu, the proper designation of the aggressive Queylus, was continuing to display belief that his appointment as vicar-apostolic by the Archbishop of Rouen made him the clerical head of all New France. This was a state of affairs which the scion of the noble house of Montmorency could not tolerate. A believer in action, Laval was not content to leave any doubt as to where he stood. Receiving no response after summoning the recalcitrant abbé to Quebec, he persuaded the governor to take a squad of soldiers to Montreal and bring Queylus back willy-nilly. Such, at least, is the story that one school of historians tells. Others say that Queylus went to Quebec of his own free will, having an equal desire to discuss the rival claims. It all seems to hinge on the interpretation of one document and, to an even greater extent, on the sympathies of the narrators. Those who desire to keep the Laval record stainless hold strongly to the second version.

This position seems an unnecessary one. No great blame can be laid at Laval's door if he took summary action. It is clear enough that the querulous Queylus was behaving heedlessly and that Laval himself had every reason to believe in the full legality of his position. The situation, moreover, could not be allowed to drag along. The history of the day, so distressingly filled with the grim details of the Indian wars, loses one of its most diverting episodes when the struggle between the two embattled churchmen is passed over or qualified; this good, thumping fight between two men who saw only one way and did not fear consequences.

This much is certain, that there were stormy scenes between the two men. It was a bitter clash of wills; but Laval, armed with authority from both Pope and King, was the winner. The protesting abbé took the next ship back to France; some say of his own free will, some that he was given no choice in the matter.

The incident created a storm on both sides of the Atlantic. The Sulpicians protested bitterly. Queylus proceeded to unite the Gallican party behind him, with the tacit support, at least, of the Archbishop of Rouen. The hand of Laval reached back across the Atlantic, however, and shattered the efforts of the dissentients. The King, who was on his way to the southern frontier of France, where he would meet and marry the Infanta of Spain, was persuaded to write a letter to Queylus. "My will," declared the young monarch, "is that you remain in my kingdom, enjoining you not to leave it without my express permission."

Queylus disregarded the royal command and set out for Rome, hoping to win the Pope over to his side of the controversy. This action seems to have been anticipated, and the inner papal circle had been told that Queylus and his supporters were secret supporters of Jansenism. The disobedient Sulpician received a decidedly cool reception when he reached Rome.

But the militant abbé was a fighter, a worthy opponent for the stern protagonist at Quebec. He seems to have made a good impression in the Eternal City. Gradually he won some support for his claims and was given bulls from the Congregation of the *Daterie*, an office of the *Curia*, confirming the independence of the Sulpicians in Montreal. Armed with these, he took passage on a ship sailing for Canada and on August 3, 1661, he arrived at Quebec, triumphant and belligerent; the bulls under his arm, figuratively speaking, to be employed as weapons in the resolving of his dispute with Laval.

It would be an understatement to say that Laval was angry when he discovered that, in spite of all the precautions and the definite orders of the King, the unpredictable Queylus had returned to New France. His first move was to charge that the Sulpician had obtained the bulls by fraud and misrepresentation. An order was issued that the abbé was to remain in Quebec until the authorities in France had been notified of his illegal entry. Argenson was supposed to act in concert by placing the abbé in confinement pending the disposition of his case, but the young governor, caught between two fires and having divided sympathies, temporized. Laval waited no more than a day and then sent a peremptory demand to the governor. Before Argenson could make up his mind, the turbulent Sulpician took matters into his own hands. His servants obtained a canoe, and during the hours of darkness he started off on his way up the river to Montreal.

If Laval had been angry before, his ire now grew by comparison to extreme heights. He suspended the abbé from the exercise of all priestly duties. This order, sent off early the next morning, overtook the runaway Sulpician before he reached Montreal. Not at all perturbed, Queylus sat himself down to wait whatever might befall. He had not long to wait. Laval had sent wrathful messages to France and in course of time he received the needed authorization. Argenson had from the King a command to give his full support to Laval. This left the governor with nothing to do but obey. He brought Queylus to Quebec and sent him back to France on the first ship.

The bulls from the Congregation of the *Daterie* were withdrawn. The Archbishop of Rouen gave in and renounced his claim to any form of supervision over the Church in Canada. Queylus remained for the next seven years in France in an unhappy semi-obscurity. Laval had won a complete victory.

2

It must be said at the outset that the first few years of Laval's rule in New France were contentious and quarrelsome ones. This determined priest, who was to prove himself a powerful and effective head of the Church and to become in time mellow and gentle, considered himself at first under the necessity of fighting with the temporal officers over the duties and privileges of his office. He was breaking new ground and as vicar of the Pope he felt that he took precedence over any state official. The two governors who served in this period considered for their part that the dignity of the kingship lay in their hands and that they must not yield on points of observance.

There was, first of all, the question as to where they should be seated in church. Argenson contended that he should be in the sanctuary, that section of church close to the altar. Laval did not agree. They finally called in the Sieur d'Ailleboust to act as arbitrator. After much consideration D'Ailleboust gave the decision to the head of the Church: the bishop would sit inside the rail, the governor outside.

A bitter incident occurred during midnight Mass on Christmas Eve when the deacon sent a subordinate incense carrier to the governor. In this instance the head of the Church, realizing that his officer had gone too far, ruled that in future the deacon must do the honors personally. He was adamant, however, in the matter of Argenson's desire to be an honorary churchwarden. This could not be allowed.

One dispute flared up openly, and on Palm Sunday there was no procession. The governor had demanded that he and certain other gentlemen of temporal office should precede the churchwardens. To this the young bishop would not agree.

An even more flagrant display of disagreement occurred on the Feast of Corpus Christi, which fell on the sixteenth of June. The procession was to stop at various points in the town where altars had been raised, and this brought up the point as to what the soldiers should do about removing their hats when the procession reached the citadel. Laval declared positively that no stop would be made at the citadel if the proceedings were to be marred by covered heads. The governor, realizing perhaps how fond the people were of the strict observance of church ritual, gave in finally. Laval discovered, however, that his victory had been only a partial one. The soldiers refused to kneel when the procession, headed by the sumptuously vested officers of the Church, stopped at the entrance to the fort. The governor had been prevented from attending by ill-health, and so the proceedings were halted while word of the situation was dispatched to him. He replied shortly that it was the duty of soldiers to remain in an upright position, that vigilance was their excuse for being, and that he would not permit what the bishop demanded. Monseigneur Laval ordered the procession on at once without performing the customary service at the altar of the garrison. The following comment on this clash is found in the *Jesuit Journal:* "On such occasions the King's guards kneel down on one knee without removing their hats. . . . This matter should have been previously elucidated and agreed upon."

It was during Avagour's brief term of office that the incident of the blessing of bread threatened to develop into an open rupture. The new governor, who was older than Argenson and somewhat obstinate, liked to do things his own way. On an occasion when he had supplied the bread to be blessed, he had it carried into the edifice during the celebration of Mass to the sound of drum and fife. Laval was incensed at this interruption and resentful, moreover, of a form of ostentation like the carrying in to music of a Yuletide boar's head or the piping in of a dish of haggis to a laird's table. The two officials disputed the point with a great deal of bitterness. Again the bishop prevailed. At any rate, it was decided that, if the governor must have his fifes and drums, it should be all finished and done with before Mass began.

The bickering did not stop with matters concerning church observance. During February a public catechism was held in the school and, as both governor and bishop were to be present, it was decided the pupils would disregard them. It was rather solemnly engaged that the infant hands would be kept too busy for a salute to either man. This was carefully explained to the children, and it was believed that the difficulty over precedence could be skirted successfully. Two of the boys, however, got out of hand. Charles Couillard and Ignace de Repentigny, scions of two of the best families, had either been secretly coached by their parents (as was later contended by the church officers) or they were carried away by the arrival of the governor in all the glory of plumed hat and velvet doublet and the sparkling of jewels on his sword hilt. They stood up and saluted the governor with a brisk flourish.

It would be pleasant if the episode could be closed with an intimation that the mistake was passed over with good-natured indifference. But, alas, such was not the case. The sequel is thus dealt with in the *Jesuit Journal:* "This greatly offended Monseigneur the Bishop. We tried to appease him; and the two children were whipped on the following morning for having disobeyed."

This far from flattering incident must be told because it is part of the picture of this early phase of Bishop Laval's life. It should not be used, however, except as contrast to a later episode. When the bishop had become an old man and was so badly crippled that walking was a matter of great difficulty, he found himself one night unable to sleep. Muffling himself up in his threadbare cloak, he hobbled out on the silent streets. It was in the middle of winter and a cold wind was blowing down from the battlements. He encountered on his walk a small boy who had nowhere to go, having been turned out of his home. The child was thinly clad and was shivering with the cold. The old man took him back at once to his own quarters at the seminary, where he removed his clothes and gave him a warm bath. Then, while the boy slept in the bishop's own bed, the latter found in the supply of wearing apparel which he kept for charitable distribution a suit of clothes as well as stockings and shoes. All through the night the gentle old man sat by the bedside while the boy slept, and the next day he made arrangements for his permanent care. This incident, a true one, was used in one of the better known of the many novels which have been written with early Quebec as a background.

Bishop Laval, in his first phase, was another Thomas à Becket, determined to assert the supremacy of Church over State, and so convinced of the importance of the issue that he was prepared to war unceasingly with governors and to be severe with school disobedience. Much stress has been laid on this unsympathetic period, but viewed with the perspective of time, it seems of small importance. It was soon over and done with, although to the end of his days the bishop would not tolerate any interference with his work and was always prepared to carry an issue to the ear of the King. The stern eye, the determined mien, which seemed at first the earmarks of an inflexible severity, were recognized as the years passed as the armor of his devotion.

The difference between the two ranking officers of the colony did not end with such relatively small matters as the incidents quoted above. There was, above everything else, the question of supplying liquor to the Indians. From the first moment of his arrival Bishop Laval found it necessary to protest on this point. In spite of the willingness of the governors to assist him, the traffic continued and the Indians were reduced to ever-lower depths of degradation.

Laval finally took an extreme step. He announced that all Frenchmen convicted of sharing in the profits of this nefarious trade would be excommunicated. This at first had the desired effect. It is recorded in the *Relations* that "one of the most remarkable occurrences is the almost complete suppression of drunkenness among our savages. . . . After the King's orders and the governor's decree had proved ineffectual, he [Laval], by excommunicating all the French who shall give liquor to the savages, suppressed all these disorders."

This was taking too rosy a view of the situation. The suppression proved to be temporary only. The traffic was not confined to the relatively few traders who dealt directly with the Indians. It was deep-seated, going right back to the sources of supply. Most of the colonial merchants were concerned in it in some degree. A large proportion of the sober citizens who heard Mass with earnest faces had money in their pockets which could be traced to the illicit sale of brandy. The traffic, accordingly, went on in spite of civil ordinances and ecclesiastical thunderings. Death and violence followed in the wake of the canoes of the white men.

Matters came to a head after the arrival of Baron Dubois d'Avagour to succeed Argenson as governor. He was an old soldier, blunt of speech and hasty of temper, but honest and sincerely anxious to fulfill his oaths of office. He had heard all about the difficulties his predecessor had experienced with the unbending head of the Church and he came to his post with his guard raised. They got along well enough for a time, but in due course the major issue of the liquor traffic came up to place them in open antagonism.

The excommunication threat had not done more than put a temporary check on the trade. A tangible form of punishment was needed, and Laval did not hesitate to demand that the death penalty be exacted. The new governor found that a current of strong opposition to this step ran under the surface. The citizenry did not dare stand openly against the zealous bishop, but they were prepared to show their opposition in other ways. Avagour hesitated and temporized. Finally, however, he was overborne; he gave in and authorized the decree.

Traders who had broken the law were brought before him at once. In the *Jesuit Journal* the results were briefly recorded as follows: "On the 7th [of October] Daniel Will was hanged—or rather shot—and on the 11th another named La Violette; and one was flogged on Monday the 10th." The brevity of this announcement bears no relation to the feeling which had developed in the colony. There seems to have been a general impression that such measures were excessive. The good citizens were uneasy. Where, they asked themselves, would such severity end?

Then a woman was brought in for illicit selling of brandy. The death penalty was not exacted in this case, but she was sentenced to a term of imprisonment. There were extenuating circumstances— she was a widow with a family to support—and Father Lalemant went to the governor with a plea for clemency. This was too much for the blunt soldier. He had been harried into confirming the decree in the first place, and now he was being asked to discriminate in carrying it out. He listened to the Jesuit with an impatience which culminated in an indignant outburst. No longer, he declared, would he be subjected to such contradictions.

"Since it is not a crime for this woman," he exclaimed, "it shall not be a crime for anybody."

The governor stuck to his word and refused to allow any further punishments. As a result, the sale of brandy was carried on openly and reached proportions greater than ever before. The bishop thundered from the pulpit, but to no avail. D'Avagour obstinately refused to listen. Finally Laval took the drastic step of returning to France and demanding the recall of the governor.

The sins of the colony were popularly believed to have been the cause of the great earthquake which shook the whole country on the night of February 3, 1663. It seems to have been a most violent one, although many of the reports recorded were obviously the result of inflamed imaginations. The clay beds of the St. Lawrence were disrupted by the shaking of the surface, and earthslides occurred everywhere. Streams were diverted from their courses, new waterfalls appeared in the most unexpected places, houses rocked back and forth, and the bells in church spires were set to ringing madly by the motion. Fissures opening in the earth sent people running for their lives, believing that the devil with a mighty pickax was opening new gateways to the fires of hell. No one seems to have been killed in spite of all the violent shaking of the hills and all the mighty winds, but people flocked to the churches, crying out that the end of the world was at hand and begging divine forgiveness for their sins.

It did not take long for the conviction to enter all minds, except perhaps the most hardened, that the brandy trade had been the cause. God had expressed His disapproval. The earthquake was no more than a warning of what would come to pass if men did not mend their ways.

The deep and passionate voice of the Bishop of Petraea had been at work in France in the meantime. He was given his way. Not only was Avagour recalled, but the young bishop was granted the right of selecting his successor.

3

It is a more pleasant task to write of the private life of François Xavier de Laval-Montmorency than to deal with the constant struggle he waged to maintain the dignity of his office on the level he deemed necessary. Even his greatest admirers are inclined to say that he sometimes erred in his official demands, but there can be nothing but praise for the exemplary life he led.

He has often been compared to Thomas à Becket, who strove in

QUEBEC, the Capital of NEW FRANCE, 1690

St Charles River

River

St. Lawrence

Comte de Frontenac

Samuel de Champlain

BISHOP LAVAL

Cardinal Richelieu

Jacques Cartier

IBERVILLE

LA SALLE

JEAN TALON

MADAME
DE LA PELTRIE

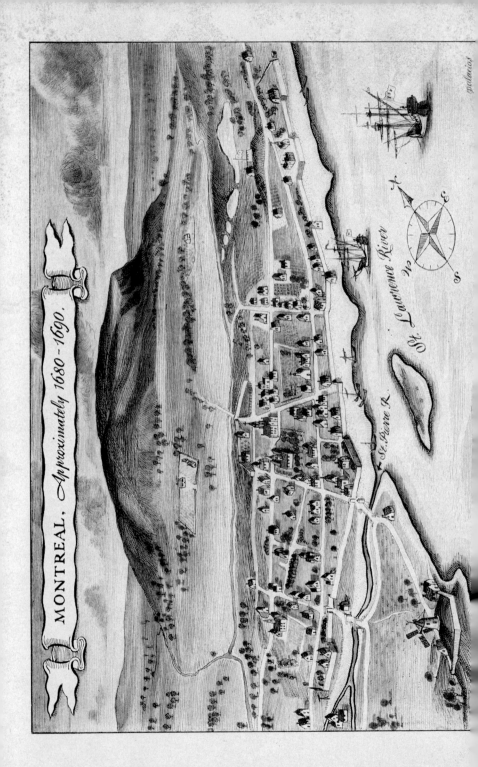

MONTREAL. *Approximately 1680–1690.*

St. Lawrence River

St. Pierre R.

the same cause against an arbitrary and very able king and who came to his death as a result. But there was one great difference between them. Becket had been the same king's chancellor and a man of mighty pride before he was made Archbishop of Canterbury. Laval was destined for the Church from the start and was only nine years old when he received the tonsure. At the age of fifteen, when he was already known for his devoutness, he was appointed canon of the cathedral of Evreux. When his two older brothers were killed in battle, his mother begged him to abandon his clerical intentions and take his place as head of the family. The prospect of so much wealth and power would have been irresistible to almost any other young man of his age. He not only refused, but he surrendered his titles to the seigneuries of Montigny and Montbeaudry to his younger brother, Jean Louis. Thus he stripped himself of all property, and when he was given his appointment in Canada he depended entirely on the small pension paid him out of the funds of the Queen Mother.

"He is certainly the most austere man in the world and the most indifferent to worldly advantages," wrote Marie de l'Incarnation of the young bishop; and this high praise was well deserved.

He rose always at two o'clock in the morning. Such an early start was particularly trying in the winter, because then the fires had burned out in the inadequate braziers and a frigid cold gripped the houses. But the bishop made no distinctions in the seasons. After dressing he would rekindle his fire—a very small one, for he was frugal even in the matter of fuel for his personal use—and then pray until four. Promptly at that hour he went out into the dark and the cold, lantern in hand, and walked to the cathedral. Here he opened the doors and rang the bells himself for the first Mass of the day at four-thirty. These were duties which devolved ordinarily on minor servants of the Church, but to assume them was a matter of personal satisfaction to the bishop. For the remainder of the day he immersed himself in the work of his office, which he administered with ability and dispatch. Not content with this, he ranged far afield to find menial and dangerous work for his ready hands, making beds in the hospitals, washing the feet and bandaging the sores of the patients, visiting the ships in the harbor and tending the ill members of the crew. It was always late at night when he went to bed. So determined was he to lose as little time as possible in the luxury of sleep that he would fend off drowsiness in the last hours by walking up and down as he talked to those about him or told his beads.

"There is no village priest in France," wrote one of his most fervent admirers, "who is not better nourished, better clad, and better lodged than was the bishop of New France."

This was in no sense an exaggeration. He had two meals a day only, never indulging in breakfast despite the early hour of his rising. They were extremely frugal meals. He subsisted largely on soups, but the favorite bouillons of the colony were never found on his table. It is probable that he did not know the taste of the rich bisques of pigeons and clams or the *boullie de blé d'inde*. The plainest of broths were served to him and, when they seemed too rich and savory, he diluted them with hot water. He never indulged in fresh meats, saying that his teeth were too tender for such fare. Accordingly his meat was kept a week after it had been cooked, and in hot weather it had to be washed in warm water to remove the worms which swarmed in it. He drank the thinnest of wines. The poorest habitant often indulged a sweet tooth with such delicacies as *crêpes de Tante Marie* or cakes filled with almond paste, spices, or raisins. The bishop refused desserts and even on feast days or special occasions he would thrust aside the *gâteau d'anis*, the aniseed cake which was the pride of the French-Canadian housewife.

The bishop laid on himself a stern injunction never to spend a sou on his own comfort. Although over the years he became shabby and threadbare, he did not buy clothes. All his small income went for alms, and so he depended on the stores of the seminary he had established for the training of native-born priests as much as the poorest novice. His faithful servant, Houssard, who was with him through his final days, wrote that in the course of twenty years the good old man had possessed only two winter cassocks and that when he came to die the last one was mended and ragged from long wear. Always, however, he had a supply of clothing on hand for distribution to the poor, purchased out of his inadequate income.

The austerity he inaugurated when he moved into the little house of Madame de la Peltrie was continued throughout his life. A straw mattress spread on hard boards was his couch, and he never allowed himself the luxury of sheets. No touch of luxury or graciousness was seen about his rooms. The furnishings were plain and cheap and practical. His supply of books was too small to warrant the designation of library. He read every day in the *Lives of the Saints* but rarely indulged any excursions into discussion of mundane matters. He refused to have a carriage and so he was, perhaps, the only bishop in the world who walked about his rounds. In his later years, when the weakness of his legs, tightly bound because of varicose veins (he bound them himself by the light of a candle when he first rose), made walking almost an impossibility, he would sometimes borrow a carriage or allow himself to be carried by the *engagés* at the seminary.

Such was the life of this stern disciplinarian who was always harder on himself than on anyone about him. Despite his personal austerity he believed in maintaining to the full the splendor of the Church. In the vessels of worship he wanted the glow of gold and the luster of silver. Rich coverings and the deep colors of stained glass pleased him beyond measure. The way he governed his own life was a compact between himself and his Maker, but he was eager to contend that when men gathered to worship God they should do so with proper majesty and opulence.

He had brought to his new post a conviction that the Church in Canada should be molded along new lines. The rigidity into which the mother church had settled over the centuries would not serve in this strange new land. The practice in France, to quote one of the major points, was to allow a curé to remain a full lifetime in the parish to which he was first assigned and to remove him only if his unfitness was unmistakably revealed; with the result that a slothful or indifferent priest could chill the spiritual zeal of his flock into an enduring apathy. Laval was determined to keep in his hands the power to remove a priest from any post where he was failing to function with zeal and understanding. He wanted also to have supervision over the selection and training of the priests who were to carry on the work in the colony. All this pointed to the need for a seminary where young men born or reared in Canada could be trained for holy orders under his own stern eye.

This was the first major change which the vicar-apostolic brought into effect. He was sadly hampered for funds in the early stages. Perhaps he regretted the excess of zeal which had induced him to part with all his personal property, for everything which remained to him would undoubtedly have been applied to the cost of the building and its maintenance. Having nothing, he raised funds among his kinsmen and friends in France and he strove, not too successfully, to impose a tithe on the settlers. In later years, when the seminary was firmly grounded and was fulfilling its function to his satisfaction, he put himself in the way of receiving land grants which

he turned over in perpetuity to the institution. In this way the valuable acres of Beaupré, the Island of Jesus, and what was once the
seigneury of the Petite Nation remain today among the possessions
of the school.

Ramparts now circled the crest of the rock. Reaching the top, a
visitor saw to the left the jumble of stone and framework which was
called the citadel of St. Louis and over which the white flag of
France waved. To the right was the Couillard house, occupying some
of the land originally granted to Louis Hébert. Between the Couillard property and the square on which the Jesuit college and the
cathedral fronted was an open stretch of land. This the young bishop
selected as the site for his seminary and here he built a far from pre-
tentious training school for the first of the youth of New France who
offered themselves to the Church.

One of the finest things about Bishop Laval was his intense love
for this institution of his own founding. He planned and directed
it on the soundest lines. It was to be not only a school but a sanctuary
to which the clergy of Canada could turn in sickness or weariness of
spirit and where they could spend their last years. Around it he
gradually created subsidiary establishments: a school for the ele-
mentary education of boys who might elect to join the priesthood,
which was started in 1668 in the Couillard house, and a farm school
for manual training. Out of this system of schools came in time Laval
University, which stands as proof of the farsightedness of this stormy
and controversial figure.

CHAPTER XXI

*Mazarin Dies and Louis XIV Decides to Rule
for Himself—Colbert Becomes His First Minister
—A Great Plan for Canada*

1

MARCH 9, 1661. Young King Louis XIV had been alone in his rooms ever since Cardinal Mazarin had succumbed earlier in the day to his illnesses and a final attack of gout. The courtiers and officials who had flocked out to the castle of Vincennes, which occasionally served as a royal residence, stood about in low-speaking groups and discussed the meaning of this long seclusion. The King had been grief-stricken over the death of his able minister but had recovered quickly enough after a brief outburst of tears. He had been dry-eyed when he announced his intention of giving himself up to solitary thought; and so, clearly enough, it was not sorrow which was occupying him. What problems, then, filled the royal mind?

The courtiers sometimes abandoned their nervous speculation on the lengthy absence of the King to discuss the passing of the chief minister. Was it true that the dying man had been impatient with the Queen Mother because she sat so faithfully at the side of his couch? Could it be that he said in a final attack of umbrage: "This woman will kill me with her importunities. Will she never leave me in peace?" Poor Anne of Austria had accepted this upbraiding with resignation, for it was known that she still sat by the bedside and wept bitterly. The whole nation knew, of course, that she had loved the cardinal devotedly, and in a very few hours the streets of Paris would be resounding with coarse songs and scurrilous couplets.

Another point of discussion in the crowded anterooms was the disposal of Mazarin's great fortune. Did he actually possess two

hundred million francs as well as his many houses, his fabulous art
treasures, and his great library? Was it a fact, people asked themselves anxiously, that the young King had been foolish enough to
refuse when the cardinal offered to will everything to him? Surely,
surely, he had displayed more common sense than that! Did he want
this huge accumulation of wealth to be divided among Mazarin's
nieces, the avaricious Mancinis?

It was two hours before the King emerged from his secretarial
closet. There was an air of gravity about him as he halted and
glanced around the room. That he had changed into a close-bodied
black velvet coat with white lining did not detract at all from his
appearance. The color, in fact, set off the lines of his fine legs, and
this led him to strut a little. There was a single sheet of paper in
one hand. Pausing in the doorway, he motioned to a few of his immediate circle to draw in close about him.

He had been considering the future, he said in a low tone. Here—
on this sheet of paper—he had set down the decisions at which he
had arrived. First—glancing particularly at a man in a green frock
coat who had placed himself directly under the royal eye as though
conscious of this being his right—he had made up his mind to follow
the advice of the late cardinal. Another quick glance at the man in
green and he added that he was going to be his own first minister.

There was an almost incredulous gasp at this announcement.
The debonair young King was very popular, but he was not regarded
as in any sense intellectual or ambitious. It had been assumed that
he would do as his father had done before him. Had not Mazarin
been quite open in declaring that Louis would not be *trop instruit?*

The King then proceeded to pledge himself to a life of effort and
hard work, checking off the items on the paper as he spoke. His days
were to be so divided that no aspect of his life would be neglected;
so many hours for sleep, so many for meals (like all the Bourbons,
he was an enormous eater), so many for recreation, a quite considerable time for prayers. The most important stiuplation was six
to eight hours a day for work, and under this heading he was not including such kingly duties as receptions and appearances. The young
monarch, in other words, was dedicating himself to a life of assiduous
toil.

The one member of the royal staff who felt the most surprise, and
the most disappointment, was the man in the green coat, Nicholas
Fouquet, the Intendant of Finance. This brilliant official had fully

expected to succeed Mazarin. In addition to such expectations, he had good reason to dread any innovations in the order of things. Change might lead to an investigation of the affairs of his department. He desired above everything else to avoid this, for he had been despoiling the country and at the same time robbing the King in the process of accumulating a large personal fortune for himself. It would be demonstrated later that only a very small percentage of the taxes collected ever reached the royal coffers. The showy and venal Fouquet had been uneasy for some time. He had been so conscious of the corruption in his department that he had begun to build a great fortress on his island off the coast of Brittany which was known as Belle-Isle. His plan (or so it was whispered) was to provide himself with an impregnable sanctuary in the event of the King's turning against him.

The minister who felt the least concern at the announcement was Jean Baptiste Colbert, who was in almost all respects the exact opposite of the handsome and vulnerable Fouquet. Colbert claimed to have Scottish blood in his veins and gave credit to this mixture of ancestry for his extraordinary aptitude in the field of finance. He was a rather glum individual who dressed in frumpish clothes and had the reputation of being a heavy drinker. Wherever he went he carried a black velvet bag with him from which he could produce at any moment all the figures and documents which might be necessary. He was farseeing, sound in his judgment, an undeniable wizard with figures, and absolutely without scruples. It had been by acting on his advice that Mazarin, after impoverishing himself in the civil wars of the Fronde, had succeeded in creating for himself an immense fortune in the years which followed.

Colbert was already deep in the King's confidence. He was in a position to produce from his invaluable bag the proofs of Fouquet's astounding peculations. Fouquet could feel the hot breath of this rival on the back of his neck and was struggling to shake him off. The struggle between them was a matter of public knowledge, and at court men were taking sides. The general public, which of course was made up of dupes, favored the glittering minister who robbed them. Having nothing but contempt for the unimpressive Colbert, people jeered him on the streets and saw to it that scurrilous verses were on his desk every morning.

The outcome was never in doubt. One day a certain Monsieur d'Artagnan, who served as lieutenant of the King's musketeers and was destined to receive much posthumous acclaim which would have astonished him very much, tapped the great Fouquet on the shoulder and said, "I arrest you in the King's name."

Colbert, unassuming and efficient and the longest of workers, was found at the King's right side very soon afterward. Gradually he took all posts of importance into his own hands: the superintendence of public buildings, the controller-generalship, the Ministry of Marine, the Ministry of Commerce and Colonies, the management of the royal household.

The young monarch in the meantime had been working with corresponding zeal. He rose at eight o'clock and dressed himself (except on stated occasions when hereditary rights to assist at the royal toilet had to be considered), gave interviews, went to Mass, and then sat down with his council until noon. The midday meal of the monarch was eaten alone at a small table and took some time. After a drive he went back to work and did not desist until the hour for dinner, which was sometimes as late as ten o'clock. While he dined, generally in the company of the liveliest ladies of the court, the royal servants stood about in impressive files, their handsome livery of blue velvet laced with gold and silver lending a note of ostentation. On state occasions the King himself wore his fabulous black velvet coat, which was so encrusted with jewelry and gold that it had cost twelve million francs.

The court, it will be realized, was becoming a brilliant one. Colbert was producing the funds necessary to allow the youthful ruler his chance to dramatize himself in his role of absolute monarch. In the first two years the minister had nearly doubled the royal income by sweeping out most of the hundred thousand tax farmers who had been absorbing the money wrung from the poorer inhabitants of the country. He had discovered, moreover, the efficacy of indirect taxation and by this means was making the nobility bear the share they had haughtily refused to assume before.

2

And this was the situation which Laval faced when he arrived in France. It was made clear at once that he stood high in royal favor. The reports which had been received of him had pleased the Queen Mother and the pious young King. The will to dominate which he had displayed was in accord with the policy which Louis himself was following. They listened to his harangues with ready ears and agreed, in principle at least, with everything he suggested.

The vicar-apostolic had a list of changes which he desired to put into effect. First he asked for the recall of Avagour, using the latter's obstinacy in the matter of the brandy traffic as the reason. This was granted readily enough. The King, in fact, went a step farther and left the selection of a successor in Laval's own hands; a rash step, because the militant head of the Church was unlikely to look for more than one qualification in his candidate, a pliant attitude in regard to procedure and their mutual responsibilities. Laval, it developed, had his man already in mind, one Saffray de Mézy, commander of the citadel at Càén. When the young bishop had been imbibing Jesuitical teachings at the Hermitage in Càén he had known Mézy and had seen in him a man of deep religious feeling. Mézy was, moreover, of humble origin and it might be a relief to deal with a man who lacked the haughty convictions of the aristocrat. The appointment was to prove a failure, from Laval's viewpoint at least, as will develop later.

On the second point which he pleaded before the King he scored a partial success only. He made a vigorous appeal to be appointed Bishop of Quebec, contending that the purely nominal title of Bishop of Petraea did not lend him the prestige he needed. The young monarch was willing to accede to this request, but it developed immediately that the question was still a prickly and controversial one. Would a Bishop of Quebec be under the Archbishop of Rouen or under the direct supervision of the Pope? It was the old controversy reborn, the Gallican viewpoint against the papal, and the French Church divided again into rival camps. Tongues clacked about the throne, voices were raised high in violent disputation. The King made the discovery that to find the solution to an ecclesiastical problem was a far different matter from resolving the disputes which came up in his council. He could not put his foot down and say simply, "This is my will." There was also the will of the Pope to be considered and the wills of many proud and powerful churchmen. The dispute went on and on.

It was to go on, in fact, for ten years more before Quebec would be made an episcopal see with Laval as the first bishop.

The latter had immediate success with a civil issue. It had become painfully apparent by this time that the machinery which Cardinal Richelieu had set up to control Canadian affairs, the Company of

One Hundred Associates, had been a failure. The company still functioned in a restricted way. The monopoly of the fur trade had been
transferred to the leading citizens of New France with the stipulation that the Associates receive a certain proportion of the profits. In
return for this they were doing nothing at all. The provisions which
Richelieu had so carefully imposed were being disregarded. No
settlers were being sent out. No supply ships were provided. Even
while they brushed aside their obligations, the greedy Associates
were striving to increase the return they received from the domain of
King Castor. An agent of the company named Peronne Dumesnil had
been sent out to the colony in 1660 to investigate conditions there.
Dumesnil had uncovered plenty of evidence that the leading citizens
of New France were doing very well indeed out of beaver pelts
and refusing to make more than a token yield to the company. There
had been a great deal of trouble as a result of the agent's activities.
Charges and countercharges had been brought. Arrests had been
made, including one episode when Dumesnil himself was laid by the
heels.

Laval placed these facts before the King and his council, asking
that the life of the company be terminated once and for all.

By royal edict in April 1663 the Company of New France was dissolved, and never after were the heavy hands of the Hundred
Associates felt in Canadian affairs. To replace the absentee control
of the investors, a council was to be set up, consisting of the governor
and Laval as head of the Church, who were to select five councilors
from among the leading citizens of the colony and a new civil official
who was to carry the title of intendant. Armed with the necessary
authority, Laval and Mézy sailed for New France on September 15
to set the new wheels to turning.

But before Laval left, a matter of even greater importance was
discussed in the royal council. On his journey back to France following his dismissal, Avagour had prepared a statement on conditions
in Canada; a vigorous appraisal which had caused Colbert some
hours of serious reflection and had brought a light of new determination into the eyes of the youthful King. The ex-governor had stated
his belief that the country along the St. Lawrence could become in
time "the greatest state in the world." To realize the imperial possibilities of this overseas domain of the Crown, it would be necessary,
he pointed out, to establish peace first by defeating the Five Nations.
To perpetuate the security which this would establish, it would be

essential to build strong forts along the St. Lawrence and on the southward-flowing river which the Dutch controlled (the Hudson), so that the French Government could use it as a trade outlet to the sea, not to mention the encirclement which this would bring about of the seaboard lands which the English were taking over.

Avagour had presented a detailed plan. Three thousand soldiers should be sent out at once to New France to carry on offensive operations against the Five Nations. The soldiers were to be discharged after three years' service and to be given land. This would turn the St. Lawrence into a vital source of food supply as well as the life line of the trade with the natives. The retiring governor had gone even farther and had prepared an estimate of the cost of thus turning a struggling colony of puny health into a new empire. Four hundred thousand francs a year for ten years would suffice.

This bold plan had been debated while Laval was in France, and there can be no doubt that his voice was raised in impassioned support. Before he left he had the satisfaction of knowing that the King had decided to follow it in its broad outline. A regiment of soldiers would be sent to New France to bring the Iroquois war to a final end. The officers would be given large tracts of land and would be expected to portion their holdings out to the men of their own companies.

New France was to have at last the full support of the Crown. A new day was dawning.

3

Monseigneur Laval and Saffray de Mézy were soon at loggerheads.

Arriving on the same ship and on the best of terms, they proceeded to erect the new machinery of government. It was Laval who made the selections for the council. Jean Bourdon was made attorney general, an engineer who had risen from such posts as barber, painter, chief gunner at the citadel of St. Louis, and collector of customs for the Hundred Associates. He was a deeply religious man and thoroughly in accord with the bishop's views. The first of the councilors appointed was Royer de Villeray, who had been valet to Lauson when the latter was governor. It was said in the colony that Lauson had taken him out of prison at La Rochelle, where he had been incarcerated for debt. Whether this was true or not, he was now counted the richest man in the colony. The other members were Juchereau de la Ferté, Ruette d'Autueil, Le Gardeur de Tilly, and Matthieu Damours.

The council as thus constituted proceeded at once to take the measure of Dumesnil, the investigator sent out by the Associates, who was still at Quebec. Although the company had ceased to exist, it was known that Dumesnil had papers which he intended to use in charging citizens of Quebec with embezzlement of funds which should have been paid to the defunct concern. He was prepared, it was known, to point the finger of proof at members of the council.

This could not be allowed. At the second session of the council Bourdon made a demand that the papers of Dumesnil be seized. Villeray was sent to carry out the order, Bourdon going along for good measure, and the governor supplying them with ten soldiers. They arrived at the house of the investigator early that evening.

"Robbers!" cried Dumesnil, who guessed immediately what their errand was. "Robbers!"

The soldiers took him in hand, holding him fast in a chair and covering his mouth. While he struggled to get free, the locksmith who had been brought along broke open his cabinets. Everything they contained was seized, including his private papers. Among them were the documents he had intended to use against members of the council.

Dumesnil did not accept this bold proceeding quietly. He raised such an uproar, in fact, that another meeting was held and it was decided to put him under arrest. No word of this resolve was allowed to get out, the plan being to wait until the last vessel had left in the fall. Their hope was that the affair would cool off before spring, which would be the earliest it could be brought to the attention of the King's ministers. Dumesnil received a hint of their plan and got away on an earlier ship. Arriving in France, he took his complaints to Colbert, and it looked for a time as though a first-class scandal would result. Nothing came of it in the end, however. In the meantime the Dumesnil papers were held in Quebec. They were never released.

The illegal seizure of the papers had been carried out with the consent of the new governor, but Mézy soon became convinced that at least some of Laval's selections for the council were unfortunate. He appealed to the bishop to give his consent to the expulsion of Bourdon, Villeray, and Autueil and to an election by the vote of the people of new men to take their places. To this Laval returned an emphatic refusal.

Mézy seems to have been a man of singleness of purpose. Once committed to a course of action, he could not be diverted. Determined that the councilors he considered unfit should be dismissed, he placed placards about Quebec, stating his views. This was followed by the proclamation of an election with beating of drums.

It can be imagined that a light appeared in the stern eyes of the bishop and a hint of a smile showed at the corners of his tight lips when this happened. The governor had made a fatal error. The King would be furious at the suggestion of selecting councilors by popular vote. He, Louis XIV, who was being called Louis the Invincible by the languishing ladies of his court, he alone had the power to appoint officials. It followed that in the breach which opened between the bishop and the governor, Laval had the full support of the King.

It happened that the bishop, in proceeding with his plans for the seminary, had laid a tithe of one thirteenth on the incomes of the people. This measure had to be changed to one twenty-sixth because of the inability of the people to pay more. They were wrathful about it and so were inclined at this point to give their support to Mézy rather than the bishop. Mézy prevailed temporarily, therefore. He secured a new council by again posting placards about the city and sending criers to summon the people to vote. For the period of a year the new appointees functioned. Then the governor made a second mistake. He banished Bourdon and Villeray from the colony. They took back with them to France reports on the unorthodox policy Mézy was following. The King fell into a fury and signed an order at once for the governor's recall. An inquiry into his conduct was to be held as soon as he reached France.

He was not to be faced with the necessity, however, of defending his conduct. He fell ill and died before the time came for him to return and meet the accusations of the affronted King.

The militant churchman was seated firmly in the saddle. It had required no more than a hint of his dissatisfaction to remove the Baron d'Avagour from office. Mézy, being his own appointee, had been a more difficult case. But now poor Mézy, honest of purpose but fumbling of method, was gone. On his deathbed he had confessed to Laval and had received absolution from him; and the moment of death had found them once more in accord. But Laval's position was not quite as secure as it must have seemed to everyone at this point. Louis XIV was a complete autocrat and could not tolerate about him any minor exponents of absolutism. He was beginning to wonder about this solemn man of strong purpose whose iron hands controlled New France; as certain instructions which he sent out later will attest.

---

CHAPTER XXII

*The Grand Plan Comes to a Head with the
Arrival in Canada of the Carignan-Salière
Regiment and the Defeat of the Iroquois*

1

ON MARCH 18, 1664, Colbert had written to Laval in Canada: "Since the Italian affair was happily terminated to the King's satisfaction, His Majesty has resolved to send to Canada a good regiment of infantry, at the end of this year or in the month of February next, in order to destroy the Iroquois completely; and Monsieur de Tracy has been ordered to go to confer with you on the way of succeeding promptly in this war."

Alexandre de Prouville, Marquis de Tracy, had been appointed lieutenant general of the French dominions in the New World. It was necessary for him to go first, however, to the West Indies, where things were quite stirred up and mutinous. He arrived there in 1664 and spent the year in restoring order. Having successfully fulfilled his mission, he set out the following year on his northward journey. The Carignan-Salière regiment had been selected for service in Canada, and four companies had already arrived at Quebec when Tracy put in an appearance. The ships with the lieutenant general and his additional forces dropped anchor in the Quebec basin on June 30, 1665. As the Carignan regiment had not been assigned to New France until after Tracy's departure, the troops he brought with him did not belong to that justly famous organization. They were made up of veterans from the regiments of Poitou, Orléans, Chambellé, and Lignières. A group of eager young noblemen had come out also, looking for adventure, glory, and perhaps quick fortunes.

On this day, therefore, the Grand Plan of the young King reached its first stage of fulfillment.

The city on the rock had never before seen so much excitement. As the representative of royalty, the marquis came ashore under a white flag with the fleur-de-lis embroidered magnificently upon it, while behind him came the colonelle (the number-one company of a regiment under the direct command of the first officer) with its special pennant. The commander was a majestic man, almost mountainous in build if the comments of beholders can be believed, carrying himself with soldierly ease in spite of his sixty-three years. He was surrounded by the afore-mentioned young noblemen, all of them attired in their handsomest clothes and so presenting a rare front: white wigs and coats of all colors sticking out as stiffly as the hoop skirts of women, swords protruding even farther under the tails of the coats.

The soldiers were veterans of the Turkish war, and some of them could even claim to have fought in the Fronde. Their discipline was perfect and they marched in splendid order through the Lower Town and up the steep incline to the summit; blue coats piped with white, plumed hats, buff leather bandoleers, muskets carried on slings over the shoulder, long leather boots turned back halfway of the calves. The drums were beaten furiously, the pipes screeched, the trumpets blew with a flourish which said, "Thus begins the King's triumph and the ruin of the wicked Iroquois."

The bells on Cathedral Square were ringing exultantly, and a procession behind Laval issued forth to bid the King's men welcome. The Marquis de Tracy went down on the pavement on one muscular knee to receive the benediction and the holy water offered by Laval, wincing a little with the effort, for he was beginning to feel his years in such bodily use and he was sallow of face from the fevers which had entered his veins in the hot and noisome Indies. The Chevalier de Chaumont followed suit and so in turn did all the noblemen, wondering, no doubt, if colonial paving stones would be clean enough to leave their satins and velours untarnished. Twenty-four guards in royal livery stood at attention while the ceremony was performed. It was, in short, a spectacle which gave great satisfaction to all and offered to the eager inhabitants the assurance that the King's mind would not waver nor his resolution weaken until the rejuvenation of the colony had been completed.

It is not known how the eight companies of soldiers now in Quebec were accommodated. As many as possible were quartered in the Château of St. Louis, but at best it was not a commodious building.

The inns, without a doubt, were filled to overflowing. After this was done there would still remain more than half of the rank and file to be housed, and it seems certain that they were billeted on the town. Tracy was lodged in a house which had been reserved for court sessions and was called La Senechaussée. With him were the Chevalier de Chaumont, who was captain of his guard, and most of the volunteer noblemen; with them the valets and pages and cooks without whom life would indeed have taken on the grimmest aspects of pioneering.

Until the forces were complete there could be no question of commencing military operations, anxious though everyone was to see the full might of the King employed against the Iroquois, who had held Canada in fear for so many years. The problem of maintaining order became, therefore, of the most serious concern. The town had no more than seventy private houses, and it was estimated that when all the ships had arrived there would be more than a thousand professional soldiers; a situation before which Morality had been known to shrink and hide her pallid face. That Quebec emerged from this phase without a stain (only one illegitimate child came into the world in the course of a year) is proof of the often-repeated assertion that this was a crusade and had true religious fervor behind it. Under the stern eye of the corpulent marquis the carefree veterans of many continental campaigns restrained their customary impulses. Tracy set an example of piety which clearly had its effect. Marie de l'Incarnation wrote happily in one of her revealing epistles that he had been known to remain six hours at his devotions. The chief concern seems to have been the religious beliefs of the troops, some of whom were discovered to be Huguenots. There was immediate pressure to convert them.

Eight more companies arrived in August. At the same time came ships filled with settlers and mechanics and girls of marriageable age to provide wives for those who lacked them. Ships came also with livestock and all manner of supplies. If the town on the rock, which had been so long neglected and had remained so patient, had seemed crowded before, it was now a madhouse, a hurly-burly of excitement and confusion.

Two more companies were expected, and anxiety grew as week followed week with no glimpse of new sails in the estuary. It was known that a new governor was with them, Daniel de Rémy, Sieur de Courcelle, and another official named Talon, who was to fill a new post known as the intendant. It may be taken for granted that there was much speculation about the new governor and comparatively little interest in the other man; a division of speculation which would be reversed later, for Courcelle was just one more in the long succession of more or less futile governors, and Jean Talon was to breathe a new kind of life into the colony and to impress himself indelibly on the pages of its history.

It was not until September that the tardy ships arrived after having been one hundred and seventeen days at sea. Courcelle and Talon landed and were greeted with suitable pomp. After them tottered ashore a very sick lot of soldiers. It had been a hideous as well as an interminable voyage. The ships had been constantly buffeted by storms, with the result that the private soldiers had been compelled to remain in the malodorous holds and had suffered beyond description. Scurvy had attacked them as well as the customary diseases. Twenty of them died almost as soon as they set foot on shore, and there were one hundred and thirty so ill that they had to be put in hospital. The Hôtel-Dieu was not prepared for a test of this magnitude. The attendants worked so hard that many of the nuns were reduced to the point of death. Most of the sick soldiers had to be bedded in churches and in such of the houses as were not filled to the eaves already.

The situation in the meantime was becoming clarified with the Five Nations. Missions had been established in the Iroquois country and were making progress. Some of the tribes were manifesting what seemed a sincere desire for permanent peace. When the word spread down through the woods and along the rivers and lakes that soldiers were arriving in Quebec in numbers like the sands of the sea (the Iroquois being much addicted to metaphor) and that they marched together like one man and the sound of their musketry was louder than thunder, a peace party was organized by three of the five nations to go to Quebec at once. The three concerned were the Onondagas, the Cayugas, and the Senecas. The embassy was headed by Chief Garakontie, who had been converted by the Jesuits and was anxious for an understanding. The envoys saw the soldiers marching in the streets, they counted the muskets, and their thirst for peace became deeper.

There were no delegates, however, from the bitterly antagonistic and contumacious Mohawks. It was understood, therefore, that the Mohawks would be the first to feel the blow when the vials of the royal wrath were finally uncorked.

2

To appreciate what the King was doing for Canada it is necessary to understand the importance of the Carignan regiment.

The Thirty Years' War had plunged Europe into a period of intense militarism. Men of adventurous spirit turned more readily to soldiering than ever before, making it possible for governments to organize large professional armies. No longer were unwilling and badly trained levies from the farms and the towns sent into battle; instead the armies which fought back and forth over middle Europe were well paid, well armed, well trained. War had become almost a sporting contest, a sanguinary game of chess between old men who sat in chancelleries and plotted new alliances.

It happened that the seemingly endless religious war which had converted all of Germany into a shambles produced a coterie of brilliant generals: Gustavus Adolphus of Sweden, Wallenstein, Turenne, Condé, Pappenheim, Tilly. The genius of the generals was the lodestar which attracted men to the profession of arms. It was at this stage that the tradition of French supremacy in generalship was born, largely on the exploits of the skilled Turenne and the dashing, headstrong Condé. Later it would be jolted badly by the victories of England's great Marlborough, but it would survive even that shock.

A strange development of the period was the method often followed of recruiting armies. That brilliant and strange leader, Wallenstein, raised armies on the Catholic side of the argument; he trained and equipped them at his own expense and then offered himself and his forces to the Holy Roman Emperor. In France individual noblemen of great wealth followed the Wallenstein example by recruiting regiments, which sometimes bore their names, and offering them to the King as a gift. It was in this way that the Carignan regiment came into existence.

It was raised in 1644, the year after Condé's tremendous victory at Rocroi, by Thomas François de Savoie, Prince of Carignan. It consisted of ten companies of one hundred men each, and it is said that most of the "rankers" were men of exceptional physique and boldness of spirit. It was, at any rate, a picked lot who marched under the flag of Savoie when the regiment was offered to the French King, or rather to the Queen Regent and Cardinal Richelieu,

for Louis at this time had not graduated entirely from wooden blocks
and toy soldiers. The civil wars known as the Fronde were dividing
France, and the Carignan regiment was nothing short of a godsend
to the harassed cardinal. It marched under Turenne to Etampes and
took part in the fighting around that ancient city, and it fought also
in the suburb of St. Antoine, where it covered itself with glory. It
seems to have created for itself a legend of invincibility. To belong
to such a dashing body was deemed an honor.

After the Thirty Years' War was brought finally and officially to
an end by the Treaty of the Pyrenees, the Savoie family could no
longer support such a costly luxury and gave the regiment to Louis
XIV. There seem to have been some strings to the gift, however,
for the head princes of Savoie always took a proprietary interest in
it, which extended even to those remnants which returned to France
after the Canadian adventure.

In 1657 the regiment was combined with one which had been
organized by a bold soldier of fortune named Balthazar, who came
from Transylvania but had joined the French Army. He was noted
for his horsemanship and rode a black stallion which became almost
as famous as its master under the name of Demi-Diable (Half-
Devil). The Carignan veterans remained under the command of
their own officers, but the regiment became known at this juncture
as Carignan-Balthazar. Whether that bizarre soldier was still in command when the regiment was sent to help the Austrians against the
Turks is not made clear in the records, but it is told to the credit
of the veterans that they fought brilliantly on the banks of the Raab
and were praised for the trouncing given the Turkish Grand Vizier
Achmet Kapruli.

When the Turkish campaigning was over and the troops were
back in France, King Louis was making his arrangements for the
carrying out of his Grand Plan, and his eyes fixed themselves on the
Carignan. By this time the Savoie family was thoroughly out of con-
ceit with the idea of continuing the financial drain and Colbert was
pressing the King to economize on the army and put the money into
strengthening the French fleet, which, as always, was being neglected in favor of the land forces. There seemed no sense, certainly,
in allowing such a splendidly trained outfit to rust in garrisons, so
the King decided to reorganize the regiment and send it out to
Canada under Henri de Chapelas, Sieur de Salières. The veterans
were given the option of dropping out or re-enlisting under the

Salières command. The latter had been first captain as long as the dashing Balthazar remained in command, but now he was gazetted colonel and the name of the regiment was changed to Carignan-Salière.

Most of the old soldiers remained in harness, and the ten companies were up to full strength when they were sent out to the New World.

3

The first phase of the campaign against the unregenerate Mohawks was a failure, and the blame is laid on the shoulders of Courcelle, the new governer. He was in too much of a hurry to act, leading the Carignan veterans into the land of the Finger Lakes in the dead of winter and suffering heavy losses as a result.

There were reasons for acting quickly, however, and some of them, no doubt, had seemed good to the governor. Tracy was in bad health. Men noted with alarm that he walked slowly on the way to his devotions from the Senechaussée and that some tropical disease was giving him a jaundiced look. It was clear that he would be unable to command any foray against the enemy, and so Courcelle saw his own chance to monopolize the glory. There was a much more practical reason which unquestionably was in all minds. Quebec was hopelessly overcrowded. More than two thousand people had arrived during the summer—soldiers, civic officials, settlers, mechanics, King's Girls. Talon was proving himself a tower of strength in facing the problems thus created. That somewhat plump and genial-appearing new official, crowded with his staff into a restricted share of space in the citadel, was the busiest man in Quebec. The intendant knew what he was about, but no human being had the capacity to fit five people into space intended only for one.

The sooner the chastisement of the Iroquois was attended to, the better, therefore. Not until the redskins had been taught their lesson could the apportionment of the new inhabitants be started. New forts could then be built and the land along the St. Lawrence broken for agricultural use. It may have been ambition which actuated the impatient governor, but it was a question of expediency which won a reluctant assent from Tracy.

It should be made clear that war in Europe at this period was strictly a seasonal affair. When the rains of fall began to teem down and the ground became boggy so that artillery could not be used, the rival armies by mutual consent would suspend operations. The troops would be moved into cantonments and the officers would seek the comforts of the home fireside. Condé, that headstrong genius, always spent his winters at court, occupied with his gallantries and the feud with his long-suffering wife. Turenne had been known to remain at the front, but there was a distinctly professional note in his approach to war-making.

It will be seen on this account that the Carignan regiment was not prepared for the test to which it would now be put. Courcelle waited until the surface of the St. Lawrence had been solidly frozen over and then started out with a force of five hundred men. It was on January 9 that the march began, straight up the river in the teeth of bitter winds and with the storm king extending a tumultuous welcome. The veterans of a stylized and relatively comfortable kind of war-making had never experienced anything like this. They suf- fered terribly. Marching up the sheer icy surface of the great river, they found that any part of their anatomy which was exposed to the blistering snow and numbing winds was quickly frozen. Backs bending with the weight of muskets, snowshoes, and supply bags, they staggered into Three Rivers finally and many of them were unable to proceed farther. If a good percentage of the force had not been Canadians—it was estimated that about two hundred were native-born—the project would probably have been abandoned at this point. The places of those who were physically incapable of proceeding were filled by Canadian volunteers; and so in due course they started out again, to be greeted with a blinding snowstorm. On reaching the Richelieu River, where they turned south into hos- tile territory, Courcelle placed the Montreal contingent in the van. Seventy strong, and under the command of that wise and courageous paladin of the woods, Charles le Moyne, the Blue Coats proceeded to show that they understood this kind of warfare. The plodding veterans were glad to follow the colonial lead.

They passed all the French forts on the Richelieu—Sorel, Cham- bly, and Ste. Thérèse—made their way across the blinding white of Lake Champlain and through the bitter storms which greeted them at Lake George, and came to the Hudson River after nearly eight weeks of indescribable hardship. There were few Indians about and no hint of organized resistance. As the Algonquin guides who were to direct the way had deserted at Ste. Thérèse, the army was now lost in the wilds. Somewhere to the south and west were the Iroquois villages, but the leaders had no idea how to find them.

The chief result of this ineffectual push into enemy territory was that they encountered a party of English officers. The latter informed them that all the Dutch possessions in America had been ceded to Great Britain by treaty. They, the French, were trespassing on British territory and must be prepared to return at once.

As soon as the sadly harassed force had turned about and started back in the direction of the St. Lawrence, the Mohawk warriors put in an appearance. They hung on the flanks and rear, picking off stragglers and making the frozen woods echo with their blood-curdling cries. Sixty men died of the cold or under the Mohawk hatchets before the unhappy band reached the shelter of Fort Ste. Thérèse.

Courcelle had been befuddled at every stage, but now he conceived the idea that the Jesuits had been at the bottom of his ill fortune. He openly charged them with having conspired to make the expedition a failure. This was the height of absurdity and can be credited to the chagrin from which the leader of the expedition was suffering and the unbalancing effect of the hardships he had sustained.

One of the junior officers, Chartier de Lotbinière, voiced the real reason for the ignominious result in the course of some doggerel verse which he wrote and which, for some curious reason, has survived:

> Victory would have spoken well
> Of the expedition and the marching
> That you have accomplished, great Courcelle,
> On horses made of string [meaning snowshoes].

Then he proceeds to the determining factor:

> C'est un tour, dit-on, de coquin
> Et, n'en deplaise a l'Algonquin
> Qui s'arretair a la bouteille
> Alors on aurait fait merveille.

Translated quite literally, this is as follows:

> It is, said they, a dirty trick
> And if it had not been for the Algonquin
> Who delayed over the bottle,
> Then they would have accomplished wonders.

But the expedition had not been entirely a failure as things turned out. The Mohawks had not liked what they had seen of the new French power. There was something uncanny about so many men dressed exactly alike. Even during the harassments of the retreat there had been times when the teachings of discipline had prevailed and the troops had marched in line. Sharp black eyes had watched from the wooded cover and had been both mystified and disturbed. Nor had they liked the looks of the many hundreds of muskets they had seen slung over the bent shoulders. There was a lesson in this which sank deeply into Mohawk minds and from which great benefit would come when the second drive was made.

4

Because of Courcelle's failure there was greater need than ever for a decisive victory. Rallying from the ills which disturbed his huge frame, Tracy began to make his preparations for a major drive. The Carignan veterans received training in forest fighting and in the life of the trail. This occupied the spring and early-summer months.

In the meantime the overcrowding in Quebec continued to be a serious problem. The floor of the Ursulines' chapel gave way on one occasion from the weight of the people who had come in for the service. Some of them fell right through into the vault, which was quite deep, but fortunately no one was seriously injured. In an effort to make life more endurable for the newcomers, the people of Quebec strove generously to introduce a gayer note into the hours of leisure. On February 4, while Courcelle was away on his ill-fated mission, a ball was held, the first to be given in Canada. A solemn note creeps into the *Jesuit Journal* in recording this event: "May God grant that it do not become a precedent."

During the summer, realizing the might of the blow which was poised over them, the Iroquois made efforts to establish peace, depending for the most part on the forensic gifts of a half-breed chief who is never called anything but the Flemish Bastard. He seems to have been an orator of parts, this gentleman of mixed blood. The first mention of him is found in a letter to the *Relations* by Father Ragueneau. "This commander," wrote the good father, "the most prominent among the enemies of the Faith, was a Hollander—or, rather, an execrable issue of sin, the monstrous offspring of a Dutch heretic father and a pagan woman." The mother was a Mohawk woman, and the son seems to have combined the cunning of the natives with the towering bulk of the Hollanders; a formidable figure with the ferocious expression of a medicine man but the possessor of a silver tongue which gave forth the most studied verbal passages.

It was the Flemish Bastard, in fact, who had eloquently described the Iroquois hegemony. "We compose but one cabin," he said, referring to the fact that the name which the Five Nations had for themselves, the *Hotinonsionni,* meant the Completed Cabin, "we maintain but one fire, and we have from time immemorial dwelt under one and the same roof."

Early in the summer the "Annies," as the French had fallen into the habit of calling the Mohawks, attacked a party of Frenchmen hunting in the neighborhood of Lake Champlain. They killed one of them, a nephew of Tracy named Chasy, and carried the rest off as prisoners. Realizing at once the ill timing of this unfriendly incident, the Mohawk council sent the Bastard to Quebec to make amends, taking the prisoners with him. Unfortunately for the Mohawk cause, another chief was in the peace party, a loud-mouthed specimen named Agariata, who succeeded in nullifying the eloquence of the head envoy.

During the course of a meal at the Senechaussée, to which the heads of the Mohawk party had been invited, Agariata felt called upon to boast of the fact that he himself had killed Chasy. "This," he declared, raising an arm in the air, "is the hand that split the head of that young man!"

The face of Tracy became suffused with an angry flush. "You will kill no one else!" he exclaimed.

On an order from the commander, Agariata was seized forthwith and taken out and hanged without a moment's delay. The nonplused Bastard looked on as the heels of his comrade danced on thin air, for once finding no words to express his feelings. This incident seems to have ended the efforts to bring about a peaceful understanding.

Early in October the second expedition started, with Tracy himself in command. There were thirteen hundred men in the party and it took three hundred boats and canoes to carry them. Only six hundred of the regimental veterans were in the little army, the pick of the ranks. There were as many colonists, including one hundred and ten from Montreal, again under the command of that doughty interpreter, Indian fighter, and merchant, Charles le Moyne. The Sieur de Repentigny was the leader of the Quebec contingent. One hundred Indians had been brought as scouts. Most of them were Christians and they seemed filled with as much zeal in the cause as the white men.

There was one notable recruit in the ranks of the Montrealers, a Sulpician priest who had arrived from France just a week before the expedition started. According to a regulation of the order, he had been included in the list as Monsieur Colson. Perhaps Tracy recognized the tall priest who came ashore with three other Sulpicians at Quebec. The newcomer was François Dollier de Casson, who was as tall as Tracy himself and much stronger. Born in 1620, Dollier had served with singular bravery as a captain of cavalry under Turenne. Becoming a priest because of the abhorrence he conceived for the cruelties of warfare, Dollier joined the Sulpician Order in the diocese of Nantes and had been selected for service in Canada.

Dollier de Casson was due to play a great part in the annals of New France, particularly during the years when he was Superior of the Sulpicians in Montreal. Third of the three tall men whose names are associated with this particular period, the other two being Father Brébeuf and the Marquis de Tracy, Dollier became the Samson of New France, and legends gathered about his name. On one occasion he was attacked by two "Annies" who had stolen up behind him. Lifting them up in the air, one in each hand, he crashed their skulls together and then tossed them aside, to recover later with aching heads and a respect for the brawny priest which grew as the story was told around the hunting fires.

No sooner had the French forces reached the difficult part of the journey than their leaders became incapacitated. Tracy was taken with an attack of gout, which was a most inconvenient form of seizure at such a time. He had to be carried when the need arose to leave the boats. Once he nearly lost his life when the soldier to whose back he had been strapped lost his footing in the rapid water. Courcelle suffered from cramps and had to be carried also. The Chevalier de Chaumont accumulated blisters on his back through the pressure of the load he was carrying. Altogether it was a good thing that there were French-Canadian leaders to assume the burden of command through these early stages.

The tall new priest was nearly worked to death in spite of his great strength. Food supplies were running short and he refrained from eating so that the men would have more, with the result that his great frame became gaunt and thin. To quote his own third-person account, which appeared later in his history of Montreal, "a scoundrel of a bootmaker had left him barefoot through a villainous pair of shoes that no longer had any soles to them." He spent his nights in hearing the confessions of the men and had little or no time for rest from his labors.

The French attacked the first Mohawk village in a dismal rainstorm. Without waiting to bring into action the cannon which had been laboriously brought along in the boats and over the portages, they rushed at once to attack the walls. It had been the intention of the Iroquois to make a stand here. The platforms back of the palisade were black with fighting men. Steam rose from the kettles of hot water which would be poured on the attacking party. Then a panic took possession of the defenders, an almost unheard-of manifestation with these doughty warriors. They vanished by the rear gates as the French came on to the attack with twenty drummers beating a loud tattoo.

Three more villages were captured with the same ease. The Indian garrisons lost heart as soon as they saw the French filing out through the trees. Not a shot was fired, not a blow struck. "It is done," said Tracy reverently after the exodus of the Indians had been completed from the fourth village. But it developed that there was one village left, the largest and reputedly the strongest of the lot. This information was conveyed to Courcelle by an Algonquin woman who had been a prisoner of the Mohawks for years and who knew the country well and the habits of her masters. She led the way at once through the forest to this last stronghold.

Andaraqué was the name of the last village. It had quite clearly been fortified with the advice of the Dutch, for there was a hint of European methods in the quadrangular shape and the triple palisades nearly twenty feet high. There were four strong bastions at the corners which made it possible to enfilade the whole line of the walls with gunfire, an idea which had not been hatched in a native skull. It would have been a tough nut to crack if the resolution to defend it to the bitter end had not deserted the garrison.

Panic swept over the crowded platforms when the uniforms of the French came in sight. The chief in command, who had been exhorting his men to fight, was the first to yield to it. "The whole world is coming against us!" he cried. He was the first to run and the first to make his way through the rear gate.

Andaraqué had been well stocked for the winter. The houses inside the palisades were unusually large, some of them being one hundred and twenty feet long. These had underground cellars filled with dried meat and smoked fish and huge stores of corn meal, enough to provide the tribe with food for the long season ahead. The presence of these necessary stores had provided the reason for the determination of the "Annies" to defend the town; but when the first of the Frenchmen forced their way in through the ponderous oak gates, they found only a very old Indian, two ancient crones, and a small boy hiding together under an upturned canoe.

After reserving as much of the food as would be necessary for the return trip, Tracy had the place set on fire. The bark on the roofs was as dry as tinder, and the trickle of fire which ran along the walls grew almost instantaneously into a devastating blaze. It lighted up the sky for many miles around. The somber Mohawks, watching it from afar, drew the anticipated conclusions from it. The power of the French King, that great white chief whose home was dragged behind the mighty hornless buffalo, was too great to be withstood. Here he had reached no more than a hand across the water and the woods were filled with demons in blue coats. The country of his enemies was being reduced to ashes. War against the French had become unprofitable.

5

The Five Nations had no will left for war. The Mohawks, after the burning of Andaraqué, managed to survive the winter but were now as much disposed to smoke the pipe of peace as the rest. No move was made to send delegations to Quebec, however, until Tracy sent word that, unless something was done quickly, he would hang all the chiefs he had been holding as hostages. The men of the Five Nations took this threat seriously, having acquired a proper respect for this massive old man. Had he not hanged Agariata the boastful in the presence of the other members of the peace party which had gone to Quebec the year before? Clearly he meant what he said.

The four more pacifically inclined of the confederacy were prompt to send delegates, who arrived in subdued mood and did not indulge in any bluster or swagger. It was not until April that the Mohawks followed suit. The inevitable Flemish Bastard had been selected for the task, and he proved himself as persistently eloquent as before, addressing himself to the French with high-flown turns of speech and impressive gestures. When the toplofty oratory of the Chief of the Bend-sinister failed to accomplish the desired end, a full delegation of Mohawk chiefs was sent to Quebec to get matters settled. An agreement was reached and, after the usual preliminaries, a treaty of peace was ratified. It was maintained for twenty years.

One indication that the Mohawks were at last inclined in all honesty to bury the hatchet was the settlement of some of their number near Montreal. Even the Flemish Bastard brought his family up to take land near the junction of the great rivers.

Colbert had fallen into the habit of addressing most of his communications to Talon. On April 5, 1666, he wrote to that hardworking official: "The King is satisfied at seeing that most of the soldiers . . . want to establish themselves in that country with the aid of some supplementary help which will be given them." It was intimated that His Majesty would be even happier if all of them decided to stay. This, however, was asking too much. The bulk of the Carignan veterans wanted to get back to France where, if they decided to remain at the trade of soldiering, they would know what to expect. The number who finally elected to remain was nevertheless surprisingly large, a total of 403, including officers. The spell of the land—this wild and beautiful land, this land of biting winds and of great rivers and forests—was upon them. They wanted to have land of their own, to marry and raise families. In addition, four companies of seventy-five men each were organized to remain in the country and act as garrisons.

Tracy returned to France in 1667, taking with him his two picked companies known as the colonelles. Most of the soldiers who went back enlisted again and were used as the nucleus of a new regiment which was given the name of Lorraine.

The officers who remained were given seigneuries, mostly along the banks of the Richelieu, where they formed a belt of settlements connecting the forts along the river. Some, however, were granted land on the St. Lawrence in close proximity to Montreal. The officers in turn portioned out tracts of land to the men who had served under them. There are few records of these transactions left, and such as exist are confused by the fact that many of the men were registered under the nicknames they had acquired during their years of military service. Thus it is known that *La Bonté* (Goodness), *La Doceur* (Sweetness), *La Malice* (The Wicked One), *La Joie* (Blythe Spirit), and *Pretaboire* (The Drunk) were among those who decided to become permanent citizens of the colony.

Little is known of their ultimate fate. Some, of course, were killed, for the trouble with the Indians continued in spite of pacific pow-wows and all the pipe-smoking which had gone on. It was the recognized right of any single Iroquois brave to go out on the warpath at any time he saw fit. When the urge to collect scalps rose to boiling point in a suppressed warrior, all he had to do was to sink his tomahawk in a post in the village clearing, and all who desired to go with him would follow suit. Where they went was completely a matter of individual preference. Peace or no peace, these little buccaneering parties were generally on the prowl around the outposts of French settlement.

Some of the soldiers, after giving farming and matrimony a trial, returned to France. A few heard of the milder climate of Acadia and removed themselves there. An occasional one vanished into the woods and presumably went native. A very few rose to posts of prominence in the colony.

A few of the seigneuries of the regimental officers became prosperous and were held by descendants of the original grantees through many generations. Descendants of at least six of them are to be found in French Canada today: Raby de Ranville, Tardieu de la Naudière, Dugué de Boisbriant, Olivier Morel de la Durantaye, Gautier de Varennes, Monet de Moras.

CHAPTER XXIII

A Great Man Comes to Canada Who Is Neither
Soldier, Missionary, nor Explorer—
Jean Talon, the Able Intendant, Who Introduces
the Elements of Normality

1

THE office of intendant was an important cog in the Grand
Plan, that grandiose conception which had lighted such a fire
of enthusiasm behind the eyes of Louis the Invincible and
which had been inaugurated so successfully by the humbling of the
Iroquois. Perhaps the best indication of the magnitude of the Grand
Plan was the cost of it. In 1664 Colbert had begun a new policy by
creating the Company of the West, which was to have control of
all French dominions beyond the seas—New France, western Africa,
South America or the parts of it which Spain had not pre-empted,
Cayenne, the Antilles. It was the same old idea on a much larger
scale, a company richer and more powerful than the Hundred Associates which would have a monopoly of trade and would in return
supply settlers, build forts, appoint and pay administrators, and provide priests. Colbert was filled with visions of a huge trade empire
such as the world had never seen before. It became necessary almost
at once, however, to adjust the vision as far as New France was concerned. The new company showed immediate signs of operating in
the old ways which had been so disastrous. The directors wanted
to collect all the revenue and forget the obligations. A compromise
was soon made so far as Canada was concerned: the company would
pay the cost of administration, with no control over the conduct of
the main officers, and find reimbursement out of taxes levied on
beaver skins, le droit du quart, and on moose skins, le droit du
dixième. The figures made available by the discussions over this

arrangement show that the sums expended each year in the direction and control of the colony amounted to something just under 50,000 livres. To carry the cost of the Grand Plan, the King had created what was called an Extraordinary Fund, the inroads on which were to prove quite as extraordinary as the fund itself. In the year 1665 alone the sum of 358,000 livres had been expended. This, of course, had been the year of greatest effort which had seen the arrival of the Carignan regiment and of one thousand other people. This would never have to be repeated (or so they hoped), but the carrying out of the royal designs would continue to cost the ambitious monarch staggering sums year after year.

An operation on this scale demanded careful supervision at both ends of the horn of plenty. No longer could the control of the colony be left to the proud and generally futile aristocrats who had been serving as governors, nor to zealous churchmen whose concern was the saving of souls. France now had in Colbert a remarkable administrator. New France must have the same, and so the post of intendant was created. The first man selected for the office was one Sieur Robert, about whom nothing much is known save that for some reason he never assumed the duties of his office. Colbert looked about him for a replacement and he recognized in the brilliant controller of Hainault a kindred spirit. He dismissed all other possibilities from his mind; Talon, obviously, was the man.

Jean Talon was not a soldier, a missionary, or an explorer. He did none of the spectacular things which remain on the pages of history while services of much greater importance are overlooked or dismissed with a dry paragraph. He was, instead, an administrator, a man of far vision who realized that the mere act of sending settlers out to New France would not bring growth and prosperity to the colony. It was Talon's great contribution that he saw the need of making the colony a small replica of the mother country, a place where employment could be found and opportunities for useful and gainful small businesses. There had to be prosperous little shops and small but busy factories and inns where the food was good. Talon provided the colony with what it had always lacked, a solid background of sound money and honest barter, where a man and his wife and his children could strive together for a secure future.

Jean Talon was born at Châlons-sur-Marne about the year 1625 and as a young man secured employment in the commissariat of the French Army. His ability was so remarkable that he soared rapidly in the service and soon became chief commissary under the great Turenne. In less than a year a promotion came his way and he was made intendant of the province of Hainault, a post of major importance.

His looks, if he can be judged by the one portrait which is granted authenticity, belied his character. He is shown as a stocky man, with a full and rather round face peering out with amiability from the background of an elaborately curled wig; a hook nose, lips which curled up at the corners with a promise of joviality (which on occasions proved highly misleading), a pleasant enough eye under an arched brow. There was more than a hint of the dandy in him. He might have been a minor aristocrat, the owner of a small estate in the provinces, an opulent attorney. There was nothing of the ruffler about him; he wore a sword, of course, but it did not clank against his plump calves as though conscious of pride and privilege.

Jean Talon was a businessman, a fair imitation of the resourceful Colbert—cool, able, hard-working, and blessed with that greatest of gifts which is known as sound judgment. He was absolutely honest and fearless and he had a sense of vision which the soldier governors of New France had lacked. His coming was to prove the turning of an important leaf in the history of New France.

2

Talon's first activities were in connection with the need for a steady increase in the population. He was full of schemes, some of them as bold as anything which had ever entered the soaring brain of Richelieu. He conceived a plan to have the holdings of the Dutch, which had been taken over by the British, transferred to France instead. It was a decidedly Machiavellian idea which he outlined in letters to Colbert. When the time came for the three nations to make permanent peace settlements France should insist on the return of the New Netherland colonies to Holland. In the meantime a secret understanding would be reached with the Dutch Government by which the colonies would then be ceded to France. Once this had been accomplished, the intendant pointed out in his communications with Colbert on the subject, the English would be hopelessly hemmed in and France would have a strangle hold on the Atlantic seaboard. As a corollary of this devious plan he suggested that five

hundred settlers be sent out each year without fail, an addition
which would soon assure Canada of a thriving population.

Colbert reached the conclusion that this appointee of his was
going a little too fast. He cautioned the new intendant not to expect
too much, to be content with less ambitious strides. Sending out
five hundred settlers a year would in time "unpeople France." Colbert, it may be taken for granted, was too shrewd to believe anything as untenable as this. Obviously he was using the argument
as a means of meeting the importunings of the overbrisk Talon.

Failure in this direction did not quench the enthusiasm of the
intendant. He began to work out plans himself, the most ambitious
being the establishment of new settlements around Quebec, selecting the neighborhood of Charlesbourg for the purpose. Forty houses
were erected in three separate communities called Bourg-Royal,
Bourg-la-Reine, and Bourg-Talon. With Quebec still hopelessly
crowded, there was an immediate demand for all of the houses.
To show his faith in the plan, Talon bought a tract of the land himself. He had it cleared and erected thereon a large house, a barn,
and other farm structures.

A shrewd plan to make these new villages easy of defense had
suggested itself to Talon. The tracts of land for individual use were
cut in triangular shape like wedges of cheese. The houses were
built at the narrow angle where the tips of all the tracts came together, which provided a solid core of settlement at the center, with
the shares of land widening as they progressed outward. Security
was what prospective settlers demanded first of all, and so this
unique idea took hold at once. This was putting in concrete form
a plan which was being tried out elsewhere; and it established a
pattern which persists to the present day, the very long and thin
type of farm, with the farmhouse itself in close proximity to neighbors.

The settlers who swarmed to the Charlesbourg developments, to
borrow a modern term, were given a supply of food to keep them
going while clearing the stipulated two acres of land. They were
paid something for their time as well and the necessary tools were
supplied to them. In other words, a man could start with nothing
save the will to make himself a landholder. The money to pay for
all this came out of the King's Extraordinary Fund. One obligation
was assumed by the new settlers: each must clear two acres of land

on other tracts, to ease the strain on those who came later. On these terms the Talon villages began to fill up rapidly.

The King viewed these steps with paternal approval. As Colbert phrased it in one of his letters, "The King regards his Canadian subjects, from the highest to the lowest, as his own children." He wanted them to enjoy "the mildness and happiness of his reign." The intendant was directed, in order to make sure that this beneficent design was being observed, to visit the people in all parts of the colony, "to perform the duties of a good head of the family" and so put the people in the way of "making some profit." It was a generous thought, and the young monarch was to be commended for his intentions. Carried to an extreme later, however, the paternalistic design was to prove the basis of a cramping and irksome tyranny.

The resourceful Talon proceeded then to attack a problem created by the increase in population. An industrial background was needed to supply some of the necessities of life and at the same time to provide employment. He started the farmers to growing hemp and then created demands for the crop. This was done by an arbitrary method which, fortunately for all concerned, worked out very well. The hemp seed was distributed to landholders with the understanding that they must plant it at once and replace the seed next year from their own crops. In the meantime Talon went to all the shops and seized the supplies of thread. It was given out that thread could be secured only in exchange for hemp. As the mothers of growing families had to make clothes for their children, they either saw to it that their husbands raised hemp or went into the market and bought it. This highhanded procedure was maintained for a brief period only, as it resulted in starting a steady crop of hemp and provided the demand for it at the same time.

It was very clear in the practical mind of the intendant that the colony should reap some of the profits that fishermen from European ports were still sharing evey season. Cod-fishing stations were established along the lower St. Lawrence, and the "take" was good from the very beginning. Settlers were encouraged to go out to the sea where the seal and the white porpoise could be caught. The oil extracted was a valuable commodity and could be sold readily on home markets, thus creating a balance for the purchase of needed goods in France.

One of his most ambitious moves was the creation of a shipbuilding plant at Quebec. New France, he contended, must no longer be entirely dependent for supplies on the ships which plied to and fro from French ports. The men of the colony must be in a position to venture out under their own sails and to establish trading connections with the French colonies in the West Indies. The first ship completed was at Talon's own expense. The cost of the second, a much more ambitious attempt, was borne by the King. The latter does not seem to have complained at the size of the withdrawals for the purpose, which reached a total finally of forty thousand livres. The venture had provided the colony with an excellent vessel and had at the same time given employment to three hundred and fifty men. It is recorded that in 1667 six vessels of various sizes and kinds were finished and put into use.

Having thus provided the colony with a thriving industry, the creative mind of the intendant turned in another direction. The brandy trade was still a bitter bone of contention in the colony. There seemed no way of preventing independent traders from using it as their main item of barter, and the colonists themselves liked it almost as well as the Indians. Talon conceived the idea that there would be less demand for brandy if fresh beer were available. He decided to build a brewery and, having every confidence that the plan would prove profitable, supplied the funds from his own purse. The idea found instant favor. In commenting on it, a correspondent in the *Relations* spoke of the beer as "this other drink which is very wholesome and not injurious." The brewery had been erected in the St. Charles section of the town. This was in 1668, and three years later the output had reached substantial proportions. The intendant reported the plant capable of producing four thousand hogsheads of beer annually, although there is no indication that this high level had been reached.

In many of his letters to Colbert the intendant stressed the need for livestock as a means of putting agriculture on a broader base. His demands fell on attentive ears. The supplies of cattle, sheep, and hogs which were sent out kept mounting. A few horses were supplied also. This led to the establishment of tanneries. To make use of the wool, the housewives were given looms, and this was the beginning of the carpet weaving which has been a characteristic activity in Quebec ever since. Potash was extracted from wood ash. Tar from the trees was collected and sent to France for sale.

3

There is behind every colonizing venture a hope that easy wealth will be discovered. The world still watched enviously as Spain grew ever richer on the easy gold of Mexico and Peru. North America had beaver skins and an abundance of sea fish, but there was no easy profit in either field; hard work and not luck was the key to financial returns there. The hope was never abandoned in France that ultimately Canada would provide natural resources from which wealth would flow eastward. This had always been behind the formation of the commercial companies to whom colonization had been entrusted.

Knowing this, Talon was always alert to any rumors of the discovery of mines. When it was reported that lead had been found on the Gaspé peninsula, he had investigations made at once. The search proved unsuccessful. It was found that iron ore existed at Baie St. Paul which was sufficiently high grade to be profitable, and immediate steps were taken to begin mining operations.

A thrill of excitement ran through the colony when it was rumored that coal had been found—and, of all places, in the Rock itself! The first trace of it had been stumbled on in the cellar of a house in Lower Town. Talon was swept along by the enthusiasm which had gripped the place and wrote to Colbert: "The coal is good enough for the forge. If the test is satisfactory, I shall see to it that our vessels take out loads of it." He was seeing rosy visions: the colony well supplied with coal for the heating of homes, the ship building industry receiving impetus on being freed of the necessity of buying coal from England. There was one drawback: if the shafts were carried into the heart of the Rock, the security of Upper Town would be imperiled. Talon began to experiment with the possibility that the shafts could be extended in other directions. His last letters to France indicated that he was convinced the grade of coal being found burned well enough to be used, at any rate, for industrial purposes.

If there actually was coal in the Rock, it is still there. After the initial excitement subsided, Talon wrote no more reports, favorable or otherwise. Any attempts at mining were abandoned. Even the location of the cellar where the initial discovery had been made was forgotten. It can be taken for granted that later tests had not been

as encouraging as the first. It is even possible that the whole thing
was a hoax.

The coal of Quebec has been one of the favorite topics of speculation down the years, but no explanation of the mystery has been
found.

There was plenty of evidence that copper existed in the country
in large quantities. Jesuit priests returned from the missionary fields
with persistent stories of great mines and sometimes they brought
specimens of the metal with them. These stories tantalized the intendant with dreams of great wealth to please the King as well as the
merchants of France who had never yet given wholehearted support
to the colony.

The most exciting reports came from the islands formed by channels between Lake Huron and Lake Superior. Father Claude
Dablon, who had been assigned to the upper Algonquin missions,
wrote a letter for the *Relations* which created an immense amount
of excitement. Copper was to be found in great quantity, in particular
on the island of Michipicoten. This fabulous isle had one drawback:
it was a floating hill of ore and shallow vegetation, never to be found
in the same location because it shifted its position with the winds.
The Indians seldom went there because they regarded it as the
home of evil spirits. On one occasion some hardy natives ventured
to pay it a visit and came back with large pieces of reddish metal
which was found most useful in cooking food. The squaws would
heat it to a ruddy glow and then throw it into the kettles, where it
would set the water to boiling. But they never went back for more.
As they paddled away from the shore on their one visit, they heard
a wrathful voice as loud as a thunderclap speak to them from the
sky. "Who," demanded this dread voice, "are these robbers carrying
off from me my children's cradles and playthings?" They knew it
was the voice of Missibizi, the evil god of the north winds, who thus
complained that they were removing the slabs of bright metal which
children liked to collect and which were sometimes used as the base
of cradles. The natives were careful not to arouse the wrath of the
god again.

More reliable reports about the abundance of copper began to
come back as the missionaries pushed on farther west. They found
an island which did not shift with the winds and which Missibizi
did not haunt but which had enormous stores of the metal. It was
called Minong (later named Isle Royale by the French), and the
engineers who inspected it on Talon's orders found that its hills

had large deposits of copper. Father Dablon reported the existence there of a copper rock which he had seen with his own eyes and which weighed seven or eight hundred livres.

In the spare little office he used (there was not yet in Quebec enough space to go around) Talon kept specimens of the copper on his plain oak desk, using them as paperweights for the piles of letters and documents, with official seals dangling from them, which always lay in front of him. They were both a challenge to him and a puzzle. Here was the wealth which had so long been sought. But how could it be mined and smelted and brought from these far-distant islands? Talon had plenty of plans for solving the difficulties. He saw visions, no doubt, of the copper islands so black with the smoke belching from smelters that even the wrathful eye of Missibizi would not be able to see what was going on. He pictured fleets of flat-bottomed barges being towed all the way to Quebec through the Great Lakes. He saw mills in the colony where the muzzles of great cannon would be cast for King Louis to use in his European wars.

If this resourceful man had lived a hundred years later he would have been able to solve the difficulties and to turn his dreams into actualities. He might have converted French Canada into a busy industrial country. As it was, he made the colony a going concern and created a background of prosperity and content. But New France, still no more than a precarious toe hold on the edge of a continent, was not ready for a Talon.

4

What was Governor Courcelle doing while this energetic man of business turned the colony upside down and gathered the control of things into his own hands? Courcelle grew more antagonistic all the time and more ready to display his disgruntlement. He sat in his cabinet in the citadel behind the handsome rosewood desk which had been brought out from France, unhappily aware that it was more likely to have on its polished surface a set of chess men or a tricktrack board than communications from France. The candles burning in the crystal chandelier above his head reflected the marks of chagrin which had become habitual on his features. Sometimes he lashed out furiously at the intendant when they met to discuss business, and often he allowed his resentment to show in his letters to France.

The reason for Talon's increase in official stature and the shrinkage in Courcelle's is easy to understand. The governor never lived down the failure of his invasion of the Mohawk country and the heavy losses which had resulted from his rashness. It soon became apparent to Colbert also that when he referred matters to Talon they were attended to promptly and satisfactorily, while in Courcelle's hands they dragged along interminably. The notes which the King scribbled on the margins of the reports from New France (the busy monarch read them all carefully) and the decisions which were arrived at in the morning meetings of the royal council were referred, therefore, to the intendant and not to the governor. Talon always knew what was going on in France and the latest ideas which had sprouted in the mind of the monarch. Courcelle was frequently in the dark. The governor often went to Talon for information, even for instructions. It was inevitable that Courcelle would complain to Colbert of the way he was being pushed aside. Talon found it necessary at times to complain also of the jealousy of the governor and the obstructive attitude he was adopting.

It must seem that the progress recorded in Talon's period of administration was the work of many years. In point of fact he was in Canada for two terms, each of no more than three years. It is no exaggeration to say that he had accomplished more in these brief years than all the officials, glittering with jeweled orders and resplendent with lace and velvet, who had preceded him; with one exception, of course, Champlain.

It was due partly to his frequent disagreements with Courcelle that Talon asked in 1668 to be recalled, partly also to ill-health and the need to attend to personal affairs in France. Reluctantly the King agreed, and in November of that year Talon sailed for home. He was most sincerely regretted. Marie de l'Incarnation, who seems to have commented on every event of importance in her revealing letters, was very much disturbed. "It is a great loss to Canada," she wrote. ". . . During his term here as intendant, this country has developed more and progressed more than it had done before from the time of the first settlement by the French." This high praise of the departing official was echoed by all, with the probable exception of the Sieur de Courcelle. Certainly it was shared by the two who counted most, the King and Colbert.

A new intendant sat after that in the small office with the plain furniture which had been made for Talon by industrious artisans (with a fine eye for design and proportions) in Quebec, a Monsieur Bouteroue. But in actuality the reins were never out of the former's hands. The King and Colbert saw to that. Instead of engaging himself immediately in the straightening out of his properties in France or in bolstering his health in the balmy airs of the south (he had always disliked cold weather), Talon was kept in constant attendance on his royal master. It was natural that it should be so. The King's interest in Canada had been growing all the time, and now he had available the one man who understood the problems of the colony intimately and could give advice out of this practical knowledge. Day after day, week after week, the conferences went on among the trio, the aggressive and lordly King, his ubiquitous minister, and the ex-official who was supposed to be recuperating.

During these protracted talks Talon succeeded in committing the King to a remarkable program. In the first place, Canada was removed from the control of the Company of the West. Colbert may have gibed at this, having been responsible for the company in the first place, but Talon fought the issue vigorously, making it clear that the moneygrubbing merchants who composed the company had no concern for the welfare or the future of the colony.

It was decided to reinforce the remnants of the Carignan regiment who remained under arms in New France with six companies of fifty men each and thirty officers, all of whom were expected to settle down in the country after their terms of enlistment were over.

In addition the King agreed to send two hundred more settlers and a great list of supplies. A steady program was laid out for the sending of "King's Girls" to provide the unmarried men of the colony with wives, an initial shipment of 150 being arranged.

In a burst of enthusiasm over his success in accelerating the royal design, Talon wrote to Courcelle, "His Majesty has appropriated over 200,000 livres to do what he deems necessary for the colony!"

One outcome of these extended deliberations was inevitable. Talon had been a bare three months at home when he was reappointed to the post of intendant. Perhaps he had foreseen it would work out that way. It is even possible that he had arranged things with this development in view, realizing that he must sit face to face with the King to get the royal assent to his program. At any rate, he accepted the responsibility for the second time without any outward show of reluctance. On July 15, with his new commission signed, his brief instructions in his pocket, he set sail from La Rochelle.

But he did not reach Canada that year. The ship was buffeted about by a succession of heavy storms and finally had to put back to the port of Lisbon to be refitted and revictualed. Starting out again, it was wrecked in shoal water no more than three leagues out from port, and those on board were rescued with great difficulty. This ended the effort to get to Canada that year. Talon and the military officers with him returned to France, and it was not until August 18 of the following year, 1670, that the intendant arrived at Quebec for the second time.

The mind of the great intendant was filled with plans of magnificent proportions, for he was confident now that he would have the backing of the King in anything he undertook. Above everything else he wanted to stimulate exploration, and his accomplishments in that field will be recorded in a later chapter. His immediate task was to see that the steps already discussed with the King and duly ratified were properly carried out. The work involved was heavy and seemingly never-ending. The health of the intendant was not good, and it was clear from the start that the burden of so much detail weighed heavily upon him. It is easy to picture him at this important stage of his work: seated at his desk, his luxuriant and heavy wig removed and his hands clutching at times of stress at his lank and not too abundant hair, his face gray and showing a multitude of lines. He felt it wise to look after everything himself, leaving practically nothing to the initiative, or lack of it, of his subordinates. There were the King's Girls, for instance. It had to be seen to that they found husbands. The full first shipment, 150 of them, had arrived. ("All the girls who came this year are married, except fifteen," he reported to the King.) More and more were to be sent out, this batch under Madame Bourdon, the next in the care of Madame Etienne ("*Canaille* of both sexes," wrote Marie de l'Incarnation in speaking of some of the newcomers.) The division of the land was to be attended to, and the wholesale bestowal of seigneurial rights which Talon took upon himself in the last few months of his second term (thirty-one were handed out on one day, November 3, 1672) will be noted later. There was, finally, the matter of creating a proper system of education. ("They take to schools for sciences, arts, handicrafts, and especially navigation.")

For three years Jean Talon worked incessantly to accomplish all the things which had been discussed and agreed upon during the many conferences with the King. By the fall of 1672 he had done

as much as was humanly possible; and the relationship with Courcelle had reached an irruptive stage. He again begged for his recall
and again the request was granted. He was rewarded on his return
with the title of Comte d'Orsainville and given an easy post as
captain of Mariemont Castle. For twenty-two years he enjoyed the
ease of this kind of existence, but undoubtedly he longed at times
for the excitement of life at Quebec. He died on March 24, 1694.

CHAPTER XXIV

The King Becomes the Paternal Tyrant of Canada,
Making Regulations for Every Phase of Life—
The King's Girls—Rigid Police Restrictions

1

"SOME of them are *demoiselles* and tolerably well brought up,"
wrote Talon to Colbert in France, in speaking of the 109 King's
Girls who had been sent to New France that year. He had
asked for young ladies, knowing that those who had come earlier had
too often deserved the comment of Marie de l'Incarnation, *canaille.*

The King's Girls were the young females who were shipped out
to provide the unmarried men of the colony with wives. It was not
a new idea when Louis the Paternal Tyrant began it: the English
had sent King's Girls to Virginia and the Spanish to their colonies
in the Indies. It was a situation made to order for writers of romance,
and many stories have since been published over the years about
girls of great beauty and good family who ran away from home and
escaped by joining the colonial shipments, always finding the husband of their hopes and dreams.

It is doubtful if any girls of the nobility came to Canada under
such circumstances. The closest approach to a romantic atmosphere,
in fact, is contained in the brief reference above by Intendant Talon.
The *demoiselles* he mentions were girls with good backgrounds and
even a little education. They were wrangled over and selected and
married, probably to military officers or men of more than average
property. They were happy or unhappy thereafter according to their
dispositions and the luck they had had in finding compatible mates.

Many hundreds of the King's Girls were sent out over the two
decades when the need for them was felt. As many as 150, in fact,
arrived at one time. They came mostly from the northwestern

provinces of France, from Normandy, Brittany, and Picardy. The preference seems to have been most decidedly for peasant girls because they were healthy and industrious. Girls from the cities did not prove as satisfactory; they were inclined to be lightheaded, lazy, and sometimes sluttish, and the sturdy young habitants had no desire for wives of that type even though they might be prettier and trimmer than the broad-beamed candidates from the farms.

It is very doubtful if any girl of high degree fleeing from an elderly suitor (the reason most often employed in the romantic stories) or for political reasons could have succeeded in enrolling for Canada. The candidates were looked over carefully, their birth certificates were examined, and their recommendations from parish priest or confessor were read and considered. There were a few occasions when mistakes were made and girls were admitted who had either been guilty of loose conduct or had criminal records. The exceptions had been frequent enough to justify the comment of Marie de l'Incarnation and to explain the slighting descriptions of an officer named La Hontan who visited the colony and wrote a book which contains the fullest information available on this matrimonial traffic. There were even a few cases where women who had been married were brought out. What happened to them when they were caught is not explained. Probably they were submerged in the ducking stool or publicly whipped before being sent back. A wife's status under French law was pretty much that of a chattel. It was almost impossible, for instance, for her to regain her freedom. Infidelity on a husband's part was not acceptable as an excuse. Only if he beat her with a stick thicker than his wrist could she claim the right of separation.

It is La Hontan who tells what happened when the girls arrived in the colony. They landed, of course, at Quebec, where they were looked over by the local swains. There were sometimes bitter complaints that the best were snapped up in Quebec and the culls were then sent on to Three Rivers and Montreal. On first landing, after making the long journey under stern duennas appointed by the government, they were placed in three separate halls for inspection. What basis was used for determining to which hall a girl should be sent is not stated, not even by that arrant gossip, La Hontan. Were they divided according to weight or coloring or even according to social background? Whatever the arrangement may have been, it permitted the authorities to direct the young men who came seeking brides to the particular hall where they were most likely to find a suitable choice.

The girls had the privilege, of course, of refusing any candidates who might want them. It is on record that they did not hesitate to ask questions of the embarrassed swains who paused in front of them; presuming that the girls were drawn up in lines or elevated on platforms like slaves at an auction or as they were on occasions in the French provinces when the glove was up for a Giglet Fair and candidates for domestic service were scrutinized by questing employers. Among the questions they were likely to ask were the following:

"How many acres do you have cleared?"

"How many rooms are there in your house?"

"Does it have wooden floors? How many windows? Does the hearth draw well?"

"Have you a proper bed and plenty of blankets? How wide is it? Is it made of cypress wood or sassafras or cherry?"

"Have you a horse? How many cows, pigs, and sheep? How many chickens?"

"How much money have you saved?"

"Are you addicted to drink?"

"Are you of clean habits?"

It was seldom, however, that they carried things to the point of a refusal, for that was a chancy proceeding. They had come out to find husbands, and it behooved them to take advantage of an offer. They did not want to be among those who were passed over by all the shuffling, staring, arch males who filed through the halls. Some, alas, failed to find favor and had to be content with domestic service for the rest of their lives. An unwanted King's Girl was a tragedy, her lot sadder than that of a confirmed spinster, for she had publicly proclaimed her willingness to be chosen. She invariably became soured and ill-tempered, the target of sly jokes and innuendoes as long as she lived.

La Hontan says the plumpest girls were taken first, and this undoubtedly was true. The bachelors wanted healthy partners who could be depended on to do their share, or a little more, of the work. A bad complexion or a squint could be overlooked if the figure was buxom.

The truth might as well be stated at once: there was little of romance in the coming of the King's Girls and their absorption into

THE FRENCH REGIME IN CANADA 285

the life of the colony, little more than at a sale of livestock. The marriages followed immediately after the selection, priests being on hand to conduct the ceremony and notaries to make out the necessary papers. The girls would be dressed in their best; but their best, poor forlorn waifs, would not be very gay or suitable. Some undoubtedly would have nothing to wear but the cardinal cloaks they had used on the sea voyage, with the hoods folded back. None of them would have the finery of a bride with parents to fit her out properly: gloves with drawstrings of silk, three-cornered hats with jaunty pompons on top, whalebone stays to make her look slim or *criardes* to stiffen out her skirts. Perhaps a few of them would be lucky enough to have trussing chests, the equivalent of the modern hope chest, with a few treasured odds and ends in the secret compartment, the *till*, as it was called.

The men, on the whole, would be better dressed. They would have on their long-tailed coats (of red cloth in Quebec, of course) with turned-up cuffs and immense side pockets or, if they had saved up enough to be a little festive, a cool ratteen capot which was made with stiffeners and flared out from the waist.

Each couple was given an ox and a cow, two pigs, a pair of chickens, two barrels of salted meat, and eleven crowns in money. This started them off well.

The result of these hasty marriages was to create a belief that the bracing climate of Canada was particularly advantageous to women. "Though the cold is very wholesome to both sexes," wrote Dollier de Casson from Montreal, "it is incomparably more so to the female, who is almost immortal here." The need for children was considered of such importance that the innumerable letters carried back and forth across the Atlantic, many of them in the King's own hand, were concerned largely with the problems of multiplication. It was even believed that marriages between Frenchmen and Indian girls could be a useful factor, and Mère Marie was said to favor the idea of finding husbands among the colonists for the Indian maidens. Talon conducted an inquiry into this before he returned to France the second time. But he reached an adverse opinion. The young squaws, he reported, did not bring many children into the world because they nursed them too long. This was a fortunate finding: otherwise the resourceful monarch would have found some ingenious regulation for the encouragement of miscegenation.

Talon's reports on the King's Girls were more favorable. In 1670 he stated that most of the young women who had arrived the year before were pregnant already. His information proved to be perfectly sound. In the following year nearly seven hundred children were born in the colony.

2

It had been confidently expected that the King would tire quickly of the ceaseless attention to detail which he had inaugurated after the death of Cardinal Mazarin. It was now found that, on the contrary, he was concerning himself more than ever before in the business of administration. It was true that he was finding time for other pursuits, but always at the accustomed hour in the morning he was at his desk, and there he stayed. At a later stage of his reign he would acquire a most useful servant, a man who had the knack of imitating the King's signature so perfectly that he attended to a large part of the royal correspondence, creating the impression that the letters had all been written by Louis himself. At the point now reached, however, the King had not discovered the Pen (the name by which this rather mysterious assistant became known at court) and so he was in the habit of writing a large number of the letters which went out in seemingly endless quantity every day.

By thus keeping his hand on every phase of administrative activity, the young monarch was hardening his resolution to rule. "I am the state!" he declared. He did not mean this as a rhetorical flourish. He was the King and he intended to rule. The seeds of a despotic intent had been contained in the statement he made immediately after Mazarin's death, and now the plant had grown and was showing the buds of tyranny. It was Canada which felt his will in its most determined phase. The people of New France were existing on the royal bounty. Why, then, should they not be treated as children and made to toe the line of kingly whim? It was, in addition, much easier to write a letter saying that such-and-such must be done, much easier than to impose the same rules on the millions of France who had ways ingrained in them by generations of ordered living. He proceeded, therefore, to lay down a series of regulations for Canada which seem utterly fantastic today.

Parents were ordered to see to it that their sons were married by the time they were twenty and daughters at the age of sixteen. Any father who failed to do so was hauled into court and fined. What is more, he was compelled to appear in court every six months until such time as the unwed child had found a mate. With one flourish of a pen the little despot of Versailles took away the right of bachelors to live as they chose. All single men were under orders to get themselves married within two weeks of the arrival of a shipload of King's Girls. Marry, declared the King, it is my will! Bachelorhood ceased immediately to be a state of single blessedness and became instead a state of persecution. Bachelors were not allowed to fish or to go into the woods on any pretext, to prevent them from trading with the Indians. They were taxed as long as they remained obdurate.

Colbert wrote to Talon that special burdens should be found for bachelors, that they should be excluded from all opportunities for advancement and from all honors. He went a step farther and declared that some measure of infamy should be imposed on them. Perhaps he had a seat in the stocks in mind or even a term of imprisonment. The persecution of the bachelor was never carried to that extreme, however.

To the habitants Cupid had always been a sly and rather bumbling little fellow with a far from taut bow. To have him turned into a scowling busybody with a rawhide whip (and bearing the features of the Sun King) was unpleasant medicine. To them a wedding had been a gay and festive occasion and they had brought with them from the French provinces many quaint beliefs and customs. Great care was always taken to have no brooms used about the house after the ceremony because that would condemn the couple to a lifetime of poverty. They firmly believed that the first one of the newlyweds to get into the nuptial bed would be the first to die, but they do not seem to have evolved any way out of the difficulty. Did they sit up all night? Or did the bride take one side and the groom the other, slithering in between the sheets at exactly the same moment?

The King displayed benevolence on the other side of the register, however. Handsome bounties were offered to those who bowed to the royal will. Twenty livres went to both contracting parties when they were within the stipulated age. This was called the King's Gift, and it was surprising how general was the desire to take advantage of the offer. Louis then proceeded to make it worth their while to have plenty of children. Any couple with ten children received a yearly pension of three hundred livres. The size of the pension grew with further increases. Twelve children entitled the parents to four hundred livres a year.

The number of families enjoying these bounties was surprisingly large. If the climate did not make the women immortal, it perhaps had some part in the fruitfulness they displayed. One of the New Year customs was to scratch the names of all the children in each house on the frosted panes of glass, and it was not at all unusual for the record to continue from window to window until every bit of glass had been filled.

Dollier de Casson, that amiable giant who had given up soldiering for a life of self-sacrifice in the garb of the Sulpician Order, cites the classic example of the haste to marry which the insistence of the King had engendered in the public. In Montreal a woman had been widowed while still young enough and comely enough to consider a second venture. He reports that she "had banns proclaimed once, was exempted from two other callings, and had her second marriage arranged and carried out before her first husband was buried." He did not seem to find such haste unseemly. In fact, he held it up as an example of what was entirely proper and admirable.

3

It has been stated earlier that Louis XIV was a heavy eater. He continued to be a mighty trencherman to the end of his days. His dinner always began with three or four soups, all of them rich concoctions made with wine and fine herbs. He was very fond of soup and never failed to have a bowl of each kind. Several varieties of fish followed, with savory sauces of course, a ragout, a deviled leg of capon, a wide selection of roasts, a meat pie with truffles and mushrooms and a crust so flaky that it melted like the first prismatic flakes of snow, game browned to a turn, and steaming golden platters of shellfish. He professed to be a light eater of desserts, but this was purely comparative. He never failed to pay full tribute to the pastry and he acknowledged his supreme addiction to rich conserves. His consumption of fruits in season was likely to be enormous.

When the last luscious peach had vanished down the royal throat and the final sip of wine had followed it, Louis would lapse into a state of profound melancholy. He had little to say, and all the beautiful ladies who sat about him were wise enough to be very restrained. The only reasonable explanation for his determination to dictate every phase in the lives of his French-Canadian subjects is perhaps to be found in these moments of dejection. In this gray state of mind, gazing at life with austere and censorious eyes, he may very well have set himself to concocting his plans for the unfortunate habitants.

At any rate, he was guilty of imposing laws and restrictions which attained a high level of absurdity. And they were not in any sense theoretical; they were meant to be enforced. "You are to lay the blame on yourself," wrote the King to one of the intendants who followed Talon, referring to some breach of laws, "for not having executed my principal order." The insistent monarch was completely in accord with the sentiments expressed by Intendant Meules in one of his letters. "It is of very great consequence," wrote this sycophant, "that the people should not be at liberty to speak their minds."

As it was essential that the land be cleared and cultivated, the habitant was forbidden to move into town on pain of being fined fifty livres and having all his goods and chattels confiscated; and a corollary order made it illegal for townspeople to rent houses or rooms to tenants from the country, the fine in their case being fixed at one hundred livres. No one could return to France without leave, and such permission was rarely given. The farmer must not own more than two horses or mares and one foal, because he might not then raise cattle and sheep in sufficient quantities.

The townspeople were fairly smothered with picayune restrictions. Merchants were not permitted to hold meetings for discussion of business matters. No one could trade in foreign goods, and any article purchased abroad, except from France, would be seized and publicly burned. Innkeepers were not permitted to serve customers during High Mass or any church service, nor were they allowed to serve food or drink to anyone residing in the town. Bakers were ordered to make dark brown bread although there was little demand for it. Dark brown bread was never served at the royal table, but the King believed it was doubly nutritious; and so bake it in their ovens the poor bakers must.

Every house must have a ladder so that assistance could be rendered when fire broke out in town. Citizens had to dig a gutter in the middle of the street in front of their property. Chimney sweeps had to be employed twice a year by each householder at a price of six sous. Dogs had to be kept off the streets after a certain hour on Sundays. People were not permitted to sit on the benches in front of their houses after nine o'clock in the evenings. Licenses had to be obtained to hire domestic servants.

Many of the regulations seem traceable to clerical influence. The habitant was an excitable and voluble fellow who liked to vent his feelings in loud ejaculations such as *"Palsambleu!"*, *"Sacre bleu!"*, and *"Corbleu!"* The King, nevertheless, reached the decision that no form of profanity was to be allowed. On the first four occasions that a citizen was charged with blowing off his feelings with rough words he was fined on an ascending scale. For the fifth offense he was sent to the pillory. For the sixth his upper lip was seared with a red-hot iron. The seventh lapse led to the upper lip being branded as well. After that the offender was considered hopeless and mercy could no longer be extended. An eighth offense was his last. He would be led out, his arms bound with ropes, and in the sight of everyone (all people were under orders to go whether they wanted to or not) his tongue would be cut out so that no longer could he profane the air with his violence and blasphemies.

Women had to be home by nine o'clock of an evening. This was designed, no doubt, to nip in the bud any tendency to hold evening entertainments and balls, but it was the one restriction which seems to have been disregarded. Visitors to Quebec wrote glowing reports of the social gaiety of the place and the beauty and vivacity of the ladies.

Unmarried girls were permitted to dance with one another only, in their own homes and with their mothers present. Ships from France were not permitted to bring in rouge (but they brought in everything else in the way of new fashions and beauty aids).

A society was formed in Quebec known as the Congregation of the Holy Family to which only women belonged. They met every Thursday at the cathedral, where a room carefully protected from eavesdropping was provided for them. The purpose of the meetings, although this was never openly acknowledged, was for each one present to tell everything she had heard about others, good or bad; a practice borrowed from the convents of earlier centuries. It is probable that the members were more likely to recite the bad deeds than the good ones, and certainly disciplinary measures were followed only when misdemeanors were retailed. The fathers and husbands of the good ladies who belonged to this gossip mart became highly incensed and tried to put a stop to it, even securing the aid of Talon in the matter. They had no success. The ladies enjoyed the tattling and they had the support, or so it was whispered, of Bishop Laval.

One of the hardships which caused the men of the colony to complain was the number of church holidays and saints' days when they were not allowed to work. "How can we cultivate our land," they cried, "or build a thriving business in our stores when we have no more than ninety working days!"

Gossip La Hontan, who found all this highly objectionable, was particularly bitter about a prohibition which had been put on the possession of any books save the *Lives of the Saints* and similar volumes of a devotional nature. He was himself the victim of this regulation which the priests carried out with unrelenting severity. It was in Montreal that he ran afoul of the King's orders.

Printing being still in an infant stage, certain kinds of books were extremely expensive, particularly those which appealed most to this avid purveyor of spicy detail. There was one book which had to be printed in secrecy and sold from beneath the counter with blinds drawn, being probably the most pornographic and obnoxious in the world at that time. La Hontan possessed a copy, a perfect one, which made it very valuable. One day he returned to his rooms and found the curé there. The good priest had taken the book in hand and was just tearing out the last of the offending pages!

4

Most of the information with reference to the regimentation of the people of New France is found in the multiplicity of letters and memoranda exchanged between the King and his minister Colbert on one hand and the men who acted as intendant in Canada, most particularly while Jean Talon filled that post. Laval does not seem to have figured to any extent in what was being done, although his influence can be felt in many of the regulations. The King had become increasingly wary of the militant head of the Church. He, Laval, was too sure of what he believed to be right and too willing to battle for it. The King preferred men who nodded their heads promptly. Not that Colbert was obsequious in his attitude. He understood his master and knew how to get his own way without seeming to oppose or press.

When Talon left the colony for the second and last time, Laval had two more years to wait for the honor he had desired so much. He was fifty-one years of age when he finally became Bishop of Quebec. It cannot be said, therefore, that he had attained his vintage years when the King was tinkering with the lives of his New World

subjects like a boy with his toys, but there can be no doubt that he
was mellowing. It was possible now to detect a hint of sweetness
back of the severity of his eyes and some of the same quality in his
smile. Needless to state, the man who had fought with Montmagny
over trifles was still willing to fight with the King over issues of
importance.

A never-ending dispute was being carried on between the new
bishop and the head of the state over the position of the parish
priest, the curé. The King wanted the priest to be more the servant of
his flock than of his bishop; a fixture who could not be removed
except for unusual cause, which was the system prevailing in France.
Laval wanted the priests in the field to be subject to change so that
a man could always be fitted into the niche where he would be most
useful. The King refused to understand why the Canadian priest
had to be paid twice as much as the rural curé in France. Laval's
answer was to demand (and finally to obtain) as much as five hundred francs a year for his priests, even though many humble priests
in France had to be content with two hundred. Did the French
curé minister to a flock living over a hundred-mile stretch of river
country? demanded the logical and outspoken bishop. Did he need
a body servant strong enough to carry a portable chapel about with
him?

Despite his willingness to fight when the need presented itself,
Laval was finding that his interests had shifted to some extent at
least. He was deeply concerned now over the schools he had established. The seminary at Quebec, which was devoted to the training
of young Canadians for the priesthood, was the point to which he
invariably turned with quickened footsteps when he had any time
to spare. He delighted in conversation with the neophytes, and
nothing pleased him more than to welcome the missionaries who
came once a year from their distant fields for a week at the seminary,
to be spent in retreat and contemplation.

The other educational institutions he had inaugurated were doing
well, the school for boys and the manual-training school which had
been set up under the shadow of Cape Tourmente down the river.
In the latter establishment young men and boys were instructed in
the work they desired to undertake in life. A few had come who
showed artistic gifts, and they were being given full opportunity to
develop them. It was to Laval's open-mindedness on this point that
the credit must be given for the fine artists the colony produced,
the men who made the classically simple but beautifully propor-

tioned silverware of Quebec, the vessels for clerical use, the handsome silver platters, the *écuelle* (a porringer) with its typical points
of design, the characteristic papboat.

Although Bishop Laval lived on a sparse minimum, he was becoming a rich man in spite of himself. The grants of land which the
Crown had insisted on conferring on him were becoming valuable.
When the bishopric of Quebec was finally set up, a quarter of the
population lived on his seigneurial lands at Beaupré and on the
island of Orleans. Laval had a plan locked away in his mind. He
would keep his land, allowing it to increase in value, and at his death
he would will it to his much-loved schools. So well managed was
this purpose that after his death these institutions continued to grow
in scope and influence over the years, free of financial strain because
of the acumen of their founder.

5

If the people of Quebec had heard on the evening of November
19, 1671, that the candles had blown out during the services at the
cathedral, they would have said at once that Madame la Fondatrice
was dead. There was a superstition, in which they all firmly believed,
that this was a sure sign of death; and they knew that Madame de la
Peltrie, who had founded the Ursuline Convent, was mortally ill.

When this earnest lady of great refinement and charm had turned
over all her wealth to the endowment of the convent in Quebec
and had come to Canada to devote the rest of her life to it—accomplishing this revolutionary change in her life by hoodwinking
her suitors and going to law with her grasping relatives—she was
filled with a great sense of devotion. With the zeal, however, had
gone an understandable belief that she would walk always in shining
spiritual armor. That she had a desire to assume spectacular roles
was made clear by the zest with which she embraced the Montreal
adventure and by her desire to go out to almost certain death in
the Huron mission field. It took her a time to reach the realization
that service is more often a matter of daily attention to monotonous
tasks; that, like Mère Marie de l'Incarnation, she must be prepared
to labor incessantly, unnoticed and unrewarded. When she was instructed to return to Quebec from Montreal, she began to see the
light and from that time forward she was content to share the
drudgery of dedication.

For the last eighteen years of her life Madame de la Peltrie lived in her tiny house in a corner of the convent grounds and had charge of the wardrobe, a task which kept her extremely busy. She did the work so well that the little Indian girls always had warm and suitable clothing, although the Fondatrice herself went about in old and patched garb.

"Why don't you give these things you wear to the poor?" she was often asked.

"I prefer," was her answer, "to see the poor in new clothes."

She had become, in fact, very humble and even contrite. Perhaps she believed that pride had played too large a part in her previous attitude. "I am the most sinful creature in the world," she said once. "Certainly I have been unfaithful to God's gift of grace."

She always took a humble place at the long table in the refectory so that she would be one of the last served. Her place in the choir was an inconspicuous one.

On November 12 she had an attack of pleurisy and sank so rapidly that all hope for her recovery was abandoned. Knowing that her end was near, she had everything which might be thought ornamental removed from the room, it being her desire to die in the atmosphere of poverty into which she had directed her life.

The consistency with which she had observed the principles of self-sacrifice became apparent when an inventory of her few personal belongings was made after her death. The list was as follows:

> A mantle of serge d'Aumale.
> A dress of serge de Càên.
> Two old serge aprons.
> Three old silk caps.
> One old velvet cap.
> Three pairs of old woolen stockings.
> One old cape.
> Three pairs of old slippers.
> One pair of corded slippers.

It must have been apparent to Jean Talon, who went to her bedside on November 15 to assist in the drawing of her will (she had almost nothing to leave), that all the regulations he had put into effect on the orders of the King, all the restrictions which aimed at improving the tone of life in the colony, would prove less effectual in the long run than the example of a life such as this.

Two other lives came to an end soon afterward to add to the

weight of the lesson. Mère Marie de l'Incarnation, who had faithfully and tearfully remained at the side of her dying friend, passed
away eighteen months later. She had been the active head of the
convent; in fact, her determination to do everything needful for the
good of the institution had led her to master three Indian languages,
Huron, Algonquin, and Iroquois. Thus equipped, she had been like
a mother to the Indian girls who came under her charge, as well as to
the French children who paid their 120 livres a year for instruction
in *les ouvrages de goût*, the finer things, such as painting, embroidery, and the making of lace. When Mère Marie came to die it
was a misfortune in which the whole colony shared. Everyone came
to bid her a last farewell, until it seemed to those in attendance that
the chamber of the dying woman was always crowded. This remarkable woman, whose seventy-one years had been years of devotion,
did not care; they were her friends, and she was dying, as she had
lived, in harness.

All of Quebec, weeping and disconsolate, came out to attend her
funeral services, which were conducted by Father Lalemant, and
to stand at the grave where she would know the rest that life had
always withheld.

"The Angel of the Colony," Jeanne Mance, passed away on June
18, 1673, thus bringing to an end the epic story of the three great
women who had played such useful parts in the founding of New
France.

6

The efforts of the King to evolve by decree the kind of state he
desired in the New World have been defended on the ground that
strict laws were indispensable. The land was far removed from
civilization, and the conditions encountered were in every way
extraordinary: a continent of vast extent thinly populated by savages,
the climate severe, the means of sustenance small. It was hard to find
volunteers for a life so different and so terrifying. Among those who
were induced by one means and another to go out, there were few
like Louis Hébert, men with a wholehearted desire to take up land
and to make a living by their own efforts. The bulk of the colonists
were so averse to agricultural pursuits, in the early stages, that they
had to be fed from France or so liberally endowed that they were
dependents of the Crown. There was very little general employment,

and so the idle hands of the men in rusty coats and patched knee-length stockings who loafed in the streets of Quebec and Montreal could not be kept out of mischief. Nothing but the strictest discipline by regulation, say the apologists, could keep such communities from falling into economic and spiritual chaos.

There is some truth, of course, in these observations. Strangely enough, however, the strongest evidence which can be advanced to excuse the royal policy is that it drove men into the woods, and this form of disobedience proved in the best interests of the colony. The opening up of the North and West had always been among the chief aims of the French in the New World. The Jesuits thought of the whole continent as their field, and the eyes of the statesmen fixed themselves resolutely on the ultimate goal, the discovery of the Northwest Passage. Unwilling to be told what they could and could not do, the *coureurs de bois* set out in ever-increasing numbers, their canoes filled with goods for trading with the Indians, their resentful eyes fixed on the waterways and the woods ahead of them. The exodus was so great that at one time the loss to the towns was estimated at a quarter of the effective male population.

This can be cited, therefore, on the credit side of the ledger for the Martinet of Marly, that as a reverse effect of his incessant interference the frontiers were rolled back and the North and the West were slowly opened up.

CHAPTER XXV

The Conflict over the Fur Trade—The Coureurs
de Bois—*The Annual Fair at Montreal—
Opening up the West—Du Lhut and Nicolas Perrot*

1

THERE had always been a conflict of interest over the fur trade. New France offered no other source of revenue to provide for the costs of administration and colonization, and so the proper method of encouraging the traffic was the problem which caused the most knitting of brows among the King's advisers and the issuance of more regulations than on any other point. Unfortunately the departmental thinking ran in a single groove: to centralize the trading, to make the Indians bring their furs to the market, to "farm" the profits as the easiest way of assuring an adequate return to the royal treasury. This was the accepted method in France, where even the taxes were farmed. It may have been an easy way, but it was a costly one, as they would discover in France in time. The system was doomed to failure from the start in the New World.

In the first place, the Indians could not be depended upon to bring their furs to the French markets. During the Iroquois wars they were prevented from doing so by the craft of the warriors of the Long House in setting up a patrol on the Ottawa, the one corridor open to Indians of the North and West. There were several years when practically no pelts reached Montreal and Three Rivers. Even after the epic sacrifice at the Long Sault it was only the opportune arrival of the fur brigade headed by Radisson and Groseilliers which saved the situation. The ships going back to France that fall would have had no cargoes at all if the heaped-up canoes of the two young rapscallions (the official view of this enterprising pair) had not arrived just in time.

Even after peace had been brought about by Tracy's devastation of the Mohawk country, the fur trade did not fall into the easy pattern designed for it at Versailles. The Indians of the North and West still had a choice in the matter. The English had taken over the Dutch country and had entered into an alliance with the Iroquois. They were making shrewd efforts to divert the trade down the Hudson. Even more important was the fact that the English had become established on Hudson's Bay. How this came about is a curious and complicated story which will be told in full detail, but at this stage it is sufficient to say that they had three forts on Mort Bay (the name commonly used by the French) and the French had none, which meant that the English were in a position to monopolize the trade of the North.

It was no time for the French to sit back and wait for the fur to be laid on their doorsteps. The people of New France understood the situation. When they found that Versailles was stubbornly adhering to the old policy, they took matters into their own hands. Disregarding the regulations which had been imposed to keep them from acting as individuals, the young men began to reverse the Versailles pattern. Instead of waiting for the Indians to come to them, they began to go to the hunting fields themselves. The canoes would start in the early fall, or in the spring if a distant destination was aimed at, and would not come back for eighteen months or longer. They began to construct small forts as rallying points and supply depots. The first was at Detroit. Then Michilimackinac became the center of trading in the West, and the free traders congregated there. That island began to serve as the point from which the free traders fanned out to cover the whole western territory.

This was free enterprise, the only way to save the fur trade for France. Angry at this disregard of royal policy, the King and his advisers strove, nevertheless, to prevent the participation of individuals by still more rigorous regulations. The *coureur de bois* was declared a criminal. In an order bristling with despotic ire the King declared that anyone going into the woods without a permit should be whipped and branded for a first offense and sent to the galleys for life for a second.

2

The term *coureur de bois* was first used by the Récollet Gabriel Sagard-Théodat in his *Histoire du Canada* in describing the start of missionary work among the Montagnais. This was as early as 1615, and it seems to have been used in reference to the act of traveling. Probably the first official use of the term was in one of Talon's letters in 1670, and it is apparent from his manner of use that it had been employed for some time to describe individuals. It was applied only to those engaged in trading without permits and who accordingly had made themselves outlaws. Later it took on a wider application and was used to mean all French Canadians who ventured out on the long trail.

Certain admirable qualities of the French people came out unmistakably in the *coureurs de bois:* their courage and élan, the combination of curiosity, restlessness, and acquisitiveness which gave them the instinct for adventure, the capacity for adapting themselves to any environment. They were remarkable woodsmen. In fact, in some respects they began to excel the Indians as hunters and trappers. They even improved on that one great invention of the North American native, the bark canoe.

A writer in the *Relations* describes the canoe as shaped "like the crest of a morion." The morion was a helmet worn by French soldiers in the seventeenth century which lacked both visor and beaver. It must have had a very long crest, if the description is an accurate one; for the French, because of the need for space to pack the supplies of trade goods they took with them, were making their canoes longer than the Indian model. The white men seemed to have learned all the tricks of the trade and to have added some improvements of their own. They achieved the perfect balance which made the frail craft easy to handle as well as the lack of weight which cut its draw in the water to less than half a foot. They had learned how to make the hulls watertight by the use of resin. The decoration of the hulls had become an art in itself, and a French flotilla was a gay affair, from the pennant flying at the prow of the first in the procession to the brightly stained stern of the last in the line. The French were such expert users of the birch-bark canoe that it is said they could make from thirty to forty leagues a day, provided they had an unbroken stretch of water and the weather was good.

The first move made by the Crown to prevent this dabbling in free enterprise was to issue permits, or congés as they were generally called. This was a compromise measure; if the tendency to roam could not be eradicated, it must at least be controlled. The number of permits issued each year was limited to twenty-five. At first the permits allowed holders to take two canoes, but later, when the rush to the woods got completely out of hand, this was reduced to one. The competition for permits was so great that the prices paid for them went higher and higher, like stocks on a bull market. The high point seems to have been reached around eighteen hundred livres. There undoubtedly was a great deal of jobbing in the sale of these prized official sanctions. Friends of the high officers of the state bought them up and then resold them secretly to the highest bidders.

As might be expected, the attempt to limit trading by such efforts was not successful. Those who could not get permits went off without them. Illicit traders evolved a plan of staying out for four years at a stretch, counting on official forgetfulness to escape penalties on their return. When it was found they could not count on leniency, they established themselves in little settlements north of Montreal and Three Rivers and never came in to the larger posts at all. Here they were found to be dangerous competitors because they could intercept the Indian canoes on their way to the bigger markets. They were always ready to trade brandy for the furs, and this was an infallible lure. The pelts from these unofficial camps were smuggled out of the country. Ships' captains had false bottoms made in the hulls of their ships for the purpose.

The *coureurs de bois* capture the imaginations of all who read about them. They were a gay, devil-may-care lot, completely lacking in fear, singing their songs which were sometimes sad, like the *Lament of Cadieux* (an early version of that well-known ballad), but generally rollicking and wild. They were true sons of the wilderness, having a love for the woods much more real than any emotion of which the stoic Indian was capable. They were mercurial in the extreme, sometimes kind and sometimes cruel, sometimes loyal and sometimes treacherous. They believed in countless superstitions. The northern lights were the marionettes to them, and they were convinced that the skies lighted up and danced because they, the bold vagabonds of the woods and waterways, were filling the evening sky with their songs. They believed in the legend of the *loup-garou*, the hound of the skies. It was a *coureur de bois* who bowed to the limp and decaying body of a criminal swinging in his cage and invited him to supper, and who was not disturbed when the spirit of the hanged man accepted the invitation, bringing his cage along with him—or so the story goes, a favorite one with the habitants.

But there was another side to the picture. Many of the *coureurs de bois* were wild and dissolute, addicted to drink and so loose in their morals that they had Indian mates wherever they went. They debauched the natives with brandy and then threw the profits away in drunken carousing in the towns. Having hair-trigger tempers, they fought among themselves with the fury of wildcats, and their ability to knock an opponent out with a well-directed kick to the head was proverbial.

All this has been forgotten. The dark side of the shield has been turned to the wall and the picture which remains is of the gay and courageous hunter sallying out to risk life and limb in the struggle for the conquest of the wilds. He will never be forgotten, this daring cavalier of the bark canoe, paddle in hand, his pack at his feet, his heart filled with high courage, a song on his lips.

3

The King and his advisers tried to meet the challenge of the *coureur de bois* in many ways. The most successful—and the most picturesque, incidentally—was the establishment of fur fairs. The largest of the fairs was, naturally, at Montreal, the meeting place of the rivers.

Trade fairs were a device carried over from medieval days. In all European countries the cities and towns set aside two weeks when merchants from all parts brought their goods with them and set up booths wherever they could find space. It was very much like a carnival. Dancers, jugglers, magicians, and mummers followed in the wake of the merchants and entertained in the streets for the largesse of pennies. The town merchants were against the fairs because they took business away from them, but the citizens loved the institution and entered into the carnival spirit with a will.

The Montreal Fair was conducted on the same principle. The Indians came down the Ottawa in one huge flotilla, sometimes as many as four or five hundred canoes at once. All who witnessed the spectacle agreed that it was both exciting and frightening. The Indians were painted and feathered and, having always something of the actor in them, fully conscious of the drama of their arrival. There was much shouting and singing and quarreling as the seemingly endless canoes came in to the landing place just outside the town. Here they pitched their tents and set up their kettles.

In the meantime the town of Montreal took on a gala air. Merchants from all parts of the colony had brought their goods for barter and were occupying temporary booths along the muddy streets or backed up outside against the tree trunks of the palisade. No word of business was spoken until the customary ceremonies had been conducted with suitable solemnity. An official welcome was extended to the visitors on the open space known as *La Commune* between the town and the river. The governor would be there, seated in an armchair and attired in his most imposing raiment, a plumed hat on his head, a sword across his knees. The chiefs would seat themselves about him according to rank, and there would be much smoking of pipes and endless solemn oratory. Perhaps the Flemish Bastard, that golden-tongued spokesman, would come over the river from Caughnawaga, where he was growing old and fat in peaceful living with the Iroquois who had abandoned their own people and their beautiful lakes to settle down on the doorstep of the white men, and add his flowery passages to the glut of simile and metaphor.

As soon as the ceremony of welcome was over, the trading began. It lasted for three days, the braves being as deliberate in making up their minds to sell as they were in all other dealings. A sinister note soon crept in. The sale of brandy could not be curtailed, and the sounds of savage revelry would be heard along the riverbanks. When this phase of the fair began, the people of Montreal took to their houses. They locked the doors and clamped the windows tight. This was what had brought the Indians to the fair, the desire to feel the white man's firewater racing through their veins. The intoxicated savages would strip off their scant articles of clothing and parade through the streets in bronze nakedness, brandishing their tomahawks and screeching their wildest woodland notes.

The *coureurs de bois* who had come with the Indians behaved as badly as their dusky-skinned friends, enjoying the drinking and fighting and showing just as much readiness to strip off their clothing for intoxicated parades of the town.

It might have been a wise thing if the King's officers had put the maintenance of order for the duration in the hands of a special court as had always been done with the medieval fairs. In France there was an institution known as the Pied-poudre Court (the Court of the Dusty-footed Men), the name stemming from the fact that the proceedings were in the hands of the itinerant merchants themselves.

On the visitors was laid all responsibility for the maintenance of law and order and the punishment of offenders. The same was done in England, where the name became corrupted to Pie-powder Courts. In course of time peddlers were called "pie-powders."

The advantage of this system was that the men who organized and conducted the fairs understood the quirks and fancies of those who came to sell the public their goods or to entertain. They could be counted on to curb the rabble of the fairs better than the stiff-necked magistrates of the towns. For Montreal to employ the Pied-poudre system would have been an interesting experiment. A colorful and effective bench of judges could most certainly have been set up: Dollier de Casson to represent the Sulpicians, his great shoulders nearly bursting out of his black robe, his broad face benign and yet alert with the need for curbing the excesses and ribaldries; Charles le Moyne to act for the citizens, with his fine, courageous face and his own hair hanging in long curls to his shoulders; one of the men from the woods, the holder of a congé, of course; a chief to act for the Indians.

Lacking this kind of guidance, the town fell into a chaotic condition as long as the fair lasted and for some time thereafter. The feudal courts, with their attorneys, clerks, and *huissiers*, could do nothing to check the drunkenness and madness in the streets.

4

It must be clear at this point that the spirit of Montreal had changed. The deeply religious feeling of the early days had not been lost, but it was not as generally shared. There were few to maintain the chivalrous attitude of the Sieur de Maisonneuve and his first little band. Perhaps it was not with complete regret that the gallant governor received a letter from Quebec (this was in Tracy's term), advising him that he should pay a visit to France "to look after his interests there."

Maisonneuve had undoubtedly expected something of the kind to happen. The tension between red-coated Quebec and blue-coated Montreal had grown rather than diminished with the years. Never inclined to push for his rights and prerogatives as the Abbé Queylus had been, the Montreal governor had stood firmly for the autonomous position of Montreal. Another source of dissension had been Maisonneuve's position on the brandy traffic. No consideration of expediency had been allowed to temper his actions. Selling brandy to the Indians was devil's work, and he sought to suppress the traffic with every bit of his power. This made things difficult for the administrators in Quebec, who had been inclined from the start, with the exception of Bishop Laval, to take an elastic policy.

After notifying Maisonneuve of his decision, Tracy made an announcement which read in part: "Having permitted Monsieur de Maisonneuve, governor of Montreal, to make a journey to France for his own private affairs, we have judged we can make no better choice of a commander in his absence than the person of Sieur Dupuis, and this as long as we shall judge convenient."

There was nothing temporary about this. Maisonneuve sailed for France at once and never came back. The people who crowded the shore to see him leave and who wept openly as the river barge pulled away from the wharf knew quite well they would never see their brave and gentle governor again. The gravity of his expression was a clear enough indication of his own feelings. His life's work, performed in the shadow of the great cross he had raised on the crest of the mountain, was finished; no more would he hear the roar of the rapids, no longer observe the climaxes which ushered in the changes of season, no more carry the responsibility for defense against the red menace in the south. He knew that this was a last farewell.

There was tangible proof of this in the absence of the blue silk coverings draped over the well of the barge and the customary armchair in the prow. These marks of honor were meticulously adhered to when an official of high rank traveled on the St. Lawrence. The Sieur de Maisonneuve, it was only too clear, was making the journey as a private citizen.

The discharged governor was sixty-three when he returned to France. Having been in no position to watch his private affairs during the twenty-one years he served in Montreal, he was a poor man when confronted with the necessity of making a new life for himself. All he could afford was a very modest house at the Fossé St. Victor, with one servingman who acted as cook, valet, and general factotum. Here he lived for eleven years. It was a lean and dull existence. He seldom went out, and his thoughts dwelt constantly on the outpost town which owed its existence to him, the sturdy little community which had braved the Iroquois terror so long.

The people of Montreal heard very little of him. When Canadians returned to France, they sometimes paid him visits at the Fossé St. Victor, where they always received an eager welcome. It was a rare thing, however, for a colonist to visit the mother country, and so the news he gleaned in this way was meager and infrequent. The last intimate glimpse which history supplies of him, through a friendly and discerning eye, came from Marguerite Bourgeoys.

"He was lodged," she wrote in describing her visit with him, "near the church of the Fathers of Christian Doctrine, and I arrived at his house rather late. Only a few days before he had constructed a cabin and furnished a little room after the Canadian fashion so as to entertain any persons who should come from Canada. I knocked on the door and he himself came down to open it, for he lived on the second floor with his servant, Louis Frins, and he opened the door for me with great joy."

Marguerite Bourgeoys was lacking in discernment on one point. The brave old gentleman had not built his cabin for the reception of colonial visitors. They would not need a familiar background to keep them in countenance. It is clear enough that he desired this retreat for himself, so that he could sit there alone and feel himself again at the meeting place of the great rivers and perhaps recapture at odd moments the feeling of the brave old days.

5

The determination of the King to keep the young men of New France at home to work the farms and raise large families did not stamp out the urge in the colony for expansion and discovery. If there had been nothing else to keep it alive, the spirit of the Jesuits would have done so. After the shock of the destruction of the Huron nation had been absorbed, they continued to cast farther afield for converts, as grimly determined as ever to banish Indian idolatry from the face of the American earth. It did not take long to establish themselves on the islands clustering in the waters connecting Lake Huron with that mighty inland sea which lay beyond and became known later as Lake Superior. Here Father Dablon conducted a mission at Ste. Marie du Sault (now Sault Ste. Marie) in a square enclosure of cedar logs with a house and a chapel. At the other end of Lake Superior a young Jesuit priest, Jacques Marquette, who was to win lasting fame later, had charge at La Pointe at the mission of St. Esprit.

This latter point was important, because here the pathetic remnants of the Hurons fleeing from the Iroquois had settled down. Existing in indolence and sloth, they hoped that they were safe at last. They had been joined by some bands of Ottawas who had left the country of the turbulent river for the same reason.

Here the scattered tribes were free of the hostile attentions of the Iroquois, but they were still to learn a bitter lesson. The men of the Long House were not the only aggressors in the redskin world. Out of the West there came suddenly a band of Sioux, who have been called the Iroquois of the Plains. Father Marquette led his terrified flock in a hasty race across the waters of the great lake. They took up their quarters on the channel islands, "the earthly paradise," according to Father Dablon, and here they were free for a brief spell from the deadly pincers of the Iroquois on one side and the Sioux on the other.

Another name comes into the story of the West at the same time. Louis Joliet had studied for the priesthood but had not completed his vows and was now devoting himself to the fur trade. He had been deputed by Talon to locate the copper mines, of which so many fabulous stories were being told, and had made a journey to Lake Superior for the purpose. On his return he encountered the man who was destined to become the greatest of all French explorers, René Robert Cavelier, Sieur de la Salle. This strange and fascinating figure had come to the colony in 1666 and had established a fur-trading post a few miles from the shelter of Montreal. This was for him no more than a pastime, a method of filling in time until he could begin to put into operation the resplendent plans which filled his head for the conquest of the continent; in which plans both Marquette and Joliet would play important parts.

It was impossible for the King and his advisers to ignore this impulse which animated the French-Canadian people, and it was decided finally to take official possession of the lands of the West. Daumont St.-Lusson was sent to perform the duty with a handful of men, including one of the boldest of the adventurers, named Nicolas Perrot, who went along as interpreter. A great conference was held with the Indians at the fort which Father Dablon had set up at Ste. Marie de Sault.

There was much oratory and smoking of peace pipes, and in the end St.-Lusson raised a large wooden cross on the highest point of land while the Frenchmen sang the *Vexilla Regis* with intense zeal.

A second post was then planted close at hand with a metal plate containing the royal arms. St.-Lusson stepped to the front and in a sonorous voice declared that possession had been taken of all the lands and waters of the West in the name of the Most Christian King of France and Navarre.

The Indians stood in silent clumps or sprawled uneasily on the ground, suspecting what this was all about and not liking it at all.

6

In addition to those whose names have been mentioned, there were many other French Canadians who were achieving a share of greatness in the exploration of the wilderness. In the forefront was Daniel Greysolon, Sieur du Lhut, who has been called the King of the Woodsmen. Little is known about him in his early years. The barest of statistics: born at St.-Germain-en-Laye, of the Reformed faith, became an officer in the King's bodyguard, and came to Canada to join some relatives in 1676, going first to Three Rivers. In the later stages of his career he held many important posts, being at various times commandant of the forts at Lachine, Cataraqui, and Mackinac. He died in 1709. He was a man of such honesty and fairness that he never had any trouble with the Indian tribes he encountered, and of such great courage that one of his sayings may be accepted as the true measure of the man: "I fear not death, only cowardice and dishonor."

His main achievement was the opening up of the country west and south of Lake Superior, although the honor of being first on the ground cannot be accorded him. Before he reached Canada those two stormy petrels, Radisson and Groseilliers, had been over this ground briefly, although they are sometimes said to have been the first to trace out the source of the Mississippi. It was in 1680 that Du Lhut, with a party of four Frenchmen and one Indian guide, spied out the land of the Brulé River and the St. Croix. He established a trading post at the mouth of the Pigeon River, and because of this the city which was founded there later was named Duluth in his honor.

During the next ten years he remained in the West, engaged in further explorations and in trading with the Indians. One of his most noteworthy feats was a peace meeting between the warring Sioux and Assiniboin tribes which was so successful that they re-

mained friends and were the allies of the French in the wars with
the Iroquois which broke out in the years 1684 and 1687. His last
years were spent in the East, in the relative peace of the fort which
Frontenac established at Cataraqui, now Kingston, Ontario.

The *Relations* speak of Nicolas Perrot as "one of the most prominent among the early voyageurs," thus placing him as one of the
men of official standing and not among the irresponsible *coureurs
de bois*. Perrot was a man of humble degree, born in the year 1644,
in the colony, in all probability, for by the year 1660 he went into
the employ of the Jesuits as an *engagé*. He remained with them until
the year 1665, when he removed to the Sulpicians.

The character of Perrot has been presented in various lights, but
there can be no doubt that he possessed in an extraordinary degree
the power to win and hold the confidence of the Indians. It was
due to his efforts that the tribes gathered in such numbers at Ste.
Marie du Sault to meet St.-Lusson. Having a glib control of several
Indian languages, he went to Green Bay on Lake Michigan to urge
attendance at the ceremony arranged for the spring. He was received
there with every mark of favor. The Miamis put on a tribal game
for his special benefit. It was played with long sticks curved at one
end to contain a webbing of catgut, and the object of the game was
to keep possession of the ball. This rugged contest gave the Indians
a chance to display their agility and their speed and was seen on
many occasions thereafter. The French coined for it the name of
La Crosse. In a very much improved form it became the national
sport of Canada.

Late in April a large flotilla of canoes started northward from
Green Bay. The skillful offices of Perrot had secured representatives
from all the tribes, the Miamis, the Sacs, the Winnebagos, the
Menominees, and the Potawatomi. They arrived at Ste. Marie du
Sault on May 5 and remained for the ceremonies the French were
staging there. It was no reflection on Perrot that, after the departure
of St.-Lusson, the Indians proceeded to tear down the royal arms
from the post on which they had been elevated. All Indians had
a certain perceptive sense, and they had on many occasions shown
their dislike of these high crosses which the French liked to set
up at strategic points, realizing that this was their way of establishing a claim to the land.

A different picture of Perrot emerges from a memoir dealing with an early stage of the career of the great La Salle. The latter had established himself at Fort Frontenac and was on bad terms with the Jesuits, being convinced that they aimed at monopolizing the fur trade. When a salad was served to him at his table containing a mixture of hemlock and verdigris which made him very sick, La Salle was disposed at first to suspect the Jesuits of a scheme to get rid of him. It developed later that one of his own followers was to blame. This man, whose name is given as Nicolas Perrot but who was generally called *Jolycoeur*, confessed his guilt and the episode seems to have ended there. It has been assumed that the man *Jolycoeur* was none other than the interpreter and voyageur, but the story is out of keeping with everything else known about him. No stigma seems to have attached to him later because of it. Four years before the death of La Salle, Perrot was appointed commandant of the whole Northwest. This post was of such importance by that time that it would not have been conferred on one who had been guilty of such a low form of crime.

As commandant he seems to have been eminently successful. He retained the good will of the Indians and kept them true to their French alliance. In the year 1693, wandering far afield, he discovered the lead mines on the Mississippi.

After taking up land near Becancourt, Perrot married a girl named Madeleine Raclot, who presented him with nine children. He began to accumulate property, having so much family responsibility, but like Job in the Land of Uz, who had excelled him by bringing ten children into the world and whose wealth was swallowed up in the attacks of the Sabeans and by the great wind which came up out of the wilderness, the last years of the voyageur's life were filled with misfortune. Twice stray parties of Indians looted his personal stores, and in the year 1687 a fire destroyed the Jesuit mission at De Père, wiping out a large supply of furs which Perrot had deposited there. Finally, in 1697, a bolt from the blue descended upon all Frenchmen who were engaged in the Northwest trade. Without any earlier notification of such intent the King abolished all trading privileges in that territory. Perrot was the hardest hit of them all. In his official capacity he had been giving expensive gifts to the Indians to hold them in line.

Perrot protested to Versailles. There was no response. The King, having made up his mind, paid no attention to the clamor of indignation which rose. There may have been reasons for this sudden change of policy, but there can be no doubt that great injustice was visited on many of the men in the government employ. Perrot spent his declining years in poverty.

Although his exploits in the field entitle him to a permanent place in Canadian annals, Nicolas Perrot is chiefly remembered for a quite remarkable manuscript he prepared during the final years, when he had little to do and nothing to expect. These memoirs, which were not printed until 1864, presented a detailed and accurate picture of the Northwest at the period when he acted as commandant and gave much important information with reference to the Indians of the lakes and plains.

CHAPTER XXVI

Radisson and Groseilliers Leave New France
and Go to England—The Formation of
the Hudson's Bay Company—Forts Are
Established on the Bay

1

IT WILL be recalled that the arrival of Radisson and Groseilliers in the early summer of 1660 with a large cargo of furs had temporarily saved the credit of the colony. They had passed the Long Sault on the way home a few days following the slaughter of Dollard and his brave handful. The pair were in high favor for a time. Elaborate plans were made for another voyage into the wilds, and the talk flew about the offices in the citadel and radiated out into all the commercial shops and the religious institutions and the houses of the town that the objective of the new venture would be Hudson's Bay. The two *coureurs de bois* were certain they could lead the way there.

But before the time to leave came they were hearing rumors which discomfited them not a little. Another party was being organized to make an overland dash for the bay. It was to be headed by two prominent Jesuits, Fathers Gabriel Dreuillettes and Claude Dablon, and the route they proposed to take was that of the Saguenay River.

The next development was equally disconcerting. The Sieur d'Avagour was governor at this time, and it was known that he had a willingness to improve his own fortunes; a weakness shared by a number of the governors of New France. He came to them in great secrecy with a proposal. He would give them official permits for their next excursion if they would give him half of the profits. The answer he received was that they would be glad to have the governor's company if he desired to share in the proceeds. This, at least, is the story that Radisson tells; there were no doubt denials later from the official camp. There is such a nice fitness about the answer of the voyageurs that it is easier to believe the Radisson version than the denials which came from the other side.

Whatever the truth may be, the resourceful pair did not delay. Convinced they had nothing to gain by further parleys and feeling the pinch of time, they stole away in the night as they had done before. They left Three Rivers with a cheery message from the guards in the lookout tower, where no doubt there was much grinning and winking in the dark. When a member of the party named Larivière became separated from the rest and was found later in a state of semi-starvation, the governor displayed his pique by clapping him in prison. Whereupon the good people of Three Rivers, who knew enough of the story to have decided sympathies and who seem, moreover, to have been an independent lot, broke open the jail and released him.

The expedition was a great success. The party struck for the hunting grounds north of Lake Superior, where Radisson was prompted by the beauty and richness of this stretch of primeval land to write in his diary: "It grieves me to see that the world could not discover such enticing country to live in. . . . The Europeans fight for a rock in the sea against one another or for a sterile land. . . . It is true, I confess, that access here is difficult, but nothing is to be gained without labor and pains."

The party returned from this idyllic land in 1663 with a wonderful store of furs and a secret. Some intimation of the secret leaked out at once; it had to do with a new land route to Hudson's Bay. As the Jesuit party had failed in their venture up the Saguenay, there was much interest in what Radisson and Groseilliers might know.

The governor acted promptly and with a degree of severity which showed that his resentment still ran deep. He ordered them arrested and had the cargo impounded. The upshot was that they were fined almost up to the full value of the fur they had brought back with them. Some of the money was to be employed in building a new fort at Three Rivers, this being intended perhaps as a measure to rob them of the sympathies of their fellow citizens. As a sop to the pair, it was stipulated they could put their respective coats of arms on the gate of the new fort. A second slice was to go at once into the treasury, and a special fine of fourteen thousand pounds was imposed. From the figures available, it seems that the value of the furs ran very high—some place it at sixty thousand pounds—and out of this the woodsmen were left no more than four thousand, from which the expenses of the expedition had to be met.

Radisson and Groseilliers were not men to sit down under such treatment. Radisson had been nicknamed *Dodcon,* which meant Little Devil, when he was prisoner of the Mohawks, and both he and his partner had shown highhandedness and temper in their dealings. Groseilliers departed at once for France in a state of high dudgeon to appeal their case before the King's ministers. It is said that he spent half of the capital remaining in the partnership in his efforts to get the Quebec decision reversed. The ministers gave him the cold shoulder and refused to do anything about a decision which had brought into the treasury such a comfortable sum. It is clear they gave no thought to the future, to the possibility that these men, the most spectacularly successful traders the colony had produced, might be capable of bringing continuous revenue into the royal coffers if allowed official co-operation. The stand they took was a grievous error and was to cost France a huge price in war and bloodshed as well as financial losses so enormous that by comparison the amount of the fines seems of no more consequence than the scratch of a bookkeeper's pen.

Groseilliers returned to New France and rejoined his partner there. They were now almost devoid of funds, and their position seemed so hopeless that they reached a momentous decision; with considerable reluctance, it is believed. They decided to see if they could secure backing in the colonies of New England. With this in mind they went to Acadia by way of Nicolas Denys' fort at St. Peter and then by Canso. At Port Royal they met a New England sea captain named Zachariah Gillam, who encouraged them in their purpose to do their trading in future from England's colonial ports. Their reluctance still nagged at them because this meant going to Hudson's Bay by sea and abandoning the land route which they had learned from the Indians of the West, the direct and easy way through a very long lake now called Winnipeg and then straight to the bay by a river which would be given the name of Nelson. Zachariah Gillam offered to take them in his ship, and together they got as far as the straits which Sir Martin Frobisher, the great Elizabethan navigator, had found in 1577. The straits led straight into the West and perhaps would open up for them the way to the Northwest Passage. Gillam, according to Radisson's account, began to complain that his ship was not fitted out for winter sailing and to say they should turn back. Radisson, who does not seem to have been afraid of anything, wrote in his picturesque reports that Gillam was frightened by "the mountains of sugar candy," by which he meant the icebergs. At any rate, turn back they did, arriving in due course in Boston.

A deal was made in the latter city by which two ships were supplied for another effort to reach Hudson's Bay by sea. One of the ships was wrecked and the crews lost heart. They did not reach the bay, and on their return the New England backers of the venture entered suit against the French Canadians.

At this low point in their fortunes—they were now almost destitute—they met an extraordinary man named Sir George Carteret. He had been born and raised on the island of Jersey and during the English civil war had fought with the greatest zeal and vigor on the royalist side, with so much zeal, in fact, that he went on fighting after the King's banner went down finally. From his headquarters on the island of Jersey he waged a privateering war on English shipping and was proclaimed a pirate by the victorious parliamentary party. His activities were maintained until the restoration of the Stuarts put Charles II on the throne. It was to be expected that among those rewarded by the new King was the hard-fighting buccaneer. Carteret was made a baronet and given various posts of importance. He was granted "a certain island and adjacent islets in perpetual inheritance to be called New Jersey," and he was one of the lords proprietors to whom the King assigned the colonization of the Carolinas.

Pepys calls him "the most passionate man in the world," and Clarendon has described him as "the most generous man in kindness and the most dexterous man of business ever known." There seems to have been a basis for both descriptions. One thing is certain: in one way and another Sir George Carteret became one of the wealthiest men in the world.

He was in the American colonies on business concerned with his New Jersey grants when he met Radisson and Groseilliers. His keen mind jumped at once to the great possibilities of the northern trade. He saw the French Canadians undoubtedly as men of his own kidney and was certain they could be employed to great advantage. He persuaded them to go to England with him.

2

They arrived in England after many adventures, including their capture by the Dutch, with whom England was at war, and a period of detention in Spain. It was in 1665 when they arrived, when London was in the throes of the Great Plague. The most acute stage of that terrible visitation had been reached, when people were dying at the rate of six or seven thousand a month, when the red cross was marked on most of the houses and at nights the carts rumbled through the streets and the summons was intoned, "Bring out your dead!" Those who could afford to leave the city had already done so. King Charles was at Oxford, and Carteret repaired to that city, taking his two new friends from the French colonies with him.

Radisson acted as spokesman, and the King listened to him with the closest attention. There can be no doubt that this young adventurer had a way with him. He probably deserved to be called *Dodcon* and certainly he had a tongue with which to spin glowing pictures. He seems, sensibly enough, to have dwelt on the great profits to be made out of the fur trade in the northern waters, but through the recital ran a golden thread, the speculation that out of the bay running ever westward on its way to the East would be found the Northwest Passage.

The King was sufficiently impressed to order that for the balance of the year, by which time he expected to have definite plans made for the conquest of the North, the sum of forty shillings a week was to be given the two Frenchmen.

The next important step was their introduction to Prince Rupert at Windsor. This was done on the King's instructions. Charles was anxious to relieve his famous cousin of the financial worries which beset him and saw in the fur trade the chance he had been seeking. Prince Rupert needs no introduction: the brave and headlong commander of cavalry who led the royal horse for his uncle, Charles I, in the battles of the civil war. He was without a doubt an able and dangerous fighting man, although he seems to have been continuously on the losing side; beaten by that much abler soldier, Oliver Cromwell, and later as an admiral engaged in some hard-fought but not too successful naval battles with the Dutch fleets. A son of Elizabeth, the beautiful granddaughter of Mary Queen of Scots who lost a German throne in the Thirty Years' War, Rupert bore her a close resemblance: his stern features beautifully chiseled, his skin ivory, his eyes brown and passionately warm. He was living now at Windsor Castle and had turned his apartments into workrooms where he tinkered with inventions and developed his gift for making mezzotints.

King Charles felt very sorry for this cousin who was so poor that he had to remain a bachelor, although the Merry Monarch knew what all England had heard, that Rupert maintained a fine house in London for a gay and pretty actress named Peg Hughes, a great friend of Nell Gwyn. He felt that the Hudson's Bay adventure offered the best method of providing his exiled cousin with an income apart from the royal funds.

Rupert, abrupt in manner, sardonic in speech, somewhat lacking in sense of humor, listened to the tales of Radisson and shared his royal cousin's reaction to the skill of that articulate tongue. Radisson and Groseilliers (the English found the latter name a difficult mouthful and even allowed it to get into one official record as "Mister Gooseberry") were kept at Windsor for the better part of a year while the plans matured. King Charles paid visits to his royal castle, where he played tennis with Rupert and went for long walks with him, surrounded by a screen of dogs; and sometimes he saw the two adventurers, who were now pensioned at an indeterminate figure running from two to four pounds a month. The royal interest in the plan did not lessen, but there were delays because the continuance of the war with the Dutch made sea ventures unsafe.

The two promoters were fortunate that Prince Rupert had as his secretary a very shrewd and farsighted man named James Hayes. The latter took fire almost immediately over the plans of the Frenchmen, and it may have been that his enthusiasm was transmitted to the more conservative Rupert. At any rate, Hayes became the strongest supporter of the plan and was allowed a prominent part in the affairs of the company which was formed finally. He it was who pried out of the strongbox the sum of five pounds which paid for the publishing of Radisson's book. It was a just thing that Hayes acted as second-in-command to Rupert for the first ten years of the life of the company.

The first exploratory venture was in the nature of a test. King Charles ordered his brother, the Duke of York, who would later succeed him on the throne as James II, to loan the *Eaglet* of the South Seas fleet for the purpose. It was a small vessel, forty feet

by sixteen, with a war complement of thirty-five men. This was put under the command of a Captain Stannard. A second ship called the *Nonsuch* was put into service in addition, a vessel of much the same size, which was assigned to the same Captain Zachariah Gillam who had tried once before. A start was made for the West on June 3, 1668, after the investors had tested the contents of some of Gillam's best bottles of Madeira wine.

Radisson was on the *Eaglet,* which was unlucky for him. The ship was disabled early and had to put back to Plymouth. The *Nonsuch* with Groseilliers on board reached the northern waters and penetrated as far south as James Bay at the southern end of Hudson's Bay. Here, at the mouth of a river which they named after Prince Rupert, a small fort was raised and the business of trading with the natives began. On the advice of the Frenchmen, the cargo included all the right articles for barter. Half a pound of beads or five pounds of sugar were given for one beaver skin, twenty fishhooks for five skins, a gun for twenty. As the result of a year's trading the *Nonsuch* returned with a cargo valued at nineteen thousand pounds, which was ample to meet all expenses and leave a margin of profit to be divided among those who had contributed the funds. The result, certainly, was good enough to convince everyone that there was money to be made in the bay.

On May 2, 1670, the famous charter of "the Governor and Company of Adventurers of England, Trading into Hudson's Bay" was introduced and signed. And thus one of the most profitable and fascinating ventures in the whole history of business the world over was begun.

This historic charter was a document of five sheets, written in curiously involved sentences, and giving the Adventurers practically the whole of the North and the waters and seas thereabouts. There were eighteen men listed as members, including the Duke of York, Prince Rupert, Carteret, Colleton, Sir James Hayes, Sir John Kirke (whose daughter Mary became Mrs. Radisson shortly thereafter), an assorted lot of peers, the Duke of Albemarle, the Earl of Craven, Lord Arlington and Lord Ashley, and a number of plain baronets and knights. John Portman, listed as citizen and goldsmith, was made the treasurer.

What of Radisson and Groseilliers? They were not mentioned, although it was understood they were to continue on some kind of dole, and the King himself gave each of them "a gold chain and meddall." They were treated throughout in such a cavalier manner, in fact, that ultimately they went back to the allegiance of their birth, as will be told later.

The company was handled in a casual way for a time. The members met at unstated intervals at any one of three places, the White Tower in the Tower of London, at Whitehall, which the King used as a town residence, or at the Jerusalem Coffee House. The financing seems to have been quite hit-and-miss at the start. Several of the original Adventurers did not put in money for the shares they held. The company made profits almost from the start and very shortly paid dividends as high as 50 per cent. The sales they held were colorful and exciting events, and the buyers who came to them were treated much better than the two men who had made all this possible. On one occasion Sir James Hayes purchased three dozen bottles of sack and three dozen of claret to be used in slaking the thirst, and perhaps unloosening the purse strings, of the buyers who attended one auction.

Rupert continued to experiment with his inventions and worked on his mezzotints, taking little interest in the company. His visits to London were infrequent and were mostly to see Peg Hughes. On one occasion, however, several years after the charter had been engrossed and signed and the posts on Hudson's Bay had begun doing a thumping fine trade with the northern Indians, he wandered into one of the auctions. They were not using the candle method of auctioneering by which the last bid heard before the light on a mere thumb-point of tallow went out was declared the winner. This was a highly exciting method and led to a pandemonium of bids as the light guttered low. The sale, however, was brisk enough, and staccato offers filled the room as three thousand pelts were disposed of at good round prices. The prince, being still as straight of back as ever, looked as though he would have been more at ease on horseback. He did not seem to understand just what was going on. He listened courteously but without comment, bowed to his associates and gave a stiff inclination of his head to some of the eager, clamoring buyers, and walked out. It was clear that he was unconscious of the fact, and quite indifferent to it, that what he had been witnessing would put many hundred sound, jingling guineas into his own pockets.

He went away without any thought that in years to come the Adventurers would be known as the Lords of the North, with an empire of their own and the best-managed and -controlled string of trading posts the world had perhaps ever seen, and that for centuries thereafter money would jingle in lordly amounts in lordly pockets because of the unprecedented success this company, of which he was the head, would enjoy. Certainly he had no appreciation of the fact that the two down-at-heels Frenchmen, who may also have been present and watching with the resentful reflection that at least some of these lordly guineas should be going into their pockets, had been responsible for creating all this welcome prosperity.

CHAPTER XXVII

The Divided Loyalties of Radisson and Groseilliers— The Policy of the Hudson's Bay Company and Its Great Success

1

THERE can be no doubt that Radisson and Groseilliers were an unscrupulous pair, but their side of the much-vexed question which developed is not hard to see. Knowing the value of their services to the English, they believed they were entitled to a fair share of the profits they were making for other men; for men who stayed comfortably at home and toasted their fat shins in front of warm fires and avidly drank their claret to the toast of bigger dividends. "We were Caesars," wrote Radisson the Irrepressible. Like Caesar, they were conquerors. But grasping hands in high places were taking the rewards from them.

The French habit of impoverishing them with fines because they were so successful drove them to England and to the formation of the Hudson's Bay Company. The suspicions and the social contempt of the English drove them again to the French service. They shuttled back and forth until the story becomes too complicated to follow in detail. Yes, they were unscrupulous, crafty, and glib. Their heads were filled with schemes, and so the men they dealt with had to be wary. But the French officials were as blind as bats, seeing these brave and somewhat mad adventurers as nothing but disobedient servants of the Crown. The English looked down their noses at these "renegades" and refused to give them any share in the company, fobbing them off with small and reluctant doles. In view of the bureaucratic stubbornness of the French and the cheese-paring of the English, there is some excuse for the pendulum-like course of these disgruntled pioneers.

The issue has been fought over so vehemently down the years that no clear pattern of the story emerges. One thing only is certain, that the blame must be divided. The censure of history cannot be withheld from any of the parties concerned.

2

Hudson's Bay was a prize worth struggling for; Versailles knew this now as well as London. The Adventurers had been sending ships to the bay every year, and those which came back (the percentage of loss by shipwreck was heavy) carried wonderful cargoes. Although the system of having a governor on the ground had been started, the first being a certain Mr. Charles Bayly, the direction of trading and the matter of policy were still in the hands of these two superlative pioneers, or the two bold knaves, according to one's reading of what happened.

In 1672, just before the Comte de Frontenac arrived in Quebec to become governor of New France, a disquieting state of affairs developed. The number of Indians bringing in their furs to Fort Charles on the Rupert River and the posts which had been established on the western side of the bay began to fall off. Radisson made an uneasy survey of the western shore where the Moose and the Severn and the Nelson emptied their waters into the bay, and on his return found a Jesuit priest, Charles Albanel, at Fort Charles. Father Albanel, a native of Auvergne, was one of the boldest of priestly explorers and had been sent to the North by Talon to claim the land for France. Coming overland by the Saguenay route, he had arrived some time before and had sat himself down to wait. He presented his credentials to Charles Bayly in the form of passports. At the same time he turned over some letters he had been carrying for Radisson and Groseilliers.

The explanation for the diminution in pelts now came out. French traders were striking north from the St. Lawrence, some by way of the Saguenay, others following the route which Radisson had wanted to take, by way of Lake Winnipeg. They were thus cutting across the lines by which the Indians converged on the bay and were getting the major share of the furs. They could not cover the whole of this vast expanse of muskeg and snow, but they were getting enough to leave holes in the holds of English ships returning to London.

England and France were not at war, and so Bayly had to accept the credentials of Father Albanel. He heard, however, of the letters which had been handed to Radisson and Groseilliers and his suspicions were aroused. Bayly, it appears, was a man of small tact. He summoned his two collaborators and charged them with being responsible for the irruption of French traders into the territory which the company now regarded as its own.

This was not true. The arrival of Father Albanel had been as much of a surprise to them as it had been to Bayly himself. It happened, moreover, to be a singularly inappropriate time to level such charges. The letters which the priest had conveyed to them contained proposals from Colbert for their return.

The upshot of Bayly's charges was that the two Frenchmen returned to London at once to discuss this situation with the directors of the company. Protracted negotiations followed. It becomes clear enough that Radisson and Groseilliers would have remained in the service of the company if satisfactory terms had been offered them. They remained in London throughout the winter of 1673–74, pressing their claims during an interminable series of talks and conferences, the letters from Colbert burning holes in their pockets the while.

The company, however, remained adamant. The best they could do was to promise Radisson one hundred pounds per annum (this apparently was to be a joint fee, for no mention is made separately of Groseilliers) and "if it pleases God to bless the company with good success hereafter that they come to be in a prosperous condition that they will reassume considerations."

Some authorities contend that the company had not been paying dividends and that this was the reason for the seeming niggardliness of their proposition. Others declare that the profits had been large and that dividends up to 100 per cent had been paid.

Radisson and Groseilliers slipped quietly across the Channel and paid a call on Colbert. He greeted them cordially and made it clear that the severity which had driven them to London in the first place was now regretted; as well it might be, for it had thrown the empire of the North into the hands of France's great rival. He made them an offer: come back into the service of France and receive a salary three times as large as the Hudson's Bay Company was offering. He wanted them for the navy, Colbert having been from the start the advocate of a powerful sea branch, even at the expense of the army.

A deal was made on that basis.

3

The attitude of the directors in London is hard to understand unless they had reasons, which have not come to light, for suspecting the intentions of the two Frenchmen. This does not seem likely in view of the resumption years later of a relationship with Radisson. What makes it difficult to understand is that they were already establishing the sound policies which were to remain in force up to modern times and to prove so extremely successful. They had a conception which can be described only as feudal. The charter which King Charles had granted to them gave the company a monopoly of all trade in the North, the right to build forts, to organize and equip ships of war, and to pass their own laws and duly enforce them. The people of the lands thus handed over to the company became their subjects. The company had the power of life and death over them.

A stern policy would slowly evolve as a result of these sweeping concessions. Free trading would not be tolerated and no one would be allowed to invade the territory, either as settler or transient trader, without the consent of the officers of the company. The rights which had been granted them would be maintained and the laws laid down would be sternly enforced. Under the iron hand of this autocracy the Indians of the North would live for nearly two hundred years. The power of the white gods of the trading posts would be respected and feared. There would be bloodshed occasionally and a succession of incidents, but in the main peace would reign in the North; for the directors also laid down the rule that, if they must be stern and unyielding, they must also be just.

The germs of other basic ideas were already blossoming. To make the rule in the North truly feudal, it must be conducted with pomp and splendor. The first indication of this was in the selection of governors. Prince Rupert filled the post in the early years. He was succeeded by the King's brother James, Duke of York, later James II. The third was John Churchill, the great Duke of Marlborough.

The governors of the posts maintained a considerable amount of pomp. Their food might be plain and scarce, but it was served with great state, with much piping and drumming. They met the Indians in velvet capes and with swords clanking at their sides. The poor natives were properly impressed and remained that way for the two centuries of company supremacy. Later the natives would begin to depend on the posts for the food they would need during the winters and would find themselves in an almost perpetual state of indebtedness.

This feudal policy was carried into the relationships with employees. If a man was injured he received "smart money," or a pension if he had been permanently incapacitated. The widows of those who died in the service or were lost at sea were treated in like vein. It is strange that the effort to be fair did not extend to the relationship with Radisson and Groseilliers. If the two Frenchmen had been kept reasonably content, the company would have been spared much fighting and trouble and endless expense. This was, at the least, a serious error of judgment.

4

In the year 1680 an important conference was held in New France. Where it took place is not known, but it was probably at Montreal, for at least three of the men included in the group were of that town. It was not an official conference; none of those in attendance held posts in the royal service. They were, instead, the great figures of the colony, the bold and the farseeing, the wise and the courageous men. Among them were the Sieur de la Salle, about whose exploits much will be told later; Joliet, joint discoverer of the Mississippi; a successful fur trader of Quebec named Aubert de la Chesnaye. Then there was that brave and solid citizen of Montreal, Charles le Moyne. His seigneury at Longueuil was in a flourishing condition and his trading enterprises in Montreal were making a prosperous man of him. He now had six sons, all of them destined to play truly glorious roles in the tumultuous years ahead. And, to give point to the gathering, there were Radisson and Groseilliers.

These two stormy petrels of the North had been for many years in the employment of France. They had not been allowed a chance, however, to return to the bay. As long as the two countries were at peace a fiction of neutrality had to be maintained and, as the English were in possession there, nothing could be done to disturb them. Radisson had been with the navy and had spent one year in the West Indies. He had been unhappy, for his heart was always in the North. He had happened to encounter La Chesnaye, and the latter had urged him to fall in line with a plan which he himself had been hatching. Radisson had agreed willingly enough, and this had carried with it the consent of his faithful partner as well.

The importance of this informal gathering can be judged by the fact that out of it came *La Compagnie du Nord*, the Company of the North, an organization which represented the will of the French-Canadian people to contest the lordship of the fur country with the Hudson's Bay Company. La Chesnaye was persuasive and glib, and it is probable that he shared with Radisson the major role in the deliberations. Ordinarily it would have seemed strange to see the Sieur de la Salle and Charles le Moyne sitting by and allowing other men to monopolize anything as momentous as this. But the former's mind was set on the South, and he was present largely for the weight of his name. Charles le Moyne would watch the proceedings with a wise and wary eye, even though he may not have much to say. He was getting a little too old and heavy to take a personal part in anything as exacting as this, but his oldest sons were ready.

The first step after reaching the decision to organize a company for the conquest of the North was to go to the Comte de Frontenac for the necessary permission. No one could have had more eagerness for the bold and the unusual than this great governor, but he was, after all, the King's representative in New France and he had to consider that the King was at peace with England. It would have been a grave mistake to give the new organization an official blessing and the commission they asked. On the surface, therefore, he took an aloof attitude, refusing to issue the commission and withholding his approval of the plan.

His decision seems, however, to have been delivered with a wink. If they, the applicants, chose to send ships into Hudson's Bay without official sanction, that clearly was their own business. He, Frontenac, must know nothing about it. They should understand that if they got into trouble they must get out of it themselves.

Frontenac was a shrewd man. He had, of course, heard a great deal about Radisson and Groseilliers, these legendary figures who were either loved very much or held up as renegades and hated. While the applicants were grouped about him in the citadel of St. Louis he cast many appraising glances in their direction. He could not fail to be impressed by them. Radisson, never a large man, was beginning to look actually rather small. Time, that shrinker of spines, had taken an inch from his stature at the same time that it sprinkled his hair with gray; but a penetrating observer would not miss the occasional blaze of fire in his eye. Groseilliers, the older by some years, was growing heavy and slow. He had little to say, leaving the matter of spokesmanship to his more dexterous partner, but there was never any possibility of a mistake about this man who had taken his title from a patch of wild berry bushes in Three Rivers. He was always one to be reckoned with; a doer of deeds, a fighter who struck hard and often.

Having thus obtained a left-handed blessing from the governor, the little group got down to business. La Chesnaye, a great promiser, assured them that he could produce the necessary funds and the ships if Radisson and Groseilliers would take the command. Their consent was readily obtained. This was what they wanted to do more than anything else in the world: to see once more the strait of the icebergs, to cruise along the shores where the fast-flowing rivers brought down the Indian canoes piled high with pelts, to strike the blows which would redeem them forever in the eyes of their fellow countrymen.

It was decided, therefore, that Radisson and Groseilliers would go into semi-retirement for the winter. In the spring they would repair to Isle Percé, where the fishing fleets congregated, and there they would wait for the twin ships La Chesnaye had promised to fit out and man.

La Chesnaye, it developed, was better at making promises than in the fulfillment of them. The two ships which finally came heaving and pitching into Isle Percé like a pair of veteran porpoises were the smallest and oldest and the crankiest to handle that could have been produced by a search of the offcasts of all nations. They were called the *St. Pierre* and the *Ste. Anne* and they could hold no more than thirty men between them; which was perhaps just as well, because the men La Chesnaye had recruited were for the most part raw and inexperienced landlubbers. The rigging was rotten, the holds were unseaworthy, and there was a stench about these derelicts which only long service in the fishing trade could produce. Was it possible for even inspired leaders to accomplish anything under these circumstances? Could Radisson and Groseilliers win back the bay with ships redeemed from naval junk piles and with the culls and misfits who made up the crews?

They decided to try. Radisson took the *St. Pierre*. Groseilliers, having a grown-up son, Jean Chouart, with him, took the *Ste. Anne*. After suppressing a mutinous outbreak among the crew, who were finding the service quite different from what they had expected, they finally reached Hudson's Bay in September.

Dependence must be placed on Radisson's narrative for the story of what happened after that, and it has to be avowed at the start that there was always a hint of vagueness and more than a tendency to exaggerate in everything he put down on paper. Briefly, therefore, what happened was as follows. The Frenchmen in their inadequate little tubs came limping into the waters where the Hayes and the Nelson rivers raced to the bay. They found there a ship, the *Bachelor's Delight*, which had come from New England under the command of Ben Gillam, a son of the captain who had figured in the early years of the company. They were poaching, these bold colonials, and the delighted Radisson saw at once that he had a hold over young Ben Gillam which could be used to advantage. By his glib talk he had "come over" young Gillam and won his confidence when a vessel owned by the company, the *Prince Rupert*, completed the triangle. It sailed into the estuary of the Nelson with two men of some prominence on board, Governor Bridgar of the company and old Zachariah Gillam himself.

The newcomers should have sensed the situation at once because the directors of the company had made plans for just such an emergency as this. On sailing, the captains of company ships were given sealed orders which contained among other things the harbor signals. Ships on the bay which did not hoist the proper signals were to be fired on as poachers and interlopers. Neither Radisson nor Ben Gillam was in a position to fly the right signals—in fact, they did not dare fly any flag at all—and the *Prince Rupert* should have blown them out of the water.

Radisson took advantage of the opportunity thus presented to him. He built a high fire, which was the Indian way of announcing their presence with furs to trade, and in response the *Prince Rupert* came in to anchor. Radisson then succeeded in getting the ear of old Zachariah Gillam and acquainted him with the news of his son's involvement. Zachariah was distressed, for he knew that his son could be shot if his identity was discovered. He did not, therefore, let Bridgar know that this bearded stranger was none other than Pierre Esprit Radisson, that well-known turner of coats.

Then nature took a decisive hand. A storm drove the ice from the bay into the estuary, and the *Prince Rupert* was sunk. Fourteen of the crew, including Captain Zachariah Gillam, were drowned.

At this point the story that Radisson retails becomes too involved for recapitulation or belief. By devious means, which he makes more ingenious than any pirate ever contrived, he took possession of a fort which Ben Gillam had built on shore and captured the whole New England crew. Not a blow was struck, not a drop of blood spilled. Then he made prisoners of Bridgar and most of his men (this one does justice to Münchhausen himself), and putting all of them on board the *Bachelor's Delight,* and all the furs which the poachers had secured, he sailed away in triumph.

It is almost impossible to believe what Radisson tells of the methods by which he brought about this miracle, but there is no denying the results. The *Bachelor's Delight* reached Quebec. Bridgar and Ben Gillam were on board in the role of prisoners. There was a valuable cargo in the hold.

This much also is certain. The people of Quebec went wild with enthusiasm when the terror of the North, who had always been a hero in the eyes of most of them, came into the harbor with his loot and his prisoners. But in high circles there was no trace of enthusiasm at all. In the citadel of St. Louis there was at this time a governor named Le Febvre de la Barre, an old soldier who completely lacked the qualifications to deal with situations like this. To Governor la Barre the success of Radisson was a complication which he solved by doing the obvious thing. He fined the victors and ordered that they return at once to France and report to Colbert, who would know how to deal with them. He restored the *Bachelor's Delight* to Ben Gillam and allowed him to sail for Boston. Bridgar was set at liberty with diplomatic apologies.

La Compagnie du Nord came very close to a premature collapse as a result of this decision on the part of Governor la Barre. When Radisson, impoverished a second time by the fines imposed on him, reached Paris he found that Colbert was dead and that the King was in a state of fury over the whole episode. Louis was angry with La Barre and wrote to him demanding to know why the latter had thus publicly surrendered the French claim to Hudson's Bay. He was furious with Radisson because he had been too successful but a little later ordered him to go back to the bay and do what he could to help the English restore order. The English Government furiously bombarded Versailles with demands for damages and the punishment of the men responsible for the losses of the company.

At this point Groseilliers drops out of the story. Some say he retired to Three Rivers and lived out the balance of his days there with his faithful Marguerite and his brood of children. Others believe that he died in the North while Radisson was performing his feats of legerdemain. Whatever the reason, he dropped for good from the pages of history, and from that point on Radisson traveled alone.

Radisson was, needless to state, very unhappy over this break in a friendship which had withstood for so many years the strain of great successes and the bitterness of defeat. It had been a truly remarkable alliance, a David and Jonathan epic of the north woods and waters. Radisson was the showy partner, the dynamic leader. Groseilliers had carried the heaviest share of the burdens. That the entente had not been impaired is evidenced by the fact that Radisson left young Jean Chouart in charge of the captured forts in the North when he made his victorious return to Quebec.

5

In the spring of 1684 there was a meeting of the directors of the Hudson's Bay Company at which a most unexpected announcement was made. Pierre Esprit Radisson was back in London. Like the Vicar of Bray, "he had turned a cat in a pan once more" and he was back for good. He was no longer willing to trust himself and his fortunes to the mercy of French colonial governors. The directors, willing to forget the past, welcomed the prodigal and made an agreement with him by which he received stock to the value of two hundred pounds, a salary of one hundred pounds in years when dividends were not paid and fifty when they were, and the sum of twenty-five pounds to set himself up again. They were so glad to see the rolling stone on their side that they made a present of seven musquash skins to Sir William Young, who had persuaded Radisson to return. They even took the Frenchman to meet the Duke of York, who had succeeded Prince Rupert as governor of the company. As a shareholder he had to take the customary oath of allegiance, which began, "I doe sweare to bee true and faithful to ye Comp'y of Adventurers: ye secrets of ye Comp'y I will not disclose. . . ."

In the years that followed Radisson seems to have been an active and faithful servant of the company, although he was still to wage many battles with the directors over his share of the proceeds and to secure a pension for his wife. He went out to the bay immediately in the *Happy Return;* and a happy return it was, for he brought back twenty thousand pelts. He made many other trips to the wild north country which he loved so much and was a factor, without a doubt, in the successes which now crowned the company efforts. There were years when his dividends on the two hundred pounds of stock he held amounted to one hundred and fifty and there were years when he received, probably as a result of the loss of ships, no more than fifty.

As he grew older he ceased to accompany the ships to the bay. He had more arguments with the directors, as a result of which his income was cut to a regular one hundred pounds a year. On this he was able to live reasonably well although he had nine children to support. He drew his last quarterly installment in July 1710, when he was in his seventy-sixth year.

His last years could not have been happy ones. In London, his ears were filled with the cries of the streets, and this must have been a poor substitute for the sound of dipping paddles and the swish of water along the sides of a birch-bark canoe. From his windows he saw sooty chimney pots and lowering skies instead of the green line of trees and the flash of the northern lights.

Of all the characters produced by New France, and there were so many of them, he seems the most picturesque. He had in him much of the stuff of greatness.

CHAPTER XXVIII

Frontenac, the Great Governor, Is Appointed— His Early Life—His Character

1

THERE now appears on the scene the leading character and the most colorful actor in this drama which was being enacted against the backdrop of Canadian solitudes. The Comte de Frontenac has been accepted as the greatest in the long list of governors who for various periods controlled the destinies of the colony. He was a man of positive qualities, a curious blending of strength and weakness—in fact, one of the most contradictory of men to attain such a degree of fame. He came to New France at a time when a strong hand was badly needed at the helm. If his record, reviewed at this late period, seems rather lacking in solid achievement to deserve the acclaim which has been accorded him, there can be no doubt that he had in full degree the strength which was needed and that he brought the colony through a period of desperate crisis.

Frontenac was a soldier with a remarkable record, brave, aggressive, and astute. As a courtier he had been less successful. As the controller of his own far from adequate fortune he had been a failure. As a man he had positive virtues and as many obvious faults.

It will soon become apparent that the Comte de Frontenac was a keen judge of men. He quarreled with the other heads of the state and from the first seems to have been on the worst possible terms with the Jesuits. His coat of arms carried an imaginary animal, half griffon and half lion. "I will yet make the griffon fly above the crows!" he cried on one occasion, the crows being the Jesuits. He had no difficulty, however, in winning and holding the affections and the obedience of the common man and his industrious wife. He strove always to improve the position of the patient habitant and succeeded to some extent.

He seems to have had an instinctive understanding of the Indians. The shrewd and fearless policy he adopted in dealing with them brought the colony through its darkest days. The Iroquois admired and feared him. He knew when to call them his children and play the indulgent parent, but he never failed at exactly the right moment to slip off the velvet glove and strike with the iron hand. He sometimes indulged in horseplay with the braves from the Finger Lakes and even joined with them in an imitation of a war dance. At other times, when hatred ran high, he did not hesitate to authorize the burning of prisoners at the stake.

On the reverse side, he was haughty, quarrelsome, absurdly boastful, unable to stomach opposition (it was said he sometimes frothed at the mouth with rage when his views were disregarded), and at most times unstable. He was impetuous in some of his decisions and always bitterly unwilling to acknowledge a mistake. There seems no doubt that he had accepted the post in the first place as a way of improving his own fortunes. The charge was made against him that he was in secret alliance with some of the *coureurs de bois,* but no proof of venality has been established.

This bold and imperious man, whose character showed in his darkly handsome face, remained in Canada for ten years, a decade of bitter controversy but at the same time a period of peace with the Iroquois and of steady if not spectacular growth in population and wealth. When the patience of the King was worn out with the constant bickering among his officers in Canada, Frontenac was recalled. But seven years later, when the mistakes of the governors who followed him had brought about the most desperate phase of the Iroquois wars, he was hurriedly summoned from his retirement. It was apparent to all men that Frontenac, and Frontenac alone, could repair the blunders which had been committed. In his seventieth year he returned to Quebec to take up the burden again, a tired old man. Despite his poor health and his lack of strength, he took the situation in hand with the same indomitable will he had displayed during his first term.

Nine years later he died at his post in the citadel of St. Louis. The clouds of defeat had been dispelled. Once again men could walk in the woods without fear or launch a canoe on the rivers. His earlier mistakes and shortcomings were forgotten. Only his accomplishments remained in the minds of the people.

Father Goyer, a Récollet, of course, delivered the funeral oration. "I will not seek to dry your tears," he said to the weeping congregation, "for I cannot contain my own. This is a time to weep, and never did people weep for a better governor."

2

The word "gasconade" was long ago applied to the habit of boastful speaking in which the men of Gascony were prone to indulge, being very sure of themselves but at the same time very conscious of their lack of worldly advantages. It would be unfair to suggest that the temperament of Louis de Buade, Comte de Frontenac et Palluau, would mark him unmistakably as a Gascon, but it must be allowed that he possessed some of their characteristic traits and was not above this kind of vainglorious talk. And he *was* a Gascon, born at Béarn in the year 1620.

His family had come down a little in their fortunes. Antoine de Buade, his grandfather, had been quite a ruffler at court and a close confidant of Henry IV. He was sent in 1600 to Italy to convey to Marie de' Medici a portrait of his King when negotiations were under way for a marriage between them. Apparently the courtly Gascon conducted whatever ambassadorial duties devolved on him with due skill. The Medici heiress decided in favor of the match and became the second wife of that great King.

Although the family fortunes were beginning to shrink, Frontenac's father also played a conspicuous part at court. In addition to being colonel of the regiment of Navarre, he held a post in the household of Louis XIII. The latter acted as godfather to the son of the family, honoring the lusty infant with his own name. Henri de Buade had a house in Paris on the Quai des Célestines, but it does not seem to have been a showy establishment. The early age at which the young scion of the line was put into the army suggests that the need was felt to get him out into the world to seek his own fortune, as in the case of another Gascon who left Béarn in his early years, one Monsieur d'Artagnan.

Frontenac was a born soldier. He was brave, audacious, and cool. When he was fifteen he was sent to the wars in the Netherlands and began to distinguish himself at once. His record was so exceptional, in fact, that at the age of twenty-three he was appointed colonel of the regiment of Normandy. Four years later, because of the success with which he led his men in the Italian campaigns, he was made a *maréchal de camp*. He had always been in the thick of things and had been wounded often, including a broken arm at the siege of Orbitello. When peace was finally made, young Louis de Buade found himself without an occupation. He returned to his father's house in Paris and seems to have been concerned for some years with the possibilities of advancement at court. He had not achieved much in that direction when he allowed himself the interruption of a romantic attachment.

Close to the Quai des Célestines lived the Sieur de Neuville, who had one child, a daughter of sixteen named Anne de la Grange-Trianon. She was a lively little beauty, a slender girl with fine dark eyes and the most charming manners. As though these advantages had not been deemed sufficient, she had as well an audacity of wit which made her quite irresistible when she was young and kept her one of the most-sought-after women in fashionable France to the end of her days. The young soldier took one look at this vivacious charmer and fell deeply in love. He went at once to the Sieur de Neuville and begged permission to address his attentions to her. The father seems to have been well enough disposed to the idea at first, for Frontenac attacked him with the methods he had learned in siege warfare, planting his storming ladders of persuasion and swarming over the paternal battlements. As the girl's father was a widower, however, he had placed his only child in the charge of Madame Bouthillier, the wife of Leon Bouthillier, who had been chancellor to Gaston d'Orléans, the brother of Louis XIII. She was a woman of hard practical sense and not to be won over to such a match for her pretty ward. She went most thoroughly into the finances of the Buade family and found that they lacked the resources to make this handsome and imperious soldier a suitable match for the lovely Anne.

The father behaved with small resolution. He had been won over at first by the vigor of Frontenac's campaign and he realized that his daughter returned in some degree at least the sentiments of her suitor. He temporized but in the end allied himself with the unbending Madame Bouthillier and refused his consent. Most suitors would have accepted this decision as final and given up. But Frontenac was made of sterner stuff. He did not give up. Instead he started on an illicit courtship, employing all the usual methods, no doubt: sending notes to his lady through the instrumentality of servants, watching for her at church, and following her home at a respectful distance, perhaps stepping beyond these limits of decorum and arranging meetings where he could pour into her far from unwilling ear the story of his devotion.

There was in Paris at this time a church called St. Pierre aux Boeufs which disregarded all the usual rules imposed on matrimonial candidates. It was, in fact, the Gretna Green of Paris, and the priests in charge exercised the right to perform marriages without publication of banns and even without the consent of parents.

One day in October 1648, Louis de Buade and Anne de la Grange-Trianon appeared at the church of St. Pierre aux Boeufs and were made man and wife. The radiant pair pledged their vows without the consent or knowledge of the bride's family. Her father was furious when he learned of it and indulged in many threats. Being a man of easy temper, however, he did not harden his heart permanently. Before long he was on easy terms again with this ardent soldier who had thus taken another citadel by surprise attack. The Sieur de Neuville was a proud and happy grandfather when the union resulted in the birth of a son who was given the name of François Louis.

The birth of this unfortunate child was not to be accepted as proof that the marriage was proving a happy one. The bride who had been so gently reared was as adverse to the monotony of domesticity as the soldier who had donned armor at the age of fifteen. She craved the excitements of court life, the intrigues, the witty chatter of the salons, to a life of simple wedded bliss. Frontenac had fallen out of love also. With full mutual consent they concluded their union had been a mistake and that the best thing they could do was to acknowledge it by going their separate ways.

The poor little son who had been ushered into the brittle and corrupt world of the seventeenth century through this mutual error was placed in the charge of a nurse in the village of Chion, and here he died at a very early age, although one report says he grew up to be a soldier and was killed fighting in the French Army. One thing is clear, that he never enjoyed a mother's loving care nor benefited by paternal guidance. The young wife left her husband almost immediately and, through the influence of Madame Bouthillier, joined the household of the daughter of Gaston d'Orléans. The willful and sprightly Anne became almost immediately the favorite of her royal mistress, who was popularly called La Grande Mademoiselle.

3

Anne Marie Louise d'Orléans, Duchess of Montpensier, was a first cousin of Louis XIV. Her father, the King's uncle, was a horrible beast who led his friends into conspiracies in his interest and then abandoned them to the block with a grimace and a jig step. He had been married to the greatest heiress in France, and so the one child born to them, who had grown up to almost Amazonian proportions, was also a wealthy woman in her own right.

It was just before the civil war known as the Fronde that the Comtesse de Frontenac joined the household of the young duchess. Monsieur Gaston was in the excitement, of course, intriguing against his nephew and Cardinal Mazarin, and as ready as ever to betray anyone who might be drawn in to his assistance. La Grande Mademoiselle was the first to fly to his aid. She went to Orléans and captured it almost singlehanded by having a gate broken through and being carried across the moat in the arms of a very muddy waterman. The second to enter through this break in the gate was the twenty-year-old Comtesse de Frontenac. The latter took a prominent part in everything that followed, reviewing troops on horseback and making plans with her mistress; and having, no doubt, all the excitement she had always craved so much.

It is not surprising that the Amazonian duchess became very much attached to the lively young comtesse, but she did not have any liking or regard for Frontenac. His assurance angered her, being so full of it herself, and his gasconades, uttered in praise of himself and all his possessions, filled her with scorn.

Frontenac, freed of the care of a wife, had acquired a small estate known as Isle Savar on the River Indre. Its chief advantage lay in the fact that it was close to Blois. That picturesque medieval city, standing up so high above the Loire that the old quarter had to be approached by steep flights of stone steps, was a favorite resort of the people of the court. A huge chateau belonging to the dukes of Orléans stood on the crest, to which Gaston had added a comfortable wing. His tall daughter liked to reside there with her ladies in waiting, including the Comtesse de Frontenac. On one of her visits she was entertained at Isle Savary and came away amazed at the arrogance of its owner. "He affected to hold court," she confided to her notes, which were published after her death, "and acted as if everybody owed duty to him." He was full of plans for improving the place and enraged La Grande Mademoiselle by enlarging on his ideas to the exclusion of all the things she wanted to talk about herself. They were good plans, too, except for the fact, which everyone understood, that he lacked the means to carry them out.

It may have been due to the dislike that the willowy princess conceived for the self-assured Frontenac that she began to lose her affection for his wife. It may instead have been a proof that she shared to some extent her father's willingness to desert friends. Whatever the reason, the relations between them became strained, culminating in accusations of ingratitude showered on the head of the unhappy comtesse. The King's cousin finally dismissed the disconsolate Anne from her service.

The comtesse proceeded then to get herself established on a basis which gave her freedom to live as she desired. There was in Paris a large building which had once been the residence of Sully, Henry IV's minister. It was now called the Arsenal but was used for the housing of people of the court. It was deemed a great privilege to be among the occupants, and Madame de Frontenac was lucky enough to receive the right to assume a handsome suite of rooms there. She moved in at once, taking a favorite companion with her, one Mademoiselle d'Outrelaise, who also had much liveliness and charm. They established a salon which drew all the great people and the wits of the court. They remained there for the balance of their lives and were so much admired that they became known as *Les Divines.* The comtesse lived for nine years after the death of her husband in New France.

Little is known of the middle years of Louis de Buade, Comte de Frontenac. He was occasionally seen at court. As his habit of living beyond his means had depleted his resources, he was no longer able to keep up appearances properly; although it is on record that his admiration for the opposite sex remained unimpaired. His services as a soldier were no longer in demand and he seems to have languished in obscurity and idleness. This made him acutely unhappy, for his temperament called for a field in which to display his mastery and his talents.

A chance to serve came to him in 1669, when Venice became embroiled with the Turks who had invaded the island of Crete. The

Turkish armies had encamped around the city of Candia and, despite the care with which Venice had fortified that old city, it was in grave danger of succumbing. The Venetians felt they needed an experienced French officer to command the forces holding out so bravely against the Ottoman attacks. Turenne, to whom they applied, had a sincere regard for the soldierly qualities of Frontenac and recommended that the command be confided to him. This was done, and the Gascon soldier, thus summoned from obscurity, went gladly to assume his impossible task. He found Candia so vigorously beleaguered by the troops of the Grand Vizier Achmet that nothing remained but to fight on grimly in the hope of securing favorable terms. This purpose was achieved and the allied forces were permitted to evacuate the city, taking with them all their guns and supplies. Frontenac had handled the defense with such bravery and skill that he emerged with his reputation enhanced.

This was a factor in securing for him the appointment as governor of New France in the year 1672. It was not the kind of post he had wanted, for it amounted almost to exile and the salary was only eight thousand livres a year. But beggars cannot be choosers, and by this time the Buade fortunes had worn very thin indeed. Two factors had stood at first in the way of his selection. A certain Monsieur de Grignan, who had married a daughter of Madame de Sévigné, the famous writer of letters, wanted the appointment very much and proceeded to pull strings to get it. It was clear to the ministry, however, that a man of strength and boldness as well as address was needed in the colony at this juncture; and Frontenac, with all his faults, had these qualities. He was so well suited for the governorship, in fact, that the second objection was overlooked. It is worth telling about if only for the light it throws on one side of the character of the brilliant but somewhat unlucky Gascon.

Louis XIV was now launched on his career as a great lover. When his romance with Louise de la Valliére began to wear thin, the royal eye rested with ardent appreciation on the perfections of one of his spouse's ladies in waiting, Françoise Athénaïs de Pardaillan, Marquise de Montespan. This opulently beautiful creature, with her golden hair and large blue eyes and voluptuous figure, had been angling for the royal favor with every known wile. In fact, it had been whispered about the court, where every kind of gossip flourished and grew, that in her determination to attract the roving royal eye she had submitted to the Black Mass. This had entailed appearing at an altar naked and reciting her dark desires to the powers of evil: "I ask for the friendship of the King and Dauphin, may it ever be granted to me; may the Queen be sterile; may the King leave her bed and table for me." The story of the Black Mass is probably apocryphal, but the fair Athénaïs was detected later in some shady associations. The King had not deserted the royal bed but he had established his fair charmer in rooms above those of the Queen and visited her there every afternoon.

The royal lover may have had one regret in thus surrendering his heart to the blue-eyed siren. It was said in court that she had been partial at an earlier phase of her career to an aging but still handsome and fascinating member of the nobility; none other than Louis de Buade, Comte de Frontenac. When the infatuation of the King became common knowledge, there was much snickering in corners and discreet singing of a bawdy verse which some wit had composed. It began:

> I am enchanted that the King, our Sire
> Loves the Lady Montespan:
> I, Frontenac, with laughter I expire.

and went on with some ribaldries, ending with the lines, "Tu n'as que mon reste, Roi, Tu n'as que mon reste."

Because of this complication it was believed that the King was only too glad to get this one-time favorite of the lovely and willing Montespan as far away as possible; and no other post was as far away as Quebec. This story was generally accepted at the time, but there is small reason to assume that pique would have been allowed to sway the King's judgment. It is safer to think that the appointment was made on the unquestioned qualifications of Frontenac for the office, the same reasons which caused the shrewd Turenne to select him for the difficult assignment in Crete.

4

The Comte de Frontenac displayed his mettle on first sighting Quebec. It might have been expected that he would be disillusioned and disturbed by its smallness and complete lack of grandeur. From the deck of the ship it could be seen that the capital of New France lacked the spires and the glistening roofs of impressive cathedrals, the somber but strong castles, the battlemented walks of all old

French towns. It looked drab, crude, a huddle of hastily constructed buildings.

This, then, was a poor setting for a man who had seen life pass him by although he knew that in himself he had the germs of greatness. This appointment was his last chance to retrieve his reputation as a valuable servant of the state and to mend his fortunes. Could either be done in this little outpost?

It had been recognized at Versailles that he must be assisted in making a proper entrance. The King had given him the generous sum of six thousand livres for his equipment and a further grant of nine thousand livres to provide him with a bodyguard of twenty horsemen. The guard preceded him down the gangplank on foot, resplendent in new uniforms. Frontenac had dressed himself with the greatest care. His close-cropped hair, now thin and gray, was completely covered by his well-curled wig. The tapabord hat he was wearing had a brim which turned up off his face and thus showed the costliness of its scarlet silk lining, in keeping with the fineness of its plume. His coat was of levantine cloth, a rich gray, not damasked beyond the severity of good taste. His shoes were of fine gray leather. The curious eyes of the people who had gathered at the docks to catch a glimpse of the new governor must have noted with approval his impeccable attire.

They must have observed also that this man the King had sent them had a keen and intelligent eye, a strong line to his jaw, a commanding nose. They had heard stories of his haughtiness and his other idiosyncrasies of temperament and so they watched him with a definite reserve. The impression he made, in spite of this, was a favorable one. They were certain of one thing, that he had courage and strength.

Frontenac himself seems to have been well impressed with what he saw. His keen dark eyes had been busy. As a soldier he had seen that this great rock was almost impregnable. Now he looked about him at close range and found the people friendly and pleasant.

Something was stirring excitedly in his mind. This great new land was his to rule. In his first letter home he commented on the superb location of the town, which "could not be better situated as the future capital of a great empire."

CHAPTER XXIX

Frontenac Takes Matters into His Own Hands—
The Breaking of All Records in Building
Fort Cataraqui—The Raising of the White Flag

1

THE success of the Comte de Frontenac in Canada can be traced to his capacity for understanding people. It did not matter that he was haughty and arrogant in manner, that he was sure of himself in everything, that he could be as unyielding as Laval of his rights and prerogatives. He saw into the hearts and minds of those about him and knew how to make them respect and obey him. The inhabitants of the colony, who had become accustomed to mediocrity in the post, sensed at once the different mettle of this imperious nobleman.

The Sovereign Council, which transacted the business of the colony, consisted of seven members: the governor, the head of the Church, the intendant, and four councilors selected from the citizenry. It met every Monday morning at the citadel, the seven members being seated at a round table. At his first session Frontenac had Laval on his right hand, Talon on his left. The latter conducted the proceedings and in the main dictated the decisions reached; a state of affairs which left the new governor in a thoughtful mood. Having heard many stories from France about him, the others were wary of him and watched intently. He returned the compliment, being especially attentive to the plump-faced intendant. He left the meeting with his mind made up that the machinery of government would have to be overhauled.

He took no immediate steps, however. First he must acquaint himself with this sparsely settled belt of forests and streams over which he was to rule. He went into every nook and cranny in Quebec, inspecting the offices and warehouses and even the homes of the residents. He cast a shrewd and appreciative eye over the innovations for which Talon had been responsible. He even went as far inland as Three Rivers to visit the mines. While on his rounds he talked to everyone and listened as intently to the most humble habitant as to the wealthy landowners and merchants. When he arrived back in Quebec he felt that he understood at least some of the problems of the colony. His head was filled with plans.

It had been on September 17 that he attended his first meeting of the Sovereign Council. By October 23 he was ready for his official inauguration and for an innovation which would lead to the abolition of the Council. This project was the establishment of an assembly or *parlement* which would be known as the Three Estates of Canada.

This was not a new idea. The Three Estates had existed in France through the Middle Ages, but after 1614 they had not been convened. The idea of a popular body had been anathema to Cardinal Richelieu. Louis XIV had never been under the necessity of contending with such an assembly, and his truly royal countenance would have turned purple with rage at the mere whisper of reviving it as a permanent institution. Frontenac had one trait which was to stand him in good stead but which proved highly unsatisfactory in this case: he acted on his impulses and explained matters later. He did not notify Colbert of his plan for the Three Estates of Canada and he did not consult any of his colleagues. His plan had two considerations back of it. He desired to set up a less confined form of government than the little group he had watched in operation and he wanted to begin his own term with what seemed to him suitable pomp and ceremony.

The Three Estates were, of course, the nobility, the clergy, and the commons. Some of the seigneurs belonged to the lesser nobility and so were qualified to act with the first group. The Jesuits, Sulpicians, and Récollets would all be represented in the second class. To act for the people, he summoned a number of merchants and citizens of substance.

It was clear to men with more subtle minds than Frontenac's that this innovation was going to rub Versailles the wrong way. The rumbling of the approaching storm sounded clearly in the ears of Talon, and that shrewd old fox became conveniently indisposed when the day of convocation arrived. Although not present, he saw to it that he was well informed of what went on. He promptly relayed all that he heard to the home departments.

Frontenac astutely turned the first meeting into a glorification of the King, allowing himself no more than a chance to impress his listeners with a brief display of eloquence. He told of the victories which Louis had scored in Flanders and predicted that peace would soon be established, which would leave the monarch free to devote himself to more pacific aims, particularly the welfare of his colonies.

The reaction at Versailles, in spite of this, was distinctly hostile. Colbert's letter to the new governor was a severe blow to the pride of the latter. The King's minister pointed out that Canada must be governed in accordance with the forms in use in France and that at home the States-General had been abolished long before. He, Frontenac, must "never give a corporate form to the inhabitants of Canada."

That the high-tempered governor, who could not brook opposition in any form, took this rejection of his plan to heart goes without saying. He saw in the rebuff of Colbert the malice of Talon. This would have set off a titanic feud if the intendant had been staying in his post. As he was planning to leave on the last boat of the year, the embers were never fanned into flame.

The plan to establish the Three Estates had accomplished one purpose only: it had served to introduce the governor to the people of the colony with the full degree of pomp that the Frontenac ego demanded. The diplomatic phrases of Colbert had masked the annoyance of the King but had made the royal will in the matter unmistakable. The reprimand marked the end of the Three Estates. They were not again convoked.

2

Frontenac had all the instincts of a showman, to use a modern term. He liked to dramatize a situation. The supreme example of this is found in the establishment of a fort, later called Fort Frontenac, at Cataraqui and the use he made of it to startle and awe the Iroquois.

Frontenac knew that a plan had been mooted long before his arrival to build a fort at the eastern outlet of Lake Ontario, where the St. Lawrence took up its burden of carrying the excess waters of the Great Lakes to the sea. He was convinced from the start that the idea was a sound one. Such a fort would stand athwart the route by which the furs from the North and West could be diverted down into the country which the Hudson River drained and where the English were dominant. A strong post at Cataraqui would at the same time strengthen the defenses of the colony.

But he knew also that there was strong opposition to the plan. The King had always frowned on expansion because he believed that safety from Iroquois aggression lay in close cohesion. At Montreal there was active and bitter opposition because it would mean the diversion of much of the trade to the new post. Frontenac decided under these circumstances that this was one of the times when he should act first and talk about it later.

Although the peace with the Iroquois still continued, there was a mounting tension. The men of the Five Nations were built for war. Their hand was against every man's hand and they chafed at the restrictions and the monotony of peace. The French, for their part, were reaching out all the time, venturing farther and farther afield, pushing back the horizon. It was inevitable that incidents would occur continuously and that war fever would mount. It was clear to the new governor that the time was ripe for another demonstration of the might of France.

He let it be known that he desired to hold council with the chiefs of the Five Nations and sent the Sieur de la Salle to Onondaga to convey his wishes. The Iroquois leaders replied haughtily that they would be glad to receive the new leader of the French in their own council house. Frontenac's response showed how well he had come to understand in this short time the workings of the Iroquois mind.

"It is for the father," he declared, "to tell the children where to hold council."

The children, he added, must always come to the father. He, the father, Onontio, would never go to them. He would receive a delegation at the mission on the Bay of Quinte, north of Lake Ontario. On the advice of La Salle he changed the location to Cataraqui. The Five Nations, thoroughly impressed, agreed to meet him there.

The showman now emerges in his full colors. Frontenac decided to go to Cataraqui with a display of force and magnificence which would amaze the tribesmen. He was planning also to demonstrate the ingenuity and the infinite resource of the French by constructing a fort in the few days allowed for the peace talks. A miracle would be brought to pass before the very eyes of the Iroquois delegation. He laid his plans for this double lesson with great thoroughness.

The governor did not have funds available for carrying out anything as ambitious as this, and he peremptorily ordered the citizens
to provide him with what he would need—boats and canoes, arms
and men, ample supplies of food, the artisans and tools required for
his display of constructive magic. Grumblingly they obeyed; they
were not yet won over completely to this man of whom they had
received such mixed reports and who had already impressed them
as of many and conflicting moods. By June 3 everything was ready
and the flotilla left Quebec on its majestic journey to Montreal. Not
yet fully aware of the purpose back of this fanfare, the citizens of
Montreal turned out to give the governor a warm welcome, the reception being planned and carried out by the local governor, François Perrot. There was nothing but cordiality on the surface. It had
been arranged in advance that a quota of blue-shirts would accompany the expedition under the leadership, as usual, of Charles le
Moyne. The latter was to act as interpreter during the sessions with
the Iroquois chiefs.

It was an imposing show they made in approaching Cataraqui,
where the Iroquois delegation waited. It was July 12, a warm sun
overhead but a brisk breeze blowing across the waters of the lake
which set the French pennants to much excited flapping. In the lead
were four squadrons of canoes filled with scouts and woodsmen, all
very noisy and exuberant. Next in line were two large barges which
had been constructed for the occasion and were used, no doubt, to
convey the materials needed in the hasty construction of the fort.
Frontenac and his staff came next, making a brave show with their
burnished breastplates and glistening swords, and such raiment as
had never before been seen on American land or sea.

The troops followed in canoes, the regulars in the center, guns
slung to shoulders and helmets glistening in the sun. The contingent
from Three Rivers was on the left flank, the Indian allies on the
right. Bringing up the rear were two more squadrons of canoes filled
with men of the woods, whose garb was as varied and multicolored
as the doublets and cloaks and plumed hats of the aristocrats surrounding the governor.

Nothing like this had ever before been attempted in this land of
vast open spaces and deep silence. The Iroquois delegation, waiting
on the shores of Cataraqui, stood in silent awe as the white men
landed and proceeded to set up their tents. No effort was made to
open negotiations immediately. Frontenac was too shrewd for that.

He allowed the copper ranks to stand and stare while the tasks of settling were carried out, and he then retired to his pavilion, which was large and imposing. The standard of France was set up in front. The great flag, rearing its head high above the pavilion, was of heavy white silk, suitably powdered with the gold of the fleur-de-lis. It rippled in the strong breeze, folding and refolding with a cracking sound. To savage eyes it seemed a perfect symbol of the greatness of the French.

3

The *drapeau blanc* came in with the accession of Henry IV, who, as will always be remembered, had worn the white plume of Navarre. White had been the flag of the Huguenots, and at first the French people had looked askance at it, having a fond memory for the red flag of St. Denis, which was called the Oriflamme, and even for the ancient blue Chape de St. Martin. But the fourth Henry proved himself a great king and his ways became accepted, even his flag. There was unmistakable majesty to this great white standard with its golden flowers.

It is probable that Frontenac, having been a soldier all his life, had a preference for the sky-blue banner of the cavalry, to which had been added recently the golden sun of Louis. But he had a very sound understanding of psychology and he knew how much could be accomplished by the proper use of flags. Certain colors have stood from the dawn of time for certain things. Men everywhere, even the inhabitants of remote islands and dark continents, have known that an all-red flag means mutiny and revolution, bloodshed and fighting, and, above all, change. To the Iroquois red meant the quivering of tomahawks in the challenge post, the laying out of the sticks before battle, the quick twist of the scalping knife, the blaze of the torture fires. Black is the color of death.

Frontenac could calculate the effect the royal standard would produce on the Iroquois, this tall banner of white and gold streaming in the breeze. White was the color of peace and the anticipation of amity; gold signified wealth and power. The white and gold of France against the blue of the sky and the vivid green of the trees!— what else could drive home the lesson so effectively and temper the savagery in unblinking black eyes, placing there a hint of fear and awe?

4

The engineers and their small army of helpers did not delay in beginning their work. The thump of axes and the screech of saws were heard in the woods from the moment of the first landing. The construction of the new fort was well under way before the governor's staff laid sails on the ground for the feet of the chiefs in approaching Onontio, even before the perspiring staff and perhaps Onontio himself had begun hasty baths in the seclusion of the tents, sitting naked on huge sponges and swathing themselves with smaller sponges held in each hand.

There were sixty delegates from the Five Nations. They stalked haughtily over the flattened sails the next morning at seven o'clock and seated themselves under the canvas canopy which had been raised in front of the pavilion. The haughtiness was on the surface; in their minds they were consumed with curiosity about this new leader who came to them with so much pomp and magnificence; perhaps they even knew a little unease. Nothing was said when Frontenac emerged into the light of the sun with his plumed hat on his head and his sword by his side. He seated himself on a much-gilded and decorated chair in the center of the semicircle of chiefs. Nothing was said as the calumet, the pipe of peace, was handed along the ranks, but the carefully laid plans of Frontenac were having the desired effect. There was a definite hint of uneasiness in the set of their naked shoulders when Chief Garakontie opened the proceedings with a long speech of greeting to the French.

Frontenac started his reply with a word which had never before been addressed to the proud men of the Five Nations. "Children!" he began. It had been the rule to address the chiefs as brothers. When Frontenac uttered the less complimentary greeting, the squatting braves stirred in surprise and muttered among themselves. Well aware of what they were thinking, the governor proceeded.

"I have a fire lighted for you to smoke by and for me to talk to you. You have done well, my children, to obey the command of your father. Take courage: you will hear his word, which is full of peace and tenderness. Do not think that I have come for war. My mind is full of peace, and she walks by my side."

This was good talk, it was flowery talk, the kind that Indians understood and liked. The Iroquois found it so much to their liking that the first feelings of dissent passed. They noticed the shadows about the eyes of the new governor. It was part of the Indian creed to respect the wisdom which comes with the years. Onontio was an old man, and it was right for him to address them as his children. They said, "Ho!" and settled back to listen.

The discussions went on for four full days, and all the time the Iroquois were uneasily aware that something strange and completely beyond their understanding was going on around them. Raudin, the head of the engineers, had trained and coached his men to do the fastest building operation the New World had ever seen. As soon as the trees were cut down they were trimmed and sized and put in place. Raudin had marked the outlines of the new buildings on the ground; and now, plan in hand, he directed where each log and plank was to go. The outer palisade went up while the moat was being dug. The living quarters inside the walls were under way before the sharp peaks of the barbican had been brought into line. Everything was going up as though by magic, walls and bastions and battlements, with loopholes for musketeers and emplacements for guns.

Handicapped by their lack of tools, the Iroquois had always found construction a long and tiresome task; but here it went along so easily that they could not take their eyes away from what was going on about them. It was impossible for them to give their undivided attention to the speeches being droned over the long pipes of tobacco. Were the French the possessors of secrets which had not yet been suspected? Were they sorcerers to raise walls almost as fast as the squaws could set up a wigwam?

By the end of the fourth day everything had been said which needed saying: the veiled threats, the boasts, the bravado, as well as the promises and the mutual compliments. Presents had been given to all the Indians and yards of wampum had been exchanged. And standing against the line of the sky, where before there had been nothing, stood Fort Cataraqui with only the occasional tap of a hammer to indicate that a few finishing touches remained to be supplied.

The conference had been a success. The continuance of peace had been mutually conceded and assured. There would be no attempts, outward at least, to divert the fur trade down into the country where the smart English traders had established themselves.

It had cost ten thousand francs, but that seemed a small price to pay for such satisfactory results. Frontenac's method of acting first and explaining afterward had been successfully applied. His letters to France after the event exhibited a personal satisfaction which seems thoroughly justified.

The feeling in the colony, however, was not unanimously in favor of what the governor had done. Men engaged in the fur trade were convinced he was attempting to establish a new monopoly. To the merchants of Montreal the presence of the new fort at Cataraqui was both a threat and a challenge.

CHAPTER XXX

La Salle, the Greatest of Explorers—Marquette and Joliet Discover the Mississippi—La Salle's Only Friend, the Man with the Iron Hand

1

RENE ROBERT Cavelier de la Salle was born at Rouen on November 21, 1643, of a noble and wealthy family. It must have been apparent from the first that this boy was destined for an unusual life. He had an elongated face and a nose too long in proportion and brows which slanted down at the outer corners at an angle most often associated with bloodhounds. Under these heavy brows were eyes which either smoldered with the tension of his innermost thoughts or flashed with animation and excitement. He was fairly pulsing with energy and filled with the desire to do things, to keep forever on the move, to achieve the ambitions which could be sensed behind those remarkable eyes. It became certain early that nothing could divert him after his mind was made up. He was always ready to face any odds, and expostulation had no manner of effect on him.

In his early youth he conceived a desire to join the Jesuit Order and fit himself for the mission fields. Perhaps he had been reading the *Relations* and had become fired with zeal, perhaps it was sheer love of danger which made the thought of service in distant lands attractive. He entered the Jesuit novitiate at the age of fifteen and two years later took the vows of evangelical poverty, chastity, and obedience. After three years of intensive study at La Flèche he was sent as a teacher to Alençon, being transferred later to Tours and finally to Blois. He was not successful as a teacher of others, being too impatient, too filled with vibrant energy. All through these years of preparation, in fact, he had been a problem to his superiors. He was too much of an individualist, too opinionated, too active of body and mind to fit the rigid rules of the order. They sought to subdue him to the proper philosophical attitude, but the only result was a demand to be sent at once to take up his work in the missions. When this was denied, he wrote to Jean Paul Oliva, the General of the order, asking to be allowed to finish his studies in Portugal. When this also was refused, he asked his Superior to grant him his release. The Superior realized by this time that the determined and head-strong La Salle would never achieve the necessary discipline of mind. Acting on this conviction, he obtained permission to accept La Salle's resignation.

At the age of twenty-four, therefore, La Salle found himself free, with his life ahead of him and his prospects rather blank. Following the customary practice, he had surrendered his property rights to his brothers when he entered the novitiate, and they now showed no inclination to return him his share. The best they would agree to was to contribute a small amount which would earn him a yearly income of three to four hundred livres. On such a meager income he could not hope to accomplish anything in France, and so his thoughts turned to Canada where an older brother, Jean Cavelier, had joined the Sulpicians in Montreal. He arrived in the New World during the summer of 1667.

This was the land to which fate had been beckoning him; he was sure of it at once. He knew, moreover, the role he was to play. There were still so many things to be discovered about the new continent: the Northwest Passage, the great rivers farther inland, the lands of the West. This, then, was what he would set himself to do: he would solve these mysteries and open up new dominions of incalculable grandeur for France. The story of the mighty river which had its rise beyond the Great Lakes and then rolled majestically southward took a special hold on his imagination. The Father of Waters drew him, it gave him no peace of mind. To see the Mississippi with his own eyes, to follow it wherever it led, was the task of all tasks for him.

He never lost sight of this objective. It was the Mississippi which called to him all the time, which drew him finally like a lodestone across the lakes and the smaller rivers and the endless forests.

2

La Salle reached Montreal at a most opportune juncture. The Sulpicians were looking for men of spirit and determination. They wanted to develop the country around Montreal and they were beginning to cast eyes farther afield. The Abbé de Queylus had returned and was now the Superior, filling the post with dignity and resolution, and being on the best of terms with Bishop Laval. He became interested in La Salle, seeing in him the type of man they needed.

The result was a grant of land to the newcomer on Montreal Island. Some miles west of the town the St. Lawrence indulged in one of its most tumultuous antics, forming the cataract of Sault St. Louis. A little farther still it widened out into Lake St. Louis. It was on the north shore of the lake that La Salle was allotted his land. So handsome was his grant that he was able to set aside four hundred arpents for himself, two hundred along the river as common grazing land, and still retain enough to portion out farms of sixty arpents to all settlers who applied. This was indeed a *fief noble* and a demonstration of the respect the messieurs of the seminary had conceived for him. The only stipulation made was the payment of a medal in gold of the weight of one mark and an understanding that similar amounts would be paid with each change of ownership. La Salle was so grateful that he chose the name of St. Sulpice for his seigneury.

The new landowner started with characteristic vim to develop this wide and valuable domain. He cleared some of the land and built a house for himself with a palisade around it; a temporary habitation, far removed from the manor he expected to possess someday. He worked hard and long but always keeping an eye on the future and the great things he intended to accomplish. To prepare himself he studied a number of Indian languages, beginning with the Iroquois.

Almost from the first, however, he was hearing things which set his mind to wandering and gave him an itch in the soles of his feet. He heard the talk which went on in Montreal, particularly in what was now called Upper Town, around Citadel Hill and the Place d'Armes, where new streets were being laid out and the well-to-do were building houses. Here he heard speculations about the great future of the land. What kept his mind most keenly aroused, however, was the arrival of some friendly Seneca Indians who camped on his land for a whole winter and became sociable and garrulous. They talked about the Beautiful River (the Ohio) which ran due west and was much greater even than the St. Lawrence, although this was a claim no true French Canadian would allow. He could not be sure whether this was another name for the Mississippi or whether they were speaking of another stream which emptied into the Father of Waters. The Senecas were quite positive on one point, that the Beautiful River flowed finally to the Vermilion Sea. The Vermilion Sea! Could such a name be applied to anything but the warm waters of the Orient?

La Salle's mind filled with new dreams. Here, without a doubt, was a substitute for the Northwest Passage which men had sought in vain for such a long time, a route leading straight to the teeming continent in the East.

The result of these provocative rumors was a decision to toss away the orderly living he now enjoyed, to sacrifice to his dreams the certainty of ultimate comfort and wealth. He went to the Abbé Queylus and told what was in his mind. He must somehow organize a party to visit the lands of the West, but all that he possessed was now sunk in the development of his seigneury. The Superior was not only sympathetic but very generous. He agreed to buy back all of La Salle's lands save the four hundred arpents where he planned to settle finally, fixing the price at one thousand livres, payable in merchandise. If the worthy abbé had accomplished nothing else during his term of office, this transaction would serve as a monument to his memory.

But La Salle realized quickly that still larger sums would be needed. He decided to sell the balance of his land and found a purchaser in Jean Milot, a resident of the town, who paid him twenty-eight hundred livres, a generous enough deal. Now the indomitable La Salle had sufficient ready money to make a start. He went post-haste to Quebec to secure the necessary permit from the governor. This was in 1668, and Courcelle was still in office. The latter not only extended every encouragement but suggested that he join forces with another expedition which the Sulpicians were sending out to open a mission among the Shawnee Indians. Dollier de Casson, soon to succeed Queylus, had been placed in charge. These two men, the youthful dreamer and the gigantic ex-cavalryman who had turned from war to serve the Prince of Peace, found themselves at once in complete accord.

On July 6, 1669, the combined expedition started out. La Salle had four canoes and fourteen men, Dollier de Casson three canoes and seven men. Some of the Senecas who had remained all this time at La Salle's seigneury went along as guides. Despite the strength of the party, it proved to be a hazardous undertaking from the very beginning. The Iroquois were turning hostile and they detained the French party for a full month in the Seneca village of Tsonnontonan. Getting away finally, La Salle led his men across the Niagara River, hearing in the distance the roaring of the Great Falls. By the end of September they had reached the Indian village of Ganastogue, close to the site of the modern city of Hamilton, Ontario. Here La Salle was told by a Shawnee prisoner of a direct route to the Ohio which would not take longer than six weeks.

It happened also that Louis Joliet joined them here on his way back to Quebec to report to Talon on his quest for copper mines. Joliet was full of praise for the friendly Indians he had found in the land where the three Great Lakes touched, particularly the Potawatomi, all of whom were thirsting for the white man's gospel.

A clash of wills arose at this point between La Salle and Dollier de Casson. There was no room in the mind of La Salle for anything but the purpose with which he had started, and nothing but chains on his ankles could have held him back. On the other hand, the Sulpician was certain that the hand of God was in this meeting with Joliet. How otherwise could it have come about that they should meet in the middle of this huge continent when there were trails and waterways galore to follow? Joliet, coming straight to this exact point like iron filings to a magnet, had been guided by the divine will so that they, Dollier and his men, would hear what he had to tell of the spiritual needs of these great tribes. To Dollier it was a Macedonian call. It was God's desire that he change his course and carry the gospel instead to the Potawatomi.

This gentle priest, who was as stout in his faith as he was powerful of body (he could have raised La Salle from the ground on the palm of one hand), did not allow himself to engage in any arguments. His eyes were filled with a steady and exultant light. Although the anxious month they had spent as semi-prisoners had supplied the best of reasons for traveling in force, La Salle gave up the effort to keep the Sulpician party with him. It was with regret, but with no

diminution of his resolve to follow his star, that he saw the equally
determined Dollier lead his party westward. Deserted by some of
his men who had lost all stomach for such adventures, La Salle
calmly turned his canoes in a southerly direction. He must find that
direct route to the Ohio.

He was away for two years, and there is considerable doubt as
to how he employed all of that time. It is certain that he reached
the Ohio and continued down that broad and powerful stream. Some
historians have contended that he went as far as the junction with
the Mississippi, but there does not seem any reasonable ground for
assuming that he progressed as far as that. A paper prepared by
La Salle himself some years later affirms that he reached the Ohio
and followed it until a waterfall, which he describes as *fort haut*,
made it impossible to continue. This must have been the falls above
Louisville.

Other writers have read into the scanty bits of evidence which
survive (La Salle's own notes of this period are lost) that he followed his exploration of the Ohio by turning north to Lake Michigan, and that he then pursued the course of the Illinois River until
it was joined by another which flowed southeasterly and must,
therefore, have been the Mississippi. This would make him the discoverer of that mighty river and take the credit away from Marquette and Joliet (not to mention the shadowy claims of Radisson),
who found it two years later. There does not seem any clear justifi-
cation for placing this additional laurel wreath on the La Salle brow.
The evidence, in fact, points the other way. He himself did not make
any such claim, nor did he ever dispute the right of the others to
priority of discovery.

3

The Jesuits were turning to exploration with all the vigor they
had shown in earlier years in their missionary work. This had become necessary because they were now laboring with tribes far
afield. Their missions clustered about the upper lakes, but far beyond
Michilimackinac and Green Bay were regions where the buffalo
roamed in countless herds and where the Indians had never heard
the white man's gospel. It had become a duty, therefore, to reach
these distant lands so that the ignorant tribes could be redeemed.
They heard the stories which the natives were telling of the Missis-

sippi and reached the resolution to locate it and trace it to where it emptied into the sea.

For this purpose they selected Louis Joliet, who had been responsible for Dollier's change of plan. Joliet was Canadian-born (Quebec, 1645) and of humble birth. His father had been a wagon maker in the employ of the Company of One Hundred Associates, by which token it may be taken for granted that he had been poorly paid all his life. The son was given a good education by the Jesuits on the expression of his desire to become a priest. He had a great desire for learning and a keen mind to assimilate what he was taught. In particular he had an aptitude for mathematics and he distinguished himself in debates at the school where he had been placed.

Like La Salle, however, young Joliet found the lure of the West irresistible. When twenty-one years of age he decided he must renounce his ambition to become a priest. His Jesuit instructors, sensing in him the kind of energy which could be better employed in other work, consented to this change of plan. They even aided and encouraged him when he took to the life of a fur trader in the West.

To accompany the virile and experienced Joliet, they selected one of their order, a priest named Jacques Marquette. Father Marquette, born at Laon and educated at Nancy, had come to Canada in 1666 and after some years spent in studying Indian languages had founded the mission at St. Ignace. He was a gentle and eloquent man. His frailness of physique was not considered a handicap, for it was realized that men of limited virility often survived the strains and privations of the wilds better than those of rugged frame and greater strength.

Joliet and Marquette were, in point of fact, a perfect combination: the one keen, alert, experienced in woodcraft, the other sustained by a spiritual force which impressed even the savage tribes they were destined to encounter.

They set out on May 17, 1672, in two canoes and with five companions. Encountering on their way such strange tribes as the Wild-Rice Indians, the long-haired Miamis, the uncouth Mascoutins, and the wild Kickapoos, they came one month later to a spot of great beauty where the Wisconsin, which they had been following for a considerable time, joined a new river, one which seemed to roll along with a sense of purpose, even a consciousness of ultimate destiny.

This was the Mississippi. The Indian guides indicated by gesture and much eloquence of speech that this was indeed the Father of Waters. The Indians themselves were awed by it and urged the white travelers to go no farther. The two explorers, realizing that they had attained the first part of their objective, were not to be dissuaded by the tales of terror and violence that the guides poured into their ears.

They followed the course of this mighty river until they reached the mouth of the Arkansas. It was rich country through which they had been gliding, and the Indians they encountered seemed to live in comfort and plenty. On one occasion the white men were given a feast of several courses, beginning with a dish of Indian corn, followed with fish from which all the bones had been removed, a roasted dog, and a platter of buffalo meat, fat and strong and to the white palates decidedly rancid.

On reaching the Arkansas they decided to turn back. They had been convinced by visual evidence of one point which La Salle had discovered by deductive reasoning, that the Mississippi did not turn eastward to the Vermilion Sea but flowed instead to the Gulf of Mexico. The river was the dividing line of the continent. It would have been abundantly clear to them, if they had been concerned with such matters, that with the placing of the fleur-de-lis above forts at intervals along its course, France could cut off her rivals from the greater half of the continent which lay westward.

Marquette and Joliet returned to their starting point by way of the Illinois River, reaching Green Bay before the end of September and after a journey of twenty-five hundred miles in all, a truly titanic feat. Joliet continued on at once for Quebec to carry a report to Frontenac and the heads of the Jesuit Order. By an ironic twist of bad fortune, this intrepid traveler got into his first serious difficulties when he reached the Lachine Rapids just below Montreal. After passing safely no fewer than forty-two rapids, by his own count, his canoe was overturned in the Lachine. Two of his companions were drowned, and all the papers he carried, including his own notes and those of Father Marquette, were lost.

Father Marquette returned to his mission work at the head of the lakes. He had for a long time desired to open the Mission of the Immaculate Conception in the country watered by the Illinois. Although fully aware that the rigors and hardships he had survived on the Mississippi had taken heavy toll of his strength, he set out

again to accomplish this purpose. Returning to St. Ignace, he died
on the way on May 20 at a small island near the mouth of the river
now named after him.

Before setting out on his final journey, Father Marquette had
written another report of the discovery of the great river which he
sent to his superiors at Quebec. This reached its destination, and
so a detailed report of this epic accomplishment was preserved.

Joliet led an active life thereafter, although his collaboration with
Marquette remained the high mark of his career. In 1675 he married
Claire Françoise Bissot and raised a family of seven children. He
made at least one voyage to Hudson's Bay and was a strong advocate
of measures to recover that great trading field for France. As a reward for his services he was granted the Mingan Islands along the
north shore of the St. Lawrence and later the island of Anticosti.
He moved his family to Anticosti and made it his permanent home.
Sustaining losses through the English invasion, he was said to have
spent his last years in poverty. He died in 1700.

4

The turning point in the career of René Robert Cavelier de la
Salle came with the arrival of Frontenac as governor of Canada.
The young explorer had returned from the wilds, filled with a new
purpose, a grand plan by which the whole of the West could be
secured for France. He saw every step by which this could be
accomplished. First the great river would have to be explored from
source to mouth. Forts would then be erected at strategic points
to be used in the dual role of trading posts and units of defense.
This would fence the English and the Spanish into the territory of
the eastern seaboard.

It was a grandiose conception. Although other French Canadians
with vision would share this dream, notably the sons of Charles le
Moyne, it is La Salle who must be given the credit for originating
the plan.

La Salle returned, therefore, from his long exploration of the
West, his whole being filled with the vision. It was fortunate that
the new governor, who had arrived while he was away, was a kindred spirit. Where or when La Salle first met the Comte de Frontenac is not known, but it must have been at Quebec and at an early
moment. La Salle, the most impatient of men, was disposed to

trample on obstacles and to rebel at the unnecessary loss of a day or an hour. It is safe to assume that he took the first opportunity to meet the new governor and enlist his support.

An alliance was established between them at once. Frontenac, his energies and ambitions blunted by the long years in which he had vegetated with nothing serious to engage his mind and nothing constructive to occupy his hands, had plenty of the fire and fury of the trail blazer in him still. It was not hard for La Salle to convince him that a western empire was to be won by seizing control of the Mississippi; and incidentally to show him the personal wealth to be achieved at the same time.

The establishment of the fort at Cataraqui may have been part of the program they discussed between them. The feeling in the colony was not unanimous in praise of this remarkable achievement of Frontenac. Most of those engaged in the fur trade were certain that he was attempting to establish a new monopoly. To the merchants of Montreal the presence of the fort at Cataraqui was a serious threat. Even men of the high caliber of Charles le Moyne and Jacques le Ber changed from a dubious support to open opposition.

To meet this antagonistic attitude La Salle went to France the following year. He took to court a proposition: place the new fort in his hands with an ample stretch of territory about it, islands and mainland, and he would pay back out of his own purse the ten thousand francs of government money which had been spent in the building of it. In addition he would guarantee to maintain at his own expense a garrison there as numerous as that of Montreal. He promised also to send out artisans and build a church when the number of inhabitants at the post reached a total of one hundred.

The offer was accepted. All that the youthful La Salle, fired now with new zeal and determination, had to do was to raise the necessary funds. He had nothing in his own purse but he had wealthy relatives and connections. His brothers contributed more generously than might have been expected in view of their attitude over his share in the family estates. Afterward they declared that his operations in New France had cost them five hundred thousand livres; and, needless to state, they were very bitter about it. A cousin, François Plet, loaned him eleven thousand livres, demanding interest at the rate of 40 per cent. Cousin Plet received no interest and did not get his money back, and it is not hard to withhold sympathy from him in his losses. Some outsiders contributed shares amounting to over twenty thousand livres. La Salle now had ample funds. He paid the government the stipulated sum and returned to Canada to claim Fort Frontenac and the lands adjoining it.

The consummation of this pact was the signal for a storm of protest in the colony. The cards had been laid on the table for all to see, and it was clear that the two interested parties had dealt themselves a winning hand. Frontenac had built the fort with government money and had then turned it over to his new ally, the visionary La Salle. Between them they would have a monopoly of the western fur trade. They would become wealthy at the expense of Montreal, where trade would be cut in two.

Paying little heed to the uproar, La Salle proceeded to carry out his promises. He replaced the wooden palisades, which Raudin had raised at Cataraqui with such remarkable celerity, with a wall of hewn stone. Inside this he erected a barracks for the men of the garrison, a mill, and a bakery. The staff he maintained at the start consisted of two officers, a surgeon, and ten soldiers. There were in addition thirty workers and two Récollet fathers, Luc Buisset and Louis Hennepin. Cannon frowned through gun emplacements in the walls. Outside the fort a village was established and in short order one hundred acres of land had been cleared and crops planted. La Salle carried on the work, in fact, with as much energy as Frontenac had displayed in the erection of the first fort.

It became apparent at this point that these two outstanding men had joined forces with more in mind than making a profit from the western fur trade. They had a far greater objective, the conquest of the West. The establishment of Fort Frontenac was the first step in this magnificent design.

5

While La Salle was in France making these arrangements and living in Spartan style because his personal purse was almost empty, he was introduced by the Prince de Conti to a man who was to play a large part in his life. This was a young Italian named Henri de Tonty, who had come to France under unusual circumstances.

The father of this brave officer was a Neopolitan banker, Lorenzo de Tonty, who got into trouble in his native city by dabbling in politics and involving himself so deeply on the losing side that he had to flee with his family. He chose France as a place of sanctuary because his fellow countryman, Cardinal Mazarin, was in power at the time and might be agreeable to assisting the exiles. Lorenzo de Tonty was longheaded, a man of ideas and schemes and stratagems, all having to do with money. He was carrying in his clever brain a plan which he called a form of insurance but which was, in reality, an ingenious gamble. He proposed to Mazarin that a public loan be promoted by which ten different classes of subscribers would pay in a certain fixed amount, bringing the total subscription to something in excess of a million livres. The first class was to consist of children under seven years of age, the second from seven years to fourteen, and so on up to the last class, which would be limited to people of sixty-three or over. The money thus raised would go to the government and a rate of interest would be fixed. The interest would be divided among the subscribers in each class and, when deaths occurred, the share of the deceased in succeeding payments would be divided among the survivors. As the circle narrowed, the lucky ones would find their incomes mounting and the last few would be able to live, literally, like kings. When the last subscriber in any class passed away, the capital would revert to the state.

This scheme was indeed an enticing form of gamble, and both Tonty and Mazarin were convinced that it would have a strong appeal for the public. The cardinal saw in it a great advantage for the state and took the scheme to Louis XIV. The young King was equally enthusiastic, and the plan was duly authorized. But the Tontine Royale, as it was called, found no favor in other administrative circles, and in Parliament registration was denied. The King, it now developed, had put some money into the promotion fund and this had all been spent. The royal enthusiasm shriveled and was replaced by such an acid viewpoint on the scheme that the ingenious banker was sent to the Bastille, where he remained for a number of years; during the whole period, in fact, of his son Henri's youth.

The idea of the tontines was not destined to oblivion. It was revived in 1689—many years after La Salle's meeting with the banker's son—and was carried out successfully. The widow who outlasted the other subscribers received the shares of all the rest, an income of 73,500 livres a year! It is not surprising that gambles of this kind became very popular and that tontines were organized in all parts of the world, even in a country which was then beginning to emerge in the form of seacoast colonies and would later become the United States of America.

Henri de Tonty, the son of Lorenzo, was a sailor. He had entered the French service as a cadet and through sheer merit and bravery had advanced rapidly to the rank of captain. At the battle of Libisso a grenade shot away his right hand. Knowing that he could not expect medical aid at once, the gallant young officer cut away the jagged flesh with a knife and kept on fighting. He had an iron hand made and thus, at a time when rumors still circulated in France about a mysterious prisoner who was called the Man in the Iron Mask, Tonty became known as the Man with the Iron Hand. He wore a glove over it and was believed to be capable of handling a sword just as well with his artificial hand as before.

When he met La Salle, Tonty was in his late twenties. He was a tall fellow with a prominent nose jutting out from gaunt cheeks. His mustache had waxed ends that turned up sharply. In appearance he had something of Cyrano about him and in character an even more pronounced resemblance to that inspired poet and swordsman. He had never known fear, and no man had ever been more completely free of selfish instincts.

La Salle conceived an immediate liking for Tonty and offered him a post as his lieutenant in America. Tonty accepted gladly. They remained friends until the early death of La Salle separated them. The brave Italian seems to have been the only real friend the reserved La Salle ever had.

CHAPTER XXXI

The Building of the Griffin—La Salle's Creditors Seize All His Assets—The Tracing of the Mississippi to Its Mouth

1

LA SALLE never seemed concerned over the ease with which he made enemies. He was too engrossed in his dreams to care what other men thought of him. At his seigneury of St. Sulpice, which already was called La Chine in derision because he had failed to reach China, he had stalked about in solitary absorption, his hands behind his back, his head bent forward, his brows knitted, neither seeing those he encountered nor returning their greetings. It was the same in Montreal, where he paced the streets in frowning silence. He was so completely the slave of his ideas, so driven by his ambitions, that many people thought him unsettled mentally. Subsequent events deepened this impression and led to a conviction in some quarters that he was actually mad; a belief that his enemies were only too ready to embrace.

On his return from France with Fort Frontenac in his pocket as well as the western concessions, including that of buffalo hunting, the feeling against him intensified. The men of the colony declared that this young madman was planning to establish a personal empire, a great new world of trade for his own aggrandizement. The merchants of Montreal had taken serious alarm, believing that La Salle had stolen a march on them. Jacques le Ber and Charles le Moyne, the most fair-minded of men, joined in the chorus. When the new intendant Duchesneau, who hated Frontenac and opposed him at every turn, presented evidence that the governor had formed a partnership with La Salle to control the trade which would now flow through the new fort at Cataraqui, the outcry became general.

Were these ambitious and money-mad men to be allowed to gather the valley of the Mississippi into their eager hands as well?

La Salle was practical enough to know that money was needed in large quantities to carry out the plans which filled his head. He was willing to go to any lengths to get it. But a study of this strange man and the short life of spectacular adventure which fate allowed him leaves the conviction that he had no concern over money for its own sake. It was never more than a means to an end. His was the true pioneering spirit, and the almost demoniac passion with which he fought to claim the Mississippi was not inspired by a consideration of future profits. He saw glory in the accomplishment and he would have been content if no other reward had offered.

At the same time he was sufficiently farseeing to know that mere possession of the waterway would not be enough. The country beyond must be opened up for trade; and to that end he had many plans.

After he had won his patents from the King and had extracted such considerable sums from his far from liberal relatives, La Salle took ship for Canada. With him were Henri de Tonty and another recruit who had expressed willingness to join in the adventure, La Motte de Lussière. On the ship with them was a pertinacious priest, a Récollet named Louis Hennepin. Despite the fact that La Salle had occasion during the long voyage to reprove Hennepin for interference in matters which did not concern him, he listened later when the priest manifested a desire to join them. La Salle was not a good judge of subordinates and seems to have had about him always some intractable and useless adherents, among whom Hennepin must be numbered. It was La Salle, nevertheless, who obtained for the priest the consent of his Provincial to going on the expedition. Hennepin, an inveterate busybody, constituted himself later the historian of the party.

No time was to be lost in setting out for the West. La Motte was sent ahead with a party of volunteers to prepare a base on the Niagara River. Hennepin went with him and has left a long and characteristic description of their adventures and difficulties. La Salle and Tonty followed with the bulk of the party, finding that La Motte had succeeded in erecting a warehouse on the west shore of the Niagara in a fold of the hills. La Motte was having eye trouble and was already weary of this kind of pioneering. It was with relief that the rest of the party saw him depart for home. There was no way of getting rid of Hennepin, however. That busy recorder of events and of his own personal reactions was in the middle of everything, preaching, exhorting, interfering.

The next step was to build a boat above the Falls, one large enough to take the whole party with their supplies over the waters of the Great Lakes. La Salle had received disturbing intelligence from the colony that his enemies, now including his brother at Montreal, who was standing like a watchdog over the family funds, were combining actively against him. He felt it advisable to return at once and do whatever he could to repair his fences. This meant a trip on foot, across the face of the Iroquois country and over the frozen surface of Lake Ontario, a matter of many months. The task of constructing the boat, therefore, fell to the lot of Henri de Tonty.

The Man with the Iron Hand rose nobly to the need. He was not an engineer but he had several good mechanics to rely upon and he seems to have possessed all the qualities needed—a stout heart, a resolute will, and a deep conviction of duty. While La Salle was plowing on snowshoes over the Iroquois trails, in constant danger of his life, his Italian-born friend was performing a miracle of another kind, the construction of the forty-five-foot vessel which had been designed.

Maître Moyse, the head carpenter, set his crew to work on the ribs of the vessel. The blacksmith, who is designated by no other name than La Forge, set up a workshop and proceeded to hammer out the metal parts needed. Father Hennepin had a small chapel built for him and did a great deal of preaching in addition to training some of the party to supply the chants. He continued to have time to set down his impressions of everything that happened.

It was a good thing for posterity, if not for his fellow workers, that Father Hennepin was along. He has left some picturesque impressions of the winter work. Unfortunately he went to the ludicrous extreme later of boasting that he, and not La Salle, had discovered the mouth of the Mississippi and so placed everything he had put on paper before under suspicion. In his narrative of the days along the Niagara he tells of the uneasiness of the Indians thereabouts who were sure the wooden monster boded them no good. Some Mohawks came over to observe and took alarm at once at the great spread of the ship's ribs. They refused to leave and settled themselves down in sullen disapproval, muttering threats to burn the strange monster before it could be put into the water.

One of the warriors made the mistake of attacking the black-smith at a time when the latter was engaged at his anvil on a red-hot bar. La Forge was a stout fellow with no fear of these copper-skinned watchers. He raised the heated bar above his head and invited the brave to come on. The Mohawk hesitated long enough to enable Father Hennepin to administer such a stinging rebuke that he gave up his evil design. This was the priest's version; but it was noticeable that the brave kept an uneasy eye on the heated bar while he lent an ear to the rhetoric of the cleric.

By spring the resolution of the Man with the Iron Hand had prevailed. The vessel was ready. It was christened the *Griffin* as a compliment to the Comte de Frontenac and it seems to have been a fine and shipshape achievement. Father Hennepin pronounced a blessing and the hull was shoved out into the middle of the stream. Here, safely anchored against the strong Niagara current, the ship provided the Frenchmen with a snug sanctuary. They hunted and fished and loafed through the spring and early summer, waiting for La Salle to return. It was not until late in August that the leader put in an appearance. He brought with him three Jesuit missionaries (to the chagrin, no doubt, of the scribbling Récollet) and no other tangible assets.

He had much bad news to tell. His brother, the Montreal Sulpician, had ordered all the pelts stored at Fort Frontenac to be seized and sold at auction in Quebec. Of the amount realized, which was considerable, La Salle himself had been allowed only 14,990 livres. François Plet, maker of loans at 40 per cent interest, had come over from France to protect his investment and had located himself at Fort Frontenac, where he was watching everything that happened with what might be termed a 40-per-cent eye. This last item of news did not seem to disturb La Salle very much. He liked Plet, even though the latter had cheated him in the sale of a cheap grade of cloth at an exorbitant price. The material was so shoddy that it became a byword in the colony, being called "Iroquois cloth." Other creditors in the colony were clamoring for dividends—among them Migeon de Branssat, Giton, and Peloquin.

What course should they follow now? The indomitable La Salle declared that they must go on. They had the *Griffin*, they had food in the hold, they had a stout crew. They had nothing to lose but their debts.

2

There has never been a story to excel that of La Salle. It was adventure piled on adventure, misfortune added to misfortune, curious quirk imposed on twist of malign circumstance. It was a tale in which stout friends and unrelenting enemies played their parts, an epic of cruelty and suffering and privation. Through it all La Salle displayed a grim determination to succeed in spite of everything and a courage which at times strains credulity and defies comparison.

When the *Griffin* reached the head of the Lakes, the La Salle party found themselves balked at every turn by open opposition. The Jesuits, who had come to distrust and even hate Frontenac, regarded this partner and favorite of the governor with an equal degree of resentment. Even the Indians had been poisoned against him in advance. In spite of the suspicion they encountered at every step, La Salle and his companions threw themselves into the fur trading with so much success that the hold of the *Griffin* became filled with prize pelts. La Salle decided then to send the ship back so that the cargo could be used to pay off the most pressing of his debts.

After the departure of the *Griffin* with its vital cargo the explorer took various steps in preparation for the main effort. He made himself familiar with the course of the Illinois and at a strategic point near what is now Peoria he built a strong post and called it Fort Crèvecoeur. The construction of a new ship to be used in the navigation of the Mississippi was begun. Father Hennepin was sent off with two companions to follow the Illinois to its source.

In the meantime disturbing rumors began to percolate down from Michilimackinac and Green Bay to the effect that the *Griffin* had been lost with all on board. Leaving Tonty in charge at Fort Crèvecoeur, La Salle set out on foot with a few companions only to discover what had happened.

This reckless journey proved to be a long series of adventures. He reached his headquarters at Fort Frontenac finally with one distressing fact established: the *Griffin* had vanished; no one knew where or when or how. Obviously it had foundered on its way down from the head of the Lakes and the crew had been lost. The only other explanation was that it had been scuttled by the malice of his enemies and all trace of it skillfully covered up. The first seems to have been the truth, although it took nearly three hundred years for the fate of the vessel to be determined. Less than a quarter of a century ago six skeletons were found in a cave on a Lake Huron island. The crew of the *Griffin* had consisted of Pilot Luc as master, four sailors, and a boy; as further proof the hull of a ship was found nearby at the bottom of the lake. This evidence seems to be reasonably conclusive.

When La Salle reached Fort Frontenac there was news of other disasters to greet him. A ship coming out from France had been wrecked in the St. Lawrence and everything it held, including supplies for his use to the value of 22,000 livres, had been lost. The supply depot he had left on the Niagara had been broken open and rifled. The final blow which this seventeenth-century Job was called upon to bear was news from the West that most of the men under Tonty at Fort Crèvecoeur had mutinied. They had destroyed the fort and carried off all the goods which had been stored there. The mutineers, it developed, were on their way east and were planning to attack and destroy Fort Frontenac. They had even announced their purpose of killing La Salle himself to prevent any reprisals on his part. La Salle resolved the last menace by waylaying the mutineers. Two of them were killed and the rest were made prisoners.

The great explorer now faced difficulties which seemed insurmountable. The arrangements made in the West for the proposed expedition down the Mississippi had been nullified by the mutiny. His supply depots had been wiped out, his main base at Fort Crèvecoeur had been burned to the ground, his men had scattered. His creditors and ill-wishers were either exulting over his misfortunes or clamoring for their money. All he could hope for was to find the hull of the unfinished vessel on the Illinois and to meet with the ever-reliable Tonty.

Somehow he overcame all these difficulties. He placated his creditors by sheer vigor of argument. He secured from unstated sources the funds to provide for a new start. He gathered together a party of twenty-five men, and on the tenth of August, 1680, he started off again.

3

La Salle reached the Illinois country on the heels of a major tragedy. The Illinois Indians had been scattered, their great city on the river (it was spoken of as a city because of the density of its population) had been destroyed with a fury which passes belief. Only blackened ruins and mutilated bodies remained where once this teeming community of friendly aborigines had stood. The silence of death and desolation reigned over that once fruitful countryside.

The perpetrators of this unprovoked attack had been the Iroquois. After wiping out the Cat People and the Andastes, the *Ongue Honwe* had been left without a purpose; no foes to overcome, no new worlds to conquer. This was a situation which the fierce warriors of the Long House could not abide. They were men of the conqueror breed, like the fighting armies from the heart of Asia which had come so often on their irresistible way to shake the very pillars of civilization. The leaders had cast their eyes on the West, where the Illinois lived in peace and prosperity. Distance held no terrors for these indomitable men.

It seems possible that the selection of the Illinois as the next victims was due to the friendship they had displayed from the start for the white men. Back of the ceaseless war-making of the Five Nations was hate of the interlopers, these men of white skin with their superior weapons who had come to steal the land from its rightful owners. The thought may have been expressed in the council house at Onondaga that to destroy the Illinois would be to serve notice on all men of red skin: make no peace with these grasping strangers who come in the guise of gods but with conquest in their hearts, or feel the might of the Five Nations.

La Salle's arrival followed soon after the departure of the triumphant Iroquois. There was something strange and macabre about the sight that greeted him. The Iroquois, as he learned later, had found the great canton practically deserted. They killed the few old people who had lacked the strength to flee and then, for fuller measure, dug up the graveyards and disinterred the moldering bones of the dead. From the burial scaffolds they tore down the bodies of the recently deceased. These grisly trophies had been mutilated with incredible savagery. The skulls of the long dead had been nailed to the tops of charred stakes, to stare with empty sockets at this sudden terror which was robbing the grave of its sanctuary.

Not a living soul was encountered in the wide district where the fury of the conquering bands had been vented. Where was Tonty? Had he and his few faithful followers been among the victims of the murderous onslaught? If this proved true, it would be for La Salle the final blow, the one loss for which there could be no compensation.

But Tonty was not dead. He had striven fearlessly to act as mediator between the Illinois and the invading hordes and had been close to death on several occasions. The Illinois had been filled with suspicion, conceiving the idea that this iron-handed man had been sent ahead by the Iroquois to spy out the land. While still convinced of this, they seized the supplies of the Frenchmen and even destroyed the forge and tools to which Tonty had clung in the hope of using them in the construction of the new ship. His efforts to avert a clash failing, he fought bravely with the Illinois and survived by luck which verged on the miraculous. He found his way back finally to Michilimackinac.

La Salle perceived at once the need to defend this beautiful and fruitful country against further aggression, and to that end he called a meeting of the tribes thereabouts. With all of his usual eloquence he succeeded in persuading them to lay aside their intertribal feuds and join in the common cause. The leaders of the assembled tribesmen seconded his efforts, professing the utmost confidence in him. "We make you the master of our beaver and our lands, of our minds and our bodies!" they cried. The tribes thus cemented into an alliance included what was left of the unfortunate Illinois, the Shawnees, the Miamis, the Mascoutins, and even some fragments of eastern tribes who had fled westward to escape the enmity of the Iroquois.

Having thus created a measure of defense against further attack, La Salle journeyed north to Michilimackinac. There, to his great joy, he found Tonty and what was left of his party.

Everything had gone wrong with La Salle up to this point, and the usually resolute leader had been sunk deep in despair. Finding the Man with the Iron Hand alive was sufficient to balance the scales. With Tonty beside him he felt that he could face the future with confidence. With the armor of his faith refurbished and shining brightly again, he returned to Fort Frontenac to start over again.

It seems necessary at this point to pause for reflection on the extraordinary course La Salle was following. At every stage of his adventures the courage and determination of this man shine in conspicuous splendor. No more daring human being, surely, ever lived. He was impervious to disappointment, immune to the shafts of ill fortune. This must be conceded. But what of him as an organizer?

The regularity with which his plans fell apart could not have been due always to bad luck.

It has already been said that he had a genius for making enemies. They sprang up wherever he went. This could not have been due entirely to the machinations of the Jesuits who feared and hated him. It was the iron quality of the man himself which set so many to working against him; his willingness to ride roughshod over everything.

Unquestionably there was lack of care and foresight in his planning. Why otherwise would it have been necessary for him to halt so often and take those interminable journeys back to his base in the face of desperate weather and always in personal jeopardy?

By way of contrast there was no fuss, no delay, no turning back on the part of Marquette and Joliet. That unpretentious pair had quietly loaded two canoes and set off on their mission.

In fairness to La Salle, however, it must be assumed that he had more than exploration on his mind. It would not be enough to trace out the course of the Mississippi. That river and the rolling lands lying back of it must be claimed for France and the first steps taken to plant the fleur-de-lis firmly on its banks.

4

It was late in the fall of 1681 that the expedition started which was to crown the long series of failures with the shining chaplet of success. La Salle, who never seemed to fail in what might be termed the promotional aspects of his plans, had smoothed away his financial difficulties. He had even secured fresh backing from a source which must have seemed the least likely of all: from the shrewd François Plet himself. That hard-bitten investor, Cousin Plet, was doing what the cautious man so often does when he has once made a rash investment: he was throwing good money after bad. La Salle made a will in his favor, it is true, but as clever a man as Plet might have suspected that what the explorer would have to leave would resemble nothing so much as a wheel of cheese in which a family of mice had spent the winter. By wile and perhaps by guile La Salle had found all the supplies he would need and had hired an ample party of men.

There were a dozen canoes in the long line which took to the water at Green Bay. In the party were twenty-three Frenchmen, eighteen Indians of the Abnaki and Mohegan tribes, ten squaws, and three children. La Salle could not cut down to the levels of efficiency and easy subsistence; he must travel in state, with his helpers and vassals about him. The Sire de Beaujeu, who will appear on later pages, expressed it this way: "He is a man who wants smoke."

The weather was good, the men were in good spirits, all the portents were favorable. In this spirit of confidence they crossed the Chicago River, reached and passed the Illinois, left Lake Peoria behind them. On February 6 they sighted for the first time the broad surface of the mighty Mississippi.

An early spring was vouchsafed to help and encourage them. There was softness in the air when they passed the junction point where the brown and sluggish Missouri swelled the volume of the parent stream. A month later they reached the Arkansas, and the promise of summer was all about them. The trees were green, the songs of awakened nature came from the woods, flocks of migratory birds filled the skies.

The most interesting of their adventures was a visit to what seemed a new civilization, the main town of the Taensas. It consisted of dwellings of baked mud with rounded domes, grouped in circular form about the temple of the tribe and the house of the venerable chief. The Taensas were sun worshipers, a form of religion new to the Frenchmen. This was their first contact with the customs which had crept north from the lands of the Aztec. A perpetual fire burned in the temple, and there was a niche on which no eyes rested save those of the priests and in which the wealth of the tribe and their prized relics were kept. The rites practiced were cruel, including human sacrifice.

Early in April the party came to a point where the great river broke into three channels. The paddles of the weary men were lifted at once with renewed energy; their voices reflected a gain in spirits. This, they knew, was the beginning of the end. Below this division of the waters must be the ocean or gulf into which the river emptied. The flotilla was divided into three equal parts. La Salle chose the western channel, Tonty the center, and D'Autray, third in command, the east. It was La Salle's canoe which first issued out on the surface of the salt water, his eyes which first sighted the broad green gulf.

When the three parties came together, La Salle followed the example of all great explorers who had preceded him in opening up the unknown places of America by erecting a tall cross on the shore. It carried the arms of France and the words:

*Louis le Grand, Roy de France et de Navarre
Règne; Le Neuvième Avril 1682.*

All voices joined in singing "The banners of Heaven's King advance!" and all arms were raised in the air. The whole of this unknown land which stretched in majesty to the western horizon had been claimed for France.

But more important than the question of which nation would reap the benefit was the fact that at last the mystery of the Mississippi had been solved.

CHAPTER XXXII

The Seigneurial System Creates an Atmosphere of Romance—The Rise of the Seigneurial Class—La Durantaye—The Fabulous Le Moynes

1

THE annals of North America, brief as they seem in comparison with the histories of older continents, have nevertheless created many romantic backgrounds. Life on the hacienda of Mexico and on the Spanish ranchero in California was filled with the color that wealth and privilege create. The plantation days in the southern states remain in the memory because of the gracious living the owners enjoyed. Life in Quebec through the seventeenth and eighteenth centuries seems fully as romantic; and this can be traced to the seigneurial system which grew out of the determination to perpetuate in Canada the feudal fabric of France.

The seigneurial system was, however, a natural development. The first settlers were completely dependent on France and continued so for many decades. Few of them had any aptitude for the difficult task they were supposed to perform—the clearing and cultivation of the land—and so they had to be fed and endowed and pampered. New France became a luxury which the French kings found highly expensive, and only the pompous determination of Louis XIV to set up a state modeled on the lines he conceived to be perfect kept the Canadian experiment from being abandoned. It was too much to expect that people who existed under these conditions would have any capacity for self-government. The paternal system suited them. It was familiar to them and it was workable. It seems to have been accepted without serious question or grumbling.

It was started early in the hope that men of initiative would take over the land and make it productive. But the early seigneurs were mostly partners in the various companies set up in France to "farm" the fur trade, men who entertained the hope that the colony would flourish (without any effort or expense on their part) and that the land in time would become valuable automatically. They did not send out settlers and they made no effort to clear the land. They do not seem to have gone through the ceremony of swearing fealty to the King for their holdings except in rare cases. King Louis had been very definite on this point. The owners of grants must repair to the citadel of St. Louis and on bended knee before the governor, as representative of the King, take a solemn oath to obey him in all things.

When Talon became intendant, he proceeded to put things on a sounder basis. The grants which had not been developed were confiscated. To take the place of the absentee landlords, the new administration developed the plan of granting fiefs to the officers of the Carignan regiment in the hope of persuading them to settle permanently in Canada and thus provide protection by their presence from Indian aggression. This resulted in the dotting of new seigneuries along the shores of the St. Lawrence and between the forts on the Richelieu, which was the route the Iroquois took in attacking the French. Twenty-five officers in all and nearly four hundred soldiers elected to stay in the colony. At first glance this seemed to offer the solution which had been sought; but the soldier does not often make a good settler, as has already been pointed out in referring to La Bonté, La Doceur, and La Male. The officers were even less suited to the life. Olivier Morel de la Durantaye, who will be mentioned at some length later, was one of the few exceptions. The training of the average officer had been along the wrong lines. He considered himself a *gentilhomme* and was convinced that he must not soil his hands with labor. Some of them nearly starved as a result. Certainly there was little or no romance in the life of the seigneur in the first days. Writing to the King as late as 1687, Intendant Champigny said: "It is pitiable to see their children, of which they have great numbers, passing all summer with nothing on them but a shirt; and their wives and daughters working in the fields." Ten years earlier Duchesneau had supplied the reason for this in one of his reports. The seigneurs, he declared, "spend most of their time in hunting and fishing. As their requirements in food and clothing are greater than those of the simple 'habitants,' they mix themselves up in trade, run into debt on all hands, incite the young habitants to range the woods, and send their own children there to trade for furs. . . . Yet with all this they are miserably poor."

The success of the effort to turn swords into plowshares was, therefore, short-lived. Gradually a more realistic view was adopted and the land was portioned out to men who had already demonstrated their capacity, settlers of the stamp of Robert Giffard, Jacques le Ber, and Charles le Moyne.

The system followed was liberal in conception. The seigneur paid nothing for his land, and his only obligation, other than to clear a stipulated amount each year and to collect settlers about him, was to pay a *quint* or one fifth of the value of the land if it were sold or passed out of the hands of the immediate family. The seigneur in turn parceled it out to settlers or *censitaires* at a nominal rate which was paid to him yearly on St. Martin's Day and consisted of half a sou and a pint of wheat, or sometimes a few capons, for each arpent of land. It was part of the bargain that the *censitaire* must bring his grain to the seigneurial mill and that he must submit to the ancient corvee by which he worked six days each year without pay on the seigneur's land. Certainly this plan was not burdensome on the settlers who thus paid no more than ten or twelve sous and a bushel of grain for their farms. Because of this nominal rent, the seigneur had to find other means of achieving an income instead of living off his land. It should be added that at the inception of the system the manor house of the seigneur was often no more than a log cabin of two rooms.

The policy of Talon was successful in the long run. In 1667, a few years after he had assumed the duties of intendant, a census was taken which showed 11,448 arpents under cultivation in all of New France. There were in the colony 3,107 head of cattle and 85 sheep. In the course of another year the acreage rose to 15,649. An arpent, it should be explained, was both a unit of length and of area. The lineal arpent was 192 feet, the arpent of area about five sixths of an acre.

Gradually the system began to take hold. Many of the seigneurs became prosperous and their houses took on manorial proportions. Furniture was imported from France. Elegant chandeliers, snowy napery, and fine table appointments became the rule rather than the exception. There was never a great deal of wealth in the country by continental standards, but the land, helped out by participation in the fur trade, provided enough for the seigneur to become a *gentil-*

homme in practice as well as in name. The system was feudal, it is true, but it supplied the merits of feudalism rather than the faults. A share of the prosperity certainly was handed down to the habitant. He lived in reasonable comfort, if not ease, and he was able to provide for the large families he brought into the world. There was always a dot for the daughters and a parcel of land for the sons when they were ready to assume the burdens of life for themselves.

This reflection of the elegance of French life was maintained against an adventurous background: the coming and going of the *coureurs de bois,* the fur flotillas arriving for the annual fairs, the gallant efforts of the bolder spirits to destroy boundaries and horizons and set the flag of France over the great West. The people, rich and poor, settled and footloose, were gay and mettlesome. Their customs and habits and conceits have conveyed to later ages a picture of life which was highly picturesque; their songs echo through the pages of their history.

It is not strange that an aura of romance still clings to the stories of these early years.

2

Among the soldier seigneurs who settled down permanently in Canada was Olivier Morel de la Durantaye. He married in the colony and in 1670 was given a fief noble, two leagues square, on the south shore of the St. Lawrence close to the Bellechasse Channel. Later he received the fief of Kamouraska, making his holding close to 70,000 arpents. His importance in the annals of New France, however, does not stem from a lifetime of effort to develop his enormous tracts of land. Having enough income to reside at Quebec, he contented himself with finding settlers for his broad acres; reaping, on that account, no more than a moderate return from the land.

Durantaye is remembered and counted as one of the great seigneurs because he fulfilled the function which King Louis and the astute Talon had in mind when it was arranged to disband the Carignan regiment in Canada. Durantaye was a pillar of strength when the mistakes of Frontenac's successors reopened the Iroquois wars, bringing the war parties of the Five Nations in unprecedented numbers against the unprotected parts of the colony. Durantaye had been in command of the trading posts around Michilimackinac, although his preference was always to remain with his agreeable family in the elegance and ease of life in Quebec. When Governor Denonville took an expedition against the Onondagas in 1684, Durantaye organized a force from among the Frenchmen and the friendly Indians at the Junction point of the three lakes and came down to share in the attack. Some years later, when tension was at its peak and the Iroquois were threatening the very life of the colony, Durantaye was stationed at Montreal, the focal point of the danger.

The part he played in these troubled times brought him a pension from the French Government. He was appointed a member of the Superior Council and lived out the balance of his life in comfort, enjoying the high regard of his fellows.

The Durantaye holdings were princely in scope and in course of time they became of tremendous value. He had six sons and three daughters to divide it among when the time came for him to die, which was in the year 1727.

Olivier Morel de la Durantaye was representative of the class of seigneur who lent glamour to the colony, a man of good birth, personable and accomplished as well as brave. There was a distinct contrast between his kind and the native-born seigneurs who attained their land through their own efforts and achieved distinction and wealth by merit alone.

The most outstanding family in the second category was the extraordinary Le Moynes.

3

Five years before his death Charles le Moyne was presented with an eighth son, who was named Jean Baptiste and was later given the title of De Bienville to distinguish him from his numerous brothers. Two more were to arrive before the fine old Indian fighter and indomitable citizen came to his end, not bound to the Iroquois stake which had been kept ready for him, but peacefully in his bed at Longueuil.

The Le Moynes were a fabulous family. No other word can give any conception of this gallant sire and his ten sons. There is no adequate record of the parts they played in the drama of New France— very little, in fact, but a series of names and dates and the manner in which each of them died. But they were always there, fighting and contriving and dying, and it is clear that they were ambitious as well as self-sacrificing, keen-witted as well as fearless. What plans did they concoct when they gathered around their father's long table? What designs of family policy did they discuss? Why did Iberville give up his life in a sweltering Havana hospital and Bienville exist for forty years in the swamps of Louisiana if they had not a vision of empire between them as clear and great as that of La Salle?

Lacking such clues to this mysterious and fascinating page of colonial history, it is left only to deal with each of the ten in turn and present the known statistics.

The first-born, named Charles after his father, succeeded to Longueuil and made it the model seigneury of New France. He was a man of wisdom and foresight, a splendid businessman and financier, who not only created a fortune for himself but carried at least some of his brothers on his back. He undoubtedly acquired the funds for the historic adventures of the other nine. It was during his time that the old manor house at Longueuil was replaced by a fortified house which Frontenac said reminded him of the great châteaux of Normandy; Frontenac, who ordinarily boasted only of his own possessions. Longueuil became a cluster of rather imposing stone buildings behind a high wall, two hundred feet in length and one hundred and seventy in width, with high towers at each corner: a large dwelling house, a chapel, stables, sheep pens, and dovecotes, and outside the walls a banal mill and a brewery. This ambitious dwelling cost sixty thousand livres to build—a fortune in those days—and an astonishing contrast to the log houses where so many of the proud seigneurs existed. Charles, the architect of all this magnificence, was made a baron, served as lieutenant governor of Montreal, and was killed in action at Saratoga in 1729. Of all the leaders of New France, he best qualifies for the appellation of business titan. He had the Le Moyne courage and he was in addition wise, cool, and farseeing.

The second son, Jacques le Moyne de Ste. Hélène, was born in 1659 and was killed during the siege of Quebec by the English in 1690.

The third of the ten was the great man of the family, one of the truly remarkable figures of French Canada, Pierre le Moyne d'Iberville. The victories he won on land and sea are so remarkable that he would be ranked among the great fighting men of all time had he played to a European audience on a world stage. Iberville had the misfortune, though not counting it such, to perform his prodigies of daring leadership in the depths of the Canadian forest and on unknown seas, not on the familiar borders of France or on the English

Channel. He died of a malignant fever in Havana before he had completed the great task to which he had been assigned in succession to La Salle, the occupation of the mouth of the Mississippi.

Iberville is still a mysterious figure. His biographers acknowledge that nothing authentic is known of his appearance, whether he was tall or short, dark or fair. Fortunately his achievements are on record and, though nothing is known of him as a man, he can be accurately assessed as a leader and extravagantly praised. In later chapters his exploits will be told in some detail. The peerless Pierre was, it hardly needs saying, the leader of this Maccabean brood.

The fourth son was Paul le Moyne de Maricourt, born in 1663. Although not so rugged or strong physically as his brothers, he became the ambassador of the family in their dealings with the Indians. The Iroquois called him Taouistaouisse, which meant Little-Bird-Always-in-Motion. He was much in the woods, visiting the various tribes and seeing that the family interests did not suffer. Apparently he had some of the ease of approach which made Frontenac so successful with the Indians, an instinctive understanding of the red men. There seems to have been a mutual liking, and it is probable that he sometimes acted as a spokesman for the savages in the family councils. Maricourt had been earlier a captain in the French marines. He died in 1704 as a result of overexertion in an expedition against the Five Nations.

The fifth was François le Moyne de Bienville, born in 1666, who had without a doubt some of the great fighting quality of Pierre. He was always in the thick of things when the colony was in danger and was killed in 1691 while fighting the Oneidas at Repentigny.

The sixth son, Joseph, known as De Serigny, was born in 1668. He served in the French Navy and seems to have possessed some of the executive ability of the oldest brother Charles, becoming governor of a French naval base, where he served with distinction. He died in 1687, leaving children from whom there are still direct descendants in France.

The seventh could perhaps be called the Galahad of the family, Louis le Moyne de Châteauguay. In his eighteenth year, fighting under Pierre, the great brother he adored, in the first Hudson's Bay campaign, he charged gallantly but recklessly in broad daylight against an English fort and was killed by a musket shot. In this family, where death in action was almost the rule, the premature ending of the splendid Louis was deeply and bitterly lamented and his memory was kept green in the manor house at Longueuil—in fact, wherever the Maccabean brothers gathered.

This brings the record to the son mentioned at the beginning, the eighth in line, Jean Baptiste, who later was called de Bienville when François, who first carried the title, was killed at Repentigny. The eighth son seems to have been different from the others, a quiet and withdrawn but capable boy who was better adapted perhaps for a department at Versailles than a life in the wilds. He grew up, nevertheless, to play a part in the saga of the ten Le Moynes second only to that of the amazing Pierre. Accompanying the latter to the Mississippi, he assumed command after Iberville's death and laid out the first settlement at New Orleans. He remained governor of Louisiana for the better part of his life, a record for patience and endurance seldom equaled.

The mark of destiny was on Jean Baptiste as surely as on Pierre. They will never be forgotten, even though the other eight brothers, heroes all, have become no more than shadowy figures with the passing of the years.

Two sons arrived after the future governor of Louisiana, Gabriel d'Assigny, who was born in 1681 and also took part in the Mississippi adventure, dying in San Domingo of yellow fever in 1701, and Antoine de Châteauguay (another repetition of title), born in 1683, who perhaps survived all the others and became the governor of French Guiana.

They were unique, these ten doughty brothers, and it is a serious deprivation that detailed records were not kept of their lives, their great exploits, their meetings, their discussions, their divergent personalities. What a pity it is that some Boswellian servitor did not live in the commodious château at Longueuil to preserve for history an enduring picture of the ten paladins.

CHAPTER XXXIII

Frontenac Places the Governor of Montreal
under Arrest—He Becomes Involved in Feuds with
His Fellow Officers—His Recall by the King

1

FRONTENAC'S first term had few peaceful moments. Bishop Laval was in France and no successor had been appointed to fill Talon's post, so the strutting, imperious old Gascon had a free hand. He managed, nevertheless, to keep himself embroiled with those about him. The mails which progressed so slowly back and forth between Quebec and Versailles crackled with controversy.

There was, above all else, the case of François Perrot. Married to a niece of Talon, Perrot had been appointed to the post of governor of Montreal. He was a far different man from the high-minded Maisonneuve. He had come to Canada to improve his fortunes and he took no special pains to conceal the fact. It soon became clear that he was a man of violent temper and rough manner. Although he could not engage openly in the fur trade, he did not hesitate to turn his seigneury, an island which he called Ile Perrot, lying off Montreal between Lake St. Louis and the Lake of Two Mountains, into an important cog in the trade wheel. An officer who had served with him in France, Antoine de Fresnay, Sieur de Brucey, was placed in charge there. Brucey proceeded to collect around him a group of deserters from the colonial forces and to intercept the Indian canoes as they came down the river en route to Montreal. By offering brandy in trade, these illicit traders succeeded in getting their hands on a large part of the furs. Stories of orgies occurring on the island did nothing to improve the relationship between the governor and the citizens of Montreal.

A deputation of the citizens waited on Perrot very soon after the piratical activities of Ile Perrot became common knowledge. It consisted of men who had played courageous and important parts in the establishment of the town, Charles le Moyne, Jacques le Ber, Picoté de Belestre, and Migeon de Branssat, who acted as spokesman. Perrot took a high hand in dealing with them.

"I am not like Monsieur de Maisonneuve," he declared. This was probably the truest thing he had ever said; he was far different in every respect from the founder of Montreal. Scowling at the group confronting him, all men of better character and reputation than himself, he added in a violent tone, "I know how to keep you in your proper places."

The method he adopted of keeping them in their places was to dismiss the deputation with complete disregard of their demands and to place Branssat under arrest. When Dollier de Casson, as the head of the Sulpicians, remonstrated with him, Perrot brushed the words of censure aside. He did not free Branssat for several days.

Frontenac could not tolerate conduct such as this. He kept a watchful eye on the Montreal governor, and when the latter provided him with an adequate excuse for interfering, he did so with characteristic energy. In attempting to follow out the King's orders to lay hands on all men engaged in the fur trade without official permits, Charles d'Ailleboust, the judge of the Montreal court, had placed two of them under arrest. One of Perrot's officers, named Carion, helped the pair to escape. Frontenac promptly sent an officer of his own to Montreal with three soldiers to take Carion into custody. To this emissary, whose name was Bizard, Frontenac entrusted a letter to be handed to Perrot in which he explained his course af action in thus invading the latter's jurisdiction. Bizard, knowing the explosive nature of the Perrot temper, did not deliver the letter personally. He proceeded instead to arrest Carion and then gave the letter into the care of Jacques le Ber, to be handed to the governor after his own departure. Madame Carion sent word to Perrot that her husband had been laid by the heels and the governor arrived at the Le Ber house in a towering rage. Bizard had not succeeded yet in getting away and Perrot ordered his arrest, throwing Frontenac's letter in his face without condescending to open it. Several days later the news leaked out that Le Ber had prepared a statement of everything that had occurred and had sent it on to Quebec. Perrot retaliated by throwing the merchant into prison.

La Salle had been a witness of Bizard's arrest and of Perrot's violent actions on that occasion. Knowing that his own movements were being watched, the young explorer slipped out of his house at midnight, climbed the enclosing fence, and started off for Quebec. That Frontenac listened to his story with mounting indignation may be taken for granted, although he did not foam at the mouth, as one recorder has claimed. The course he followed indicates, in fact, that he did not rush into action without careful thought. There was a note of caution and certainly more than a touch of diplomatic guile in the steps he finally took. He wrote two letters, both couched in courteous terms, which most effectually concealed the purpose he had formed in his mind.

The first was to Perrot, instructing the latter to set Jacques le Ber at liberty and inviting him to come to Quebec to discuss the situation with the governor. The second was to the Abbé de Salignac Fénelon, a member of the Sulpician Order, and contained an intimation that he, Frontenac, was anxious to establish a better relationship with Monsieur Perrot and to clear away the misunderstandings which existed between Quebec and Montreal.

The letters had the desired effect. Perrot set off for Quebec, accompanied by Fénelon, who seemed to feel that he might be useful as a peacemaker. It was in the middle of winter, and the pair tramped most of the distance on snowshoes, a long and arduous trip. On arriving, Perrot made an official call at the Citadel of St. Louis and so discovered immediately that Frontenac, in extending his invitation, had been anything but candid. Lieutenant Bizard met him at the entrance, wearing no doubt a grin of intense personal satisfaction, and demanded his sword. He was under arrest, declared Bizard, and would remain so at the discretion of the King's viceroy. Perrot was in no position to resist and so was led away to one of the cells in the château, a small and far from comfortable habitation in such bitterly cold weather. There he was to remain in solitary confinement until November of that year. Fénelon, shocked beyond measure by the nature of the trick which had been played upon them, sought out Frontenac at once and protested vigorously. The governor was cool and withdrawn in his attitude. He listened to the heated remarks of the Sulpician in silence and then refused to allow the latter a pass to see the prisoner in his cell. Seething with indignation, Fénelon returned to Montreal on foot, where he proceeded, for the benefit of the good citizens of the town, to paint the governor's conduct in the bitterest terms.

Up to this point the sympathies of the Montrealers had been with
Frontenac rather than with the violent and openly venal Perrot.
Frontenac alienated their support, however, by proceeding to appoint
a new governor, selecting a man who had served with him in
Flanders, one Monsieur de la Nouguère. It had been the rule that the
office of governor of Montreal could be filled only with the consent
of the messieurs of the seminary, and in ignoring this Frontenac
lost the good will he might otherwise have counted upon. The attitude of Montreal hardened against him when he ordered the new
governor to arrest Brucey and to start action against all *coureurs de
bois* in Montreal, which was going over the head of Charles d'Ailleboust. The stout men of the town at the trading crossroads had no
stomach for a rule exercised from Quebec.

The new appointee went to work without any delay to carry out
Frontenac's wishes. He arrested Brucey, put him on trial, and
sentenced him to a term of imprisonment. He managed to get his
hands on the two *coureurs de bois* whose seizure had precipitated
the trouble in the first place and sent them off to Quebec to be dealt
with by the now thoroughly aroused Frontenac. The latter decided
the time had come to demonstrate the power and inflexibility of
the law. One of the pair was sentenced to be hanged, and in due
course he was led to the square in front of the château where the
sentence was carried out. It is affirmed that Perrot, who had the
benefit of a single small window commanding a view of the square,
watched the proceedings from his cell. If such was the case, the
spectacle did nothing to soften the Perrot temper or incline him
to bow before the sharp will of his antagonist.

In the meantime the Abbé Fénelon, who undoubtedly lacked discretion but had plenty of courage and zeal, was stirring things up in
Montreal. A month after the execution—on Easter Day, in fact—
he preached a sermon in the Hôtel-Dieu chapel in Montreal before
a congregation which filled it to overflowing and included the Sieur
de la Salle. It was an incendiary address and directed so clearly
at Frontenac that La Salle is said to have flushed with anger and
to have called the attention of those about him to the significance of
the abbé's remarks. The first result of the incident was that Dollier
de Casson left a sickbed to call the abbé sharply to account. The
bit had been taken firmly in the ecclesiastical teeth, however. Fénelon proceeded to circulate a petition in Perrot's behalf and secured
many signatures from among the citizens of the town. When word of

the abbé's activities reached the ears of the château autocrat, the churchman was summoned to Quebec and put on trial there with Perrot.

It might have been expected that the recalcitrant Perrot, led out for the first time from his solitary cell, would be the center of interest when the trial opened. Fénelon proceeded, however, to upset any such calculation. If a modern expression be permissible, the doughty churchman "stole the show" from his fellow defendant. He entered the courtroom with his clerical hat pulled down determinedly over his brows and proceeded at once to take possession of an unused chair. On both counts he was breaking the rules of court procedure. Five members of the Sovereign Council sat at the board as judges, with Frontenac himself presiding. The governor, according to custom, wore his plumed hat and his sword buckled at his side. He stared for a moment in complete silence at the seated defendant and then, in a voice which he strove to keep calm, informed the abbé that he must stand up and remove his hat. Fénelon stared back with equal composure and stated that priests appearing in a lay court had the right to do as he was doing.

"Not," declared Frontenac, "when they are cited to answer criminal charges."

The abbé continued to regard the presiding judge with eyes that did not flinch.

"My crimes," he asserted, "exist only in your head."

He went on to say that the governor was acting not as his judge but as his opponent and that an impartial trial of the case would be impossible under such circumstances.

Through the stormy scene that followed the governor seems to have behaved with unwonted restraint. It was the abbé who allowed himself to display an excitable temper. Rising from the chair which he had been so determined to claim, he paced up and down the space in front of the board where the Sovereign Council sat, removing and replacing his hat continuously in the course of his heated harangues. The outcome was that the defendant was instructed to leave the court, an order which he reluctantly obeyed. While he remained in an anteroom with a guard at his elbow, the Sovereign Council debated the points at issue, ignoring the presence all the while of the sardonically scowling Perrot, who had been forced to stand and to doff his hat, and who no doubt was regretting that he had no such rights as the Sulpician to fall back upon in defying the court. The decision of the Council favored Frontenac, and the abbé was removed accordingly to close custody in the brewery until further action could be taken.

After several hearings had resulted in similar altercations, it was decided to refer the case to the decision of the King. The two prisoners, therefore, were put on the last ship for France that fall, and all the records and the evidence were sent along for the royal guidance in the matter.

It looked at first as though the pressure of opinion hostile to Frontenac in the French capital would affect the opinion of the monarch. Talon was at court and openly antagonistic to the governor, and it was well known that Louis allowed himself to be guided in many things by the advice of the ex-intendant. The Abbé d'Urfe, a close adherent of Fénelon's, was connected with Colbert through the marriage of his cousin-germain, the wealthy young Marquise Marie Marguerite d'Allegre, to the Marquis de Seignelay, the minister's son. The court seethed with excitement. For a time nothing else was talked about, and the supporters of the two points of view fought among themselves for opportunities to reach the royal ear. There were comparatively few to speak for the bitter old soldier sitting in his cabinet atop the rock at Quebec and cut off from all further participation in the dispute; and it appeared certain for a time that the anti-Frontenac faction would prevail.

But Colbert's head was incapable of entertaining anything but a common-sense view of such matters, and the King himself showed an admirable resolve to consider only the main issues. There were faults on both sides, but the defendants in the case had erred more openly and more often. There could be no denial that they had defied the man who represented the monarch himself. Louis decided that he must give his support, even though it might seem little more than a token affirmation, to the viceroy he had selected and appointed. It was decided that the Abbé Fénelon should not be allowed to return to Canada, although the charges against him were dropped. Perrot was sentenced to the Bastille for the brief period of three weeks.

It was a victory for Frontenac. Later developments made it clear, however, that it was a partial vindication only. A letter from the King reached the governor by the first ship in the spring which made it clear that Louis had not been above straddling the issue. "To punish him," wrote the King, referring to Perrot, "I have put him for some time in the Bastille. . . . After having left M. Perrot some days in the Bastille, I will send him back to his government and I will order him to call on you and to offer you his apologies for all that has passed. After which I desire that you will not retain any resentment against him but that you will treat him in accordance with the power I have given him."

It was clear that the patience of the monarch had been strained almost to the breaking point by the incident.

2

Part of the troubles in which Frontenac was involved in his first term was the result of a conspiracy of his own contriving. Colbert was afraid of the power which the Jesuits had acquired in Canada. The King also was wary of the order and prepared to have them curbed in any reasonable way, but he did not feel as strongly on the point as his minister. Colbert, therefore, had a talk with the brusque nobleman before the latter first set sail for Canada. It is clear that he gave the new governor verbal instructions which exceeded the official mandates. It was agreed between them that a close eye must be kept on Jesuit activities. The conspiratorial attitude developed when they arranged between them for a code in which they could exchange news and views with the most complete frankness.

That such an understanding had been reached between them is proven by one of the passages which Frontenac used in the course of a letter to the minister. "Indeed, my lord," he wrote in the personal system of shorthand they had devised for their protection, "I recall every day to my mind the last words you spoke when I took leave of you, and I realize more and more that it is very expedient for the service of the King to oppose the least encroachments made on his authority, which are daily occurrences here. And if I were not firm in this respect this authority would be altogether lost, as there is nothing here at which they aim more eagerly than to lessen that authority. Nevertheless, to thwart such schemes I make use only of the most skillful and gentle means I can devise, according to what you prescribed I should do."

The haughty Gascon needed no further authority than this understanding with Colbert to proceed at once in checking the Jesuits. Almost immediately after his arrival, certainly before he could have acquainted himself thoroughly with the facts and before he had mastered the situation which existed, he wrote to Colbert that the Jesuits were as much interested in the conversion of beaver as in the conversion of the Indians. This was a libel which he must have regretted later.

The clashes that resulted between the volatile and choleric governor and the stern, single-minded priests arose from several causes. One of the first was the exclusive concern of the Jesuits with the souls of the Indians. There had been always a school of thought in France that claimed this attitude to be basically wrong. These theorists pointed out that the English and the Dutch, who were heretics and so must be considered children of the darkness, had succeeded in such a thorough conversion of the savages among whom they had settled that the red men lived with them amicably. The natives had fallen into European ways of living and had even taken up trades with some success. On the other hand, the French, in spite of the heroic efforts of the missionaries, had failed to civilize the natives in any degree. Mother Marie de l'Incarnation had written in one of her letters on this point: "We have not been able to Frenchify more than seven or eight girls. Others return to their homes where, however, they are leading very Christian lives."

One of the first visits Frontenac made on arriving in the colony was to the settlement of Ste. Foye, where the Indian converts congregated. He found to his astonishment that none of them spoke French. This discovery prompted a letter in which he expressed the belief that in making the savages subjects of Jesus Christ they should also be made subjects of the King; a clever approach in angling for the support of the monarch. "The way to make them Christians," continued the governor, "is to make them men first."

The Jesuit thinking was in direct opposition to this. They were interested only in the souls of the red men and they strove to keep the races apart, believing with a passionate conviction that if the Indians were brought into close contact with the French they would soon unlearn the lessons of morality they had been taught. This attitude was repugnant to Frontenac and to the active supporters in France of the policy he desired to inaugurate. To them it was a defeatist policy, a confession of lack of faith in the French way of living, even in the French people.

Frontenac was so eager to demonstrate the method he advocated that he at once gained a promise from the Indian leaders that they would send a number of children to him to be taught the French language and be raised in the French way. When the Jesuits offered to carry out the experiment for him, he said emphatically, no, he preferred to keep his Indians under his own eye. If the Jesuits desired to participate, let them find another set of children and educate them *their* way. Not content with this, the energetic governor issued orders that in all new settlements of converts an effort must be made to have French methods introduced. He insisted that the huts built for the converts have French chimneys instead of the customary hole in the ceiling to let the smoke out. It is not on record that the comfort the converts enjoyed from this change had any civilizing effect on them.

The chief source of disagreement was, of course, the traffic in brandy. Frontenac was convinced that it was necessary to use brandy for barter because the English, who were proving themselves shrewd and successful traders, supplied firewater to the natives. The fur supplies would inevitably go to the English, he believed, if the French refused to slake the native thirst. In this he had the backing of most of the citizens of the colony, who knew that their prosperity depended entirely on the fur trade. It was an opinion, moreover, which Colbert had consistently shared and in which the farseeing Talon had believed. The Church was against the sale of brandy, and on this issue the Sulpicians were as firm and outspoken as the Jesuits. "If brandy were forbidden among the Indians," wrote Dollier de Casson from Montreal, "we would have thousands of conversions to report."

The previous heads of state had dealt warily with this question, realizing the strength of the clerical position. Frontenac came right out into the open, refusing to mask his real opinion. Why, he demanded to know, was it more sinful to give brandy to Indians in trade than for a Bordeaux merchant to sell wine to the Dutch and English? The Dutch and English, he averred, got just as drunk as the Indians.

Being a fiery protagonist in all things and at all times, Frontenac went much farther. He declared that the Indians did not get as drunk as the Jesuits avowed. There was only the word of the missionaries for the orgies which they said resulted when firewater was supplied the natives, the roistering and fighting, the cruelty and the killings.

It was strange that Frontenac, who was a skillful swordsman and adept in the light thrust of the blade and the quick riposte, did not employ the finesse of the fencer in his controversies. He used instead the mace or the battle-ax, attacking his antagonists with an unabating fury. Carrying the struggle over the use of brandy to an extreme which almost defeated his own purpose, he asserted that the stand of the Jesuits was due to their desire to get the fur trade into their own hands. He charged them with bartering, and on the surface there was some basis for the statement. By no other means could the missionaries secure the bare necessities of living. Money was of no value to the Indians; they wanted trade goods and were prepared to offer food and pelts in exchange. The Jesuits accepted pelts from their red-skinned charges on this basis. Frontenac used this to charge them with a selfish design. In 1676 he openly accused the order of acquiring great wealth as a result of the trading facilities they enjoyed. They owned vast stretches of territory and valuable seigneuries, he declared.

Frontenac never knew when to stop. Having gone thus far, he threw caution to the winds and attacked the hold the Jesuits had acquired over the consciences of the people. They tormented their charges in the confessional, he asserted, demanding to know the names of accomplices in sin, informing husbands about the misdeeds of their wives and telling parents the faults of their children.

The order struck back. A complaint was lodged against the governor that he insisted the missionaries and the priests secure passports from him before setting out on their labors. It was even charged that he was intercepting the mail and reading the clerical letters in an effort to get evidence against them. They charged Frontenac with being in the fur trade himself, using the belief generally held in the colony that he and La Salle were conspiring to get a monopoly on the trade of the West and South. The result was that Colbert wrote to the governor a note of warning. "His Majesty," said the minister, "further orders me to tell you in secret that, although he did not believe what was said here that some trade and pelt traffic was being carried on in your name, you must beware lest any of your servants or any person who is near you carry on such a trade. It would be impossible for the colonists to be persuaded that you will protect them and render them the impartial justice which you owe them as long as they see a few persons who have private access to trade." This shaft was launched at La Salle, who was popularly believed to have Frontenac's support and co-operation in all his great schemes.

This unending altercation brought the King to a decision finally. The power of Frontenac must be curbed. Accordingly, late in the year of the settlement of the Perrot-Fénelon affair, 1675, a new intendant was appointed in the person of Jacques Duchesneau, who had been serving the monarchy well in a financial post at Tours. To strengthen the position of the new official it was decided further that the filling of places on the Sovereign Council was to become the direct prerogative of the King. Frontenac might make recommendations, but the King would choose the men to serve.

Frontenac and Duchesneau fought from the outset. The haughty eye of the aristocratic governor held nothing but scorn whenever it rested on the plebeian intendant. Within a month of the arrival of Duchesneau at Quebec the two men were at daggers drawn. They quarreled over the right to preside at the meetings of the Sovereign Council, and it took five years to settle the point, the final resolution being in favor of Duchesneau. They accused each other of making personal fortunes out of the fur trade. Frontenac wrote to Colbert that Duchesneau was not only incompetent but a tool of the Jesuits. Duchesneau countered with charges that the governor was using the authority of his high post to buy beaver skins at prices below market value. Frontenac complained that spies had been introduced into his household to report on his actions.

It reached a point where the two men hated each other so violently that they instinctively took opposite sides on every question. Their adherents fought in the streets. The meetings of the Sovereign Council were given over to the bitter wrangling of the two high officials.

3

To complicate matters further Laval returned to Canada in 1680. He had been granted finally the right for which he had fought so long, and it was as the Bishop of Quebec that he stepped off the ship. He was now sixty years of age but he seemed much older, a bent and frail figure, hobbling rather than walking. His face was gray and gaunt, his hair had thinned to white wisps.

But if his eye betokened the haste of the passing years, it was with no diminution of intensity that it rested on the ashes of Lower Town, which had been burned to the ground a short time before, or when it turned upward and saw the Château of St. Louis on the crest. The old man knew that he would have to struggle hard to get the Lower Town rebuilt on a better, sounder basis. He knew also that the hardest fight of his career lay ahead of him with the stormy governor who now occupied the château.

The King, on promptings from Frontenac without a doubt, had promulgated a decree the year before which had cut much of the ground from beneath the feet of the clerical leader. It had provided that the tithes should be paid to the parish priests, who were established in perpetuity, and no longer to removable priests, who came and went at the bidding of the bishop. This was the old controversy on which the King and Laval had taken opposite sides for so many years. The bishop finally had lost. He had taken his defeat philosophically, it appeared, but those who knew the intensity of his conviction of the need to keep the clergy of Canada under close control instead of allowing them to settle down in lifetime inertia in one parish were certain he was no more than biding his time. Sooner of later, when the proper opportunity arose, the fighting bishop would reopen the issue, prepared to face all the powers of earth.

Bishop Laval's attitude at first was conciliatory. If there could be peace with the autocrat of the château, he desired it. Only if Frontenac proved as belligerent as he had been in the past would the head of the Church enter the lists against him. His first step was to make a tour of the country, traveling by barge and canoe to every parish in his huge diocese, observing with joy the evidences of growth in the population. He returned after months of travel a thoroughly tired old man.

Inevitably the bishop was drawn into the conflict between the two state officials. He ranged himself on the side of Duchesneau, realizing, no doubt, that the latter needed support in the duel with his high-placed adversary and would be willing to accept the bishop's own terms. The indomitable will of Laval, the hauteur of Frontenac, the stubbornness of Duchesnau: here were the elements for a titanic battle. The colony divided into two camps. Frontenac had with him the men engaged in the conquest of the West, La Salle, Du Lhut, the leading fur traders. Laval and Duchesneau had the royal appointees on the Sovereign Council, the solid merchants of Montreal and Three Rivers. The old issues were brought out to add fuel to the fire: the brandy traffic, the proper control of the *coureurs de bois,* the right of state officials to engage in trade. Both sides bombarded Versailles with their complaints and proofs, and at first it seemed certain that the governor would prevail. At any rate, Duchesneau received a letter which was designed to put him in his place. "Though it appears by the letters of M. de Frontenac," wrote the minister, "that his conduct leaves something to be desired, there is assuredly far more to blame in yours than in his. . . . It is difficult to believe that you act in the spirit which the service of the King demands; that is to say, without interest and without passion. If a change does not appear in your conduct before next year, His Majesty will not keep you in your office."

This threat did nothing to check the turbulence of the intendant. The squabbling grew even more intense, and Versailles heard stories of violence in Quebec which shocked the King and even ruffled the composure of Colbert. Frontenac, it was claimed, had summoned the sixteen-year-old son of Duchesneau to the château to explain his part in a street brawl and had struck the boy in an excess of rage and had torn his coat, making it necessary for the intendant to barricade his house in order to protect his offspring against the wrath of the governor. Frontenac seems to have ignored this story, but his friends denied it loudly and bitterly, claiming that it had been invented.

In 1681 Colbert placed the affairs of the French colonies in the hands of his son, the Marquis de Seignelay. In order to gain the favor of the new incumbent, both sides promptly bombarded him with great masses of memoranda bearing on all phases of the long dispute. This seems to have precipitated a decision on the part of the King. He had long since wearied of the endless bickerings in Canada and the barrage of charges and countercharges. There might be different levels of guilt, but both men, clearly, were at fault. Instead of deciding openly between Frontenac and Duchesneau, he again straddled the issue. He recalled them both.

On May 9, 1882, the King sent his order of recall to the governor, saying in part, "Being satisfied with the services you rendered me in the commandement I entrusted to you in my country in New France, I am writing to you this letter that you are to return to my court on the first ship which will leave Quebec for France."

A gentle form of dismissal, indeed, but one that could not be misunderstood.

CHAPTER XXXIV

The Mistakes of Frontenac's Successor—The Death of Colbert—La Barre Is Recalled—Meules Makes a New Kind of Money

1

WHILE man-made storms kept the little colony in unhappy agitation, a real storm was brewing which threatened the very existence of New France. Its rumblings could be heard in the teeming villages of the Senecas and in the council house at Onondaga. Every wind from the south carried whispers of war. The first muffled thunderings of the trouble had reached the ears of France's allies, and so great was the dread they felt that the tribes along the Ottawa had been thrown into abject inactivity. Even in the Illinois country, so far away, the warriors scowled in fear and their women raised supplications to their ineffective gods. The evil wind blew about the ramparts of the Château of St. Louis at Quebec and carried its message of uncertainty and unrest through the narrow, sloping streets of the town.

Frontenac had known of the Iroquois unrest before his cantankerous quarrels with Duchesneau resulted in his recall. He had striven to continue and consolidate the peace by his usual methods of persuasion, summoning the Five Nations rather haughtily to a conference with him. The Iroquois held off at first. They were willing to confer with Onontio, they said, but he must come to them. He had sought the meeting, not they. Finally a great Iroquois chief named Tegannisoriens met the governor at Fort Frontenac to extend a formal invitation for talks to be held at Oswego, which lay well within the territory of the Long House. Frontenac succeeded in buttering up this brave warrior with a great wampum belt and a scarlet and gold jacket and a silken cravat. He seems to have succeeded in convincing the delegation that the proposed meeting at Oswego was now unnecessary. At any rate, he returned to Quebec confident that he had stifled the discontent. Soon thereafter he returned to France under the cloud of dismissal.

But his hopes of peace had been built on a false optimism. Tegannisoriens had been honestly convinced of the wisdom of peace, but he was only one of many. The bitter chiefs who had no scarlet jackets or silken cravats to wear were still in favor of digging up the hatchet again after its long period of sequestration.

To succeed Frontenac and to avert the storm there now came the Sieur de le Febvre de la Barre, accompanied by a self-satisfied man named Jacques de Meules, Sieur de la Source, who was to act as intendant. With the colony rent into factions and the mutterings of war all along the rivers and the forest trails, they were indeed a sorry pair to gather up the reins of office. La Barre was sixty years old and had been a lawyer most of his life. Translated to the French West Indies in charge of the military and naval forces, he had won quite a reputation for himself in some trouble with the English (who must have been most incompetently led indeed) and had begun to swagger and demand the title of Monsieur le Général. He seems to have accepted the post with the intention of making a rich man of himself.

It is not surprising that evil days soon fell upon Canada. Frontenac, with all his faults, had been the possessor of a conscience for his responsibilities. La Barre was a boastful and greedy fraud.

La Barre proceeded to make a series of grievous mistakes. He had come to Canada with a preconceived dislike for his predecessor and a determination to stand in the way of La Salle. When he received a letter from the latter, informing him of the discovery of the mouth of the Mississippi, he openly expressed his disbelief and even wrote to the King, voicing his opinion that the matter was of small consequence. He succeeded in persuading the King of this and received a letter in which Louis said, "I am convinced like you that the discovery of the Sieur de la Salle is very useless and that such enterprises ought to be prevented in future." Certain now that he had royal support, the new governor proceeded to detain the men La Salle had sent east for supplies and to refuse all requests for assistance against Iroquois aggression in the West. He even went to the extreme step of seizing Fort Frontenac and impounding all La Salle's property on the pretext that the latter had not fulfilled the terms on which it had been granted to him. Finally he sent an officer, the Chevalier de Baugis, to take possession of the fort that La Salle had erected to serve as his headquarters in the Illinois country.

His next false step was to set himself up in business with a coterie of Canadian merchants and to establish a great store of trade goods at Michilimackinac. The syndicate thus formed operated fleets of canoes and ships on the Great Lakes, and it was a matter of necessity for them to have peace. La Barre accordingly sent Charles le Moyne, the good old standby who could always be depended upon to accomplish whatever was demanded of him, to visit the Iroquois leaders at Onondaga and invite them to a conference at Montreal. As usual, Le Moyne succeeded in his efforts, and in course of time a delegation of over forty chiefs came to meet the new governor at a council held in the church of Bonsecours.

La Barre cut a poor figure in the negotiations that followed. He lacked the easy dignity of Frontenac and seemed to be very ill at ease under the unflinching scrutiny of forty pairs of intent black eyes. He showered the chiefs with presents to the value of two thousand crowns and urged them in return to respect the peace with France and at the same time refrain from attacks on the Indians of the upper lakes without notifying the French first. The chiefs agreed on both points, but in view of what happened later it is clear they had no intention of keeping their promises. The question of the western tribes was then introduced and La Barre demanded to know why the Iroquois had attacked the Illinois without provocation.

"Because they deserved to die," declared the chief Iroquois spokesman.

The issue having thus been introduced, the delegation from the hostile tribes complained that La Salle had been supplying the Illinois with guns and powder; as he had indeed, that being the only way to hold the western confederacy together. La Barre had no hesitation in declaring that La Salle would be punished. He is even supposed to have disclaimed all responsibility for the actions of the great explorer and to have left the impression with the Iroquois that they had carte blanche to deal with La Salle as they saw fit.

It was soon apparent that the tongues of the Iroquois had been in their cheeks all the time. One of the first proofs of amity they supplied was to attack and capture a convoy of French boats on their way to the upper lakes. It so happened that the boats belonged to La Barre and his associates and that they were filled with goods for trading with the northwestern tribes. The goods were valued at fifteen thousand livres and the governor was furious at this costly breach of the peace; a condition of mind which was not improved when the explanation was forthcoming that the Iroquois had thought the shipment belonged to La Salle, who could be attacked with impunity. La Barre seems to have been convinced by this episode that war with these belligerent and insolent people was inevitable.

On first arriving in Canada, Monsieur le Général had written to the King: "The Iroquois have twenty-six hundred warriors but I will attack them with twelve hundred men. They know how roughly I handled the English in the West Indies." Now the strain of bombast disappeared from his official communications. He did not like the situation at all and he wrote repeatedly to the King and to Seignelay, urging that trained soldiers be sent out to strengthen his hand.

2

The situation at home was not favorable for the carrying out of a strong and consistent policy. The great Colbert had died in 1683. During the last stages of his tenure of office and of his life he had been an unhappy man. Always a believer in peace, he had seen the warlike ambitions of Louis the Victorious mount as he listened to his war minister, the Marquis de Louvois. The funds which Colbert had accumulated by his sound policies over the long years were being handed to Louvois for use in the building of a great war machine. After a victory at Strassburg, the sun of Louvois rose high in the heavens and that of Colbert declined until it could hardly be discerned on the horizon. His spirit seems to have been crushed by a comparison the King made between what he, Colbert, was accomplishing about the rebuilding of Versailles and the success of Louvois with some construction work in Flanders. The great minister took to his bed and in a rankling of spirit refused thereafter to receive any message from the fickle King.

The news of his death was joyfully received by the public, and he had to be buried in secrecy to avoid hostile demonstrations. The French people had always hated him. They seem to have had a habit, in fact, of resenting the collectors of taxes while at the same time they took to their hearts the unscrupulous spendthrifts who dissipated the revenue in showy ways.

With Colbert gone and his much less capable son in the colonial ministry, it was difficult to get things done. Finally, however, the piteous appeals of La Barre resulted in the dispatching of three companies of regular soldiers to Canada, each being made up of fifty-two men. They were veterans of the Dutch wars, tired and disillusioned fellows who had no stomach left for further fighting and who embarked without enthusiasm. Nevertheless, they were welcomed at Quebec with the utmost acclaim, the shouts of the relieved populace merging with the not too brisk rat-tat of the army drums.

La Barre had no excuse now for postponing the punishment he had promised to mete out to the insolent Iroquois. He began to organize his forces for a drive against the Senecas, the most numerous and powerful of the Five Nations. As a first step he wrote to the English governor at New Amsterdam, which was now called New York because the colony had been handed over to the Duke of York, afterward James II, by his brother Charles II. He informed the English that he intended to attack the Iroquois and that no guns were to be supplied them in the meantime. This bit of absurdity was tantamount to saying to a fencing opponent, "Monsieur, my next thrust will be straight at your midriff, so place yourself on guard." The English governor answered that the Iroquois were subjects of King Charles and that he, La Barre, must not set foot on English territory. The threat had the result also of inciting the Iroquois to furious preparations. They were delighted, being sure they could cope with this new French leader who had failed so lamentably to impress them. Father de Lamberville, who was still at his post in the Iroquois country, saw what was happening at first hand and he sent a gloomy letter to La Barre, advising him to exercise caution. He declared that the Senecas were filled with joy and that they expected to strip, roast, and eat every Frenchman in the country.

The Iroquois front was better organized at this stage than it had ever been. The costly wars with the Andastes were ended and so the heavy drain on their man power had ceased. For years they had been enrolling the youngest and strongest men of the tribes they had attacked and beaten, training them in Iroquois philosophy and drilling them in new ways of fighting. The alliance with the English had been cemented, and the latter had a shrewd and aggressive

leader in Colonel Thomas Dongan as governor at New York. Dongan
was a realistic Irishman who saw that conflict between the English
and the French was inevitable and that it behooved him to take
full advantage of the strength of the Five Nations.

La Barre, having deprived himself of all the advantages of a surprise move, set out for Fort Frontenac with the army he had gathered about him. In addition to the hundred-odd soldiers from
France, he had seven hundred Canadian volunteers and a few hundred mission Indians. The regulars had not fully recovered from
the rigors of the voyage across the Atlantic and were as soft as putty.
The mission Indians had about as much martial ardor as could be
brewed at an afternoon tea party. "My purpose," wrote Monsieur
le Général to the King, "is to exterminate the Senecas."

The governor proceeded to handle the affair with all the military
skill that might have been expected from a leader who had spent
most of his life in a law office. After encountering great difficulties
on the way, the troops reached Fort Frontenac, and La Barre
selected a damp stretch of ground for pitching his camp. The mosquitoes made the nights miserable for the unhappy French soldiers,
and noxious mists rose from the dank soil and the stagnant water,
spreading malarial fevers. Many of the men died, and the governor
himself was reduced to a sickly condition. The supplies of food
proved inadequate, and in a very short period of time the force
was reduced to a condition of martial impotence. La Barre saw
no way out of it but to invite the Onondagas to a peace conference,
sending the ever-reliable Charles le Moyne to arrange it, hoping
that they would induce the Senecas to join the proceedings. To
await their coming, the governor selected the most healthy-appear-
ing of his men and moved them to the other side of the water, stopping at a spot most appropriately called La Famine.

The Onondagas responded to the invitation by sending a delegation headed by an orator whose fame had almost obscured the
memory of the Flemish Bastard. He was called Big Mouth and he
had such a flow of words that white men fell under his spell as
readily as his own people.

Squatting in a dignified semicircle with his fellow chiefs, Big
Mouth listened to the speech with which La Barre opened the discussions. When the governor had finished, the spellbinder rose to
his feet. For a few moments he paced up and down in silence, then
he stopped, struck an attitude, and began to speak. His manner

exuded confidence; and well it might, because there had been
fraternizing between the rank and file on each side and it had not
needed much craft on the part of the red men to discover the weakness of the French force.

"Listen, Onontio," orated Big Mouth in a voice as deep and full
as the chords of an organ. "I am not asleep. My eyes are open; and
by the sun that gives me light I see a great captain at the head of
a band of soldiers who talks like a man in a dream. He says he has
come to smoke the pipe of peace with the Onondagas; but I see
that he came to knock them on the head, *if so many of his Frenchmen were not too weak to fight.* . . . Listen, Onontio. My voice
is the voice of the Five Tribes of the Iroquois." On and on it went.
Every sentence, punctuated with sweeping gestures, was an attack
on the pride of the French.

La Barre retired to his tent in a rage. There was no answer he
could give. He *was* too weak to fight. He had no strength to fall
back upon, no tricks up his sleeve. The next day there was a shorter
session and a peace of sorts was patched up. There was to be a ces-
sation of hostilities between the French and the Iroquois. The latter
would pay for the damage they had done to French trade (they later
refused to do this). The red men asserted their determination to
fight the Illinois to the death; and La Barre could find no words to
say in support of the allies who were thus condemned to extinction.
As a final gesture of defiance the Five Nations demanded that any
future talks be held at La Famine, on Iroquois soil, and not on the
French side. Frontenac would never have assented to such a humili-
tion as this; he would have hurled the suggestion back in their teeth
with fitting scorn. La Barre weakly agreed.

This concluded the open talks. La Barre returned to Quebec,
leaving his forces to negotiate the long water trip as best they could.
His great gesture had done no more than avert an open breach for
a short spell. The peace had been purchased at too high a price, as
subsquent events would show. Big Mouth had flaunted the power
of the Iroquois and had told the French leader that he was too weak
to attack them. There had been no thunderbolts from the skies to
punish him for his audacity, and for many moons thereafter laughter would be heard about campfires where the orotund passages of
the daring orator were repeated.

The French lost face also with their allies in the West. Owing
largely to the efforts of the resourceful Nicolas Perrot, a band of

five hundred warriors had gathered to come down the lakes and join La Barre in his attack on the Senecas. The armada of canoes which brought this powerful band had reached the point where the Niagara empties into Lake Ontario when a messenger reached them with a letter from La Barre. It said, in brief:

"Go home. We have made peace."

The resentment with which the allied warriors returned to their hunting grounds was echoed all over the land. La Barre might declare that he had scored a victory. Everyone else knew that the peace was a sham to be broken at the will of the Five Nations.

The King was not deceived by the protestations of the governor. He wrote an immediate letter of recall and appointed the Marquis de Denonville to succeed him.

3

While the tenure in office of La Barre was thus being brought to an inglorious finish, the intendant Meules had been writing letters home. He had kept the King and the Marquis de Seignelay well informed of everything the governor was doing, particularly the profits he had been taking out of the fur trade. His tart epistles had played their part in bringing about La Barre's recall.

The record of Meules himself in Canada is limited to one note-worthy achievement. What he did, considered in the light of its consequences, was quite remarkable. It had nothing to do with the Indian wars and their barbarities nor with the troubled state of trade. It had to do entirely with money, and it came about in this way.

The colony was always short of currency. A supply would be sent over each spring, mostly in the form of the fifteen-*sol* and five-*sol* pieces which had been minted exclusively for use in Canada. As the settlers depended on France for all the goods they purchased and used, the silver and copper pieces invariably found their way back. The colonists had, on this account, fallen into the barter habit. Wheat and moose skins served as legal tender, and sometimes debts would be paid in beaver skins, wildcat skins, and even in liquor. The merchants preferred the barter system and certain price standards had been established. A blanket, for instance, cost eight *cats*.

It happened that the usual supply of financial ammunition was overlooked in the spring of 1685. The soldiers who were to have

aided La Barre in his extermination of the Senecas were still in
Quebec and had fully recovered their health and appetites. With no
funds available, the intendant could not dole them out their little
bits of pay, and he found the frugal inhabitants opposed to the idea
of feeding three companies of hungry soldiers on credit. Faced with
this difficulty, Meules had an inspiration. He would issue pieces of
paper as pay and redeem them later when real money was available.

Some writers have contended that this was the start of paper
money in the Western world, but this is giving rather too much
credit to Monsieur de Meules. The Chinese, of course, had used
paper currency; to quite good advantage in the reign of Kublai
Khan. Before that the Egyptians had experimented with parchment
currency. "Leather" money, which may have been parchment, had
been in circulation in Greece and Rome. There had been in England, as early as the period of the first Norman kings, paper ac-
knowledgments of private deposits with the goldsmiths, who were
the first bankers, and these had been exchangeable. There had also
been bills of exchange and lading. It must be conceded, however,
that Meules had no immediate precedents for the step he proposed
to take and that he deserves to be remembered.

He encountered a great deal of difficulty in connection with his
plan. There were no available supplies of paper in the country and,
of course, no printing presses. As a way out, he conceived the idea
of collecting all the playing cards he could find and using them for
money.

Most of the cardplaying in the colony was done by the unpaid
soldiers themselves. In France card games had become a fashionable
obsession and the cards used were glossy and of good quality. As
in England, four suits had come into general practice, although of
course they were called *coeur* (heart), *carreau* (diamond), *trèfle*
(club), and *pique* (spade). The popular game almost certainly was
maw, which had become established as the favorite on the continent.
Having nothing else to do, the soldiers played at maw continuously
in the rooms where they lived in the small frame houses in the
suburbs. The destruction of Lower Town by fire had made it necessary for everyone to move out from under the comfortable shelter
of the town walls. La Barre resided in the château, but the intendant
had been compelled to content himself with a very small outside
house. Being a man of timorous disposition, he had existed there
in much discomfort of mind, often waking in the hours of darkness

and shivering for fear that the Iroquois might be skulking outside.

The soldiers, who had nothing to do at this stage, drank a great deal and smoked even more. They quarreled noisily as they planked the soiled cards down on the uptilted kegs which served as tables, calling impatiently to be favored with the best takers of tricks, Tiddy, Gleek, Tup-tup, and Towser.

Meules gathered up all the cards he could find, had some of them cut into halves and quarters to represent the valuations of four francs, forty *sols,* and fifteen *sols,* stamped them with the word "bon," signed and sealed in wax, and appended his own signature as well as that of a treasury clerk. These were handed back to the soldiers in lieu of pay, and a proclamation was made that the cards were to be accepted as money. The experiment proved quite successful, and in the fall, when the regular supply of currency arrived, the much-thumbed and greasy bits of paper were redeemed. Meules was warned not to repeat the experiment, however. It was a dangerous thing to do, averred the King's officials, and might lead to inflation in prices.

The next year more playing-card money had to be issued in spite of this stern admonition, because once again the currency shipment was overlooked. This happened so often, in fact, that gradually playing-card money became recognized. The people in Canada were now accustomed to it and, in fact, liked it very much, finding it handier than the bulky items of barter. The idea had been followed in the New England colonies, where soldiers were paid in paper money. It continued right through the period of the French regime, and in the year 1749, in fact, an official issue was made in paper which reached a value of one million livres.

One of the disadvantages of the new money was the relative ease with which it could be counterfeited. The laws had to be made very severe. In 1690 a French-Canadian surgeon was condemned to be flogged on his naked back in all the public squares of Quebec for making card money. Death by hanging was decreed for the offense at a later stage.

The ingenuity of Meules had played a large part, beyond any doubt, in revolutionizing banking and monetary practice. It is possible that the handy bills which today repose so easily in wallets and in pockets would never have come into existence if he had not found himself with a hundred soldiers on his hands and no currency to use in paying them.

4

Bishop Laval did not long enjoy the title which had come to him after so much delay. It has already been pointed out that he was broken in health when he reached Quebec with his laurels; although it must be added that he would have resented the use of any such word as "laurels," being convinced that he had done nothing to deserve praise or reward. The long tour he made of his diocese drew further on his strength. When he returned to Quebec, it was with the conviction that he could not hope to administer for any length of time the duties of his office with the vigor demanded of the incumbent.

On August 28, 1685, the old bishop attended the meeting of the Sovereign Council in Quebec with a light in his eye which would have been familiar to the governors who had faced him in earlier years. With Frontenac recalled and out of his path, he had hopes of revoking the edict which secured the parish priests in their posts. He had accepted the edict with seeming resignation and had given much careful attention to the selection of the men for the various parishes. Deep in his mind and heart, however, the decision had always rankled.

La Barre, who was still governor at this time, was absent on his abortive expedition against the Senecas when the Council met. The intendant Meules was on hand, as were also the citizen members, all of whom were appointees of the King and submissive to his ideas. It undoubtedly was in the bishop's mind that an expression in his favor by the members might lead to a consideration on the part of the King. The verdict, however, was in favor of the edict. Disappointed, saddened, secretly bitter no doubt, the bishop realized that he must bow to the inevitable.

The defeat thus sustained in his final stand against the will of the King made it clear to the old bishop that the days of his usefulness were over. He decided to resign.

To sail the Atlantic was an undertaking of the most rigorous kind. When the weather proved rough, which could always be expected in the fall, the port lids would be closed and the tiny cabins would become dark and the air so foul that passengers were driven to the perils of the deck. Here the freeboards would be raised, but no precautions could keep the water from washing across. After the first few days the cooks had to depend on the food supplies in the rancid barrels lashed outside the galley: dried eels, salted fish and beef, and whatever such unskilled hands could concoct with flour, dried fruits, and spices. This was no hardship for the Spartan prelate who had eschewed the pleasures of the table all through the span of his years, but it seems certain that his strength suffered from it. For a man as sick and old as Bishop Laval the Atlantic crossing was a terrible ordeal.

It might have been expected that he would spare himself the adventure by sending his resignation by letter, but he never stooped to such weakness. It seemed incumbent on him to present his reasons in person and so he took himself aboard the last packet, fully conscious of the fact that he might never again set eyes on this beloved land.

Appreciating the importance of having the right successor, Laval addressed himself on reaching France to men whose opinions he valued. From each of them he received the highest encomiums of the King's almoner, the Abbé Saint-Vallier. He was young, gifted, and zealous. He was, moreover, generous to a fault and almost as free in his personal charities as Laval himself. The post that Saint-Vallier was filling at the royal court was pleasant and easy and one which could be converted into a springboard to eminence and power by an ambitious man. The bishopric of Quebec, on the other hand, offered nothing but hardships, disappointments, worries, and dangers. Any man willing to trade the one for the other would be eminently worthy. When Saint-Vallier unhesitatingly expressed his eagerness to accept, Laval was certain that he had found the man he sought.

There must have been some hesitation in the King's mind about accepting the resignation of the bishop. Laval had become a legend and he seemed essential to the spiritual life of the colony. Nevertheless, the monarch expressed his willingness to have the old man step aside and conferred on him the privilege of nominating a successor. Laval spoke up for Saint-Vallier, and in due course the appointment was made.

It had been in the old man's mind that, when freed of his duties, he would retire into the seminary at Quebec for the balance of his life and spend his time in encouraging the young priests. To his dismay he found that he would not be allowed to return to Canada. It was made clear to him in diplomatic terms that the King felt the new incumbent should have a free hand. Disappointed, and no doubt a little shocked at this unexpected turn of events, the old man bowed to the monarchial will. He saw his successor set sail for Canada in June of the following year on the same ship which was taking out the new governor, the Marquis de Denonville.

Denonville was a soldier of long experience and he was being sent out to take hold of the Iroquois problem with an iron hand. There was a companion ship, and eight hundred soldiers were divided between the two. They were packed in as tight as fish in salted kegs, and the nature of the hardships the poor fellows were condemned to suffer can easily be imagined. The King's decision to keep Laval in France spared the venerable prelate from a sight which would have wrung his heart, the conveyance each day to the railings of bodies sewed up in canvas to be committed to the deep. The fevers created by the filthiness of the holds and the scurvy (no effort seems to have been made to recover the cure for that foul disease) took heavy toll. One hundred and fifty men died before the ships put in at Quebec.

CHAPTER XXXV

*La Salle Embarks on a Wild Adventure—A Colony
Is Founded by Mistake in Texas—His Death at
the Hands of Mutinous Followers*

1

T HE bad impression of La Salle, created by the hostility and
innuendoes of Le Febvre de la Barre, had spread in France.
At first the successful exploration of the mysterious Mississippi had caught the fancy of the public and there had been general
praise of the man who had accomplished the feat. This would not
have lasted long in any event. Envy and malice are always active
at court, and reputations can be unmade in a whispering conspiracy.
The fine edge of La Salle's acclaim had been blunted, and it needed
only the animadversions of the governor to start the pendulum swinging in the other direction.

La Salle himself seems to have been impervious to such small
matters. He made a quiet entrance into Paris, restrained in mood
and deeply preoccupied. A little shabby in attire, perhaps, for his
purse was again as flat as the old skin from which the spring snake
has emerged. He went to his humble apartments in the Rue de la
Truanderie and applied at once for audiences with the King and his
ministers. Louis, always curious and with an eye for the spectacular,
decided to see the homecomer himself.

One morning, therefore, La Salle appeared by appointment in the
royal anterooms. At the designated moment (Louis being as punc-
tual as any humble clerk) he was ushered into the cabinet of the
King. He had heard much about it, mostly from men who had never
been there; how in the blazing effulgence of the Sun King casual
visitors blinked and became tongue-tied and the pretensions of the
unworthy or the unlucky shriveled to nothing. It is unlikely that La

Salle saw anything in the small room save a stoutish man behind an ornate escritoire, a man with the florid cheeks of high living and a sharp eye. As solemn as a saulie himself, La Salle had room in his mind for one thought only, the need to convince this omnipotent being of the feasibility of a great new scheme.

This was what they discussed. France and Spain were now at war, and La Salle pointed out to the King that the northwestern point of Mexico, where gold and silver mines were yielding their wealth to Castilian greed, was not far south of the mouth of the Mississippi. Why not, therefore, accomplish a double purpose by establishing on the newly claimed river a colony strong enough to command a foothold on the Mexican coast? He had a plan worked out in full detail. Give him two ships and two hundred men, half of them soldiers, half artisans. He would then recruit in Canada a much larger force of trained woodsmen. An alliance would be made with the northern confederacy of Indian tribes, and a party of four thousand warriors would be brought down the Mississippi to join in an attack on the Spanish settlements. La Salle proposed to take possession of New Biscay, the Spanish province which lay between the twenty-fifth degree of latitude and the twenty-seventh, and this would place in the hands of the French King the fabulous mines of Ste. Barbe.

Such was the scheme proposed to the ambitious King. It is hard to believe that La Salle could have advanced an idea as wild as this with a straight face or that a man as shrewd as Louis XIV could have considered it in full seriousness. If La Salle really believed that a war party of four thousand western braves could be persuaded to travel down the great river (for which they had a superstitious dread) to fight a powerful white race, leaving their own lands wide open to more mass raids by the Iroquois, he had no conception whatever of Indian nature. If he thought this unprecedentedly large native force could be fed off the land and kept in control while en route, he was the most optimistic general who ever courted failure. If he was convinced, finally, that such an army could be held together and made effective against the trained soldiers of Spain, he was indulging in dreams as ephemeral as soap bubbles. In other words, if he had faith in this preposterous plan, he was mad. The misfortunes he had suffered, the hardships he had endured had affected his brain.

On the other hand, if he did not believe in what he was proposing, he was holding out false prospects to the King in order to win the royal interest in the project closest to his heart, the colonization of the mouth of the Mississippi.

As to the judgment displayed by King Louis and his minister in accepting this harebrained scheme, the less said the better.

Louis was silent and noncommittal after his visitor left. Courtiers who considered themselves reliable barometers of the royal temper laughed contemptuously and said to one another, "Whatever his purpose may have been, this gloomy clod has failed." But they were wrong. The King might maintain an outward show of indifference, but underneath he was seething with purpose. Almost above everything else he would like to scoop into his own treasure chest a share of the easy wealth which Spain controlled. He had already sent a scorching letter to La Barre, who was still functioning in Canada, ordering him to reverse his attitude on La Salle. He, La Barre, must make it clear to the Iroquois that the brave explorer could not be attacked at will, that on the contrary he stood high in the favor of the King. La Barre must lose no time in restoring La Salle's possessions.

The royal decision was known only to three men: the King himself; his colonial minister, the Marquis de Seignelay, a son of Colbert; and La Salle. The secret was closely held during the whole period of preparation. Men might guess that the fitting out of four ships and the recruiting of a force of four hundred men (the King had doubled La Salle's conservative estimate) had to do with a settlement at the mouth of the Mississippi, but who could foresee the deeper purpose back of it?

Plans of this magnitude are seldom carried out without trouble in the matter of personnel. The Sun King, or Seignelay acting with the royal consent, proceeded to make a mistake as grave as that which put Cartier and Roberval in double harness. The Sire de Beaujeu, a commander in the royal navy, was given charge of the ships. La Salle, as usual, wanted to have every shred of power in his own hands and he glowered unhappily over the appointment, making no effort to get on a friendly footing with the naval captain. Beaujeu developed a supercilious attitude almost from the start and conceived a low opinion of La Salle. He began to write letters to vent his views. "I believe him," speaking of La Salle, "to be a very honest man from Normandy. But they are no longer in fashion." In another epistle he declared that La Salle "had spent his life among schoolboy scribblers and savages," a curious way to describe the epic life of the explorer. "He smells of the provinces," was the final summing up.

The resentment of Beaujeu mounted when his instructions on sailing bore no information as to the destination of the expedition. This secret was being held among the King, Seignelay, and La Salle, and the latter was to give the necessary instructions later. The royal captain exploded into bitter complaints over this restriction of his power, particularly when La Salle proceeded to confound him with conflicting hints. One day he would confide to the naval commander that the ships were to sail for Canada. The next day he would contradict this and whisper that the real destination was the mouth of the Mississippi or some other part of the Gulf of Mexico. Beaujeu did not need any further proof of La Salle's instability. "There are few people," he exploded in one of his letters, "who do not believe that his brain is touched."

In the meantime the upper brackets of the personnel were being filled by young nobles who wanted a chance to distinguish themselves and by men of means who desired a share of the wealth to be ravished from His Most Christian Majesty of Spain. Several of La Salle's relatives were going to sail with him. His glum brother from Montreal, Jean Cavelier, was accompanying him to keep an eye on things. A still younger brother was to be included in the party, and a nephew named Moranget. La Salle would have been much more comfortable without them. Wherever he went he could feel the critical gaze of the Sulpician boring into his back.

The expedition sailed from La Rochelle in the summer of 1684. The smallest of the four vessels, a ketch named the *St. François,* was captured by the Spaniards off San Domingo. There were plenty of other people who came around to Beaujeu's view of La Salle's insanity when the latter was struck down with a fever at San Domingo. He went out of his head and raved wildly. Finally a limp and very ill La Salle went aboard the *Joly,* his flagship, and gave orders to drive westward into the unknown waters of the Gulf of Mexico.

2

La Salle had been unable to fix the location of the mouth of the Mississippi by scientific methods. He had found the latitude by some rough-and-ready way, but the longitude had been beyond him. This is not surprising, for navigation was in a primitive stage. The speed of a ship was still reckoned by the "Dutchman's Log," which was inaccurate. As for finding the longitude at sea, a writer of the period was frank enough to say: "I would not have any think that the longitude is to be found at sea . . . so let no seamen trouble themselves but keep a perfect account and reckoning of the way of the ship."

Having nothing definite to guide them, therefore, the navigators of the little fleet took a course considerably south of the route across the gulf which would have brought them to the three-pronged mouth of the great river. On the twenty-eighth of December the lookout man in the shrouds saw land ahead, and some time later the eager eyes of the crews rested on a long stretch of flat islands ahead, behind which lay the waters of a bay of considerable size. At first La Salle was inclined to think that they had located the Mississippi (in some of his notes he calls it the Colbert River, so apparently he had selected this as the name for it), but observations soon showed him his mistake. This was Matagorda Bay, and it lay four hundred miles south and west of their destination.

The story of this ill-fated expedition concerns Canadian history so indirectly that there is no point in recounting it here in any great detail. It is sufficient to say that one of the remaining ships, the *Aimable,* ran aground on a reef in the bay while coming in under full sail, that Captain Beaujeu returned to France in the *Joly,* and that finally the last one, the *Belle,* a small frigate, was wrecked on the river shoals.

Now the colony was cut off from the world in a strange hot land, ringed about by hostile and watchful tribes, with no prospect of early relief. The soldiers and settlers had been landed on the shore and had built for themselves a stockade which they called with a complete lack of originality Fort St. Louis. They had even started to plant crops. The country was flat and marshy and it seemed impossible that there could be gold and silver here. Herds of buffalo could be seen in the distance, but with Indians lurking in the canebrakes, none dared venture out. They lived on their stores, supplementing them with alligator meat.

La Salle passed the long days in a state of despair. For the first time he had been entrusted with a royal mission and he was failing dismally. He had stranded the hopes of the Sun King for a western empire in the muddy flats of Matagorda Bay. The people he had brought with him from France were dying of the malarial fevers. The recruits he had picked up in the West Indies with promises of a share in the wealth to be won were thoroughly disillusioned and mutinous. They included Duhaut, a man of some substance, and his colored servant L'Archevêque; Liotot, a surgeon; and a Wurtemberg German named Hiems who had been a pirate and for some reason which remains obscure was called "English Jem." These men had lost all respect for the high and mighty Frenchman who had involved them in his mad adventure and whose mistakes seemed likely to cost them their lives as well as their fortunes.

A way out of this desperate plight had to be found. This, of course, was nothing new for La Salle. He had faced such dilemmas before and always had found a solution by sheer courage and perseverance. But this time the need was particularly pressing; the royal eye would turn cold and hostile to the man who had won his confidence if he did not emerge victorious from his difficulties.

The only hope left them was to get word back to France by way of the Mississippi. La Salle set out accordingly with a party of twenty men. He was playing again his most familiar role, risking life and limb in a dangerous journey to rectify the consequences of bad luck and his own mistakes. All the actors in the final tragedy were included in the party, his Sulpician brother, his nephew Moranget, and the recruits from the West Indies.

It would have been better if he had decided to leave his nephew with the colony at Matagorda Bay. The bad temper of the youth had won him nothing but dislike and was now to lead to the tragedy which brought the explorer's life to a close. A party, which included Duhaut and Liotot as well as Moranget, was sent to recover a *cache* of food. There was a quarrel, as a result of which the leader's nephew and two others were killed in their sleep. It now seemed necessary to the assassins to dispose of La Salle as well in order to cover up their guilt.

This was accomplished two days later, when the leader set out to find what was keeping the party absent. According to a friendly member who went with him, Friar Anastase Douay, La Salle was weighted down with a sense of doom. In his account of what happened the friar says that La Salle talked of nothing but "matters of piety, grace, and predestination, enlarging on the debt he owed God." When they approached the spot where the conspirators had hidden, a volley was fired from the ambuscade and the leader dropped dead, with a bullet through his brain.

"There thou liest, great Bashaw!" cried the surgeon, emerging to stand above the victim.

The body of the indomitable explorer was stripped naked and

left in the dank reeds and bushes; and above the spot the air was soon filled with the black wings of buzzards.

Thus ended the life of René Robert Cavelier de la Salle, who had compressed into his scant forty-three years more excitement and adventure than any other man of the period. Fortunately the memory of his achievements has persisted down the years while the stories of failure and of the enmities he created have faded away. One hostile belief persists, that he was mad, that an inner demoniac fever had driven him into his excesses of energy and had led to the miscalculations which studded the record of his years. Perhaps he was mad near the end; but certainly it was a glorious madness, for even his mistakes were of the kind which keeps history glowingly alive.

3

The murderers of La Salle fell out among themselves, and English Jem killed Duhaut with three pistol bullets, after which he strutted about the camp in a scarlet coat with golden embroidery which had belonged to La Salle. The rest of the party, led by the elder Cavelier, finally reached the junction of the Father of Waters with the Arkansas. Here they found two Frenchmen who had accompanied Henri de Tonty in an abortive expedition he had led to find his lost friend. Later they found Tonty himself at Fort St. Louis.

When it was proposed to Louis XIV that he send a ship to rescue the unfortunate remnants of the venture who presumably still clung to their miserable existence on Matagorda Bay, the Sun King refused to do anything about it. The failure of the mad gamble had been a wound to his pride, and the excessive cost of it still rankled. He shook his head angrily. Hoodwinked once, he desired nothing so much as to wash his hands of everything.

But the Spanish Government was not prepared to forget the matter as easily as the French King. Ships were sent out to locate the interlopers. Although they found the wrecks of La Salle's ships, they did not spy the miserable little fort inside the belt of islands where a few desperate men and women still held on. Finally, however, an energetic leader named Alonso de Leon took a party by land along the coast and came upon the last sad traces of La Salle's folly. The walls of the fort were broken down, the belongings burned or scattered, the bodies of the last three survivors still recognizable.

A recent Indian attack had brought about this violent termination to the French invasion of the Spanish realm.

Later Alonso de Leon took his band as far north as the Rio Grande River and heard that another survivor had established himself as the ruler of an Indian tribe near Eagle Pass. They lured this resourceful individual—some believe it was English Jem—into paying them a visit and promptly made him a prisoner. He was later sent back to France. The Spanish were actuated in these efforts, not by a desire to help the survivors, but by an angry determination that not a single Frenchman should remain in the well-guarded domain of Castile in the New World.

CHAPTER XXXVI

*The Duel between Denonville and Dongan—An Act of
Treachery Makes War with the Iroquois Inevitable—
The French Seize English Forts in Hudson's Bay—
Denonville Lays the Seneca Country Waste*

1

THE period of French rule in Canada divides loosely into two
parts. The conclusion of the first is now close at hand. French
settlers, living under the firm and heavy thumb of the King,
have had a chance to develop this continent of huge lakes and stately
rivers with such interference as the Indian wars afforded and no
more than an occasional clash of arms with the English colonists.
Now the time approaches when there will be open and continuous
war with the English for the possession of the continent. The seeds
of conflict have been planted. It needs only the commencement of
war between the mother countries to set the fires ablaze. The Indians
will divide into two camps; little armies will perform miracles of
daring; the rich, fair land will know on both sides suffering and
dread and despair.

There had been always a conflict of ideas between the rivals.
The French purpose was to keep America an Indian country, their
ultimate goal a peaceful land of christianized and industrious red
men bringing the results of their trapping to French posts, ruled
benevolently but sternly from forts planted at strategic but distant
points. The English intended to make America a country for white
men. They were willing to convert the Indians and teach them some
of the ways of civilization, but what they really wanted was the land
over which the aborigines had hunted, the rivers where they had
fished, the beautiful, bounteous lakes. It had been inevitable from

the start, therefore, that the daring and adventurous French would have to fight the steady, purposeful British.

The Indians were caught between these two forces, particularly the Iroquois, who were the only red race capable of playing an important role in the struggle. The Five Nations distrusted the English but they hated the French. They sided with the Anglo-Saxons and helped them to ultimate victory. Nothing could halt the British, consolidating their gains as they moved forward, taking over and settling the land and building towns before moving the boundaries farther westward, shoving the red men back slowly but inexorably. The imperial dreams of the French, demonstrated in the exploits of La Salle and the Le Moynes and in the persistence of the Jesuit missionaries, make the Canadian story warm and exciting and as colorful as a book of folklore; but dreams dissolve in impact with sounder conceptions. Courage and élan cannot prevail against equal courage backed by logical purpose.

The clash would have come sooner if a curious undercurrent of policy had not held back the colonial governors in New England during the thirty years of the second Stuart period. Charles II had secret commitments with the French which kept the two nations at peace. James II was spending his few troubled years on the throne when Denonville came out to inaugurate a vigorous policy and found Colonel Dongan watching him warily from his post in the fast-growing town of New York. James soon got himself so embroiled with his subjects that his only hope of clinging to power lay in the support of Louis XIV. He kept sending secret instructions to Dongan to maintain the peace. A few more years would see Willian of Orange at Westminster and James living in bitter sanctuary in France. When William involved England in his continental alliance against the Sun King, the dry tinder in America would catch fire instantly. It would continue to blaze furiously for the better part of a century thereafter.

Denonville was a good soldier with thirty years of honorable service to his credit. He was a devout and conscientious man, a believer in blind obedience to the King. Less adroit than the resourceful Dongan, however, and facing a situation which demanded knowledge and facility rather than sterling rigidity, he proceeded to make disastrous errors of judgment.

2

At first the two governors played a careful game, exchanging letters which ranged in tone from cordiality to bitterness. Dongan, being heir to an Irish earldom, was a gentleman but he does not seem to have been a scholar. On one occasion, in a mood of rare amiability, he wrote to Denonville, "Beleive me it is much joy to have soe good a neighbour of soe excellent temper." In another official epistle he displayed a facetious turn and answered a charge of his gubernatorial opponent that the English traders were converting the Indians into demons by supplying them with liquor by declaring that "our rum doth as little hurt as your brandy and in the opinion of christians is much more wholesome."

While thus engaging his rival in a harmless interplay of verbal fencing, and while Barillon, the French Ambassador in London was whispering in the ear of King James that Dongan must be restrained, Denonville was making secret and ambitious plans. He realized that this was the time for the French to make themselves felt. The La Barre fiasco had alienated the western Indians. Although none of them had yet withdrawn from the alliance, they no longer placed any faith in French powers or promises. Denonville wanted to cement the tribes about the Great Lakes to the French cause by building a chain of new forts, stretching from Frontenac to Michilimackinac and ultimately to the mouth of the Mississippi. The most important location was at the waterways connecting Lake Erie with Lake Huron, because the English traders could be blocked off effectually there from the Eldorado of the northern lakes and the great West.

To carry out these broad plans, Denonville needed more soldiers and more money. Louis the Ever Patient (where Canada was concerned) groaned at the need because he was already deeply involved in the continental wars which would continue as long as he lived. He obliged, however, by sending out eight hundred more trained soldiers as well as cash and supplies running close to two hundred thousand livres.

This brought Denonville to the moment of decision. He instructed Du Lhut to establish a fort in the Detroit area and to occupy it with a garrison made up of *coureurs de bois*. Did it matter that the adventurers who took the woods against the orders of the Martinet of

Marly had been fined, imprisoned, sent to the galleys, even hanged, for their disobedience? They were needed now and so they were taken back into official favor. Du Lhut obeyed the instructions by constructing a small but strong fortress at the entrance to Lake Huron. The next step had to do with the far North, where the English were monopolizing the fur trade on Hudson's Bay. The two nations were at peace, but Denonville was convinced that the precarious position of King James kept him securely under the thumb of the French King. He decided to risk sending a force of French-Canadian militia to the bay to take the English unawares and seize all their forts and posts. The chief enterprise was to be the leading of an army into the Iroquois country to exterminate the Senecas.

Before he could put all of his bold plans into execution, however, the governor committed an error of judgment. He proceeded to make a mistake of such gravity that it has remained a blot on his memory and is generally accepted as the prime cause of a catastrophe which involved French Canada soon thereafter.

The French King had intimated during the La Barre incumbency that one way to tame the Iroquois was to capture as many of them as possible and send them to France to work as galley slaves. Louis XIV has left sayings on the pages of history which do not lend luster to his name or redound in any way to his credit as a monarch or a man; but nothing he ever said or did compares for cruelty and stupidity of conception with this particular idea. La Barre was neither astute nor discriminating but he had seen the folly of the King's suggestion. At any rate, he had done nothing about it.

The galley, propelled by great banks of oars or "sweeps," had ceased by this time to be a ship of war, but France still kept a few of them in the Mediterranean as a means of punishment for criminals. The *galiot* was a tall vessel with sails as well as banks of thirty-two oars on each side. The slaves were the most unfortunate and the most pitied of men. In earlier ages they had been chained to their benches and kept there until they died. At this stage there was some slight mitigation of their lot. The galleys would go out on cruises and the slaves would pull on the oars, three or more to each, under the lash of supervisors. The supervisors had their own beds built over part of the bench they controlled, and those who sat immediately under were in luck because they escaped the indiscriminating flail of the lash. To be "under the bench," the poor criminals toadied to their supervisors in every possible way. Between cruises the slaves would be kept in prisons, so closely packed into dark cells that they would have to sit knee to knee on damp masonry. They had the word "gal" branded on their backs, but it was generally hard to distinguish the letters because of the scars left by the whips of the galley masters.

To condemn Indians to such a fate was particularly cruel. They were accustomed to a life in the open air, and their lungs soon collapsed in the fetid atmosphere of the galleys. Having as well a racial tendency to melancholia, the most powerful of them would pine away and die in such surroundings.

Frontenac, who understood the Indians, would have brushed such instructions aside with no ceremony at all. Denonville, the earnest and obedient servant of the King, decided it was his duty to carry out the orders which had come to him.

His choice of victims was as faulty as his judgment in taking action at all. If the unfortunate braves he sent to the galleys had been prisoners of war there might have been a bare excuse, for there were only differences of degree in the barbarity with which such prisoners were treated. Instead he sent the new intendant Champigny (Meules, the playing-card moneyman, had been recalled by this time) to the north shore of Lake Ontario, where there were two villages of expatriate Iroquois engaged in hunting and fishing. By various wiles these harmless people were coaxed into the waiting maw and, when the catch had been sifted out, fifty-one able-bodied men were left in the net. Until such time as they could be placed on ships and sent off to the *galiots* of Marseilles, the puzzled and frightened natives were tied to stakes and kept in this trussed-up position for many days. Some of them died of exposure.

The unfortunate prisoners were being held in this way at Fort Frontenac when Baron la Hontan arrived to take part in the final phase of Denonville's plans, the expedition against the Senecas. He reported that it was a favorite occupation of the Christian Indians, allies of the French, to burn the fingers of the men strapped to their stakes with the bowls of their tobacco pipes.

Some of the prisoners were freed later, but a large number were sent to France. It had been in Denonville's highly unimaginative mind that what he was doing would serve as a lesson and a warning to the Five Nations. When he discovered that his action had created an entirely different reaction, stirring the Iroquois tribes to a furious desire for revenge, he wrote to the colonial minister, begging that the prisoners be sent back.

Many of the prisoners had died in their cruel captivity, but even if it had been possible to send them all back, sound and well, the damage could not be undone. The Iroquois never forgave this exhibition of treachery. With them it was an eye for an eye and a tooth for a tooth; and for every one of the harmless fishermen thus sent to a lingering death, many Canadian men and women would die in torment at the stake.

3

Denonville, earnest though he was by nature and honorable according to his lights, was still not above resorting to subterfuge in the matter of the projected attack on the British at Hudson's Bay. As the two countries were at peace, he could not proceed against them openly and so he left it to the *Compagnie du Nord* to assume the responsibility. Seeing a chance at last to undo the grievous errors which had driven Radisson and Groseilliers to London and so had led to the English occupation, the enterprising merchants who composed the French company were only too ready to take advantage of the governor's compliance.

What followed has an importance out of proportion to the significance of the event itself, for this was the introduction to the pages of Canada's history of one of her truly great sons, Pierre le Moyne d'Iberville. He was third in the family in point of years but already he was recognized as outstanding among the many tall, brave sons of that equally brave father, Charles le Moyne. Born in 1661, Pierre was now twenty-five years of age and had spent his life on the wilderness trails and in the maritime service of France. It is unfortunate that so little is known about this remarkable man who was soon to demonstrate his ability to command successfully both on land and sea. To present him as he was in the flesh, to make him come alive by anecdote and story, would be a grateful task for any narrator of those stirring events. This much can be repeated: that his brief career was filled with such amazing exploits that the luster of his name would have shone with the bravest figures of French history had they not been enacted in the obscurity of an overlooked colonial backwater.

It had been decided that the command of the expedition should be in the hands of the Chevalier de Troyes of Montreal, which lent something of official sanction to the effort. The Chevalier de Troyes was a good soldier but he dropped into the background when from the ranks there emerged the figure of the daring and inspired Iberville.

In all honesty it is impossible to describe this beloved paladin of New France. Over the years stories have grown up about him and bits of description have accumulated which have served as a portrait of the man; but it must be asserted that most of this, if not actually all, has no basis in fact. It has been assumed that he was strongly built, which seems a reasonable conclusion, and also that he wore his hair long as his father had done before him; and this also seems within the range of probabilities because the close cropping of hair had not become general then and a woodsman venturing out into the wilds in a wig would be an absurdity. Perhaps, then, the gallant Iberville had ringlets falling to his shoulders. This is a pleasant assumption; but whether his hair glistened like ripe corn in the sun or inclined instead to the dark coloring more general among men of his race is open territory for personal preferences.

With Iberville were two of his brothers, Jacques de Ste. Hélène, his senior by two years, and Paul de Maricourt, who was two years younger. Ste. Hélène was destined to an early death in the service of his country, and so it is impossible to make any comparisons among these elder brothers. Maricourt seems to have been quite different from the vivid and outstanding Iberville. He was already a rare woodsman, although he had not yet acquired his nickname among the Indians of Little-Bird-Always-in-Motion. One assumes from this picturesque term that Maricourt lacked the stature of his better-known brothers and that he possessed perhaps a delicacy of physique which would set him apart from them.

The expedition left early in the spring of 1686. It had been decided, most wisely, to take the overland route to the bay, that pet project of the unlucky and unstable Radisson. The party proceeded up the Ottawa River, passed Lake Temiscaming and Lake Abitibi, and then proceeded north on the Abitibi River to strike at the nearest of the English posts, Fort Hayes, which lay about equidistant between the two other posts covering the southern portion of James Bay, Fort Rupert on the east and Fort Albany on the west. If they had sailed from Quebec, the arrival of their ship in the northern reaches of the bay would have been detected quickly and all element of surprise would have been lost. As it was, they emerged from the desolation of this unknown muskeg country like the men of Israel under Joshua surprising the city of Ai from the impassable hills or, to cast on into the future, Wolfe debouching on the Plains of Abraham.

There were sixteen men in the four-bastioned stockade of Fort Hayes and they were sleeping snugly in their beds when the eighty Frenchmen materialized out of darkness in the night attack. Troyes led his main force against the gate, which he proceeded to belabor with a battering-ram made from the trunk of a tree. What made the victory easy, however, was the fact that Iberville and his two brothers and a squad of the boldest French Canadians had climbed over one of the side walls and were already in possession of the compound when the first crash of the ram split the air. The English came rushing out to see what convulsion of nature had thus disturbed their slumbers, to find Iberville and his men scowling at them over leveled muskets.

Before news of this bloodless triumph could circulate along the swampy and dismal shores of the Great Bay by that form of forest telepathy which has never been fully explained, the jubilant French force had covered the forty leagues eastward to Fort Rupert. The same tactics were employed: a night attack, a party scaling the walls and exploding a grenade down the chimney of the blockhouse where the garrison slept, a break through the main gate at the same time. Iberville had been assigned a still more daring part of the operation. A vessel lay at anchor near the fort, and it was seen to be highly essential that it should not get away to carry the alarm to the remaining English post. The daring Pierre led a small party over the side of the ship. They found the sentry asleep and killed him, then gave short shrift to such other members of the crew as came up through the hatch to investigate. The rest of the crew, imprisoned in the hold, finally surrendered. A big fish was caught in this casting of the net, none other than Governor Bridgar, who commanded on the bay for the Gentlemen Adventurers.

The capture of Fort Albany, which lay to the west where the river of that name flowed into the ice-clogged waters of the bay, was a different matter. Somehow the garrison, which consisted of thirty men under the command of a resolute agent named Sargent, had heard what was afoot. Lacking the advantage of surprise which had made their successes relatively easy, the Frenchmen had to adopt more conventional methods. From the two forts already in their hands they brought ten cannon in the vessel which Iberville had captured and which he now commanded. The guns were mounted on a hill overlooking the fort. The fusillade directed at the fort from this protected position was so deadly that in the matter of an hour the stockade was in flames and the garrison had taken refuge in a cellar. The white flag was hoisted and terms of surrender were arranged between Troyes and the crestfallen Sargent.

The part the Le Moyne brothers had played in this remarkably successful raid was recognized in the appointment of Maricourt to remain in command of the captured forts while the rest of the party returned to Montreal in triumph.

The news of the raid shook London, and there was such clamor for reprisal that the submissive attitude of King James could not hold things in check. King Louis had to send a special envoy to London to assist Barillon, his Ambassador, in countering the angry demands made for the restitution of the forts and recompense for the losses sustained. A neutrality pact was signed finally at Whitehall. Whether the English had any intention of keeping it cannot be judged by what followed, but the French King soon made it clear that such was not his purpose.

4

Denonville had made Irondequoit Bay on the south shore of Lake Ontario the rendezvous for the forces he now intended to lead against the Senecas. He arrived there himself with four hundred canoes and two thousand men. By the greatest of good luck he reached the bay on the same day as his Indian allies from the north and west. They came four hundred strong, accompanied by a band of *coureurs de bois* led by three of the bravest Frenchmen in the West, Du Lhut, La Durantaye, and Henri Tonty.

The Senecas had been marked down as the victims of this great drive because they were the most numerous and powerful of the Five Nations and, at the moment, the most belligerent; more obdurate even than the Mohawks, who had once opposed the French with the greatest determination. There was another reason, however, which focused hostility on this single nation. Dark rumors had spread about the Senecas. Not only had more Frenchmen and their allies been burned to death in the main village of the tribe, but the place was reputed to be the scene of strange orgies. Men whispered about the dark magic practiced there, calling the village Babylon, Sodom, or Gomorrah. Witchcraft of the most foul and devilish description

was carried out in dark temples of infamy. The Senecas must therefore be wiped out first. Perhaps their fate would teach the rest of
the Iroquois tribes to bury the hatchet for good and consent to live
on terms of friendship with the rest of the world.

The strength of the invaders was so great that the Senecas, after
one unsuccessful attempt to ambush the advancing Frenchmen, retreated in panic toward the east, taking their families with them
and such food supplies as they could hastily gather. Before running
away, however, they burned the main village about which such un-
savory stories had been told. Even if it had been left standing, it
would have disappointed the least avid of the invaders. It had occupied the crest of a hill and it was neither very large nor very strong;
a tawdry affair of tanbark and logs. Where were the temples in
which the medicine men had performed their dreadful rites? Was
this the scene of the orgies in which the strange and fierce tribesmen
indulged?

All the French found were the blackened remnants of small lodgings and the mask of a medicine man attached to a bearskin. One
recorder, not to be robbed of his chance for an effect, speaks of the
many snakes slithering about the ruins and over the graves of dead
Senecas, believing them to be evidence of the evil which had existed
there.

One thing was certain: the valleys and hills of the Seneca country
were bright with warm sunshine and covered with great fields of
maize. About the stalks of the corn there crept, not snakes and
rodents, but the thick vines of the yellow pumpkin. There would
have been a bountiful harvest if the green fields had been left to the
ripening sun, but the French spent ten days of backbreaking labor
in cutting down the corn and burning the fields. Three other villages
were located and burned. Convinced then that the Senecas had been
taught a lesson they would never forget, the invaders turned and
marched to Niagara, where a fort of considerable size and strength
was built.

The Senecas did not forget. The other four nations shared in the
hatred inspired by the French attack. Nor had the Iroquois forgotten the seizure of the harmless fishermen on the Bay of Quinte, some
of whom were still tugging at their oars under the lash of slave
masters. They had never forgotten, it might be added, the first
sight of a white man vouchsafed their fathers: Champlain stepping
out from the ranks of the Hurons in his glistening breastplate and

bobbing plumes with his strange new weapon, the terrible musket. While Denonville set his men to work at Niagara, the gloomy interior of the council house at Onondaga echoed with the talk of the chiefs assembled there to decide upon measures of reprisal.

5

The demolition of the Seneca villages was followed by a period of indecision. Denonville was realizing that his problem had not been solved by the partial victory he had scored. Canada was faced with a famine. There had been no furs delivered for two years, and the revenues of the colony were at a low ebb. Finally it was obvious to the blindest of observers that the Iroquois were hatching schemes of revenge. Even the fact that the wary and active Dongan had been recalled by the British Government and that a new governor, Sir Edmund Andros, had been sent out to take charge of all the Anglo-Saxon possessions in the New World did not bring Denonville any sense of security or relief. He began to write the King in a state of panic, begging for more troops.

The Iroquois, deep in their plans for retaliation, played a waiting game and even dispatched some envoys to Fort Frontenac to discuss the patching up of the broken peace. Even if they had been sincere in these advances (and it soon became clear that they were not), there was no possibility of a satisfactory outcome. A remarkable Indian chief makes his appearance on the scene at this juncture for the purpose of defeating any peace moves.

He was a Huron from Michilimackinac and his name was Kondiaronk, which meant the Rat. There was nothing of the rodent in his nature, however. He was a good leader in war or peace, as wise as any white statesman and as crafty as the most Machiavellian diplomat trained in the wiles and guiles of European chancellories. Kondiaronk had one fixed purpose, to preserve the lives of the scattered remnants of the Huron people who existed, humbly and miserably, about the trading posts and missions at the junction of the Great Lakes. He knew, this wily old chief, that peace between the French and the Iroquois might mean his people would then be exposed to the full fury of Iroquois designs. He recalled, as did all the tribal leaders in the West, the silence of La Barre when the Five Nations, speaking with the tongue of Big Mouth, had declared their intention of making war on the French allies.

It is to the pages of La Hontan, that busy but useful gossip, that one must turn for the details of what the Rat proceeded to do in his determination to prevent a truce. He went promptly into action when the news reached him that the envoys from the Five Nations were on their way to Fort Frontenac. Waylaying them near La Famine, he killed one of the chiefs with the first volley and took the rest prisoners. The Iroquois, stunned by the unexpectedness of the attack, protested that they were on their way to propose terms of peace.

The Rat then staged a scene in which he professed chagrin and anger at the French for deceiving him. Denonville, he declared, had informed him, Kondiaronk, that a war party was approaching and had sent him out to attack them.

Kondiaronk released all of the party but one, who was to be held as a hostage. "Go back!" he said to the rest in effect. "Go back to your people and tell them of the treachery of Onontio."

The Iroquois, nearly all of whom had suffered wounds from the fire which the Rat's men had poured into them, turned their canoes about and set off for home. It was clear they believed what the wily chief had told them.

The Rat watched them go with an expression of triumph on his bronzed and wrinkled face. "I have killed the peace!" he declared.

The remaining prisoner was taken back to Michilimackinac and handed over to the French commandant there. The latter, acting on the advice of Kondriaronk, who believed in being thorough, had the captive executed publicly by a firing squad. To make sure that the Five Nations learned of this further example of French perfidy, the Rat secretly released an Iroquois prisoner in the camp and turned him loose with enough food and a supply of powder and shot to take him back to his own land.

Kondiaronk sat himself down in the shade of his wigwam, from which he could look out across the waters of Lake Huron toward that fair country where once his people had lived in ease and happiness. He was well content with what he had done. The war would go on and the brunt of it would be borne by the French. For the time being the few remaining Hurons could exist in peace.

An event occurred later in the year which was to prove highly disastrous, in the long run, to the French cause. Two days before Christmas, having seen his kingdom invaded by troops under William of Orange who were received as deliverers by the English people, James II stole down the river from London in the darkness of night. Dropping the Great Seal in the water in a fit of spleen, the unpopular King left the country forever. Britain made William and his English consort Mary (a daughter of James) joint rulers of the kingdom. It was inevitable that William, being the architect of the European coalition against France, would involve Great Britain in his foreign policy; and so it followed very soon that active warring for supremacy in America began in full earnest.

Denonville realized what this meant, and his importunings for further assistance took on a frantic note. In one letter he begged the King to send him four thousand troops, believing that with such strength he could settle the issue with a single stroke. Louis was in no mood, however, to grant such demands as this.

The King, in fact, had lost faith in Denonville. As a governor he had been on the best of terms with Saint-Vallier and with Champigny, the intendant. The love feast which had succeeded the bitter bickerings of Frontenac and Duchesneau had been grateful to the harassed monarch but it had not compensated for the conviction now generally held that Denonville was not the man to deal with an emergency such as this. His intentions were good, but he lacked the will and insight for command. Designed by nature for subordinate roles, his judgment had faltered at critical moments.

On May 31 of the following year, 1689, his recall was decided upon and a letter was dispatched to Canada, summoning him home. It did not arrive soon enough to spare Denonville from sharing in the great catastrophe which descended upon the colony as a result, partially, of the mistakes he had made.

CHAPTER XXXVII

The Grim Story of Iroquois Revenge—The Massacre at Lachine—Denonville's Weakness

1

LACHINE had changed since it had been occupied by the young La Salle. Settlers had moved in and many houses had sprung up along the shore of Lake St. Louis. It had become, indeed, the most populous outpost of Montreal. The people who occupied the small whitewashed houses with their high-peaked roofs were landowners and, in the main, prosperous. A surgeon had taken up his quarters in the little village; the curé paid regular visits. Montreal, which was now growing out of all recognition and claimed a population of two thousand, talked of the day when it would spread out from its narrow confines and envelope Lachine. In the meantime, to provide protection for the south shore of the island, there were three garrisoned stockades in close proximity, La Présentation, Rémy, and Roland.

The night of August 4, 1689, was hot and close. The good people of Lachine, before retiring for the night, studied the black clouds above them and averred there would be trouble before morning. Perhaps they shuddered at the same time, for in their minds there was always something analogous between storm signals and the black cloud of fear which hung over all of New France. The storm broke some hours before dawn. It swept across Lake St. Louis with heavy claps of thunder to announce its coming, and almost in a moment there was a pounding of hailstones on the snug little houses. Householders roused themselves and stumbled about in the dark to see that everything was closed. Some of them were up and about, therefore, when there came to their ears a sound foreign to the sharp cracking of the thunder and infinitely more terrible, the high, maniacal screech of the Iroquois battle cry. The lane running crookedly between the rows of houses was filled with naked warriors armed to the teeth, their heads close-shaved, their faces smeared with ceremonial paint.

Fifteen hundred warriors had taken advantage of the storm to cross Lake St. Louis and had arrived on the heels of the first downpour of hail, more terrible by far than any catastrophe that nature could have loosed on the unsuspecting countryside. It was said later by some of the survivors that many of the heads of families, knowing that help could not reach them in time, turned their guns first on their wives and children to save them from a much worse fate, and that when the maddened invaders broke into the houses they found that death had been before them in the dark. Those who died in this way and the many who were butchered in the first onslaught were lucky. After a few minutes of indiscriminate slaughter, during which men and women were cut down by knives and tomahawks and the brains of children were dashed out against doorframes and bedposts, the attacking braves gave thought to a still greater pleasure than this orgy of vengeful killing. In all the villages of the Finger Lakes the stakes had been raised and the fagots piled. Prisoners must be provided for the nights of torture which always followed victory. The people of Lachine, devout, kindly, and industrious, must supply this need of victims.

Three miles along the crooked road, on the way to Montreal, was an encampment of two hundred regular soldiers who had been sent out from France to aid in the defense of the colony. By an unfortunate twist of fate the officer in charge had gone to Montreal the evening before to attend a reception for Denonville, who had just arrived there. The officer's name was Subercase and he was a bold and resourceful soldier, as subsequent events would show. If he had been with his men when the blow fell, he would have hurried to the assistance of the unfortunate people and there might have been a different story to tell.

The camp was aroused at four o'clock by the ominous boom of a cannon from one of the three forts. This could mean one thing only, that Indians were on the warpath. A subordinate officer gave orders for the men to dress and arm for action. Almost immediately there was a second proof of trouble. Through the rain, which still fell with fury, came the drenched and muddy figure of a survivor crying to them hoarsely that all the furies of hell were loose in the woods and along the shores. The man in charge waved him on to carry the alarm to Montreal.

More fugitives arrived in a very few minutes, furiously pursued by a band of naked warriors. When the Iroquois saw the soldiers they turned immediately and ran back in the direction of Lachine.

The first survivor reached Montreal as fast as his stumbling legs could carry him over the six miles of muddy road. Wild fear swept the town at the news he brought. Subercase lost no time in getting back to his command, but several hours had passed when he reached the camp. The first fury of the storm had abated and light was beginning to show through the drizzle; although the sun, which had risen on so many scenes of horror and bloodshed and might be expected to have become indifferent, seemed reluctant to face the evidence of what this dreadful night had brought about. Subercase was incredulous when he found that his men had waited for his return and had done nothing to aid the victims of the Iroquois attack. Men from the three forts had joined them and many settlers from other sections had armed themselves and were beginning to reach them through the woods, ready to do what they could.

Had it been cowardice which held the troops from rushing into action or a disciplinary sense pounded into them by years of service that nothing should be done without his orders? Drawing his sword, Subercase shouted an angry command to follow him to Lachine.

2

The most terrible of sights is a community after it has been ravaged by fire and sword. At Lachine the horror had been multiplied by the incredible ferocity of the invaders and the circumstances under which the destruction had been carried out. Unable to wait for a first taste of the delights of torture, the Iroquois warriors had set up stakes and with unwonted haste (it was customary to prolong the victim's end as long as possible) had done to death some of the prisoners with the usual fiendish ingenuity. When the belated rescue party reached the scene, they found the stakes still standing, all of them tenanted by broken bodies which had once been men and women. None of the most revolting rites had been neglected, even to the slashing from the bodies of strips of flesh to be enjoyed later in cannibalistic rites. An effort had been made to destroy the houses by fire, and some of them still smoldered at the same time that water dripped from their sagging eaves. To enter any of those which were still standing was to suffer a shock never to be forgotten, for the mothers and their children had been dragged from their pitiably useless hiding places and killed near the hearths, where tidy brooms and clean copper utensils still occupied their usual places.

One of the survivors, the surgeon who had been located in the settlement, emerged from his sanctuary in the woods to meet Subercase and his men. He was soaked with water and blood and his face was white with the horrors he had witnessed and from which he had so miraculously escaped. The war party, he told them, had left Lachine but had gone no more than a mile and a half farther down the shore, where they had stopped in the shelter of a screen of trees. He had another piece of information to give which caused the trained officer to nod his head with new confidence and satisfaction. The Iroquois had delayed the destruction of the houses until each had been searched. A large store of brandy had been uncovered and all of it had been gulped down before the devil's work had been resumed. The halt behind the cover of trees had been caused by the torpor which had overtaken the Iroquois braves.

Subercase realized that this opening, in which no doubt he saw the hand of Providence, must be seized at once. Such a chance would never come again, certainly. But he had no illusions as to the odds he would face. From all reports he had received, he knew that the enemy were out in larger numbers than ever before and that, when roused, they would fight with sullen fury. He did not hesitate. He decided to take the risk, and to his satisfaction he found that his men were willing to gamble their lives in an effort to rescue the unfortunate prisoners.

At this moment, however, the Chevalier de Vaudreuil arrived from Montreal with orders from the governor. No unnecessary risks were to be taken. The forces still intact must remain on the defensive and retain the power to protect the sections which had not yet suffered from attack.

Unnecessary risks? Subercase and his men had never known of a risk which seemed more necessary than to attack the marauding braves while they lolled in drunken stupor. He stormed at Denonville's envoy and demanded to be allowed to proceed with his plan. Did Denonville know, he asked, that over one hundred white men and women were in Iroquois hands and would be herded back to the villages of the tribes for death at the stake? The governor could not have known, he contended, of the fortunate circumstances which made this moment the best for a counterattack. Vaudreuil stood firmly on the ground that the orders he bore were from the highest authority in the colony and must be obeyed.

After a stormy altercation Subercase gave in. With despairing unwillingness he ordered his men to return to the shelter of the forts. The opportunity had been lost.

For two days, while the troops under Subercase fretted in the inactivity imposed upon them and Denonville kept his considerable forces behind the new palisades which had been built around Montreal, the revengeful Iroquois roamed the countryside, capturing new victims and burning all the houses and barns. Depredations were carried out as far distant as twenty miles, an indication of the bravado now animating the invaders.

Finally the terror was lifted from the island. The Iroquois took to their canoes, their terrified captives with them, and paraded contemptuously up and down the river within sight of the three forts. They raised their paddles in the air and shouted in derision, "Onontio! Onontio!" and then screeched loudly that they had paid back the governor for the deception he had practiced on them.

Before turning for the other shore of the St. Lawrence, they paused to give vent to ninety loud shouts, one for each prisoner in their hands. This was the usual practice of returning war parties, as has already been stated. The grim watchers behind the stockade walls counted the exultant shouts and were convinced that the men of the Five Nations had been careless in their estimate. It was believed that no fewer than one hundred and twenty victims were still in enemy hands.

3

The scene now shifts across the St. Lawrence. For many years the christianized members of the Iroquois tribes had lived in mission settlements across the river from Montreal. Now they were settled finally in a section which had been given the name of Caughnawaga. They had always been so loyal and peaceable that the Jesuit recorders had gleaned much of their most gratifying evidence from among them. It was at Caughnawaga that the brave and honestly sincere Chief Garakontie had lived his last years, dying there finally in the arms of his great friend, Father de Lamberville. The high cross which had been raised over his grave still stood.

The chief interest in the community, however, rose from the fact that Catherine Tekahkwitha had spent most of her life there. She was like a character from a story of high romance, this daughter of a Mohawk father and an Algonquin mother; a slender girl of such grace and beauty that the English called her the Lily of the Mohawks, and of such a devout nature that in Canada she was known as the Genevieve of New France. She had not been dead long and her memory was green in all minds.

Caughnawaga lies almost directly across Lake St. Louis from Lachine. Just below, behind a projection of land into which the island of St. Bernard fits snugly, is Châteauguay. It was to Châteauguay that the Iroquois went on crossing the river, and so it was close to the home of their christianized kin that they paused for a further demonstration of their triumph and contempt. They had decided not to wait any longer for another taste of the fruits of victory. Pitching their camp so close to the line of the shore that the watchers on Montreal Island could see the blaze of their fires through the trees of the island, they spent a wild night around the torture stakes, killing women and children as well as men, with furious abandon. The watchers knew the meaning of the flickering lights; they were aware that the gentle and blameless people of Lachine were dying in slow torment. It lasted all through the night, and then the fires died down and the watchers knew that the orgies were ending in heavy, brutal sleep.

Whether a rescue could have been carried out at this stage is very doubtful. To attempt a crossing of the river would have been a great hazard in itself and might have resulted in such heavy losses that the Iroquois, whose casualties had been slight, might have come back in triumph to attack Montreal. The one good chance to rescue the prisoners had been lost when Subercase was forced to give up.

Nothing but a miracle would have brought success at this late stage. Close to the shore where the torture fires burned lay the bones of the Genevieve of New France, and many stories had been told of miracles which had come to pass at her grave. People watching from the safety of the other shore prayed that a miracle might happen now to save the cringing victims from further torment. But a far different kind of miracle was needed, a miracle of brave and audacious leadership; and this the French commander of the moment could not supply.

Denonville's decision had been made with great reluctance. A man of personal bravery, he was slow in making up his mind and far from inspired in his judgment. It might be said that he had lived his life for this one moment when a splendid and audacious move on his part would have enriched the history of the land with another stirring tale. But there was neither splendor nor audacity in the spiritual and mental equipment of the slow Denonville. He decided against any action which might be counted of ill-considered boldness, and so the men of New France were condemned to watch the torture fires of the Iroquois from the safety of the north shore.

It is said that the events of these few terrible days preyed on his mind and saddened the last years of his life. On his return to France he was given a post at court as governor of the children of the King's legitimate sons. The nature of his employment was not intended as a reflection on his record in Canada, nor does it seem to have been accepted in that light.

CHAPTER XXXVIII

The Beginning of the English Wars—Four Titans and a Heroine

1

SOME men are born for emergencies. They are not particularly successful when life flows easily and placidly. They are prone to display faulty judgment and almost certain to get at odds with their fellows; but when a crisis arises and courageous leadership is needed, they come into their own. Such a man was Frontenac. It must be conceded that during his first term as governor of Canada he had not been successful in many respects. But now adverse winds were blowing in the colony and its very existence was at stake, and it was to the old lion that the King instinctively turned.

Frontenac had been existing on the fringe of the court. The King had not found a post for him but had granted him a pension of thirty-five hundred livres. It was possible for Frontenac to live on this income, but most certainly it did not allow for ostentation. His rooms would be few in number and of no distinction, and he would not be able to afford more in his household than a valet and a cook. It was probably a dingy-looking old man, the very picture of an ex-official out of favor, who had haunted the anterooms of Versailles and chatted with minor officials. Certainly there would be no gold lace on his sleeves and no clean white plume in his hat.

He was seventy years old when summoned back to the presence after these years of neglect. There was still a glint in the Frontenac eye, however, and a hint of the former pride in the firmness of his step. The King himself was in his fifties and had become decidedly plump. There was no shadow between them this time. Even if there had been any truth in the story about the count and La Montespan, she had lost her hold on the royal affections some years before and had been replaced by a ripe and intelligent beauty named Madame de Maintenon. The new favorite had been governess to the brood of children La Montespan had borne the King, and it was generally believed that she had demanded marriage as the price of her compliance. The royal widower had yielded. He was a little subdued in manner now and, in many respect at least, under the plump white Maintenon thumb.

"I send you back to Canada," said the King to the old count, "where I expect you will serve me as well as you did before. I ask for nothing more."

No word had reached France at this time of the Lachine disaster, but it was recognized that the colony was in serious straits. Plans were discussed and it was decided that an offensive move would be the best defense. The drive should be made, in the opinion of the monarch, against the English and not against the Iroquois. William of Orange, now seated on the throne of England, was at war with Louis, and the latter burned with desire to find vulnerable chinks in his opponent's armor. Albany and New York and the patroon country along the Hudson had been Dutch territory and were therefore highly valued by the great Dutch leader. If the French could drive down the Hudson and capture New York, the fast-growing New England colonies would be hedged into a small corner of the continent with no outlets save by sea. There were other good reasons for the plan, the main one being that New York Harbor was open all year round and was therefore of high strategic importance.

The plan decided upon was that two warships would be sent out to attack New York from the sea at the same time that Frontenac organized the strength of Canada for a drive down the Hudson. The King saw no insurmountable difficulties in the carrying out of this military coup and felt as though Manhattan were already in his pocket.

It should have been as apparent to the optimistic monarch as it was undoubtedly to the realistic soldier who would have to carry out the most difficult part that the success of the plan would depend on a miracle of improvisation. It would take genius on the part of Frontenac to create an army of sufficient strength out of the ragtag and bobtail of military resources in French Canada. And what of the Iroquois while this magnificent turning movement was in operation? They were overrunning the St. Lawrence as it was. Could they be expected to return obligingly to their villages while Frontenac proceeded to undermine their very existence?

Such were the instructions, however, with which the old man of seventy set sail for Canada to begin his second term of office. Knowing the reasons for the wide-open breach between French Canada and the Iroquois, he had demanded that the surviving Indians in the slave ships be sent back with him. From the malodorous benches of the galleys, therefore, came thirteen bent and sick men of copper hue, all who were still alive. They were bathed and fed and dressed in the gayest of French garb. They were treated with great respect, given long fancy pipes and all the tobacco they would need, and then turned over to the governor as honored guests. Frontenac, with his instinctive knowledge of the Indian nature, made much of them in the hope of turning them into ambassadors of good will among their own people. As he had a remarkable way with him, he did succeed in establishing friendly relations with one of the thirteen, a Cayuga chief named Ourehaoué. On arriving at Quebec, where he was greeted with wild acclaim, Frontenac lodged Ourehaoué in the château with him and completely turned the chief's head with attentions and flattery.

The old governor heard for the first time now of the Lachine massacre. He realized from the panicky reports brought to him that the colony would have to fight for its existence and that the King's pet enterprise would have to be laid aside for the time being. Going up the river to Montreal, he found Denonville still there, sitting disconsolately in the ashes of defeat, saddened and unhappy and incapable of making any constructive plans. The superseded officer, in fact, had been piling mistake on mistake and had just carried out one colossal blunder which was designed to fill his successor with resentment. On demands from the Iroquois he had dismantled Fort Frontenac, leaving its smoking walls and the highly strategic country surrounding it to the marauding Indian bands.

Although Frontenac found the colony in this sorry plight, the indomitable veteran decided on an offensive campaign as the best means of retrieving lost ground. He organized three forces and sent them down into English territory in the dead of the winter which followed. One was to strike Albany or Schenectady, the second was to invade New Hampshire, the third Maine.

And so began the long series of wars with the English. Inasmuch as the struggle must be reserved for a second volume, the story of the first broad phase of the French regime has been brought to a conclusion. The narrator confesses, however, to a reluctance to leave the scene. There are still threads of narrative waiting to be tied into place, still much that the reader who has progressed thus far might like to know before closing the volume. This has been, above everything else, a story of people, of the men and women who created Canada in the face of such odds, nourishing the soil with their blood, lending to the early annals the fascination of a spirited gaiety, an instinctive touch of romance.

Many of the greatest of them were still on the scene. Frontenac, the hot-tempered old lion, had returned and with his back to the wall would win his best-deserved bays. Bishop Laval, patient and restrained in retirement but still burning with zeal, had many years still to live in the twilight. Nine of the ten Le Moynes were in the front line and the varied and magnificent achievements of Iberville and Bienville would soon be reached; almost with the turn of a page. Du Lhut, Durantaye, Perrot, Tonty were still holding in the West the outposts of an empire. On the southern shore of the St. Lawrence in a rude blockhouse there lived a delicate child just emerging into her teens whose name was Madeleine de Verchères.

At the risk of overlapping the full recital which will begin in another volume, it seems fitting to end with a few scenes about the greatest of these surviving figures. Some stories will follow, therefore, about four Titans and one remarkable little heroine.

2

October 16, 1690

An underofficer whose name has been omitted in all the records came ashore early in the morning under a flag of truce. Four canoes put out from Lower Town and the subaltern was taken ashore. Before landing him, however, the Frenchmen blindfolded him with such thoroughness that all of the beautiful October sunlight and the view of the picturesque capital on the heights were blotted out completely. Stumbling at the quay, he found himself taken tightly by both arms and led forward. A wild-goose chase up and down the town followed. He was taken through the narrowest and roughest of the streets and forced to climb obstructions which had been placed deliberately in his way, coming at last to Mountain Street, where barricades blocked off the heights above. By the time they reached the Château of St. Louis, the bewildered messenger may have been of the opinion that Quebec was a maze of defenses which could be defended easily against attack; unless, of course, he had expected something of the kind and was not surprised.

While this game of blindman's buff, as one recorder has called it, was being enacted ashore, the Basin of Quebec swarmed with English vessels; thirty-four of them, of all sizes and descriptions, geared for war and carrying twenty-three hundred men. Never had the fortress faced such danger before.

The successful attacks which Frontenac had launched against the New England colonies, resulting in the destruction of sleeping towns with atrocities different only in extent from the tragedy of Lachine, had roused the British to a decision that the French must be subdued once and for all time. A land force had marched from New York and Connecticut, joining with a band of Iroquois and moving up to Lake Champlain with the purpose of attacking Montreal. In the meantime the state of Massachusetts had equipped a fleet at a cost of fifty thousand pounds (which had to be raised by loans) to attack Quebec simultaneously by sea.

The command of the naval expedition had been entrusted to Sir William Phips, who was acclaimed in the colonies (he proudly acknowledged it himself) the greatest of self-made men. He had been born on what Cotton Mather called a "despicable plantation on the River Kennebec," one of the last of twenty-six children. First a sheepherder and then a ship's carpenter, Phips had grown into a tall and unusually strong man, determined to get ahead although handicapped by his lack of education. He had the great fists of a bucko mate and the courage to use them against any odds. Married to a widow of some means, he had promised to get her a "fair brick house" in Boston and had done so as the result of an extraordinary adventure. Having heard stories, from sources which seemed impeccable, of a Spanish treasure ship sunk on a reef off an island in the Bahamas, he interested some Englishmen of wealth in fitting out a vessel to search for the lost gold. He located the island on his second attempt; and there, caught in deep water between sunken reefs, was the wreck of a large ship. For two months divers worked continuously over the bulk, bringing up thirty-four tons of gold and silver, "peeces of eight and litters of sows and dow boys," to the value of over three hundred thousand pounds. Out of this unexpected showering of fortune Phips had secured only sixteen thousand pounds (having promised to recompense the crew from his personal share, if necessary, and scrupulously adhering to his word), but as compensation a knighthood and a fair brick house at the corner of Charter and Salem streets in Boston, not to mention the praise of a poet who sang:

> England will boast him too, whose able mind,
> Impelled by angels did those treasures find.

He had become governor of Massachusetts since this fortunate speculation and had fulfilled the duties of the office like a well-intentioned bull in a china shop, continuing, nevertheless, to hold such a share of the esteem of the citizens that they considered Quebec as good as taken when he assumed command of the naval forces.

The subaltern sent ashore by Phips was not freed from the blindfold until he stood in the reception room of the château. It was an unexpected sight which greeted him. The aging governor, an actor to his fingertips, had arranged things to impress the messenger in the stately room with its dark paneling and long embrasured windows. It is probable that the eyes of the subaltern, blinking in the sudden light, saw nothing but the people gathered there. They were grouped about their leader, wearing coats which flared out so stiffly from their waists that the use of whalebone, that great aid to feminine attire, could safely be surmised. There was no other hint of the feminine, however, about these fierce and proud men. It might have seemed that they had hackles about their necks instead of white collars of the finest lace. Their sashes were of the richest silk velours, but the function they served was to support swords which were ready to leap from the scabbards at the smallest pretext. Under any other circumstance an onlooker would have been impressed with the beauty of the setting and the mingling of three major colors— red, white, and blue—to designate the parts of Canada from which each man came.

The majestic mien of the governor offset the evidences he showed of old age: the white of his shaggy brows, the lines in his face, and the corpulence of his waist. He kept his eyes on the messenger with the hauteur of an aging lion confronted by a jackal.

It may be assumed that this particular officer had been selected for two reasons. The first was to demonstrate the belief held in New England that one man was as good as another and a subaltern as worthy of respect as an admiral. The second was the capacity of this particular underling to face a situation with aplomb. At any rate, he refused to be put out of countenance. Saluting the governor with a flourish, he looked about him at the assembled company with a not at all respectful eye before handing a letter to Count Frontenac. If the governor read English (which was very unlikely), he refused to acknowledge it. The letter was turned over to an interpreter.

It was a demand for the surrender of Quebec, couched in far from gracious terms; in fact, the kind of communication which could have been expected from a man as completely self-made as stout Sir William. He insisted on the relinquishment "of your forts and castles undemolished, and the King's and other stores unimbezzled, together with a surrender of all your persons and estates to my dispose. . . . Your answer positive in an hour returned by your own trumpet, with the return of mine, is required upon the peril that will arise."

As the interpreter finished the letter, the English subaltern drew a watch from his pocket, pointed a caloused forefinger at the time, and then handed the timepiece to the governor.

"It is now ten o'clock," he declared. "The answer must be had before eleven."

There was an angry clamor in the room at this, and one voice demanded loudly that, inasmuch as Sir William Phips was a pirate (this referred to an attack he had made on Acadia), the messenger should be hanged in full view of the English fleet.

The governor raised a hand for silence. He said in a calm voice that he would not keep the messenger waiting as long as an hour for his answer. The English colonists, he declared, were no better than rebels against their rightful King, and it was the intention of his master, the King of France, to replace King James on the British throne by force of arms. "Even if I had a mind to accept these far from gracious conditions," he continued, "would these brave gentlemen give their consent?"

The messenger asked if the governor would put his refusal in writing.

"No!" cried Frontenac in a voice which had suddenly lost all graciousness, and throwing the communication from Phips to the floor. "I will answer your general only by the mouths of my cannon."

The carefully staged scene came to an end. The subaltern was blindfolded a second time and he was escorted with the same roundabout pretenses to the waterfront where his boat was waiting.

The struggle which ensued was to prove a far from palatable but a highly useful lesson to the English colonists. Convinced of the justice of their cause—for the ravaging of their frontiers by fire and sword had been unprovoked—and obsessed with the belief that men of free democratic training could not be withstood, they had planned the campaign with all the carelessness that such optimism breeds. There was no leader of much military experience with either the land forces or the fleet. Sir William Phips might be brave and bluff and lucky (they seem to have counted on his proverbial good fortune), but he had no knowledge of naval tactics. He now found himself faced with the same situation which almost undid a splendid general named James Wolfe three quarters of a century later, and the truth must have been plain to him that he would not find success as easy here as locating a sunken ship on a shark-toothed reef.

The preparations for the expedition had been made with amateurish dispatch and unconcern. There was nothing but the hastiest organization, no established plan for co-ordination among the ships. There was a desperate shortage of ammunition, the food supplies were inadequate, no pilot had been provided for the St. Lawrence. Go out and fight, seems to have been the tenor of the instructions, and may the God Who makes men free make you victorious.

Sir William did the best he could, although he wasted a great deal of time in a nervous tendency to hold interminable councils of war. As a result of this delaying, a force of eight hundred men arrived from Quebec in time to help in the defense, marching in with much beating of jubilant drums and loud acclaim from the people and the garrison. Phips did not allow himself to be discouraged by these unexpected reinforcements (by the over-all plan Montreal should have been in English hands by this time) but decided to make a two-pronged effort. He landed troops at Beauport first to make an attack on the rear of the city. He seems to have known of the path which Wolfe took later but preferred the other approach. He did not know, however, that Frontenac had built a wall along the back entrance to the town and that strong forces would be needed to carry it. The second half of the plan was to bombard the town from the water at the same time.

While the New Englanders planned their attack Frontenac was organizing his defense with a vigor unusual in a man of his years. Even the most Plutarchian of men (and the old count deserved this appellation) are subject to the limitations of age. They must have their sleep lest they fall into naps at councils of war and startle their subordinates with their snoring, and they tire quickly of the effort involved in the personal supervision of detail. The governor was as much subject to these symptoms as any other general of seventy, but for the period of the siege he managed to rise above them. He saw to everything himself: he inspected the guns, he mingled with the troops, he went on tours of reconnaissance and often at night drew a startled *Qui vive?* from the men who stood at sentry on the new palisade around the heights.

He knew that the self-made commander of the English expedition was making all the mistakes which might be expected of an amateur soldier: that the land attack was to be launched openly and with no attempt at surprise, that the bombardment of the town could be expected at any moment and so would precede the landing of forces along the St. Charles. He was aware also, however, that thirty-four ships of war were in the harbor and that the invading force far outnumbered the garrison. Unexpected things can happen under these circumstances, and the governor did not allow himself the usually costly luxury of overconfidence.

This was the apotheosis of the venerable leader, the supreme moment of his career. He seemed to slough off the years, his gray mustaches seemed to bristle with energy, and his eyes burned with fighting spirit.

The land attack was bravely carried out under the command of Major Walley, but a defending force under Ste. Hélène, the second of the Le Moyne brothers, waged a successful delaying action and it inflicted losses on the invaders. When it became certain that the attack was going to bog down in the mud and the underbrush, Ste. Hélène was transferred to Lower Town to command the batteries there. Phips had opened fire prematurely, as Frontenac had expected, with all his guns. The batteries of the town replied in kind. Much damage was done on both sides, but the supplies of ammunition on the ships ran out quickly and their fire diminished and finally ceased.

In the meantime the land forces had not yet crossed the St. Charles and were now making an effort to get over the ford. Ste. Hélène, who moved from one point of need to another, had taken charge of the fighting along the river again and was mortally wounded at the same moment that his elder brother Charles was hit by a spent bullet. The death of the gallant Ste. Hélène was the worst loss the

French cause sustained, for the English effort was suspended the next day and the spent troops taken back to the ships.

The fleet, badly riddled by the fire from the batteries on the rock, withdrew behind the Island of Orleans to refit for the return voyage. The effort to capture Quebec had failed.

Frontenac had gambled and won. Convinced that only audacity would restore French prestige, he had risked the consequences of a direct attack on the New England colonies and had now successfully countered the angry reprisals. He had accomplished what he had been sent out to do. The white and gold standard still floated above the Château of St. Louis.

3

October 22, 1692

The particular section of Canada which was most open to Indian attack lay along the banks of the St. Lawrence from Three Rivers to Montreal and beyond. In this vulnerable area stood a fort which was called Castle Dangerous because of the excessive peril in which its inhabitants existed. This was Fort Verchères, which was on the south bank of the river, about twenty miles below Montreal. It was therefore only a short distance from the Richelieu River, the route taken by Iroquois war parties. The mouth of the Richelieu was always under watch and guard, and the wily redskins had fallen into the habit of leaving the water before reaching the junction point with the St. Lawrence and striking inland. After a few miles they would find themselves in sight of the fort and blockhouse (connected by a covered passage) of Verchères. It had suffered so many attacks and alarms that the inhabitants thereabouts lived in constant dread.

Castle Dangerous belonged to the Sieur de Verchères, who had been an officer in the Carignan regiment. He had settled down with more good will and determination than most of his fellow officers and had been reasonably successful over the years.

A curious spell of overconfidence seems to have invested the Verchères domain on this morning of October 22. The seigneur was on duty at Quebec and Madame de Verchères was in Montreal. It had been a good season in spite of the constant alarms which had kept men as well as women indoors. The fields were high with waving corn, the pumpkins were ripe and yellow, the last of the melons remained to be gathered, and the trees were laden with fruit. The sun had been so bright and cheerful this fine October morning that the settlers had decided to risk gathering this bountiful harvest. They were out in the fields, and the cheerful sound of their voices could be heard from all parts of the cultivated area as they labored with sickle and hoe.

The fourteen-year-old daughter of the family, Madeleine, was at the wharf on the riverbank, which was close to the main entrance of the fort. The settlers had a name of their own for wharves, calling them *mouille-pieds*, which meant "wet feet"; but this did not concern small Madeleine (from the descriptions available she seems to have been petite and rather pretty) because she was probably expecting her mother from Montreal and so would not have dared put on her best kid-topped shoes with tasseled drawstrings. A hired man whose name was Laviolette was with her.

A sound of musket fire reached them from the direction of the fields where the settlers were at work. Laviolette, with his greater height, could see more of what was happening than the girl. In a voice of great panic he cried: "Run, mademoiselle, run! The Iroquois!" She saw then that the fields had filled almost in the winking of an eye with naked top-knotted warriors screeching their triumphant battlecries and killing the unarmed workers as fast as they could run them down.

She turned and made for the fort, followed by the man Laviolette. Her mind was filled with supplications to God and the Holy Virgin but at the same time busy with thoughts of what might be done. There were only two soldiers in the fort, she knew, in addition to her two brothers, aged twelve and ten, a very old man of eighty or thereabouts, and a number of women with infant children. They reached the fort uninjured in the face of a heavy spatter of Iroquois bullets.

"To arms! To arms!" cried the girl.

Outside the gate were two weeping women who had seen their husbands cut down and killed by the fierce marauders, and it required a firm hand and a display of confidence, both of which the child managed to achieve, to get them inside. Madeleine closed the gate herself and drove the crossbeams into place.

She found the two soldiers in the blockhouse, which was safer

than the somewhat dilapidated fort. One had hidden himself and the
other was standing over a budge barrel of powder with a lighted fuse
in his hand.

"What are you going to do?" she cried.

The man answered in a quavering voice, "Light the powder and
blow us all up."

"You are a miserable coward!" said the girl, driving him away
from the ammunition supply.

She proceeded then to instill courage into the huddled group
about her. They must fight as though they were all soldiers and
numerous enough to hold the Indians off, she said, and perhaps God,
Who was watching them as she spoke, would send them help in
time. The rest were encouraged by her words. First her two young
brothers and then the soldiers in a shamefaced silence took guns to
the loopholes and began to fire on the Indians in the fields. By running from one loophole to another, while the women loaded the guns
for them, they were able to create the impression that a sizable garrison held the fort.

Neither time nor space is available to tell in full detail the story
of what followed. For a week the little band of defenders kept up
their brave pretense. The four men, counting the octogenarian,
the two boys, and the petticoated commander slept at intervals only
and never at night. They stood guard in the bastion of the fort and
at the loopholes in the blockhouse in the daytime, firing briskly when
the bronze skin of a hostile warrior showed in the fields or in the
cover of the trees. At night they paced the platforms to keep awake
and kept up encouraging cries of "All's well!" at regular intervals.
The gallant little band was so successful in its pretense of being an
adequate and alert garrison that the Iroquois, still lurking in the
woods, did not risk an attack. It became known later that the redskins held a council of war and decided that the chance of carrying
a fort so well defended was slight.

During this week of effort and strain the meager garrison took
their orders without question and drew their inspiration from the
girl of fourteen. In the desperate moment of time when she had
first seen the war party issuing from the trees she had ceased to be
a child. An adult resolution had taken possession of her. Knowing
the full weakness of her tiny band—the soldiers had displayed their
clay feet in the first moments of the attack, her brothers were still

children, the old man could do no more than dodder about the loopholes—she drove them with a fierce energy and never allowed them a moment's ease. She slept little herself and consumed the cold scraps of food which the women prepared with an eye on the fields and the line of trees. She preached at them and prayed with them when their will to go on wavered. She sometimes swayed unsteadily with the weight of the musket which she always carried (and used also to good effect), her face became pale and wan, her eyes were shadowed and deep-sunken. But never for a moment did she give way to her fears.

On the night of the seventh day a party of forty men arrived from Montreal under the command of Monsieur de la Monnerie, a lieutenant in the French army. They stopped at the landing place and hailed the fort, not knowing whether the defense still held out but fearing very much that they would find the Iroquois in possession. Madeleine had been dozing with her head on a table, her gun still in her arms. She roused herself and mounted the bastion.

"Who are you?" she demanded.

The answer came back in an unmistakably French voice, "It is La Monnerie, who comes to bring you help."

In a voice which seemed for the first time to show emotion, Madeleine ordered the gate to be opened. Leaving one of the soldiers there to keep guard, she ventured out alone into the darkness. When she met the lieutenant on the path, she stopped and saluted him.

"Monsieur," she said in a voice high-pitched with the first hint of hysteria, "I surrender my arms to you."

She was ready to drop with fatigue but she remained a good commander to the end. Her first thought was for those who had shared with her the long vigil. "Monsieur," she said to La Monnerie in a tone of great earnestness, "it is time to relieve them. We have not been off our guard for a week."

When she told the story later of these remarkable seven days, she made no mention of what followed immediately after the arrival of the rescuing party or of the emotions she felt. It may be assumed, however, that she did not allow herself to break down and that her tears were held back until she reached the privacy of her room. It may also be taken for granted that she slept the clock around and that the effects of her seemingly unending vigil were not easily shaken off. Did the maturity of character and mind which she had summoned so resolutely continue to govern her thereafter, or did she slip back into the fancies and humors of girlhood? One thing may be accepted, perhaps, that she began to insist on some grown-up privileges. It would be pleasant to think, for instance, that she was allowed to wear her kid-topped shoes whenever she chose and that she was allowed the right to have *considerations* on her skirts, the panniers which were deemed proper only when girlhood had been put behind.

Her full name was Marie Madeleine Jarret de Verchères and she was fourteen and a half years old when she thus earned for herself a place in Canadian annals with Adam Dollard and the heroes whose shades are in his train. She was summoned by the Marquis de Beauharnois, who held the post of governor when she was a young married woman, and told her story at his request, with proper dignity and simplicity. She was treated with the consideration she had earned and given a pension, a small one. Her husband was Thomas Tardieu de la Naudière, and she brought a number of children into the world. They lived in rather less parlous times and had no opportunity to emulate the deed of this remarkable girl who had become their mother.

4

March 2, 1699

Iberville knew that he had solved the mystery as soon as he saw the waters of the Gulf turning color. The brilliant blue in which they had been sailing had become grayish and the surface was distinctly agitated. He had no doubts that these were signs of a heavy inflow. Somewhere ahead, then, he would find the mouth of a great river; the Mississippi, he was sure—the Hid River, as the Spanish had begun to call it since La Salle's failure.

Later in the day the great French Canadian—for by this time Iberville had acquired a reputation which put him first in the esteem of his own people—saw a break in the banks ahead, marked by two tall rocks. Between these natural sentries a great body of water was rolling down with inexorable majesty. No Frenchman ever set eyes on the Mississippi without recognizing it; nor, in all probability, did anyone else. It could not be mistaken now, this turgid and magnificent stream, carrying to the Gulf the surplus water of the prairies and so much of the mud from the Ohio, the Missouri, and the Arkansas.

The small company, staring with fascinated eyes at the goal of their long voyage, crossed themselves in thanksgiving. Iberville, who had brought Bienville with him, the younger brother who was destined for great things also, found himself in a conflict of emotions. He was triumphant, of course, for he had come almost straight to the mouth of the river. At the same time he must also have been sad, thinking of the three brothers, Jacques, François, and Louis, who had died in battle and would never know that it had fallen to the lot of the Le Moynes to complete the work of La Salle.

Iberville's reputation as a military leader had grown out of a series of unusual exploits. He had led another land expedition to Hudson's Bay, which had been successful but had resulted in the death of the seventh brother, Louis, known as the Sieur de Châteauguay. Louis had been distinguished for bravery, even in this family of brave men. His was a young and heroic form of courage, reminiscent of that great figure of the preceding century, the Chevalier Bayard. It had led him to advance gaily and audaciously across open ground in an attack on the English fort, and a bullet had cut him down.

The exploits of Iberville were on the sea after this last land invasion. In charge of two small ships of war, the *Envieux* and the *Profond,* he won a naval battle off the St. John River and immediately after captured Pemaquid. Leaving these waters, he sailed to Newfoundland, taking possession of the island and sacking the towns and villages with realistic thoroughness. This unpleasant task over, he led a fleet of four ships of war into Hudson's Bay to take Fort Nelson and so made the French sweep complete. His lasting reputation is largely based on his brilliant success in this undertaking.

His flagship, the *Pelican,* carrying forty-four guns, became separated from the rest of the small fleet and found itself confronted on the somber waters off Fort Nelson with three English vessels, the *Hampshire,* the *Daring,* and the *Hudson Bay,* carrying 120 guns between them. Great naval commanders have always had two qualities, audacity and initiative. Iberville had these assets in a superlative degree and, because of the daring strategy he employed, he scored what is probably the most noteworthy victory in French maritime history; which, it must be added, is a rather barren page.

Keeping to windward of his opponents by the boldest of tactics, he sank the *Hampshire,* captured the *Hudson Bay,* and sent the

Daring into hasty flight. The capitulation of Fort Nelson followed, and so the French, for the time being, had all of the great bay in their possession.

It was after this that Louis XIV, perceiving he had in Iberville an iron leader who always carried out his orders and always won, decided to make one more effort to seize the mouth of the Mississippi. His preference was to send some court favorite with a lofty title in nominal command, with Iberville to do the work, but he was finally persuaded that this habit of divided command always led to trouble. He gave in, and the brilliant young French Canadian was appointed to an undivided leadership.

After a week's slow progress up the Mississippi in small boats, the little party saw a wide curve in the river ahead of them. Standing in the prow of the leading *chaloupe,* Iberville had been keeping an observant eye on this exotic land in its spring stage of extravagant blossoming, realizing perhaps that someday a miracle would happen hereabouts. Now he looked closely ahead, and it came to him that the land above the bend was exactly what he had been seeking. It was low at the water's edge but rose slowly and steadily back from the shore. His hand shot out triumphantly to show where the remains of Indian huts marked the southern end of a portage. It was apparent to Iberville that this was the site for the great city he proposed to establish, a view in which his keenly observant younger brother fully concurred. It is perhaps superfluous to add that on the land they studied from the deck of the *chaloupe* there now stands a much larger and finer city than anything their imaginations had conceived, New Orleans.

Great military leaders have confidence in themselves or they would not dare the improvisations and risks by which battles are won. Iberville was no exception. It was only because he had a belief in his star that he had adopted such bold offensive tactics and had attacked the three ships which came against him on Hudson's Bay. It is not unlikely, however, that his assurance had been dampened somewhat by his reception at court before the command of the Mississippi venture was entrusted to him.

Louis XIV had kept such close personal supervision of Canadian affairs that he had come to regard the men and women of the colony as puppets moving in response to his tugging on the strings. The most colorful and effective of the puppets, the most rambunctious in its response to the pressure of the royal fingers, had been Iberville, but the King still seemed to consider him no more than a rather astonishing automaton. There had been no thought, apparently, of making use of his spectacular talents in any task which did not have to do with America.

Knowing the King's attitude, Iberville was still unwilling to accept the minor role in which he was being cast. To sit in a fever-ridden jungle and wait for a tiny post to grow into a flourishing colony was not a part that the hero of New France was prepared to play; he was too pre-eminently a man of action for that. Leaving Bienville in charge of the land operations, the bold Pierre sailed off to keep watch and ward on the sea. For seven years thereafter the eighth son remained in command of small forts, first at Biloxi, then at Mobile. He grew sallow from malarial infections in his veins and many times his patience wore thin, for nothing seemed to happen and his resources were so slight that he could do no more than hold his ground against the activities of Indians under such tribe names as the Bayougoulas and the Quinupissas who were as hostile as the Iroquois.

In the meantime the legend of French invincibility on land had been rudely jolted by the appearance on the European scene of English armies under the command of a great general named Marlborough. This unusual soldier defeated the French and almost annihilated one of the Sun King's armies at the battle of Blenheim, thereby breaking the power of Louis in Germany. Two years later he won another tremendous battle at Ramillies, which resulted in freeing the Low Countries from French invasion. The Sun King, as stubborn as ever and still unshaken in his confidence, recruited new armies and continued to entrust them to the command of generals who shared his reactionary ideas. It did not occur to him, apparently, to make use of the French Canadian who had never lost a battle on land or sea. Too many Frenchmen of high degree clamored for the command of regiments and brigades, and even armies, for a place to be made for Iberville.

Fate then intervened to remove the latter forever from any of the enhanced glory which he might have won in the continental wars. He was not to live long enough even to see the first crude settlement at the bend of the Mississippi nor to observe any material results from his rediscovery of the mouth of the Father of Waters. Sailing in the Caribbean with the sixth Le Moyne, Joseph de Serigny, he cast anchor off Havana Harbor. Three members of the crew had died with suspicious suddenness, and the two brothers suspected they had the plague on board. The suspicion became a certainty when the port surgeon visited the ship. The latter found, moreover, that the plague, which is no respecter of rank or authority, had visited the captain's cabin as well.

Iberville was taken ashore and placed in quarantine. The foul disease quickly strengthened its hold. He tossed for days in torment, babbling in his delirium. Only at brief intervals did reason pay him a fitful return. His brother was not allowed to come ashore, and so the brave Pierre faced the inevitable end alone. What were his thoughts during the brief moments when sanity returned? Despite the disappointments he had suffered, he knew that he had not yet reached the peak of his powers and he did not want to end his days so soon in a stinking Spanish lazaret. He raved perhaps of the great plans he had shared with his remarkable brothers, shouting *"Pointez à couler bas!"* as in his fevered fancy he stood on the quarter-deck of the *Pelican,* murmuring in lower tones of Longueuil with its four towers and high walls, which all of the valiant sons had loved so much.

There were only five of the Le Moynes left when the body of the great Iberville was put in the death cart and hurried away to an unmarked and never identified grave.

Twelve more years passed. The Mississippi colony, now located near Mobile, languished in great discomfort and privation, and nothing seemed to come of what they were attempting to do. A miracle would be needed to turn the palisaded shacks in which Bienville and his discontented men existed into a flourishing outpost of empire.

The miracle came to pass. A spectacular banker from Scotland named John Law persuaded the Duc d'Orléans, who had become regent of France on the death of Louis XIV, that a get-rich-quick scheme of his contriving was the tonic the country needed. The regent authorized the launching of a huge investment concern in 1717 called the *Compagnie de la Louisiane ou d'Occident.* The public was offered subscriptions in it at a price of 500 livres a share (there were 500,000 shares), and as there had to be tangible assets back of the company, it was given sovereignty over all of North America west of the Mississippi. The riches of Louisiana were dangled before the eyes of investors, and the people began to buy shares so eagerly that the value went up and up and one of the great booms of history started. In a very short time the whole nation was in the throes of a madness which later caused the scheme to be called the Mississippi Bubble.

In the meantime, of course, something had to be done to turn Louisiana into a bonanza land. The ever-loyal Bienville, sitting so patiently in his toy fort, received hurried instructions. He must provide at once a capital for the El Dorado into which Louisiana was to be turned, a place to which could be sent the shiploads of settlers the government was packing out immediately, and the soldiers and the King's Girls, and the mountains of supplies and building materials, and the guns. There could be no manner of delay; the first ships were sailing at once.

The genius for organization which had been dormant in Bienville all these years came to life. Remembering the land on the broad bend of the Mississippi which his great brother, now moldering in a Spanish grave, had selected as the best site for the projected capital, he moved his men there at once and set them to work. The place which had served as the terminal point of the portage was cleared off and made into the Place d'Armes of the new town. The north side of the square, looking down to the river, was selected for the cathedral; although for the time being the young leader could contrive nothing more than a shrine under a canopy of canvas. On each side of the square he built frame *casernes* (barracks) for the soldiers who were coming on the first ships. At the southwest corner he raised a hasty single-story building which would serve for administration purposes.

Streets were then cut through the woods and underbrush and small houses were run up hastily. With the addition of a great many tents, the capital of the new El Dorado (named New Orleans for the regent) was capable of housing in one way or another all the people due to arrive. Here was a second miracle, a man-made one, the credit for which belongs to Bienville.

Then the ships began to arrive at the mouth of the river and the place was quickly overrun. The new arrivals were a thoroughly unsuitable lot, as Bienville saw at one glance. His work as governor of this hastily thrown together metropolis was not going to be easy.

Back in France the Bubble burst. The company failed, thousands of investors were impoverished, John Law had to leave France in great haste and secrecy. The only thing that did not vanish was the

capital of the new empire which Jean Baptiste le Moyne de Bienville
was building and which was now crowded with disillusioned people.
This part of the experiment had to go on.

A real and enduring miracle came about. Slowly the town grew
as ways were found to use the resources of the river lands. Permanent buildings were erected, churches and schools as well as private
residences of charm and individuality. The first personal wealth
produced sent the possessors out to fine houses and plantations along
the streams and bayous. Bienville never returned to Canada, he
never married, and when he was allowed finally to retire he was an
old man. He went to Paris to spend what was left of his life.

He was eighty-seven years old when Louis XV, who had very
slight consideration for the obligations and responsibilities of kingship, decided to hand Louisiana to Spain. Bienville tried to intercede,
to convince the King that the charming civilization which the people
of the colony had created would wither and die under alien rule.
The King would not see him, and the ministers were unsympathetic.
Bienville died before the transfer was carried out officially, and it
was generally believed that the blow had broken his heart.

5

May, 1708

Bishop Laval was dying. Quebec, which had always maintained
an air of gaiety and sophistication even when a scowl above a black
cassock had carried authority, paused and pondered what it would
mean to be without him. A deep sense of impending loss took possession of the people of the town.

Visitors had always been impressed with the volatile spirits of
Quebec. They had commented on the gay air of the town and, in
particular, on the beauty and charm of the women. This had been
in no sense an exaggeration. Often in the late evening hours, the
still, cold air would fill suddenly with the high notes of feminine
voices and with the last snatches of song as social circles dissolved
and the members took their way homeward. The shadows cast by the
high palisade Frontenac had built back of the heights were seldom
untenanted, for here young lovers went for walks, and often the
crunch of slow footsteps on the snow would evoke the same sharp
Qui vive? as the old governor had heard from the sentries in the
stone towers.

But the people of Quebec were as devout as they were gay, and so the loss of the old bishop was going to be deeply felt. They had been on his side in the main when they found that he and his successor were at odds. Laval had been so sure of the fitness of the Abbé Saint-Vallier that it had come as a shock to find that the new bishop did not share his convictions at all on certain points. Saint-Vallier was not inclined to place much importance in the seminary which he, Laval, had founded with so much enthusiasm and which he felt should be the very heart and core of spiritual life in the colony. A decree had been passed which limited the institution to the education of priests, and the number of directors had been reduced casually to five. The new bishop had accepted fifteen thousand francs from the King for the erection of an episcopal palace and the funds had been used for the purpose, so that now Laval in his bare little corner of the seminary could see the tall windows and fine glass of his successor. Saint-Vallier had been an ardent supporter of Denonville, even when the mistakes of that well-meaning but weak governor had brought Canada to the brink of ruin.

Troubles had multiplied on the head of the old man since his return from France. A scourge had carried off a quarter of the inhabitants of Quebec. The seminary had burned down, and Laval, desperately ill at the time, had been carried half clad from his bed. It had been necessary for him to accept on behalf of himself and his staff the hospitality of the episcopal palace; although he had cringed no doubt from the evidences it presented of easy living. When the walls of the new seminary were halfway up, another fire swept the neighborhood and the work had to be started over again. The Spartan old prelate had removed himself before this from the comparative magnificence of his successor's abode.

Fortunately, because two such men could not have lived in peace together, Saint-Vallier had now been absent from Canada for the better part of ten years. The King, who generally had a shrewd grasp of the situation in his favorite colony, which was also his pet extravagance, had realized the danger in the open lack of unity between the two men. Perhaps he also had been disappointed in Saint-Vallier. At any rate, he summoned the new bishop back to France in 1700 and kept him there on various pretexts. In 1705 permission was granted him to return, and he set sail for Quebec in a ship called the *Seine*, which was taking out a million francs. Getting wind of this tempting cargo, perhaps, an English ship chased and captured the *Seine,* taking all the crew and passengers back to England. Saint-Vallier had been a prisoner of war ever since and he would remain in England for two years more. In his absence two of his assistants attended to the executive duties, but for spiritual guidance the people had turned back to Laval. He ordained the new priests, he presided at confirmation, he visited the sick and attended the dying. His face, wrinkled with age and reduced to boniness by the rigor of his fasting, was seen everywhere in spite of the infirmities which had gripped him.

The old prelate's asceticism had increased rather than diminished with the years. He still rose without fail at two in the morning and dressed himself hurriedly in the cold of his room. The tendency to varicose veins had become worse with the years, and as a result an unsteadiness had developed in his legs. It had become necessary to bind them every day, and in this he would allow no help. Stooping with great difficulty in the dark (for the use of candles was an extravagance) and groaning from the pain he was inflicting on himself, he took a long time at the task. Not until he was dressed would he light the charcoal in his brazier, and even in the depth of winter he allowed himself no better than a feeble fire, above which he would huddle as he turned to his morning devotions. At four he would be ready to set out for the cathedral, where he would celebrate the four-thirty Mass.

He could no longer venture out alone as he had done when he was young. An *engagé* at the seminary, Houssard by name, devoted himself to the service of the stern old man. Houssard would come to the bishop at four, his eyes heavy with sleep, to escort his master through the darkness of the streets. Sometimes the bishop was too weak to walk and Houssard would take him on his back. They must have cast a curious shadow when the *engagé,* carrying the thin figure pickaback, emerged on stumbling feet from the twisting and narrow streets into the full light of the moon.

The prelate spared neither himself nor the back of the devoted Houssard, for always he must go to the cathedral for later services on Sundays and saints' days. He must attend all funerals and respond to every request for his presence. The people of the town had become well accustomed to the sight of the old man being thus carried wherever duty called him. Nothing could be said to convince him that the time had come for him to rest.

He continued thus to tend the spiritual needs of the ill and the dying until it became only too apparent that his own end was close at hand. This was in 1707, and during the summer of that year it seemed that he could not rally from the weakness which had seized him; but he did, and even presented an appearance of physical improvement. He smiled again and spoke much of the future and of all the things he intended to do. This improvement carried him through the winter.

Spring was late the next year. On Good Friday, Houssard carried the ailing prelate to the cathedral. There was still ice on the streets and a bitter and unseasonable wind had risen and was twirling the snow about the eaves of the houses and making it almost impossible for the eye to see the top of the spire. It was not surprising that the bishop's feet were frozen before they reached the comparative warmth of the cathedral. The old man said nothing about it until it was too late to take the necessary steps. Even had he done so, it is doubtful if any measures could have been taken to relieve him, for the swollen veins in his legs gave at best a poor circulation of the blood. Gangrene set in and he suffered terribly during his last few days on earth.

He did not complain, but the intensity of the pain wrung exclamations from him. "O God have pity on me!" he cried. "O God of mercy, let Thy will be done!"

He had no thought that his accomplishments had set him apart. The humility he had shown in his later years seemed to accelerate, in fact, as the end drew near. Someone made the suggestion that he do as the saints had so often done and voice a last message for the people he was leaving.

The dying man shook his head slowly from side to side.

"They were saints," he whispered. "I am a sinner."

He died early in the morning of May 6, 1708. There had been no gaiety in Quebec for many days, nor would there be for a long time thereafter. The spiritual father of the colony had been taken away, and with bowed heads the people prayed long and earnestly that his benign influence would not be lost to them.

The great men had been passing one by one. La Salle, Talon, Frontenac (who died in the Château of St. Louis in 1698), Iberville, and now Laval. With the death of this passionately devout churchman, who had been so arbitrary in his first years and so gentle and understanding in his last, an ending seemed to come to the period of Titans.

6

It is too sweeping a generalization to say that New France produced her great men in the seventeenth century and that the full flowering of genius in the American colonies did not come until the eighteenth. It would be even more dangerous to draw from this a reason for the ultimate success of the English in the long struggle. This much can be said, at any rate, in support of such statements: the eighty-one years from the time when Champlain founded the settlement at Quebec until the period of open and declared war began, the French colony produced a long succession of great men. Some of them were men of extreme bravery, some were wise and far-seeing, all were romantic and adventurous. There would be outstanding men in the eighteenth as well—La Mothe-Cadillac, La Harpe, Le Sueur, Varennes de la Verendrye and his sons, the Mallet brothers—but active and daring as they were, they seem of lesser stature.

The great figures of New France began with Cartier and Champlain and included those enumerated above: La Salle, Talon, Frontenac, Iberville, Laval. Of these, Iberville alone was born in the colony. The others, who might not otherwise have emerged into the bright white light of historical importance, came from France and found in Canada the setting and the opportunity for their particular talents and personal characteristics. Consider, for a brief and concluding moment, the list of the great and the near great and the picturesque minor characters who performed so actively in the wings and the fly.

De Monts made possible the continuance of Champlain's effort at colonization, but he does not stand with the others in enduring bronze or marble. Champlain's renegade servant, Etienne Brulé, made for himself an amazing record of getting first to places of importance, north, south, and west. If he had not sold himself to the Kirkes, he would have an honored place of his own. Radisson and Groseilliers have been getting more recognition as new records are uncovered, more especially Radisson, who seems to have been the greatest and luckiest of traders. It was not his way to start out with a certain number of companions and canoes and to come back with a smaller train and stories of ill fortune; rather he came back with more canoes than he started with, packed deep with furs, amid a noisy and cheerful gabble of great things done and seen. It was unfortunate for France that he lacked the patience to accept official rebuffs and injustices; and equally to be regretted that the hide-bound and high-nosed governors with whom he came in contact could not see the possibilities in this footloose genius. Now they begin to crowd the stage, these men who opened up the North and the West—Marquette and Joliet, who discovered the Mississippi, Du Lhut, Durantaye, Perrot, Tonty, the Jesuit fathers who would be found in the most unexpected corners of the wilderness to which their zeal had carried them; and, towering above them all, La Salle.

On with the list. There was Maisonneuve, unselfish and chival-rous, who saw Montreal through its first perilous stages. After him came Dollier de Casson, the gentle Sulpician giant who fled the face of war, only to find himself more deeply immersed in violence than before. Adam Dollard supplied the one story which would live if all other colonial annals were lost and forgotten. No equal can be found for the story of the Jesuit martyrs, Jogues, Brébeuf, Lalemant, Dan-iel, Bressani. Four women, all different one from another but all brave and devout, played remarkable parts, Madame de la Peltrie, Mère Marie de l'Incarnation, Jeanne Mance, Marguerite Bourgeoys. Louis Hébert, courageous and industrious, the first settler, must never be overlooked. Can other histories produce the equal of Charles le Moyne and his ten fabulous sons? Great men indeed, great days, great deeds.

Seldom has so short a span of years produced a more varied, a more exciting, a more romantic history than these eighty-one years out of the seventeenth century. Time has a habit of moving so slowly that any period of equal length in the past would have re-corded little of change in the world; a dingier color on the walls of ancient towns, a slash of tailoring scissors converting a tunic, per-haps, into a tabard, a very slight advance in habits of thought, a new song on men's lips, and a new book to be reverently kept. But these eighty-one years saw the opening of a new continent, a conti-nent of vast extent which would be taken over completely in three centuries by great men in all parts of North America and its amazing resources harnessed. In the process a new spirit of rapid change would be loosed in the world.

INDEX

Monts, Pierre du Guast, Sieur de, 50–51; charter granted to, to establish Acadian colony, 53–54; colony placed on St. Croix River, 54–59; colony moved to Annapolis Basin, 59–60; charter revoked, 60–61; charter renewed, 63–64; in new colonial company, 72, 74

Moranget, nephew of La Salle, 412, 414

Moras, Monet de, 268

Mort Bay. See Hudson's Bay

Morton, John, Archbishop of Canterbury, 2

Mouey, Charles de, Sieur de la Milleraye, 16–17

Mount Royal, named by Cartier, 32; cross raised on, 147

Moyse, Maître, head carpenter on La Salle expedition, 366

Nantes, Jean de, 45

Nantes, Edict of, 51

Navarre, Henry III of. See Henry IV of France

Navarre, in religious wars, 49

Navigation, in fifteenth century, 3; in seventeenth century, 412–13

Netherlands. See Dutch colonies in New York

Neutral Nation of Indians, 74; warfare with Iroquois, 176, 187

Neuville, Sieur de, 335–36

New Amsterdam. See Fort Amsterdam; New York

New Brunswick, discovered by Cartier, 20. See also Acadia

New England, colonies established in, 111–12; as probable location of Viking settlement, 12

Newfoundland, discovered by Cabot, 7–8; fishing trade, early development of, 9, 15, 43, 54; as possible Vinland of Norsemen, 12; visited by Cartier, 18; west coast observed by Cartier expedition, 20

New France, preliminary efforts at colonization, 51–53; colony established in Acadia, 53–61, 64; Quebec settlement founded by Champlain, 63–66; company formed with Condé as viceroy, 73–74; reorganization of company, 84–85; Jesuit order established in, 100–5; Company of One Hundred Associates organized, 105–8; first English raid on, 112–13; conquered by English, 114–20; restored to French rule, 120–22; Iroquois warfare against, 139–40, 148–51, 154–56, 164–76, 188, 206–7; struggle for control of Church in, 228–33; made royal province, 246–49; arrival of Carignan-Salière regiment and defeat of Iroquois, 253–68; economic development under Talon, 269–77; program of expansion under Louis XIV, 279–80; laws and restrictions under Louis XIV, 286–91; West claimed as part of, 306–7; conflict with England over fur trade, 322–23, 325–30;

484 INDEX

Plymouth, Mass., establishment of
colony at, 112

Pocahontas, 111, 112

Ponce de Léon, Juan, 56

Poncet, Father, Jesuit missionary,
145

Pontbriant, Claud de, on Cartier
expedition, 28

Pontgravé, merchant of St. Malo,
52; on De Chastes venture, 52;
on colonizing expedition to Acadia, 55; in settling of Quebec, 65

Port of Castles, 8

Portman, John, treasurer of Hudson's Bay Company, 318

Port Royal (Annapolis Royal), Acadia, 58; settlement established
at, 59–60; colony abandoned on
loss of charter, 60–61; charter renewed, 63–64; Argall raid against,
112–13; development under
D'Aunay, 184

Portugal, explorations of Corte-Real
for, 13–14; in Newfoundland
fishing trade, 9, 43

Potawatomi Indians, 308, 355

Poulet, Jean, on Cartier expedition,
28

Poutrincourt, Jean de Biencourt,
Sieur de, on first colonizing expedition to Acadia, 55; Port
Royal granted to and named by,
59; colonists brought over by,
59–60; charter lost, 60–61; colony reassembled after Argall raid,
113

Prevert, Captain, on De Chastes
venture, 52

Primot, Catherine, 209

Prince Edward Island, discovered
by Cartier, 20

Prince Rupert, ship of Hudson's
Bay Company, 328

Prisoners, sent as colonists to New
World by France, 40, 51–52,
105; sent on exploration voyages
by English, 6; torture of, by Indians, 69–70, 170–71; torture of,
in Europe, 70

Protestants, French. See Huguenots

Provincetown, Mass., landing of Pilgrims at site of, 112

Psalms, translation by James I of,
113–14

Puerto Rico, English repulsed by
Spanish at, 13

Puiseaux, Pierre des, 139, 142–44,
145, 207

Quebec, site claimed for France by
Cartier, 31–32, 35–37; settlement
attempted by Cartier and Roberval, 40–45; colony founded
by Champlain, 64–66; in 1620,
86–89; building of citadel, 95,
97; siege and capture of, by English, 116–20; founding of Ursuline convent, 124–30; in 1636,
138–41; soldiers sent to, 253–56,
262; English attack on, 440–46

Queylus, Abbé de, Sulpician, 228,
231–33, 353–54

Radisson, Pierre Esprit, 194; in
escape of Jesuit mission from